A STUDY OF BIRD SONG

Three-wattled Bellbird calling

A STUDY OF BIRD SONG

EDWARD A. ARMSTRONG

Dulce melos iterans vario modulamine musae,
Atque Creatorem semper in ore canens . . .
Felix o nimium, Dominum nocteque dieque
Qui studio tali semper in ore canit!

De Luscinia. Patrologia Latina, ci. p. 803

SECOND ENLARGED EDITION

DOVER PUBLICATIONS, INC.
NEW YORK

Published in Canada by General Publishing Company, Ltd., 30 Lesmill Road, Don Mills, Toronto, Ontario.
Published in the United Kingdom by Constable and Company, Ltd., 10 Orange Street, London WC 2.

This Dover edition, first published in 1973, is a revised and enlarged version of the work originally published by Oxford University Press in 1963. The author has written a new Preface and a second Addenda for the present edition.

International Standard Book Number: 0-486-20460-X
Library of Congress Catalog Card Number: 72-88733

Manufactured in the United States of America
Dover Publications, Inc.
180 Varick Street
New York, N.Y. 10014

PREFACE
TO THE DOVER EDITION

Since this book was first published nearly ten years ago much relevant literature has appeared, considerable technical advances have been made in recording bird vocalizations, and bio-acoustics has become a separate science. From being largely the concern of amateur ornithologists interest in bird song has passed, in this generation, to professionals with aviary, laboratory, and recording facilities available. By means of electronic instruments whose capabilities have been rapidly increased objective comparisons can be made and fine details can be studied, including those which human hearing is unable to detect. This new technology has facilitated rapid progress in those fields to which it is applicable but it has tended to deflect attention from some interesting environmental, ecological, and aesthetic aspects of bird song.

Some of this more recent information appears in the new 'Addenda II'. Unlike the Addenda of the original edition (now 'Addenda I'), which are signalled in the main text with daggers (see p. 6) and follow page order strictly, the new 'Addenda II' section is divided into several major topics, as follows: 'Pre-natal communication and individual recognition', 'Social functions', 'Learning and imitation', 'Song dialects', 'Species recognition', 'Song structure', 'Ecological and meteorological', 'Neurological', 'Physiological', 'Vocal organs', and 'Bird song as music and in literature'. There are no daggers in the main text for Addenda II, but each of the topic headings indicates the relevant text pages.

The notes in Addenda II are necessarily very selective. It has been possible to mention only a few of the books and papers published since the first edition. The selection cannot but appear rather arbitrary but my aim has been to call attention to well-referenced works which give a conspectus of research done in various fields and to lay emphasis on recent advances. The reader may thus trace the up-to-date literature appertaining to most aspects of a realm which gives great delight to the lover of the countryside and presents vistas of intriguing research to the scientist.

Cambridge
May 1972

EDWARD A. ARMSTRONG

CONTENTS

LIST OF PLATES

FIGURES IN THE TEXT

Figures in the Text

TABLES

ACKNOWLEDGEMENTS

I have been indebted to so many friends during the years this work has been in preparation that it is impossible to acknowledge adequately all the help I have received. I am particularly grateful to Professor W. H. Thorpe, F.R.S., for reading the galley-proofs and allowing me to use figures from his publications, and to Professor Charles Hartshorne for reading the page-proofs. They both played over to me some of their recordings. I am also indebted to Mr. J. Boswall of the B.B.C., who enabled me to hear a number of recorded bird songs. My thanks are expressed to all the authors, editors of journals, and publishers who have given permission for the reproduction of figures. I regret that in a few instances I have been unable to establish contact with those concerned.

I wish to express my hearty thanks to those who have supplied illustrations, especially to the following: Dr. Sten Bergman, Mr. P. Bourke, Dr. H. B. Cott, Mr. M. D. England, Dr. Desmond Morris, Dr. Robert J. Niedrach, Mr. Jan van Peppel, and Dr. P. O. Swanberg. I am much beholden to Dr. William Bridges and the New York Zoological Society, and to the Australian News and Information Bureau for sending me a fine set of illustrations and I thank the Director and authorities of the Pinacoteca Ambrosiana, Milan, for permission to reproduce the photograph of the painting by Alessandro Magnasco. All these kindly donated photographs. I am glad to keep in memory a pioneer bird photographer, Miss E. L. Turner, by reproducing one of her studies.

Thanks to a grant from the National Science Foundation of the United States in connexion with the thirteenth International Ornithological Congress I was able to pay another visit to the United States and to hear the songs of many species in the field as well as others tape-recorded and chosen from the collection of recordings of animal sounds at Cornell. I am very grateful to all those who helped to make this trip so enjoyable and ornithologically profitable. I am also grateful to the Royal Society for contributing toward the expenses of a visit to East Africa to study and record bird songs. The staffs at the University and Newton Libraries at Cambridge have been very helpful. It would not have been possible for me to have completed this work but for the extent to which my wife Eunice has eased my burden of responsibilities.

EDWARD A. ARMSTRONG

INTRODUCTION

Birds have evoked man's interest throughout the centuries because of their value as food, as sporting quarry and as cult objects. More than any other animals they have elicited aesthetic appreciation. Cave art testifies to the magical qualities attributed to them and Palaeolithic bone whistles suggest that our primitive ancestors may have tried to imitate the sounds made by birds with their crude musical instruments. Probably birds first became objects inspiring delight through their association with the regeneration of life. Ikhnaton's hymn to the life-giving powers of the sun concludes :

'All flowers bloom; the plants of the waste lands thrive at thy dawning; they drink themselves drunk before thy face. All cattle gambol upon their feet; all the birds rise up from their nests, and flap their wings with joy, and circle round in praise of the living Aten.'

Above all the arrival of the birds in spring aroused wonder and joy. The dweller on the tundra awoke to hear the twilit sky clangorous with the cries of geese, swans, or cranes. To him they must have seemed not merely heralds of the spring but magical creatures bringing it from afar. Now the winter was over and the community could bestir itself and begin its own annual cycle of activities.

As the centuries passed and higher cultures arose man became much more than a hunter. He began to record his aspirations in poetry. The happiness of spring inspired not only love but love-songs, and the lover found his feelings reflected in the songs of the birds. The young Hebrew's ardour mounted with the coming of the migrants :

'My beloved spake, and said unto me, Rise up my love, my fair one, and come away. For, lo, the winter is past, the rain is over and gone;

The flowers appear on the earth; the time of the singing of birds is come, and the voice of the turtle is heard in our land.'

More than two thousand years later Tennyson in well-known lines linked the burgeoning of young love with the brightening of birds' plumage but although his imagination was haunted by traditional symbolism he knew that Darwin had banished the love-lorn, thorn-pierced Nightingale and all its kin.

John Clare, born sixteen years prior to Tennyson, appreciated and even exaggerated the gulf which separates the poetic from the scientific mind. He wrote, 'For my part I love to look on nature with a poetic feeling, which magnifys the pleasure. I love to see the Nightingale in its hazel retreat, and the Cuckoo hiding in its solitude of oaken foliage, and not to examine their carcasses in glass cases. Yet naturalists and botanists seem to have no taste for this poetic feeling.' Clare misunderstood the scientist, as poets have ever been wont, for the scientist also would declare that surveying nature with a scientific eye 'magnifys the pleasure'.

Although Athanasius Kircher published a book in 1650 rendering some bird songs in musical notation (Fig. 42) and later naturalists, such as Baron von Pernau, Altum, and Moffat, realized to a considerable extent the function of song, Eliot Howard's books at the beginning of this century laid the foundation for scientific study of bird utterances in relation to other adaptations. Bird fanciers and researchers, including Barrington, Bechstein, Whitman, and Craig, had already studied such aspects of song as learning, vocal mimicry, and the use of sound signals but Howard emphasized the ecological significance of song by stressing its association with territory. The function of territory has been in the forefront of discussion ever since. As it was soon generally accepted that song announces the possession of a domain the vocalizations of birds aroused increasing attention. Naturalists realized that, apart from its intrinsic interest, bird song provides clues to the size of territories, the number of males in a given area, and the phase of the breeding cycle. No field study of a songbird can be conducted without paying attention to its utterances. None the less the *ad hoc* study of song received little attention until comparatively recently. The failure to concentrate on this field of study was due in part to the tendency of those intent on population and life history research to regard it as subsidiary, but a more important deterrent has been the widespread conviction that song could not be studied objectively. This was mistaken, as some ornithologists showed by research into such matters as diurnal and seasonal changes in song, but not until electronic methods of sound recording were developed and instruments such as the sound spectrograph invented could songs be exactly recorded, analysed, and compared. With the aid of these technical devices research on bird song is being conducted so energetically that even the specialist is finding difficulty in keeping in touch with all the work that is going forward. Now there may be some danger that concentration on the analysis of song may deflect attention from the study of song's setting in the context of the bird's life history. My viewpoint is that song should be regarded as one aspect of a delicately integrated complex of behaviour. The nature of a bird's utterances cannot be adequately interpreted without taking into account characteristics such as the nature of its pair-bond, coloration, foraging behaviour, and other adaptations. Therefore an attempt has been made to consider many aspects of bird song. Some of them have had to receive much less detailed treatment than they deserve but it is hoped that the reader may here find encouragement to explore further a realm of inexhaustible interest and delight.

EDWARD A. ARMSTRONG

Cambridge
   July 1960

I

BIRD UTTERANCE AS LANGUAGE

Many of the winged tribes have various sounds and voices
adapted to express their various passions, wants and feelings;
such as anger, fear, love, hatred, hunger and the like. All
species are not equally eloquent; some are copious and fluent
as it were in their utterance, while others are confined to a
few important sounds; no bird, like the fish kind, is quite
mute, though some are rather silent. The language of birds
is very ancient, and, like other ancient modes of speech,
very elliptical; little is said, but much is meant and intended.

GILBERT WHITE.
The Natural History of Selborne. Letter xliii.

THE *Concise Oxford Dictionary* defines language as 'a vocabulary
and way of using it', and a vocabulary as 'words used in a language'. A word is 'any sound or combination of sounds recognized
as a part of speech, conveying an idea'. When we speak of the language
of animals the only alterations necessary to make these definitions appropriate are to understand 'words' and 'speech' in the special sense of
significant sounds or gestures and, in place of 'idea' to substitute a
formula denoting that what is transmitted is an indication of the state of
the animal, such as readiness to act in a particular way, or a signal tending to elicit a specific reaction by the bird or other animal receiving it,
or both. It is not suggested that when a bird reacts instinctively to such a
signal it has 'received information' in the sense of conscious evaluation
which these words usually bear. Acoustic bird language consists of
sounds, given and received—often augmented by visual movements and
posturing. Indeed, the latter constitutes an elaborate gesture 'language'
to which only passing references will be possible in these pages. 'Display'
may be used of strictly visual signalling but when auditory signals are
associated these should be considered an integral part of the display
(Armstrong 1947).

It has been maintained that the principal difference between human
language and animal language is that the latter cannot convey abstract
ideas but we should think of bird language in terms of what it does rather
than what it cannot do, more especially as it is easy to underestimate its

1

potentialities. We have no introspective knowledge of the bird's mind and there are difficulties in deciding what is meant by an abstract idea in this context. Long ago John Locke postulated that birds had ideas in the sense in which he used the term (p. 44) and Koehler's experiments (1937, 1943, 1950) on the ability of birds to count suggest that they have 'wordless ideas'. Birds can express anticipatory associations (p. 83). However, the significance of their vocalizations is best discussed in relation to what we know of particular bird utterances, their motivation, so far as this may be ascertained, and the reactions evoked by these signals.

Next to man, birds have developed auditory means of communication to greatest perfection (Appendix). More than fifty years ago Craig (1908) drew up a list of the principal functions of the calls of doves. His paper marked a considerable advance in assessing the significance of bird vocalizations. He noted that they were effective in relation to : 1. Personal control. 2. Suggestion. 3. Stimulation. 4. Inhibition. 5 and 6. Co-ordination in space and time. 7. Proclaiming species, sex, individual identity and rights. 8. Tradition (by this he meant providing an example or a lead). Whitman and Craig realized that bird utterances could be both informative and stimulatory.

A number of subsequent writers have sought to enumerate the functions of the song of a species—as distinct from its repertoire of calls. For example, Blanchard (1941) considers that the White-crowned Sparrow's song expresses : 1. Defiance of territorial rivals. 2. Longing for a mate. 3. Sexual excitement. 4. Concern for territorial boundaries as well as communication. 5. Eagerness for the female to return to the eggs. 6. Fright. As will appear, distinctions have to be made between (a) the different items of information together with their functional effectiveness in any given type of song; (b) the changes in significance which a song may undergo according to the circumstances in which it is uttered, and (c) the different types of song, each with its own significance, which are uttered by some birds.

Difficulties throng the path of anyone who seeks to tabulate the various kinds of information conveyed by bird utterances. Apart from other considerations a bird's song may be uttered in special circumstances or in a modified manner, either of which may alter its signal significance. Even when referring specifically to territorial song we do not escape these difficulties because such song, as we shall see, may be highly modifiable. As the meaning of a sentence may vary according to the way in which it is inflected so may the signal function of a song. Enough has already been said to indicate that the song of any species must be studied in detail before we can evaluate its range of flexibility and communicatory capacity. An attempt to do this for the Wren's song has been made else-where (Armstrong 1955).*

Various attempts have been made to enumerate the sound-signal reper-toires of mammals and birds. The following are some representative estimates : Blackbird 7 call-notes , song, and sub-song (Snow 1958); Nut-hatch 12 call-notes and 3 types of song (Löhrl 1958); Black-capped Chickadee 16 (Odum 1941–42); Pied and Collared Flycatcher 17, in-cluding song (Curio 1959); Whitethroat 14 calls and four forms of song (Sauer 1954); Wren 13 calls and about 5 types of song (Armstrong 1955); Song Sparrow and Chaffinch 21 (Nice 1943; Marler 1959b); Chukar Partridge 14 adult calls (Stokes 1961). Blase (1960) lists 9 calls of the Red-backed Shrike and 3 forms of song but only 6 of the call-notes are characteristic of breeding adults and the songs are distinguishable primarily by their functions. Carpenter's investigations (1934, 1940, 1944) indicate vocabularies of 13 for the Gibbon and 15–20 for the Howler Monkey. D. Fossey (*Anim. Behav. 20*: 36–53) noted 16 types of Gorilla vocalization. Marler (1959b) considers that there is surprising consistency in the repertoires of the birds and mammals which have been studied but, although most of the species mentioned above possess signal sounds for certain common types of situation, his comment suggests a greater conformity to a particular range of significant utterance than is actually found. On the basis of available data it seems that the maxi-mum distinctive signal sounds noted in any species of mammal or bird

* To illustrate the necessity to study a species intensively if its whole repertoire of utterances is to be ascertained, some examples may be given of call-notes which change their character or significance during the breeding cycle or are uttered in circumstances in which they might be overlooked.

The Irish Dipper's display note *zur-r-r-r* is used as a greeting by both sexes early in the season but changes later to a loud rattling quality though uttered on the same occasions. After the young hatch it is confined to when the parents are flying back and forth feeding the young (Rankin and Rankin 1940). About two days before young Carolina Wrens leave the nest the female modifies her call from a twitter to a loud chatter. This alteration 'seemed to be the beginning of an attempt by the female to interest the large nestlings in sounds beyond the nest' (Laskey 1948). The alarm notes of the Robin and Stonechat change when the young leave the nest. Young Wrens are never heard to use the rattling alarm call in the nest, but they may utter it as they fly out. They do so when disquieted afterwards.

In some species, such as the Chaffinch and Whitethroat, certain alarm calls are uttered only in the breeding season (Andrew 1961b).

A practical difficulty in annotating bird vocabularies is that some call-notes are not always clear-cut in their utterance or significance. Examples are mentioned in Chapters IV, IX, and elsewhere. Mixed, composite, or intermediate vocalizations—called *Mischlaute* or *Mischgesänge* in German (Curio 1959a; Thielcke 1960)—may be uttered when birds are highly excited or confused. Avocets, and sometimes Wrens, emit an alarm call inappropriate to the kind of predator (Makkink 1936; Armstrong 1955). Whitethroats and Red-backed Shrikes may utter 'displacement activity' calls (Sauer 1954; Blase 1960). (Chapter VII. Appendix and p. 262.)

is about 20 odd. Some mammals and a few birds, including the Kiwi and vultures, have a very limited vocabulary. The number of signal sounds uttered by a species is related so closely to its social, territorial, and mating behaviour that comparisons between species with dissimilar patterns of behaviour can be misleading. We must remember that the observers mentioned above are not in complete agreement as to what constitutes a discrete signal sound. Also, those who have studied a species most intensively tend to list more signal sounds than others who have devoted less study to their chosen bird. Moreover, vocalizations are subject to minor modification in a way which renders it difficult to ascertain changes in signal significance. Bird language is flexible and one feels that, if necessary, it could be adapted to express more than it generally does in most species.

Bird vocalizations may be classified in various ways and a complete tabulation would be elaborate as it would have to show the accentuation or disappearance of certain utterances according to season, breeding cycle, and age of the individual. It would also have to take into consideration pair-bond, parent-offspring, and predator-prey relationships—and other factors. Poulsen (1958) lists Chaffinch utterances mainly according to sex and season :

TABLE I

CHAFFINCH VOCALIZATIONS (AFTER POULSEN 1958)

Male and female throughout the year	⎧ Flight call ⎨ Social call ⎪ Alarm call ⎩ Injury call (?)
Male and female during breeding season	Aggressive call
Male only during breeding season	⎧ Two alarm calls ⎨ Two courtship calls ⎩ Song
Female only during breeding season	Courtship call
Young ⎧ Nestlings ⎨ Fledglings ⎩ Juveniles	⎧ Begging call ⎨ Begging call ⎩ Escape

Useful as such a scheme may be it tends to give an unduly simplified picture of the situation. Also, in some species utterances are modified according to the degree and kind of excitement so that they intergrade in significance. No mode of classification is perfect.

Calls and songs may be classified, firstly, according as they are Social, Sexual, Domestic, or Self-expressive, and then according as they are Aggressive, Attractive, Contact, or Environmental. They may be qualified further. Thus the call announcing an air-borne predator is Social, Environmental, and a fleeing signal. Self-expressive utterances are those which express a mood rather than serve a communicatory function, as when a bird croons on the nest. This classification is unsatisfactory as the categories overlap.

Another method of tabulating the utterances of the Chaffinch has been drawn up by Marler (1956b). He divides the information conveyed into two classes—environmental and social, and subdivides these groups according to whether the identity and location of the bird are communicated. Thus we have four categories of information: Environmental, Social, Identifying, and Locating. Each type of Chaffinch utterance is considered and the number of items of each kind estimated. As a given type of utterance may not only convey information in all four categories but transmit more than one item in one or more of them a particular utterance may communicate much information. The Chaffinch's song, for example, transmits eight items. Its identifying function includes denoting its species, sex, and individual identity.

TABLE II

NUMBERS OF ITEMS CONVEYED BY CHAFFINCH CALLS, PLACED IN FOUR CLASSES OF INFORMATION (AFTER MARLER 1956b)

Environmental	Social	Identifying	Locating	
1	2	1	–	Flight
1	1	1	1	Social
–	–	–	–	Injury
1	1	1	–	Aggressive
–	–	–	1	'tew' alarm
–	–	–	1	'seee' alarm
1	–	–	1	'huit' alarm
–	–	–	–	Subsong
1	3	2	2	Song
1	2	2	–	'kseep' courtship
1	2	2	–	'tchirp' courtship
1	2	2	–	'seep' courtship
–	–	1	1	Nestling begging
1	2	1	1	Fledgling begging
9	15	13	8	Total

By this method the vocalizations of a single species may be listed but the categories are so general that the items have to be accompanied by much explanatory text. Three types of courtship call are enumerated without any indication, in the Table itself, that song attracts the female. Moreover, it is desirable that in any descriptive list of bird calls account should be taken of the identity and status of the bird receiving and reacting to the information, as a sound may convey information prompting to different courses of action according to the sexual or other relationship of the receptor to the signaller. If it be objected that we have no 'inside' knowledge to show that a bird takes account of status or is the direct recipient of items of information the answer is that what is meant is that the bird acts as if this were so. Observed reactions provide one criterion of the significance of a signal; what we know of the state of the signaller provides another.†

A more inclusive classification is required to cover the range of bird language. The main difficulty in applying the categories set out below lies in our uncertainty, in regard to some of them, as to the exact content of the information conveyed. Human observers watching a bird's response might differ concerning the extent to which they were individually 'reading into' its behaviour more than was justified. Apparently all bird utterances carry multiple information. Perhaps the main value of the categories listed is to stimulate awareness of the variety of data communicated. This classification is sufficiently comprehensive to provide room for the inclusion of items of information, the communication of which is based more on inference than direct evidence; but otherwise encouragement would be given to the assumption that the content of birds' vocalizations is less rich than it is. It may be misleading, for example, to refer to an utterance as 'territorial' or 'aggressive' without indicating the complexity of the information conveyed. To make it a rule to assume that a communication conveys only the data which are most evident on superficial observation and conservative interpretation of a bird's behaviour is to adopt an attitude of parsimonious credit which can hamper research and delay appreciation of the complexity of animal means of communication.

TABLE III

ITEMS OF INFORMATION COMMUNICATED BY ONE BIRD TO ANOTHER BY AUDITORY SIGNALS

Identity	*Motivation*	*Environment*
Species	Sexual	Location
Sex	Need (other than sexual)	(a) individuals
Individuality	Aggression	(b) objects
Status	Escape or alarm	Territory
		Predators

IDENTITY

Information indicating species

Montagu (1802) remarked that 'the peculiar note of each is an unerring mark for each to discover its own species'. He was referring particularly

† Throughout the text a † indicates a note in the Addenda.

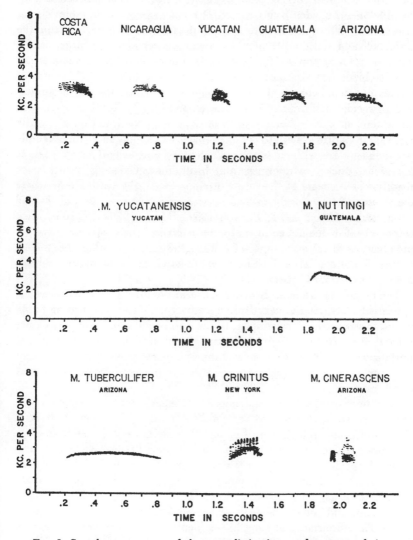

Fig. 1. Sound spectrograms of the most distinctive vocal patterns of six species of crested flycatcher (*Myiarchus*) in Middle and North America. The upper row shows the utterances of *Myiarchus tyrannulus* in five regions. (After Lanyon 1960a)

to song, and indeed bird song is the most highly elaborate complex of mechanisms precluding mistaken identity evolved by sub-human organisms. To the human observer auditory clues are often the readiest and most reliable means of identifying a bird. It was by the Wood Warbler's song that Gilbert White was able to identify it as a species differing from the Chiffchaff and Willow Warbler. Even wing-noises made by birds may be diagnostic (Johnston 1960). Distinctive utterances prevent mis-matings between birds very similar in appearance. Lanyon (1960a) in his study of crested flycatchers has shown that acoustic characteristics may be important in species discrimination in this group (Fig. 1). Territorial song in particular acts as a barrier against dysgenic hybridization (p. 118). Hybrids in nature are apt to occur in species which do not form a definite pair-bond or are without 'standard' territory and song-defence, such as lek birds, ducks, carduelines, and hirundines. Crossing occurs most readily when a mate of the bird's own species is not available or where the ranges of two closely related species or forms overlap and 'hybrid zones' occur (Mayr 1942; Lanyon 1957; Sibley 1957) (p. 105). Most commonly it is due not so much to deficiency in species-specific advertising clues, as to the acceptance of a less satisfying mate when the normal partner is not available. This is the explanation of the numerous hybrids reported by aviary keepers.

Territorial utterances, being *inter alia* long-range declarations of species identity, tend to vary from a stereotyped pattern according to the extent to which they are adapted to proclaim individual identity, or are uttered at times when their territorial significance is of diminished importance.

Information indicating sex

Most territorial utterances disclose the singer's sex. Experiments with recordings show that a bird recognizes a rival by its song; that is, it reacts to the sound as if a bird of its own species and of identifiable sex were present. Long-distance auditory signals were first evolved as declarations of species, sex, and location, as in the insects and batrachians (Appendix). Such means of communication are of special value to highly peripatetic organisms—hence their great development in birds, but in this group, and some others, these signals have acquired wider significance. The importance of song in sex identification is shown by the confusion which may ensue when an abnormal female sings (p. 178). In many species the male's adornments proclaim his sex, as in lek birds, and auditory clues perform a minor rôle or may even be dispensed with, but the hybridizations which occur indicate that in general acoustic releasers are more efficient in preventing miscegenation than visual releasers (p. 110). While the birds are still at a distance, and even out of sight, mistakes are forestalled. Mis-matings are rare in similarly plumaged (isomorphic) species in which the male has a distinctive territorial song. In such species the female's sex is usually disclosed by her behaviour and particularly her lack of song (p. 150). In the Red-necked Phalarope the rôles of the sexes are to a large extent reversed. It is significant that not only is the female more brightly adorned than the male but she has evolved instrumental territorial song (p. 154). In many species there are rather subtle differences between the calls of the male and female (Kortlandt 1940a; Gullion 1950, 1952).

Information indicating individual identity

The auditory discrimination of birds can be extremely delicate, surpassing human abilities in some respects. Young Green Woodpeckers look out of the nest hole and beg when the trunk of the tree is scratched with the claws of a stuffed Green Woodpecker but cower in fright when the scratching is made in other ways (Blume 1957). An Allied Woodhewer (Woodcreeper) can distinguish the sound of its mate alighting on a tree trunk from sounds made by other birds (Skutch 1945a). Human capacities in this respect are, perhaps, greater than we commonly realize. We have no difficulty in recognizing a familiar footstep, and a photographer in a hide by a nest may soon find that he is able to distinguish non-vocal sounds made in the vegetation by the birds he is awaiting from sounds made by other species. A correspondent in the *Daily Telegraph*, 9 June 1960, stated that the gulls at Dover quickly learned to discriminate between the sounds made by British and enemy aircraft. Buxton (1946) noticed that Great Crested Grebes were able to distinguish the noise of one motor boat from others.

Not only do birds' songs differ from individual to individual but individual characteristics are often retained for a lifetime. Thus an expert in recording songs remarks that 'the graphs provide an identification that is just as positive as a numbered band' (Borror 1960).

Very slight differences in individual songs must be apparent to birds (p. 10). Specific identity and individual identity are proclaimed in different ways. While characteristics important for specific identification must remain consistent for the species, or, at least, for populations, individual identity must be revealed by characteristics which differ from bird to bird. In some species, such as the Yellowthroat and other American wood warblers the songs are distinguishable to such an extent that the human listener can identify individuals by their songs (Kendeigh 1945a; Stewart 1953; Borror 1961). Probably this is achieved in different ways by different species—as by the use of repertoires of song versions, the temporal alteration of components or, possibly, the interpolation of mimicries (p. 77). In the thrushes the time-pattern, duration of notes, and relative changes in pitch provide clues to species, and individuality is revealed by details of pitch (Dilger 1956; Stein 1956; Marler 1959b). Studying the Chipping Sparrow's simple trill Marler and Isaac (1960a) found that one syllable type was characteristic of each individual but the syllable structure might differ from one individual to another, even if the birds were neighbours. They concluded that 'significant individual differences, which might be used in individual recognition, were found in the number of syllables per second and possibly in syllable duration and minimum frequency in some cases'. These authors also noted (1960b) that the introductory and trill syllables of Brown Towhee songs are noticeably different even when birds occupy contiguous territories.

That a bird's call has characteristics which reveal its individual identity is particularly apparent where a number of individuals nest close to one another. A Black-headed Gull recognizes its returning mate by its call and a Herring Gull asleep on her eggs in a noisy colony is awakened by the voice of her returning mate (Kirkman 1937; Tinbergen 1954). A sleepy Hawfinch reacts immediately to her mate's single note when he comes unseen to invite her to leave the nest (Mountfort 1957). A Bullfinch identifies its mate's call by criteria which the human ear cannot detect (Nicolai 1956). A Turnstone does not mistake an intruder's voice for that of his partner (Bergman 1946) and the call of a Jackdaw's mate causes it to emerge from the nest hole even when other birds are calling (Lorenz 1931). After a single day a male Pied Flycatcher recognizes his mate or another male individually (Curio 1959a). Probably vocal as well as visual clues are used. Male Cactus Wrens recognize other males by their voices (Anderson and Anderson 1957). The female Pheasant recognizes and answers her mate's call (Kozlowa 1947). Doves prospecting for a nest site are able to distinguish each other's voices although when the pair-bond is established the demeanour of the female may change so much that to the human observer she is not recognizable as the same bird (Craig 1908). A Budgerigar identifies his mate by the colour of the cere yet, if it is altered experimentally, he recognizes her by voice (Cinat-Tomson 1926).†

The extent to which nidicolous passerines ever recognize their own chicks by voice or appearance is uncertain. Such birds react to the nest-situation at first rather than to the young as individuals. A Meadow Pipit will disregard her own chicks struggling outside the nest from which the young Cuckoo she cherishes has evicted them. However, Rowan (1955) describes how a male Red-winged Starling, impatient with young which would not leave the nest, lifted two of them out and dropped them to the ground in spite of the female's efforts to protect them. Afterwards they differentiated between their parents, cowering and becoming quiet when the male approached. It is a general principle that animals do not make detailed discrimination where normally it is without practical advantage. Nice (1943) thinks that Song Sparrows probably know their young as such some days before they attain their independence. That Jackdaws and some other corvids recognize their young is more likely (Lorenz 1931, 1938). Auditory clues probably play a part. Among nidifugous species the larger gulls and terns recognize their chicks at about five days old but Noddy Terns, nesting in trees, whose chicks do not wander, never learn to identify their young (Watson and Lashley 1915). Similarly Kittiwakes, nesting on cliff ledges from which the chicks cannot stray, do not recognize them up to the age of four weeks (Cullen 1957). Goethe (1954) has shown that the Herring Gull can recognize its chick's call. When chicks hatched from substituted eggs of another species are killed or neglected the peculiarities of their call may be responsible. Palmer (1941) concluded that Roseate Tern chicks hatched by Common Terns died because their begging call resembled the sound made by the Common Tern chick after it had been fed. Sooty Terns, given the eggs of Noddies, throw out the chicks (Lashley 1938). Strange chicks of their own species are accepted during the first few days of brooding. As the chicks of the two species do not differ greatly in appearance the difference in calls may have some bearing on the treatment of the Noddies. Tinbergen thinks that vocal clues may be more important than visual in the Herring Gull's recognition of the young.

In an experiment involving the substitution of eggs a Kentish Plover chick two days old recognized the call of its Ringed Plover foster-parents. At four days it heeded their alarm call and disregarded that of its own species. A Ringed Plover chick a few hours old heeded only the alarm notes of Ringed Plovers (Rittinghaus 1953) but in some species the young will follow a very crude imitation of the parental call. Apparently nidifugous chicks recognize their parents sooner than the parents their young (Lorenz 1935) but 'recognition' is difficult to define. In general what happens is that the young differentiate stimuli more exactly as they grow older.* Chicks of the Domestic Fowl placed in darkness with several hens tend to respond to their own mother—at least when different breeds are used (Collias 1952). Ramsay (1951), experimenting with domesticated birds, concluded that the adults and young mainly acquire, rather than inherit, the ability to recognize other members of the family to which they belong, by using visual and vocal cues. The latter seem to be most important.

Turnstone chicks orientate to their parents by sound better than sight (Bergman 1946). Young Prairie Chickens have an irresistible impulse to follow when they hear their parent's call, even if she is invisible (Gross

---

* The octopus is exceptional in that the young at first respond to stimuli from particular forms of prey animal and later respond to more generalized stimuli.

1930). It seems that young Snow Buntings may possibly be able to distinguish their father's song from the songs of other males (D. Nethersole-Thompson, pers. comm.). A young Mockingbird recognized the voice of the parent who fed him and started to beg on hearing it (Michener and Michener 1935). Nestling Blackbirds know their mother by her food-call (Messmer and Messmer 1956) and apparently fledged young recognize their father's song (Thielcke-Poltz and Thielcke 1960).† Young Ring Doves distinguish one parent from the other, as is shown by their soliciting food more insistently from the female, who remains to feed them longer than the male but auditory cues may not be involved. They, and some other birds, such as Coots, learn to distinguish strangers through being rebuffed when begging for food or seeking to follow them (Craig 1908; Alley and Boyd 1950). Fledged Chiffchaffs can distinguish their mother from other Chiffchaffs (Gwinner 1961) and nestling Horsfield Bush Larks distinguish their parents from House Sparrows at six feet (Bourke 1947).

Information concerning status

This category is introduced tentatively as the concept of status is rather abstract but without it we might assume some signals to have less significance than they possess. Thus among Domestic Fowl threat sounds are used by the despot in maintaining his position in the dominance hierarchy. A given threat sound conveys to a hen that the other is aggressive and also the individual identity of the threatening bird. More than this, previous experiences of this kind have established such a situation that the threatened bird acts in a stereotyped way as a subordinate. This is what is meant by regarding the threat sounds as conveying information concerning status. Describing the behaviour of Marsh Tits, Morley (1943) refers to 'dominance-assertiveness' being expressed by a particular type of call-note. When a bird, such as a Bullfinch, paired for life, distinguishes its mate's call from all others it is not a large assumption that the call's content includes 'mated status'. In bird flocks possessing a definite social structure, as with Jackdaws, one bird is the acknowledged leader in certain activities. He has leadership status (Lorenz 1931, 1938).

In regarding bird utterances as conveying information concerning status (or relationship) we are assuming that the receptor summates information to some extent. It might be argued that the bird merely registers separate items of information, as they might be set out in Marler's Table (p. 5) or listed in accordance with Table III, but itemizations of information transmitted should not be regarded as indicating that this is how the information is apprehended. Indeed, a signal sound may have significance beyond its itemized content just as in music we may have 'not a fourth sound, but a star'. Thus it seems necessary to postulate that some sounds convey information concerning mated, parental, filial, social, or other status. In spite of the fact that a recorded call will attract a chick as its parent's call would do we should not assume that such a call merely triggers the reaction to approach. Recognition of identity may, or may not, be involved, dependent on the age of the chick (p. 10). Similarly, when a bird is attracted to feed a young Cuckoo which it has not fostered in the nest, the assumption that the call releasing this behaviour is devoid of all relational content is no sounder than the assumption that it has this content. In some birds, such as some species of geese, in which the family bond endures until the next breeding season, learning is important, and the content of the contact notes becomes richer, conveying information concerning identity and hierarchy. It is undesirable to shut our minds to the possibility that some calls have greater content than we can prove since there are utterances which can acquire additional signal significance through experience.

MOTIVATION

The main types of utterance expressing motivation are Sexual, Hunger, Contact, Aggressive, and Escape, associated with reproductive, social, and agonistic situations. It might be argued that some calls convey information concerning parental, filial, or social motivation but they can best be included, as suggested, under Status, except when they are instigatory of certain types of action.

Information concerning sexual motivation

The character and condition of the receptor of a signal sound are of special significance where the sexual relationship is concerned. Sex, maturity, pair-bond status, stage of the sexual cycle, and other factors may be important in determining the reaction to the sound. A bird not in the relevant condition and relationship may fail to register an utterance which activates powerful reactions in another individual of the same species.

The most specifically sexual utterance is the call of the male or female inviting copulation. The female Wren emits a ringing squeal, the Flicker awaits a sexual cry or movement from the female to release copulatory behaviour (Noble 1936). The male Cowbird utters a shrill descending note, the female a rattle when ready for coition (Laskey 1950). Male and female Redstart give a high-pitched hissing note, rather like the begging call of the chick (Buxton 1950). Perhaps this type of call is difficult to locate and so reduces vulnerability at this crucial time. I have noticed that the Great Tit utters varied and very subdued chirps, amounting to a pre-copulatory whisper song.† The Nuthatch may, or may not, utter a precopulatory call (Löhrl 1958). This is true of the Robin also but when a call is uttered it resembles the note emitted during courtship feeding. Perhaps the solicitation call of relatively conspicuous species with a fairly long 'betrothal' period tends to be less conspicuous than the corresponding call of cryptic birds which breed immediately after pairing. In some species, especially those in which pair-bond formation and copulation are separated in time and mated birds recognize each other individually, such as the Robin, the male may mount without preliminaries on the part of either bird.

Male courtship utterances may manifest a mingling of motivations—escape, aggression, and attraction. It must therefore be understood that in this section utterances are classified according to the dominant motivation.

A *kseep* call is uttered by the male Chaffinch during pair-formation and may accompany aggressive behaviour but a *tchirp* note replaces it later when the female dominates and the male is anxious to copulate, but timid. When the female utters *seep* he is attracted and, if she solicits, mounts, though he is afraid of her. His timidity is justified as she may attack him (Marler 1956a, b). The Corn Bunting's *kwaa* as he flies to the female to copulate is very similar to the aggressive *chaa* (Andrew 1956–57).

Sexual calls and/or songs (p. 110) are important in overcoming the strangeness or antagonism which often prevails at the formation of the pair-bond or before coition and they play a significant rôle in the progressive synchronization of the sexual cycles necessary for successful breeding (p. 149).

There are various utterances, such as those used in greeting, which probably have some sexual as well as status connotation. In some species particular calls may be effective in more than one type of situation or relationship. The Hawfinch's *quilp* alerts the female to his presence, is uttered by both sexes as a greeting, and stimulates the chicks to beg (Mountfort 1957). Some male game birds utter the same note to warn the female as she uses to warn the chicks (Schenkel 1958), and the female Canada Goose attracts the goslings with a call resembling that uttered by the gander in attracting the goose. Both male and female Rufous Whistler cheep like nestlings when courting (Erickson 1950).

Information concerning need other than sexual

These calls include many contact utterances expressing the need for company (Andrew 1961b), and are the dominant calls of young, dependent birds. In buntings there is a change in the begging call when the young are about to leave the nest (Andrew 1957). Such a change, which may occur in other species, would be adaptive if it rendered dispersed chicks more readily locatable by the parents. These location calls tend to be brief and abrupt, with wide frequencies (p. 253). Need or anxiety calls, with their descending frequencies, suggest forlornness to our ears whereas contentment notes tend to rise (Fig. 4). Distress calls attract the parents, other members of the flock in social species, and even birds of other species (Snow 1958).

Corresponding to such calls are parental or other social calls instigating in another individual action conducive to the satisfaction of a need. Chicks may thus be activated to seek food or shelter, to follow or to squat.

Information concerning aggressive motivation

Threat sounds play a particularly important part in the lives of animals with powerful armaments. The beaks of many species of bird are capable of inflicting serious injury so vocal deterrents as well as ritualized posturing have been evolved restricting dysgenic fighting. Pugnacity is probably a basic factor in the evolution of song. Aggressive calls are often harsh and strident, though seldom so far-carrying as territorial song, the motivation of which has an aggressive component (Chapter VII). The aggressive calls of some species, such as the Blackbird, Chaffinch, and probably Wren and Blue Tit, are used in defending territory and may be regarded as territorial defence calls. Sauer (1956) interprets the harsh, aggressive note of the Garden Warbler as due to the conflict between fear—the impulse to flee—and aggression. Probably many other aggressive utterances, as well as territorial song, have evolved as a product of such conflicting motivation which underlies many forms of behaviour. A number of birds and mammals make a growling noise when food competitors are near. The threat sound of the Domestic Cock is a low 'grumbling' which appears in a sound spectrogram as a long, thick band prolonged for two seconds or more. Crowing, unlike this and other warning utterances, is much less harsh (Fig. 4) (Collias and Joos 1953; Collias 1960).

At least seven species of bunting utter a harsh *chaaa* call indicative of pugnacity (Mayr, Andrew, and Hinde 1956; Andrew 1956a, b). The Blackbird's *chink* or *tix* expresses high intensity excitement. A deeper *chook, chook* is associated with excitement of lower intensity. Both are uttered when an owl is mobbed. A slightly modified *chook* announces the approach of a ground predator. Andrew (1961b) has found a correlation between these types of call and flight motivation. The fullest expression of pugnacity is a thin, piercing *seee*, lasting nearly a second. Snow (1958) thinks that the alarm rattle, often ending in a scream, has no communicatory value, but the alarm rattles of other turdines, such as the Mistle Thrush and Redwing, attract the mate, and perhaps other birds, to mob the intruder. Many birds utter ticking sounds which express alarm and convey a warning to neighbouring birds.

15

The aggressive call of the Chaffinch is a low buzzing which, in the sound spectrogram, appears as a wide band of frequencies with a nearly constant mean pitch, though on close examination it is seen to be a rapid succession of short notes. It is sustained for nearly a second. The aggressive calls of a number of other finches are somewhat similar (Marler 1956b).

Aggressive and alarm calls and behaviour are apt to increase in intensity as the breeding cycle advances (Dilger 1956a). Similarly there is an accentuation of distraction display when the eggs of nidifugous species hatch or nidicolous young are about to leave the nest (Armstrong 1949, 1954b).

Hissing is the type of aggressive or defensive expression most widespread in the animal kingdom and we may plausibly assume it to have been one of the first communicatory sounds used by land animals. Snakes hiss, the box turtle makes a hissing sound as it withdraws to its carapace, and the platypus is said to hiss under stress. The following are among large birds which hiss—Ostrich, Jabiru Stork, White Stork, some geese, Mute Swan, Bittern, vultures, Gentoo Penguin, and some owls (Collias 1950a). The Kiwi hisses while feeding, as well as aggressively (Robson 1947). Among hole-nesting birds which hiss are the Wryneck, young Hoopoes, and some tits. The suggestion of a snake is very vivid, especially when a tit, sitting on the eggs, suddenly flips out its wings (Armstrong 1947; Sibley 1955). The young Cuckoo also hisses. A gardener, who had glimpsed a Cuckoo in a nest and heard this noise, told me that he thought it was some kind of toad. A rat hears a hiss as a powerful sound because its hearing is highly sensitive to energy between eight and twelve kilocycles per second. Pumphrey (1950) comments that a snake's hiss is to a rat probably 'louder and more shattering than the lion's roar is to us'.

Aggressive calls, in common with many other calls, are normally innate. Response to them is also usually innate (p. 45).

Information concerning alarm, fear, and escape motivation

Nothing more is assumed when terms such as 'alarm' or 'fear' are used than that the birds are observed to behave as if they felt alarm or fear, or as if information of an object or situation which normally evokes such reactions were conveyed to them.

Alarm utterances may have arisen in some groups in the past, as Darwin suggested, as a concomitant of muscular movements made by organisms when surprised or escaping. A cat may give an involuntary grunt on touching the ground after jumping from a height. No doubt such sounds have evolved in some groups into communicatory signals, alerting to danger.

In a general classification a rigid distinction cannot be made between

I. Oxpeckers on Black Rhinoceros

IIb. Grasshopper Warbler singing

IIa. Whitethroat singing

alarm calls proper and calls indicating that the bird is taking flight for one reason or another. When in a flock the Great Tit utters characteristic stopping and starting notes (Hinde 1952).

There are not many species whose alarm notes have been carefully investigated. A bird may possess a vocabulary of alarm calls of several grades both in regard to their communicatory value and the extent to which escape or aggressive impulses are the dominant motivation. Thus the Yellow-breasted Chat has four calls indicating different intensities of alarm (Petrides 1938). Many species reveal degrees of alarm or the imminence of the danger by varying the loudness or rapidity of their cries. The fear calls of buntings vary according to the degree of escape motivation and are modified in different species. They range from *eee* to *see*, *seeoo* and *cheep* with intermediate sounds in many species. The Reed Bunting utters three types of call. The *see* is used as an alarm call and is difficult to locate (p. 253). The *cheep* has a definite beginning and therefore is easily located. It expresses mild fear or disquiet at being alone and therefore has social relevance as well as fear motivation. According to Andrew (1956a, b, 1956–57, 1957) the *seeoo* call may be primitive in this group and may have diverged into the other two types. There are also brief *tit* notes and rattling calls uttered by many species when disquieted or about to fly. The *tit* call may be uttered by a male before he sings. Andrew remarks that the Yellow-hammer gives the *see* call, expressing great fear, when disturbed at the nest. He accounts for this by the conflict situation in which the bird finds itself on having to remain close to, or approach, a threatening object. Calls of this kind by birds in flocks alert their neighbours and generate in them a like mood. When uttered by nesting birds they apparently warn the bird's mate, who may approach and utter similar notes. We have already remarked that a bird may use the same call in different contexts (p. 14).

Some alarm calls, especially those indicating sudden danger, such as the near approach of a swift predator, trigger an immediate reaction appropriate to the whole situation. Flying raptor warnings cause chicks of nidifugous species to rush for cover or to crouch and remain still. Adults also seek cover or crouch. The Golden-naped Woodpecker utters a call which brings the young home immediately (Skutch 1948a) whereas when the female Ptarmigan emits a certain note the chicks at once scatter into the herbage.

Many birds utter shrill calls or screams when seized or wounded. In some social species, such as Jackdaws, other members of the flock are attracted and also utter loud calls. In other species the cry of pain seems to have little or no communicatory significance though such calls may sometimes be adaptive if they surprise a predator into loosening his grip.

ENVIRONMENT

Birds are able to convey information in regard to the animals and objects in the environment and their own location. That is, a bird, by its utterances, may attract attention to another creature or object in the environment and also stimulate appropriate reactions by other animals, not necessarily of its own species. It may also signal changes in the environment.

Information concerning location of individuals

By virtue of uttering any sound a bird indicates its position to any listener equipped with hearing organs sensitive enough to perceive it, though calls vary from those which are definitely locative to others of such a nature as to reduce, so far as possible, betrayal of the calling bird's position (Fig. 43). Birds are able to locate certain calls with exactitude. A Cuckoo or an owl can be enticed from a distance to within a few feet by imitating the call (Armstrong 1940). The ears of owls are modified to facilitate the location of sounds (Appendix). Chicks are able to locate the calling hen precisely when she is out of sight (Katz 1937).

Locational calls may indicate the location of other individuals than the caller. The males of a number of species which display or nest socially give a specific call when a female approaches (Collias 1960) and the ground-predator alarm usually calls attention to the whereabouts of the animal.

Locational call-notes always carry additional content. Thus the Curlew's flight-note does not merely signify 'Here I am' but also 'Where are you?' since an imitation of it will cause a solitary bird to deviate from its course. Contact calls used by paired birds have similar significance. Certain types of locational call have been named 'sequestration calls' by Grinnell (1920). He regards them as serving to keep foraging birds apart but they are probably more correctly considered 'distance-adjustment call-notes'. When pairs of Willow Tits are observed in birch forest in Lapland it is noticeable that the frequent calls prevent the birds from foraging too close to one another or getting out of touch.

There is some evidence that in a number of species the vocabulary of calls has expanded from the calls of the chicks. Adult Blackbirds, Whitethroats, Meadowlarks, and Red-backed Shrikes utter calls developed thus. The Curlew's call appears to be a clear-toned version of the chick's distress note and the Domestic Cock's crowing develops from the chick's distress call (Andrew 1961b).

The rallying call of mature Bobwhite Quail is a modified form of the anxiety note of the chicks (Stoddard 1931). Probably all the utterances of gulls develop by elaboration and differentiation from anxiety calls (Moynihan 1959). The occurrence of call-notes in the songs of some birds supports the view that song has evolved from calls. The alarm flight call is a major component of the Skylark's song (Thorpe 1961).

Information concerning location of objects

Food

Some utterances communicate not only the location of the caller but also, together with the bird's movements in some instances, the presence of some other object. It might be argued that when a chick responds to the hen's call to food the response is mechanical but it seems reasonable to suppose that the chick anticipates food on hearing the call, at least after some experience that food is obtainable where the call is uttered. Gulls attract each other to food visually and vocally (Armstrong 1944b, 1946a). The Herring Gull utters a specific food-finding call which is said to attract individuals from up to five kilometres distant, but this announcement is not given if there is only a small amount of food (Frings and Frings 1956; Frings *et al.* 1955). Behaviour of this kind is characteristic of species feeding on locally or sporadically abundant sources such that the community gains more than the individual loses in the competition which ensues.† The response to visual and vocal food-locating calls is not necessarily confined to birds of the finder's own species. Similarly, alarm calls may be responded to by other species.

The activities of honeyguides are of special interest as information concerning a food source is communicated alike to birds of the guide's own species, to honeyguides of other species, to ratels, and to man. The utterance of a churring note as the honeyguide moves towards the bees' nest is of primary importance in attracting attention and 'guiding' a man or quadruped. Africans wishing to stimulate the birds to act as guides grunt like ratels (Friedmann 1955). An association is established between the honeyguide's movements and bees' nests. Doubtless the anticipatory images aroused differ in man, beast, and bird although the effect is the same, but man's anticipatory image or intuition may be assumed to be a refinement of capacities possessed by other vertebrates.

Water

Possibly the calls and movements of some birds indicate to others the presence of water. Sven Hedin describes how the sight of a duck flying up saved his party from dying of thirst in the deserts of Central Asia by revealing where a pool was situated. Birds may establish associations of this kind. However, it is doubtful whether any bird utters a special call denoting water. Various species may behave in odd, excited ways before a thunderstorm (Armstrong 1947) (p. 209) but there is no definite evidence that a bird can convey to another information concerning the weather by means of its calls.

Nest-sites and roosts

As we shall see later, calls or songs, sometimes specially modified or specific to the situation, are often employed to indicate a potential nest-site or more or less complete nest (p. 162). The nest-songs of some Central American flycatchers elicit corresponding songs from neighbouring birds of related species (Skutch 1951a) so information concerning the stage of the breeding cycle may be communicated. Collias (1960) noticed that Village Weaverbirds uttered a particular call only when in a place suitable for collecting nest material. Vocalizations are also used by some species to indicate a communal roosting place. When Wrens follow a leader, as he calls and sings, to a dormitory, they act as if they were aware that a sleeping place was in prospect (Armstrong 1955). Goldcrests utter specific calls as they go to roost (Nöhring 1958).

Information concerning territory

Calls as well as songs may be declarations of proprietary rights and in some species a call-note seems to be substituted for song when such motivation is of low intensity (p. 115). Territorial song conveys much information (p. 113) but its primary importance lies in its announcing to birds to whom it is relevant that an area is occupied and defended. Wrens, House Wrens, Robins, Willow Warblers, Chaffinches, and other passerines remain quiet and move unobtrusively, even furtively, when they venture into a neighbour's domain (Armstrong 1955; Marler 1956a). Such a trespasser offers no resistance if he is discovered. He flees and refrains from singing until safely back in his own territory. Female birds seeking mates may go outside the area where the male sings and return again. This seems to imply some appreciation of the restriction of the male's activities to a certain area (Marler 1956b). Mated females of a number of species soon learn the boundaries of the male's territory, partly by accompanying him but probably also by registering to some extent the places where he sings. As a trespassing male shows wariness even during the temporary absence or silence of the owner of the area an association is apparent between song as a warning and the area to which this warning is relevant.

Information concerning predators

Warnings concerning predators are the items of information most immediately relevant to survival which can be conveyed acoustically, so it is not surprising to find that predator-warning calls have been evolved to a highly specialized degree. They vary in the urgency ex-pressed, in the specificity of their information concerning the type and location of the predator, and in other respects. The nature of the alarm cry uttered is influenced by internal state and external situation, by mood, the stage of the breeding cycle, the suddenness of disturbance, and other factors. As we have already noted, most alarm notes are inborn. The response is normally also inborn. Unhatched chicks respond by quiescence to the parents' warnings. However, some of the Chaffinch's calls, such as the *chink* and the *huit* alarms, occur in variants and are probably subject to modification by learning (Marler 1956b; Poulsen 1958).

The Canary can learn the alarm call of the Roller Canary, and the flight call of the Linnet seems to be learnt to some extent (Poulsen 1954, 1959) (Fig. 14). The Bullfinch's call-note indicating 'mood' is inborn but the call used at considerable distances is inborn only to the extent that the bird 'knows' that it should be monosyllabic and fluting. In isolated birds the quality is aberrant (Nicolai 1959). Pied Flycatchers, reared in isolation, respond to the mobbing calls of their own and other species and 'freeze' when large birds fly over. Mobbing, accompanied by rattling notes is elicited by a few key stimuli (Curio 1959a). Association and learning may quickly add to the content of a signal and birds learn to connect warning calls with particular hazards. Lorenz (1952) remarks that 'on the appearance of an enemy as yet unknown to the young an old guide Jackdaw needs only to give one significant "rattle" and at once the young birds have formed a mental picture associating the warning with this particular enemy'.

Alarm calls may range from generalized cries to call-notes specifically related to different kinds of danger. Most birds utter different types of warning according to whether the predator is airborne or a ground marauder. Gilbert White (Letter xliii), in a passage commenting on the vocabulary of poultry, mentions the special calls uttered by Domestic Cocks and Turkey Cocks when a flying raptor appears. Warnings of air-borne predators are usually high-pitched and without abrupt phase- or intensity-difference—approximating to pure tones beginning and ending gradually. They are adaptive to the extent of warning companions while giving minimum clues by which the predator could locate the bird calling (Fig. 2) (Marler 1955, 1959b) (p. 253).* On the other hand the mobbing

---

* Marler (1955, 1956b, 1959b) points out that phase-difference is most valuable for sound-location at low frequencies 'because the information it provides becomes ambiguous when the wave-length is less than twice the distance between the ears'. Intensity differences are most useful at high frequencies as the head or any other object casts appreciable sound-shadows if its size is greater than the wave-length of the sound. Time differences can be used throughout the range of hearing. The most easily located signals are those which provide clues of all three kinds.

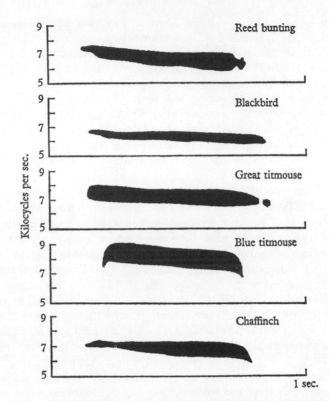

Fig. 2. The calls of five different species when a hawk flies over. Each has a relatively narrow frequency range, somewhat over-emphasized in this figure and figure 3 as a result of the use of wide-band pass filters. They all sound like a high, thin whistle, and are difficult to locate. (After Marler 1959b)

calls and behaviour elicited by a ground or static predator, as, for instance, a perched owl, are usually such as to draw attention to where it and its announcer are located (Fig. 3). The male Chaffinch utters the *seee* alarm on perceiving a flying hawk and the *huit* warning when the danger is less imminent. The alarm calls alert other species (Promptoff and Lukina 1945; Marler 1956b). Song Sparrows emit *tik* notes when a flying raptor appears and *tchunk* calls on observing other intruders, but the response is discriminatory; American Sparrowhawks, *Falco sparverius*, which are not a very serious menace to other birds, may evoke the *tchunk* warning (Nice 1943). Wrens utter a short, sharp call as they dash for cover but voice repeated *kreeee* notes when they spy a cat or stoat. As they do so they follow it around. When a hawk appears the Eastern Chipping Sparrow calls *zeeeee* but cats and squirrels are greeted with *chip* notes

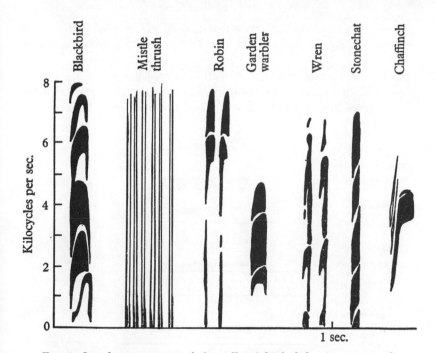

FIG. 3. Sound spectrograms of the calls of birds belonging to several families uttered while mobbing an owl. The frequency in kilocycles per second is proportional to the pitch, and the time-scale on the base-line shows the duration of each note. A thin vertical line corresponds to a short note with a very wide range of pitch, like a click or tap, which is the easiest of all to locate. Thus these calls are such as to draw the attention of other birds to the predator. On the kilocycle scale middle C occurs at about 0·25 kc., two octaves above at about 1 kc., and four octaves above at about 4 kcs., corresponding with the highest notes of the piccolo. (After Marler 1959b)

from a high perch (Walkinshaw 1944). Many other emberizines and other birds utter these high-pitched, elusive calls (Hailman 1959). Great, Blue, Marsh, and Long-tailed Tits usually emit a specific trilling *tsee* when a hawk approaches though occasionally it may be evoked by some other large bird flying over. The House Sparrow's hawk alarm differs from the call uttered when the intruder is on foot (Daanje 1941). Flying birds evoke a brief warning call from Chiffchaffs but, according to Treuenfels (1940), ground predators are greeted with alarm notes only in the breeding season.

Passerine cries calling attention to airborne or other suddenly appearing predators are very similar in their acoustic characteristics. They are brief and lack sharp phase- or intensity-differences, difficult to locate and

23

consequently unlikely to betray the location of the bird calling. Like mobbing calls and food-indicating calls (p. 19) they have community value.

A special type of non-betrayal call is uttered by young Green Sandpipers. When the chicks are disturbed they utter a sound only just within the range of human hearing but reacted to immediately by the parent

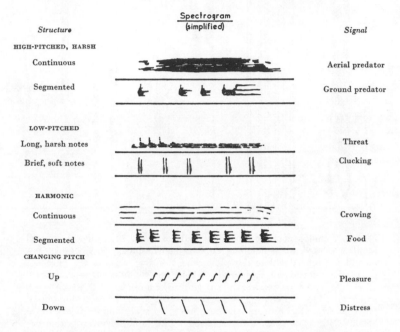

	Spectrogram	
Structure	(simplified)	*Signal*
HIGH-PITCHED, HARSH		
Continuous		Aerial predator
Segmented		Ground predator
LOW-PITCHED		
Long, harsh notes		Threat
Brief, soft notes		Clucking
HARMONIC		
Continuous		Crowing
Segmented		Food
CHANGING PITCH		
Up		Pleasure
Down		Distress

FIG. 4. Simplified spectrograms of the classes of auditory signals of the Domestic Fowl. (After Collias 1960)

when fifty metres distant (Voipio 1952). Further evidence is desirable. I have not noticed any such sound when photographing Wood Sandpiper chicks. As the upper range of hearing in cats (50 kc.) and rats (40 kc.) (Jahn and Wulff 1950) is well above that of human beings (20 kc.) adaptation by young birds to utter ultrasonic calls would not prevent their detection by some predators. Small mammals utter ultrasounds.

Warning calls differentiating flying and ground predators are characteristic of other groups than passerines, including the Crotophaginae, waders, and game birds (Davis 1942; Bergman 1946). The Golden Pheasant and Jungle Fowl utter different cries according to whether the danger is from the air or the ground. The alarm note of the Domestic Fowl evoked by flying enemies is a loud, sustained, harsh scream but the ground predator warning is *cut-cut-cut-kaaah*—the final note being like the aerial-predator warning and fear squawk (Fig. 4) (Collias and Joos 1953; Collias 1960). Calls signalling aerial danger cause birds hearing them to make for cover or to squat if the terrain is open. The Snow Bunting calls *weee* at the approach of a falcon or ground predator. If the enemy is airborne it crouches; if not it flutters around (Tinbergen 1939).

Many birds react to the warning calls of other species. Bechstein commented on this in rather extravagant terms: 'The least experienced observer of nature knows that the approach of danger is expressed by a universally intelligible cry; which, if uttered by a Wren, for instance, is understood by the Turkey-cock, and vice-versa. Of whatever species the one may be, which first perceived the approach of a bird of prey, it is able to excite the attention of all the birds in the neighbourhood by its peculiar cry of warning. As soon as the Blue Tit utters her *Iss!* so indicative of fear and terror—which, nevertheless, she seems sometimes to do from pure love of mischief—the wood is silent in an instant'. There is a general resemblance between the alarm calls of related species and these calls tend to be interspecific (Saunders 1929) but reciprocity in this respect goes much further and extends, for example, between the alarm calls of Chaffinch, Blackbird, Mistle Thrush, Robin, Wren, Hedgesparrow, Greenfinch, Bullfinch, and various tits (Marler 1956b). The alarm calls of Garden Warblers alert Blackbirds and the calls of Great and Marsh Tits warn Garden Warblers (Sauer 1956). A Bewick Wren dashed for cover when a Bluebird sounded the alarm (Thomas 1946a). Toucans, Caciques and other species do likewise on hearing the warning note of Wagler's Oropendola (Chapman 1928). The Lapland Bunting utters a fear call and eyes the sky on hearing the Chaffinch's flying-predator alarm (Andrew 1957). In nature the occasions when these species hear each other's alarm notes must be so rare as to be negligible.

The alarm call of the American Robin, which may be uttered at eighteen days old, has warning significance for other birds, even poultry (Jackson 1932). Craig (1909) thought that the Blue Jay sometimes uttered its alarm call gratuitously and 'enjoyed' the consternation of other species.

Meadowlarks cease singing when Red-winged Blackbirds give the alarm (Linsdale 1938a) and Black Woodpeckers look up apprehensively when they hear the hawk alarm of tits (Eygenraam 1947). A Red-throated Diver disregarded the usual cries of Great Skuas but at their first alarm call slipped from the nest (Lockie 1952). Black-necked Grebes cover their eggs when Black-headed Gulls overhead sound a warning (England 1960). Similarly, Turnstones respond to the alarms of Common and Herring Gulls, Common and Arctic Terns, and Redshanks. The reaction is strongest when the sitting bird is unable to see the intruder. This is adaptive because Turnstones thus avoid being seen by Crows when leaving the nest (Bergman 1946). It has been shown experimentally by playing records of the voices of gulls and crows that individuals mingling with other species learn to respond to their calls (Frings *et al.* 1958). Birds learn by association the significance of the alarm calls of other species, but the similarity of many passerine alarm calls—rising and falling in pitch (Marler 1955)—suggests that they have common characteristics to which there is an inborn response.

Mammals, and possibly crocodiles, also profit by responding to bird warnings. Mammals may also respond to the alarm calls of other species of mammal as a chimpanzee does to the orang-utan's warning (Bierens de Haan 1929). Mention has already been made of birds responding to imitations of their calls (p. 18). The calls and movements of Oxpeckers and other species which perch upon, or constantly frequent, beasts such as buffalo and rhinoceros alert them to the approach of potentially dangerous creatures, and seals and sea-lions heed the warning calls of gulls (Pl. I). Deer return to a tranquil state after being disturbed when the normal bird voices are heard around. By imitating such noises an observer can reassure alarmed animals (Riney 1951).† Prairie dogs utter an 'All Clear' signal after an eagle has flown away.

Experiments in which recordings of American gulls and crows were reproduced in France, and vice versa, showed that individuals accustomed to hear and respond only to signal calls of their own species or regional group did not respond to communication sounds of other groups, but individuals mixing with other groups of their own species or flocks of other species learned to respond to their calls (Frings *et al.* 1958).

Whether any bird utters an alarm call so specialized as to be elicited only by a predator of a single species is doubtful. Perhaps there are species which include a specific snake alarm among their calls but the evidence in regard to the Curve-billed Thrasher reviewed by Rand (1941b) is inconclusive. Certain squirrels of the Cameroon forest utter a specific call when they come across a large snake (Friedmann 1955). Kuusisto (1941) noticed that the Willow Warbler used different calls when alarmed by a Cuckoo and by a man but he thought the Cuckoo alarm might be similar to the snake warning note. Smith and Hosking (1955) found that this species reacted to the imitation of a Cuckoo's call with an odd *chee-chee-chee* cry—a remarkable response as it apparently implies some appreciation by Willow Warblers of the association between the call of the male—who never approaches the nest—and victimization by the female Cuckoo. Many passerines have an inborn response to owls (p. 23) but apparently the alarm note is not exclusively evoked by them (Nice 1943; Hartley 1950b; Hinde 1954). According to Makkink (1936) Avocets utter a specific warning cry when gulls approach but apparently different species are not discriminated. It would be interest-ing to know what cry is evoked where some other bird, such as the Magpie or Carrion Crow, constitutes the most dangerous enemy.

No doubt our appreciation of the manner in which birds communicate by means of acoustic signals will rapidly increase as scientific techniques for studying them and better methods of listing them are elaborated. There is ample justification for speaking of bird utterances as language. The ancient legends concerning birds whose language could be under-stood by those endowed with esoteric means of interpretation embodied what scientific investigation has shown to be true. Bird language is adaptable and a great deal of varied information can be communicated quickly and accurately. To some extent birds can interpret the language of other species than their own and even quadrupeds can respond to the language of birds.

II

THE STRUCTURE AND COMPONENTS
OF BIRD SONG

'Tis wonder
That an invisible instinct should frame them. . . .
Cymbeline, IV.ii.177

ANY single sound differs from another in three respects—pitch, intensity, and quality. Pitch is determined by the frequency of the vibrations of the source of the sound and of the medium transmitting it—usually the air. Vibrations succeeding each other slowly cause a low sound, rapidly successive vibrations a high sound. Intensity, loudness, or volume is due to the amplitude of the vibrations. A guitar string produces a louder sound the more vigorously it is plucked but the pitch does not change unless the string be tightened or shortened by placing a finger on it. The quality or timbre depends on the harmonics which accompany the vibrations of practically all sound-producing objects, so that it is not strictly correct to speak of a single sound. A plucked string or the air in a wind instrument reacts in a number of ways, producing not only the 'fundamental' due to the movements of its whole length but also subsidiary vibrations of higher pitch. These determine the quality of the sound. A musical, pleasing sound is heard when the vibrations are regular, a 'noise' or harsh sound when they are disorderly. Such noises are common in bird songs. When they are introduced in orchestral music, as when the triangle is played, they supply emphasis or contrast.

Pitch

It is easy to be mistaken in regard to the pitch of a sound. Many people are not endowed with absolute pitch discrimination and changes in tempo can be mistaken for changes in pitch. A bird singing faster may seem to be reaching higher notes and a song with decreasing tempo may appear to be descending the scale. Increasing loudness may give the impression of singing up the scale. Before electronic techniques were available attempts were made by using musical notation, systems of lines, nonsense syllables, and verse to illustrate changes of pitch in bird song but they all have severe limitations. Musical notation involves approximations which often amount to falsification, other systems are not easily interpreted and onomatopoeic verse or syllables may recall the lilt of a song to those familiar with it but convey little meaning to others (Fig. 42) (Armstrong 1923). Until recently bird songs were almost as difficult to capture as the music of fairyland but now records of songs obtained in many parts of the world are available and the sound spectrograph can be used to transcribe the details of such songs with accuracy. The number of notes, changes in pitch, duration, and other characteristics are clearly revealed.

Absolute and relative perception of pitch have been noted, not only in birds but also in mammals (dogs) and fish (Koehler 1956). Once the songs of Blackbirds have become established they remain constant, not only throughout a season but for many years. Even a deaf Blackbird or Bullfinch sings normal pitch, though the songs of a small proportion of Bullfinches may change in the course of a year or two (Messmer and Messmer 1956; Hüchtker and Schwartzkopff 1958). Hamersley (1714) stated that a bird never alters the pitch of its song but a Cirl Bunting while bathing may do this (Gooch 1952).† F. A. Saunders (1924) found when attracting Chickadees by imitating their call-notes that he could sometimes induce a bird to raise or lower the pitch of its response by raising or lowering his call tone. According to Knecht (1940) a Nightingale may break off its song when a note is imitated and then raise the pitch of its song accordingly. He claims that in nature the Yellowhammer, Golden Oriole, and some tits may be heard transposing. Of two Blackbirds taught by means of a flute one reproduced two notes accurately but the other sang them an octave higher (Thielcke-Poltz and Thielcke 1960). Pallis (1939) mentions hearing an unidentified species of cuckoo in the Himalayas transposing its song. Bechstein reported that Bullfinches could transpose what they had learnt. He also remarked that if Grey Parrots or Starlings pitch a melody too high for their vocal range they break off and repeat in correct pitch. An Indian Hill Mynah whistled a tune in several keys. If the tune were sung to it in E sharp it would sing in this key. Stadler (1934, 1935) concluded that many birds were able to transpose. When Koehler (1954) whistled the beginning of a seven-note melody to his parrot it would complete it in whatever key he used. Sir J. Swinburne (1920) kept a Grey Parrot which could whistle snatches of Beethoven on hearing the name of the work. When the words 'Pastoral sonata' were spoken the bird would whistle an appropriate fragment. He writes: 'I kept a sheet of paper and whenever the Parrot whistled a tune I noted the tune and the pitch. For about a week he whistled each tune approximately at its own pitch. One day, put out in the sun, he seemed to run melodious riot. He whistled most of the tunes, repeating them over and over again, and at all sorts of pitches. It is clear, therefore, that a Parrot does not work on the absolute pitch principle, but I cannot penetrate further into its mental processes'.

We should not be surprised that some birds are able to transpose, as the recognition of pitch by human beings appears to involve subconscious processes. Scholes (1938) comments on the ability of some musicians to remark, 'I don't know that piece he's playing, but it's in A flat and he's playing it in A'. He explains this by postulating that the open notes of a stringed instrument are recognized as such by those with highly sensitive hearing. 'The observer first subconsciously realizes that the open notes are below or above the pitch he regards as normal, that the instrument is therefore mistuned, and then recognizing the key of the music as played, allows for its mistuning'.

When a Chaffinch's song develops from sub-song to the mature territorial song the pitch may be raised, though the bird has absolute pitch. The extent to which elements of song may be innate, and the capacity for singing in a particular way transmitted by inheritance is shown by the difference between the songs of the wild Canary and Border Canary on the one hand, and the Roller Canary on the other. As Thorpe (1958) and Marler (1959b) point out, the Border Canary has been bred mainly for colour and shape, and its song remains close to that of the wild Canary, whereas the Roller, being the product of selection for song, sings differently from the other two in pitch, time pattern, and quality. A first-class singer should have as many as fourteen different 'tours'.

When pitch intervals in bird songs are recognized by human observers as being the same as, or approximating to, the intervals of music such songs are apt to be ranked high musically. It has been claimed that Hermit Thrushes sing according to the pentatonic scale (Wing 1951) and that a Blackbird piped the opening phrase of the rondo in Beethoven's violin concerto (Howard 1952) but it is all too easy for observers to read musical intervals into bird songs. However, the notes of the Wood Thrush are 'so pitched that they follow our musical scale very accurately' (Borror and Reese 1956). A. A. Saunders (1951, 1959) thinks that Song Sparrows commonly use the pitch intervals of human music and points out that in the Ruby-crowned Kinglet's song the interval between the first and second parts is frequently an exact octave. Miss Terry Gompertz and Miss Rosemary Jellis of the B.B.C. tell me that a Great Tit, whose songs they have recorded in detail, sings several distinctive songs in the key of F sharp major. A difficulty in forming an opinion as to the extent to which birds are sensitive to human musical intervals lies in our ignorance of the influences operative in the formulation of the various scales used by mankind. Scholes states that three processes have been suggested as bringing scales into being: intuition or instinct, reasoning, and chance. He points out that 'instinct' cannot be unimportant as 'a large number of scales, even of quite early times, have been constructed, partially at least, on lines which the discoveries of science have later endorsed as being in accordance with acoustic principle, or, in other words, natural mathematical logic; this can be nothing but an instinctive recognition of natural fact'. This gives support to the thesis advanced in Chapter XIII that human music owes characteristics to inborn rhythms and modes of apprehension inherited from our animal ancestry.

Gilbert White had a friend who noticed that Cuckoos usually sing in D but he had heard one sing in D sharp and another in C. Owls hooted in B flat but one went almost a note below A. It should be noted that Handel's English tuning fork gives the pitch A as 422·5 vibrations whereas A=439 is now standard. Gerard Manley Hopkins commented that Cuckoo calls altered in pitch when the bird called in flight.

The Pine-woods Sparrow's song is in two parts. The first varies in relation to the second. It may be higher, of the same pitch, or lower (Stillwell and Stillwell 1952).

The range of frequency within the songs of some species is very wide as is shown by some examples given by Nicholson and Koch (1937):

TABLE IV

APPROXIMATE FREQUENCY IN CYCLES PER SECOND OF
EUROPEAN BIRD-NOTES

Species	*Minimum frequency*	*Maximum frequency*
Wood Warbler	2200	6000
Garden Warbler	1500	5000
Mistle Thrush	1500	4500
Curlew	1100	4000
Woodlark	650	3750
Jay	275	1400
Stock Dove	250	550
Heron	140	550

Probably the high frequencies are under-estimated owing to deficiencies in the apparatus used for measuring them. Nicholson (1936) classifies the songs of British birds into categories thus: Very Low (up to 600 cycles per second)—Woodpigeon, Nightjar, owl hoots, and human singing voices; Low (600–2000)—Cuckoo and Carrion Crow to Rook, Jay, and Nuthatch; Medium (2000–4000)—Blackbird, Willow Warbler, Blackcap, Blue Tit, Curlew (spring call); High (4000–6000)—Wren and others; Very High (above 6000)—Robin, Starling, warblers, buntings, and finches (top notes). The top note of a male tenor attains the

Very Low class and a soprano has a range closely similar to a Jay; the violin goes to 3000 and the piano to 4000.

Brand (1935, 1938), using more sensitive instruments, studied the songs of fifty-nine North American species. A few of his estimates are set out below:

TABLE V

APPROXIMATE FREQUENCY IN CYCLES PER SECOND OF
NORTH AMERICAN BIRD-NOTES

Species	Mean	Highest	Lowest
Eastern Winter Wren	5000	8775	3300
Eastern Song Sparrow	4700	7700	1900
Starling	3475	8225	1100
Black-capped Chickadee	3300	3700	3025
Eastern Robin	2800	3300	2200
American Redstart	1200	7300	4400

According to these studies the Blackpoll Warbler has the highest average note and the highest frequency, 8900 c.p.s. and 10,225 respectively. The Grasshopper Sparrow averages 8600 and the Cedar Waxwing 8400. The average of the fifty-nine passerine songs was 4280—a quarter note higher than the highest note on the piano keyboard. For comparison it may be mentioned that the highest note attained by a coloratura soprano is 1200–1500 cycles but even thrushes do not sing as low as this. Brand (1938) estimated that the Wood Thrush's range was from 1825–4025 c.p.s. but Borror and Reese (1956) recorded 1640–8900 c.p.s. for this species. The Horned Owl's hoot is at about the middle of a baritone's range. Some birds, such as the Umbrella Bird, which has a modified trachea and syrinx (Sick 1954), and Emu pitch their notes much lower.†

Bird notes seldom remain on the same pitch from moment to moment but slur upwards or downwards, and often in both directions. Many notes are so constantly changing pitch that estimates have to be averaged (Brand 1938). In the song of the Wood Thrush there are up and down variations of pitch as rapid as 200 per second. Some phrases contain two fluctuating notes uttered simultaneously (Borror and Reese 1956). The Rufous-sided Towhee and the Reed Warbler can also sing two notes simultaneously (Borror 1960; Thorpe 1959), as may some other birds (p. 256). The Gouldian Finch seems to operate three vocal mechanisms (Thorpe 1960) (Figs. 5, 6, 7 and 8).

In human utterances loudness and pitch tend to vary together, though those learning a tone language, such as Chinese, have to discipline themselves to alter inflections natural to Westerners. Increase in pitch and

III.   Thick-billed Nutcracker singing his subdued song with bill closed

IV. An old woman teaching a Jackdaw to sing.
Alessandro Magnasco

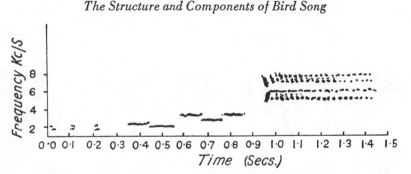

FIG. 5. Vibralyser graph of part of Wood Thrush's song. From 0·95 sec. to the end the bird is singing two notes simultaneously, one about five or six half-notes on the musical scale above the other, each fluctuating up and down in pitch 45 times a second. (After Borror and Reese 1956)

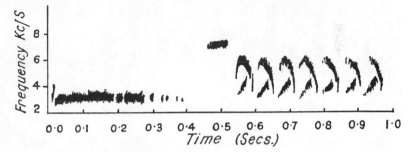

FIG. 6. Vibralyser graph of song of Rufous-sided Towhee illustrating the singing of two notes simultaneously. The bird utters an up-slurred note and at the same time a note that slurs upward and then downward. (After Borror 1960)

loudness occur during heated arguments and their conjunction is usual in creating an emotional effect on stage or screen. Composers, too, raise intensity and pitch when the heroine in opera reaches an emotional crisis. In musical composition and also in bird songs intensity and pitch may vary independently.

Intensity, volume, or loudness

There are immense differences in the loudness of the songs of different species. A Bittern may be heard three miles away (Turner 1924), a Pileated Woodpecker at a mile and a half (Bent 1939a), a Cuckoo at more than a mile (Haviland 1926), a Reed Warbler at 300 yards (Brown and Davies 1949), and a Goldcrest at seventy yards (Nicholson and Koch 1936). The courtship song of the Rose-breasted Grosbeak may be inaudible at a distance of more than a few feet (Ivor 1944). In favourable conditions a Wren may be heard singing half a mile away but its sweet

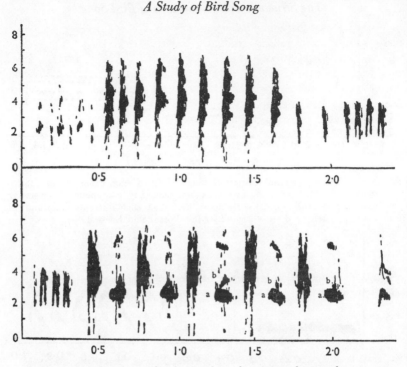

FIG. 7. 'High front' sounds of very short duration and great frequency range alternating with notes of two harmonically unrelated fundamentals (a) and (b) sounded simultaneously as produced by the Reed Warbler (*Acrocephalus scirpaceus*). Vertical scale: frequency in kilocycles per second. Horizontal scale: time in seconds. (After Thorpe 1959)

courtship song carries only some yards, and its 'whisper song' a few feet (p. 62). Within related groups there is sometimes a correlation between the size of the bird and the loudness of its utterance; the Mistle Thrush's song carries farther than the Redwing's, the Greater Spotted Woodpecker's drumming farther than the Lesser Spotted's, but no general rule can be formulated correlating size and loudness unless it be that the notes of loud-voiced large birds tend to carry farther than those of loud-voiced small birds. Ethological and ecological considerations are more important in determining the volume of a bird's utterances than its size (p. 227). The Hawfinch is larger than the Chaffinch but has a much quieter song, the Wren and Long-tailed Tit are among our smallest birds but one has a powerful song, the other has not. Some of the largest birds, such as vultures, have very feeble voices but the relatively small South American bellbirds produce an astonishingly loud clanging noise (Armstrong 1940a) (Frontispiece and Pl. XV). According to Waterton (1903) the White Bellbird can be heard at a distance of three miles.

Within a song there may be variations in intensity. Starlings will begin their songs softly, getting gradually louder, so producing a crescendo effect. Many birds, singing sub-song, utter louder notes as they proceed, as if their measure of success gave them increased confidence. The Ovenbird's song increases in intensity as it ends whereas the songs of the Worm-eating Warbler and Sharp-tailed Sparrow decrease in volume (Saunders 1929). Intensity tends to vary according to mood, increasing when a bird is vigorously defending territory against a would-be intruder and in some species decreasing as attack grows imminent or courtship becomes ardent (p. 156). Birds in a stimulated condition may sing more songs in a given period than those in a less excited state (Nice 1943).

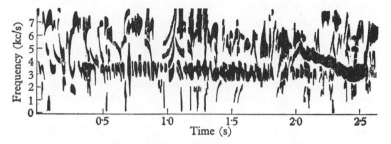

Fig. 8. Section of song of Gouldian Finch. There appear to be three different vocal mechanisms operating simultaneously, one producing a drone-like continuo, the other two an elaborate chirruping song above it. (After Thorpe. 1961) (From material supplied by F. Hall)

There are species which sing songs in which there is great difference in volume between the two sections (p. 68). **1775340**

Quality

The quality of a bird's song or call is highly important in enabling us to distinguish what species we are listening to. We may assume that tonal quality is very significant to the birds concerned. An artificial Chaffinch song, played on an eighteenth century organ, though conforming to the pitch, range, number, and duration of notes as well as length of phrase, was too different in quality to be recognized by Chaffinches (Thorpe 1958). As the Chaffinch sings forty-five notes a second the imitation was deficient in this respect. On the other hand Chaffinches learn Tree Pipit's songs—these being close in quality to the Chaffinch song (von Pernau 1707).

An indication of the variety in quality of bird voices is provided by the terms used to describe these sounds in the *Handbook of North American Birds*, now appearing. There are 373 terms in the list. Probably these are not exhaustive. Often in attempting to convey an impression of the quality of a bird's song to someone who does not know it we are forced to compare it with the song of some other bird. In describing bird voices comparisons have been made with practically every instrument of the orchestra. The names of some birds, inspired by their calls, embody references to man-made sounds—Bellbird, Whipbird, Sawwhet Owl, and so forth, or to similarities to the calls of other creatures, such as Catbird and Grasshopper Warbler. Some birds are named after phrases of human speech. A Tyrantbird in Trinidad is called the Kiskadee. Its name is a corruption of the phrase which it repeats with maddening monotony, 'Qu'est-ce-qu'il dit?' In orchestral music the instruments sometimes imitate bird notes. Bach composed a fugue, *Thema all'imitatio gallina cucca*, based on the crowing of the Cock. Handel wrote a 'Cuckoo and Nightingale' organ concerto and the Cuckoo and Quail are heard in Beethoven's Pastoral Symphony.

The tonal quality of a bird's song as apprehended by the human ear is more than a matter of fundamentals and harmonics, pure notes and noises. In many songs the notes follow in such rapid succession that what is perceived is not the sequence of individual notes, but a summation of them. Rapid changes of frequency may create a buzzing effect (Borror and Reese 1956). Similarly the teeth of a circular saw in contact with a log individually make a noise but in rapid motion they create a tone varying in pitch according to the speed of the rotation. Also the production of two or more notes simultaneously may introduce exceptional quality to particular utterances (p. 256).

Terminology and forms of song

As we are not concerned with the detailed analysis of the more elaborate songs, a complex terminology such as has been suggested by Sotavalta (1956) need not be adopted. The time is not yet ripe for the formulation of a set of terms which can claim general acceptance. In most songs there are portions which by reason of certain characteristics are registered by the ear as entities. In songs such as those of the Mistle Thrush and other turdines these components are distinguishable by their timing. The song is a succession of notes or groups of notes with detectable pauses between them. Other songs, sung more rapidly and of a more repetitive character, such as the ditties of the Yellowhammer, Chaffinch, and Wren, have other characteristics which catch the ear—the monotonous repetition and final drawl of the Yellowhammer, the rollicking changes of pitch with the final flourish of the Chaffinch's song, the repetitions and pitch changes of the Wren. The ear gains a general idea of what is happening in rapid songs but for the details we must have recourse to the sound spectrograph. What is heard as one note may be many. The Oxford

Dictionary states that 'note' in music may be used with several different meanings, but it is a 'written sign representing pitch and duration of a musical sound' and also 'a single note in a bird's song or call'. For 'written sign' we may substitute 'electronically recorded sign' and by 'single note' we must understand, unless patently popular language is being used, what the sound spectrograph, rather than the ear, records. Slurring makes it difficult to compute exactly the number of notes in many bird songs. In discussing trills some writers (Marler and Isaac (1960a) refer to 'repetitions of more or less identical syllables'.

'Phrase', as used here, signifies a discrete succession of notes commonly forming a subdivision of a complete song. In this definition 'syllables' might be substituted for 'notes' in referring to some types of song. 'Subdivisions' may be recognizable as temporal units or by pronounced changes of pitch, or both. In semi-continuous songs, as, for example, the Robin's and the Song Thrush's, the phrases are separated by intervals or rests. In more rapid songs, such as those of the Chaffinch and Wren, the trained ear can distinguish the phrases with a fair degree of accuracy but they are depicted clearly in sound spectrograms. These are essential when the analysis of complex, continuous songs is undertaken. A 'motif' is here regarded as a distinct musical element. It can often be co-extensive with a phrase.

When two or more phrases recur frequently in regular succession, as in the Wood Pewee's song, they may be called 'sentences' (Craig 1943). A song which consists of a series of phrases exactly repeated is a 'stereotyped sentence' but as many species which sing thus possess a repertoire of stereotyped sentences these should be given a specific name and called 'song-versions'. Although many species, including the Chaffinch, seem to the casual listener to sing a stereotyped song, close investigation usually reveals that there are several versions. Marler (1959b) remarks that in Europe the Woodpigeon seems to be exceptional in singing the same theme all the time. In contrast White-winged Doves vary their songs by (1) different groupings of notes, (2) different arrangements of these groups, and (3) different tempi (D. C. Saunders 1951).

Song-versions and discontinuous song

When a bird utters a stereotyped sentence at intervals as long as, or of longer duration than, the sentence itself, the song may be called 'discontinuous' to distinguish it from continuous songs, which flow or ramble along without pronounced pauses, and from semi-continuous song which will be considered presently. When speaking of these separate utterances as units they may simply, for convenience, be called 'songs'; but some writers, distinguishing between the different forms in a bird's repertoire, have styled these 'song-types' or 'songs' (Thorpe 1958). 'Song-versions' is preferable as the repertoire of such birds consists of variations on a basic pattern, and songs of a species could mean 'forms' such as territorial, challenge, courtship, and so forth. 'Song-type' is apt to be misinterpreted, on the one hand as being equivalent to 'kinds of song' in a more general sense than is intended, and, on the other, as denoting a norm from which other forms diverge. 'Song pattern' (Borror 1961) is ambiguous. It is known that a number of species—probably very many—learn the song or song-versions to greater or lesser extent (Chapters III and VI). Commonly birds with a rather restricted repertoire of versions sing a burst of one and then a series of another. This is true of birds as different as the Chaffinch and White-winged Dove (Smart 1943; D. C. Saunders 1951). Hinde (1958) has shown that the alternation of series of song-versions in the singing of the Chaffinch may be explained in terms of the competing self-inhibiting and self-facilitating effects of singing the different versions. Probably other mechanisms are also involved.* Craig (1943) comments that in his experience the clear-cut and long-continued alternation of phrases by birds of the Tyrant family is unique but Rufous-sided Towhees may alternate versions and a Yellowhammer has also been heard doing so. During a period of observation a Calandra Lark four times followed mimicry of the Swallow's song with the song of the Tawny Pipit (Alexander 1927). If this kind of linkage between mimicries can thus become established it suggests that linkages may also be formed between the motifs of a species. It also raises questions as to the extent to which a bird exercises choice in regard to the succession of motifs—and this leads on to the difficult issue—'Have birds aesthetic taste?' (Chapter XIII).

Analysis of bird song has not been carried far enough for a clear distinction to be made, applicable to songs in general, between song-versions, recurring sentences, and motifs more or less loosely linked with others. It remains uncertain to what extent the components of song can be defined on a temporal basis. Playing songs over at a reduced or accelerated rate reminds us of the subjective bias which may enter into our aural appreciation of bird song. Highly important is the extent to which in some birds' songs components are detachable from stereotyped succession, as in the songs of some turdines. Ultimately research may enable us to envisage the phylogeny of forms of song and to formulate theories concerning the development of differentiation into continuous and discontinuous song. A few examples follow, illustrating how different in number may be the repertoires of song-versions and motifs of various species.

* 'Mechanism' is used here in the sense given in some dictionaries of 'means by which results are attained'. Many writers employ this overworked term in such a way that the reader is liable to assume it to imply a mechanistic philosophy.

The Plain Titmouse has two basic patterns of song used interchangeably with no detectable difference in function (Dixon 1949). The Western Meadowlark may have up to three song-versions. A bird may switch abruptly from one to another but individuals have 'favourite' versions (Miller 1952a). The Blackburnian Warbler has five forms of song as well as a courtship song (Lawrence 1953) but here we seem to be concerned with song-modification rather than song-versions. It must be borne in mind that writers' terminology does not always render it easy to be certain how a bird's repertoire is constituted. Although to the ear the Yellowhammer's song seems stereotyped a bird may have as many as six versions (Marler 1959b). Both sexes of Lark Bunting utter eleven song-versions but repetitions of the versions may not be identical (Stillwell and Stillwell 1955). The Song Sparrow may possess twenty-four. A male 'usually goes through his whole repertoire before repeating any one song; the order in the second set of series is rarely repeated exactly' (Nice 1943). Saunders (1935) says of the Carolina Wren: 'Each individual is extremely versatile in singing, producing a large number of different songs, singing each one over a number of times, but possessing so many that it is difficult to find the same bird singing the same song two days in succession'. Borror (1956) noted twenty-two different song patterns in twenty-four series sung by a single bird. The Cardinal possesses a repertoire of at least twenty-eight different patterns. The songs of male and female are said to be indistinguishable (Laskey 1944a).

Semi-continuous song

It is convenient to regard semi-continuous songs as a somewhat loosely defined category between discontinuous and continuous songs. This usage differs from that of Hartshorne (1956). Turdines are representative of this group of singers. The order in which phrases are sung is variable, as it is also in continuous songs. One observer credits the Hermit Thrush with five motifs, another with ten (Saunders 1935; Wing 1951) but individuals vary and investigation with the sound spectrograph may reveal larger repertoires. Marler (1959b) shows that a Mistle Thrush sang twenty basic motifs (themes) in forty-seven phrases but the components could be combined in different ways (Fig. 9). He recorded a Song Thrush which gave only two repeats in eighty-five phrases and a Robin which sang a series of fifty-seven phrases without ever repeating itself. Charles Koffán informs me that in eight minutes of the continuous song of the Woodlark he found 108 distinct motifs, only five or six being repeated.

The elaborate terminology used by Sotavalta (1956) in analysing the Sprosser Nightingale's song involves inconsistencies. He defines a phrase as 'figures and groups of figures belonging together'—a figure being the smallest melodic unit with a pattern. He found that a typical Sprosser phrase consisted of introductory, antecedent, characteristic, postcadence, final, and cadence, with bridge sections between introductory or antecedent and the next section or between final and precedent sections. Such a 'phrase' was a more or less fixed unit. Birds were found to have a limited number in their repertoire. The frequency of occurrence of the 'phrases' varies greatly but sufficient order reigns for it to be possible to calculate a 'probable' order of succession in a postulated run.

Craig, whose study on somewhat similar lines is the only work of importance of this kind preceding Sotavalta's, comments on certain 'tendencies' common to the Wood Pewee and most other related species: (1) A tendency to quick tempo in twilight songs; (2) to regular rhythm in

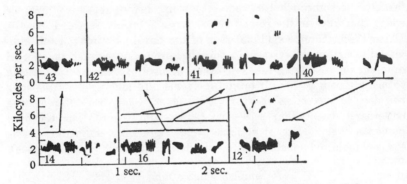

Fig. 9. The last four phrases in a sequence of 43 uttered by a Mistle Thrush compared with earlier songs in the sequence to show how new themes are produced by re-combination of components. (After Marler 1959b)

the twilight song; (3) to use special rhythmic phrases when singing rapidly; (4) and to alternate two or more different phrases—'regular recurrence'. He concludes that the tendencies are older than the phrases and have influenced the evolution of the phrases, not vice versa. This probably holds good of the songs of many birds. If we look deeper than the characteristics which have been evolved in the interests of specific distinctiveness we find similarities in other respects, such as rhythm. Thrushes all sing chains of phrases in varying succession with clearly perceptible pauses between the phrases whereas buntings sing discontinuous songs. In the buntings there are marked specific differences in song though in some species individuals differ a great deal but short song duration and very rapid repetition of notes seem to be generic or family characteristics (Thorpe and Lade 1961). Analysis of such characteristics may prove of some value in systematics.

Forms of song

Writers have endeavoured unsuccessfully to formulate a definition of bird song which would distinguish it from call-notes. Craig, criticizing these efforts, attributes their failure to the concept of song being aesthetic as well as biological. Indeed, he says of bird songs that 'they are aesthetic art and we believe that this is the essence of the concept'. Song, to our ears, is usually the most aesthetically satisfying of a bird's utterances. Reasons for this will be discussed later (Chapter XIII) but the aesthetics of bird song are so speculative a matter that Craig's view is of little help. An attempt to define bird song has been made by Smith (1959). It is 'a social utterance, long or short, simple or complex and species specific which is given by either sex or both and which functions primarily to repel males of the same species, to attract a mate, or both'. He considers that 'other musical utterances not serving to attract or repel should be considered sub-songs and all other vocalizations as calls'. This implies discarding the accepted conception of sub-song as identifiable by its low intensity. Subdued courtship songs, being attractive to potential mates, would have to be classified as song, not sub-song. As some call-notes have an attractive function it would be difficult to deny these status as song. Difficulties arise when a definition is sought in terms of, on the one hand, acoustic characteristics, or, on the other, function, and where a definition is attempted in terms of both, exceptions are numerous. Borror (1961) defines song as vocalizations with one or more of three functions—to advertise the presence of the male, to attract a female, and to repel other males. He, and many other writers, seem unaware how many functions song can perform (cf. Chapter IX).† As the writer has maintained (1947) a satisfactory, inclusive definition of bird song is probably unattainable but this need not be disconcerting. Song may be considered to constitute the major item (or items) in a bird's vocal and/or instrumental communicatory repertoire, and normally the most informative, complex and sustained. Forms such as sub-song and whisper song should be regarded as particular types under the general term 'song' (Chapter IV). It is almost invariably possible, except when our observations are deficient, and always desirable, to indicate the function of particular songs, as for example, 'territorial song' or 'courtship song' (Chapter IX) or when a definite communicatory function is not apparent to describe it in some such terms as 'developmental sub-song'. Usually when song is mentioned without qualification it can be understood to refer to the territorial utterance. A number of writers regard 'advertising song' as equivalent to 'territorial song', but some birds sing to attract a mate rather than to defend a territory (p. 151). This can be termed 'advertising song' or 'call song'. Thus 'territorial song' has greater content than 'advertising song'. Territorial song is also advertising song but advertising song is not necessarily territorial. At one extreme is developmental sub-song—often called 'juvenile song'—which usually has little or no communicatory value and, at the other, territorial song which in species uttering it is always the most informative and conspicuous utterance. It is sometimes convenient to distinguish the mature and loudest song from juvenile and other forms of song by calling it 'full song', but the 'full song' of a species may not be territorial. Its characteristics enumerated by Thorpe (1961) apply to territorial song—'loud, repetitive, of considerable duration in time, containing usually a variety of notes, and displaying a consistent overall pattern'.

Saunders (1935) classifies the songs of North American birds into twenty-six categories, based on such criteria as number of notes or phrases, uniformity at end or beginning, number of parts, trilling, warbling, slurring, repetition, and continuity. Such a classification is useful up to a point, in providing clues for identification, but birds belonging to different genera may sing the same class of song. Thus the list of two-part songs begins with Field Sparrow, Cardinal, Mourning Warbler, and Long-billed Marsh Wren. However, although the distinctions between songs tend to be marked on the species level there tend to be general similarities in features such as phrasing where the genus is concerned.

Bird songs vary in tempo according to species and in some *accelerando* or *ritardando* occurs. They vary, too, in rhythm and accent and the extent of repetition and variety. The rhythm of the Chaffinch's song has been compared to that of a bowler delivering the ball. The rate of respiration has a bearing on the rhythm of some birds' songs. The Crested Flycatcher and Wood Pewee are reputed to sing a phrase with every breath, but, as Craig points out, it is probably equally true to say that the requirements of the music influence the rate of breathing. Their rhythmic songs increase in tempo, and Craig thinks that this may be correlated with the rate of respiration after the bird has been singing for some time and has 'warmed up' to his task. The Wood Pewee's daytime song is leisurely but the twilight song is in rhythmic style with many more phrases per minute. The twilight songs of all tyrant birds tend to be in quick tempo. A third type of phrase, or motif, is introduced between the other two and the faster the Wood Pewee sings the more of these are heard. Blackbirds are constant in rhythm for years and maintain intervals between identical notes equivalent to the accuracy attainable by the most expert human musicians. In their first spring they try to imitate the phrases which they hear being used by adults but although they attain correct pitch they apparently lack the technique of respiration to imitate the rhythm in full volume (Messmer and Messmer 1956).

There are enormous differences between species in the number of notes uttered in a given time while singing and the intervals between songs. Ten minutes or more may separate the series of booms which constitute the Bittern's song, while pauses of only a few seconds occur between the rapid songs of some small passerines. The degree of continuity or discontinuity, which is important as a diagnostic characteristic to the human observer, is certainly significant to the birds themselves. In territorial song the intervals between utterances are apt to be stereotyped. Probably, in many species, this interval rhythm is inborn but is subject to modification by internal and external factors. The pauses between the songs of many species are probably adaptive in enabling the singers to listen to other individuals and acquire information concerning the approach of predators (p. 242).

III

THE DEVELOPMENT AND LEARNING
OF SONG

For to pass by other instances of Birds learning of Tunes
and the endeavours one may observe in them to hit the Notes
right, put it past doubt with me, that they have Perception,
and retain Ideas in their Memories, and use them for
Patterns.

LOCKE. *Essay on the Human Understanding,* Chap. X, Par. 10.

IN numerous species the first attempts at song begin remarkably early.
There are accounts of Red Ovenbirds, Song Thrushes, Dippers, Black-
caps, finches, and other species singing in the nest (Hudson 1892;
Heinroth and Heinroth 1924–33; Lorenz 1943)—though writers have
not always made it clear what was regarded as 'singing' in such circumstances. Presumably all these observations refer to sub-song. A Tree Pipit
about twenty-four days old is said to have uttered the complete song in a
subdued way (Took 1947) and at about the nineteenth day the juvenile
song of Blackbirds 'starts in its full variability of note and rhythm' (Messmer and Messmer 1956). A Crowned Hawk Eagle hardly out of down went
through the adult repertoire of calls (Brown 1953). Normally when very
young birds sing it is a non-stereotyped song which Metfessel (1935) has
called a 'nonsense song'. Hand-reared Song Sparrows began warbling at
ages varying from 13 to 31 days while Redstarts first sang at 18, 19, and
21 days (Nice 1943, 1945). The ages of Roller Canaries when they first
utter song vary from 60 to 148 days (Metfessel 1935). Bicknell's Thrushes
first sang at 15 and 25 days and American Robins at about three weeks
(Wallace 1939). California Thrashers began at 19 days, Curve-billed at
20 and Brown at 44 (Nice 1943; Bent 1948). At four weeks a Darwin's
Finch sang. This type of song lasted for only a few months and ceased as
abruptly as it began (Orr 1945). A female Goldfinch uttered song at 30
days and the male 16 days later. Female Cardinals sing at three or four
weeks. Young Cardinals warble in a manner totally unlike the song of the
adults (Nice 1943; Laskey 1944a).*

* Other forms of adult behaviour may be manifested precociously by young birds.
Many instances have been collected of display, nest-building, attempted coition,
brooding, and feeding other chicks by very young birds (Armstrong 1947; Nicolai
1956). Young Peacocks will display before they have acquired the appropriate

The early bird fanciers were well aware of the development of song from quiet utterances which bear little resemblance to the specific song. A bird singing thus was said to be 'recording', though this term—derived apparently from the instrument—was applied both to the developing song and to the utterance in later seasons during the phase before the attainment of full song.*

In a number of species there is indeed a rapid recapitulation seasonally of the development of song in the young bird. Bechstein commented: 'The practising, which goes by the name of learning or *recording*, consists . . . not of notes or passages which have any reference to the usual song, but of a kind of twittering or chirping, intermixed with which the well-known notes are now and then to be detected, given on every occasion with increased perfectness and facility'.

In recent years the development of song in a number of species has been studied in detail. Sauer (1954, 1955) shows that the Whitethroat has a repertoire of twenty-five call-notes and three types of song, each associated with a particular activity (Pl. II). All are inborn.** Birds isolated all their lives utter them in precisely the same situations as wild birds. All calls are identical in both sexes but song is confined to the males. It develops by maturation and begins with the continuous reiteration of one note, comparable to the food call. (A thirteen-day-old female uttered a double note—the only suggestion of female song.) Further notes are introduced and during the first month of life become integrated into the juvenile song. This is subdued and delivered rapidly. Song may develop latently so that a bird coming into song more tardily than others sings as well as they. So, too, the juvenile song of the Red-backed Shrike matures up to a certain point like the ability of some birds to fly without previous practice (Blase 1960). The full territorial song 'crystallizes' eventually as the end-product of the process of development.

This type of Whitethroat song is characteristic of the period before the attainment of sexual maturity. The first phase lasts from the late nestling

plumes. Apparently such behaviour is stimulated by the action of the gonads. The juvenile Starling has relatively active testes when it leaves the nest and Bullough (1942) has suggested that the precocious behaviour of the young of other species may be due to a comparable secretion of sex hormones. Böker (1919) found that Chaffinches sang the territorial song before spermatogenesis but there is abundant experimental evidence of the induction of song and sexual behaviour of various kinds in young birds by the injection of testosterone propionate (Armstrong 1947; Collias 1950b; Eisner 1960). Precocious sexual behaviour also occurs in some mammals, including primates (Beach 1948).

* The recorder used for teaching melodies to birds was a form of 'fipple-flute'. A small barrel-organ with pipes of high pitch called the 'serinette' was also used.

** According to Lanyon (1960b) Sauer has informed him that learning occurs during the development of the song. Messmer and Messmer (1956) pointed out that before a song can be considered innate the possibility of 'self-learning' has to be eliminated.

stage to the time of migration. It becomes more subdued during the moult in August. Captive birds begin to sing again towards the end of October. This is probably normal as Whitethroats sing to some extent in their African winter quarters (p. 174). Such juvenile song is subdued, almost continuous at times, and is uttered with the beak closed and from deep cover (p. 220). When the bird is thoroughly at ease this sub-song tends to be particularly fluent. Indeed, it is characteristic of much non-communicatory sub-song and some forms of subdued communicatory song to be expressed when the bird is apparently in a relaxed state. On the other hand some adult birds sing sub-song when they appear to be in a state of tension (p. 67). These contradictions show how far the nature of such song motivation is from being understood. Males arriving early after the spring migration sing this 'juvenile song'—developmental sub-song—in cover, but the full territorial song may be elicited by the appearance of a female or a rival male.

The territorial song is of two types—reduced and full (*Vorgesang* and *Motivgesang*). These may be considered as indicative of a lower or higher degree of stimulation, rather than as different in quality. When stimulation is at its height, as when a female lingers in the territory or after display and copulation, display-flight with song occurs. The song-flight attracts and stimulates the female.

Towards the end of April when display and nest-building have been completed, subdued or reduced song is frequently heard and during the incubation period song decreases. On the initiation of a second brood there is a recrudescence of the song-flight—as in various other species in similar circumstances. When the male comes to the nest with food he sings in a subdued way, like the Blackcap, Blackbird, and a number of other birds (p. 170). Just as increasing sexual motivation causes the change from juvenile to territorial song so the reduced and intense types of territorial song are also correlated with the degree of sexual motivation. In autumn and winter the song tends to lose its 'territorial' characteristics and to be replaced by incomplete song. The development of the Blackcap's song is very similar to the procedure of maturation just described (Sauer 1955).

Much less is known concerning the development of the Wren's song as it is difficult to rear these birds in captivity but it is probably almost entirely inborn (Armstrong 1955). The first suggestions of song heard in the field are squeaky, subdued notes but as the days pass a crude, jingly phrase develops. Gradually this becomes less formless and the birds tend to restrict their singing to a small area. They consolidate their position in it while neighbouring birds are moulting and may be regarded as holding territory, though they may not be able to retain it into the breeding season. By the autumn the song has acquired the stereotyped pattern and volume but tends to be uttered at irregular intervals. Wandering Wrens seeking to establish territory sing a version which is more subdued and melodious—as if they were timid about making their presence known. It sounds more 'finished' than the maturing song of juveniles. Contrary to what holds of the Pied Flycatcher (Curio 1959a), the Chaffinch, and some other species, Wrens singing early in the year do not utter an approximation to the developing song of the young though at the moult adults utter 'broken' songs and in winter the utterance is prone to deficiency in volume and pattern.

The Blackbird is one of the resident species in which the process of song-development is best known, thanks to the work of the Messmers (1956), Thielcke-Poltz and Thielcke (1960), and others. Newly fledged young emit a quiet *reereeree*—the preliminary stage of song. As has been mentioned, at about the 19th day the juvenile song is heard. It is quite brief at first but after a few days it may be sustained for half an hour, and later for hours on end. A young bird intersperses alarm notes and when something in the environment causes disquiet it may utter these in a subdued, imperfect way for a minute or so almost to the exclusion of the normal song notes—then returning to normal sub-song. According to the Messmers juvenile song is completely innate and the only differences between the songs of wild birds, isolates, and deaf individuals are in the duration and pitch of some notes. However, the Thielckes (1960) have found that young Blackbirds which have been isolated from other birds sing many details of the full song but are unable to arrange them in their correct relationship.* Blackbirds can sing normally only when they have had the opportunity to hear other Blackbirds sing. Birds were able to learn and reproduce motifs from about their 28th or 29th to their 122nd day. A bird produced a very accurate imitation when 67 days old. Another was able to repeat a Wood Thrush's phrase after hearing it only twelve times. It seems that for learning to occur, Blackbirds must be in a receptive mood. Wild Blackbirds learn motifs. Of seven birds trapped in October only one sang the innate form of song. Birds kept isolated but allowed to hear recorded motifs learnt them in their first winter and spring even if they had earlier acquired other motifs. Immature Blackbirds sing learned or improvised phrases occasionally from September onwards but there are deficiencies in pitch, timing, and pattern. Learned motifs are heard with increasing frequency between Christmas and 3 March and some motifs are then incorporated into the full song for the first time. In spring the birds first sing the phrases learnt the previous year, gradually eliminating the traces of juvenile song and so the song

---

* In experimental situations isolation may be of different degrees: (a) deafened birds; (b) isolated from all other birds; (c) from all experienced birds; (d) from all experienced birds of own species.

becomes loud and typical. In the second year the song matures more quickly, as in the Chaffinch and probably many other species. Some birds then lengthen components of their song.

The Messmers state that the Blackbird includes up to eight motifs in its repertoire but this is an under-estimate. The Thielckes studied a bird which sang at least twenty. The order in which they are uttered varies. Motifs may be transferred to another context and as the season advances birds seem to compose musical phrases in this way. Other turdine species sing in much the same manner but some have more extensive repertoires (p. 40).

These workers record that a deaf bird in his second spring sang loudly a motif from his juvenile song. This individual is said to have uttered a typical song but since imitation was impossible it must have been to this extent impoverished. Third-brood birds, fledged after the adults have ceased singing, copy their first learned motifs in spring and suddenly add new motifs. For the first few weeks in spring until the end of March the birds heard in the later hours of the day are nearly all young males. During that period the older birds sing a little at dawn and dusk (Snow 1958). Having reached the phase of established song the Blackbird sings with great constancy.†

Song Sparrow vocalizations develop from continuous warbling to a combination of warbling and brief songs, then a stage is reached when these songs predominate. Next almost adult songs are heard and finally the songs become stereotyped. According to Nice (1943) there is great individual variation in the duration of some of these phases. One bird progressed through the first four in eleven days in February but another took five months—from October to February. The date of attaining regular adult song depends on age, time of year, and temperature. A bird in the 'short song' phase sings full songs on arising. Territorial competition may abruptly stimulate a juvenile into singing temporarily in this style. Observations on other species confirm that competition may accelerate the development of song (p. 115). It also stimulates song learning. A Song Sparrow concentrated his learning into a week in December and in so doing acquired all six versions of his rival's repertoire. The songs of individual Song Sparrows vary from one to another. The ending of the song is less stable than the other two parts, which suggests that, as with the Chaffinch and some other species, the termination is apt to be modified through learning songs heard in the neighbourhood. The songs of a number of buntings—belonging to the same family as the Song Sparrow —are inborn (Poulsen 1951).

Nice, studying a wild population without recording instruments, found no instance of a male reproducing the song of his father or grandfather on either side. She followed the fortunes of one bird for seven years and noticed that the song remained constant. If her ear noted accurately the differences between these songs it appears that in this species the songs are not inherited from direct ancestors nor are they learned during the first month of life when a bird is in close enough contact with a parent to learn his song. In this Song Sparrows differ from Bullfinches (p. 55). Nice concluded that the pattern (form, length, and timing) of the Song Sparrow's song was inborn but that the quality was learned. This latter is probably too great a generalization. She also decided that her hand-reared birds must have acquired the learned characteristics of their songs when opportunities were very limited—in September and October.

Song Sparrows in the wild learn song-versions from their adult rivals during the establishment of territories, but some of these imitations are abandoned later and others are adopted in somewhat modified form. Nice, noting that one male sang 'a tremendous amount' for eight or nine years, especially while young birds were developing their songs, thought that this explained the widespread occurrence in the area of some of his song-versions. This may well be correct, though some of the birds may have learned the song at second hand. Other instances of vigorous singers being efficient in other respects and well able to maintain their ground in competition with others suggest that this may be a factor in establishing and disseminating song-versions (p. 117).†

The development of the Chaffinch's song has been investigated very fully (Promptoff 1930; Poulsen 1951; Marler 1952, 1956a, b; Thorpe 1956, 1958; Hinde 1958). Youngsters at first utter sub-song with two types of note, chirps and rattles, which may be continuous or in bursts of two or three seconds. Like other young and adult birds singing sub-song they often keep their beaks closed. In autumn young males commonly give a sustained series of chirping notes, varying in pitch. This is the simplest form of sub-song. Some females also sing thus. Nearly full innate song can be induced in females by injections of testosterone phenylacetate (Thorpe pers. comm.). The spring sub-song embodies single rattles. Borrowed notes appear in sub-song, especially in aviary-reared birds. Eventually it merges into full song. As juveniles the birds 'appreciate' that their song should consist of three phrases or sections and that it should end with a flourish. In sexual situations the notes follow quickly and continuously; rattles are often heard and several may be uttered in succession (Fig. 10).

Soon after the young male chooses a territory in spring he utters sub-song which develops into full song, stimulated by the singing of neighbouring males. Older birds at this season utter less sub-song and cease to sing it sooner. Competitive singing tends to elicit song and accelerate its development. Even out of the normal song season the singing of a Chaffinch artificially brought into song by hormone injections may stimu-

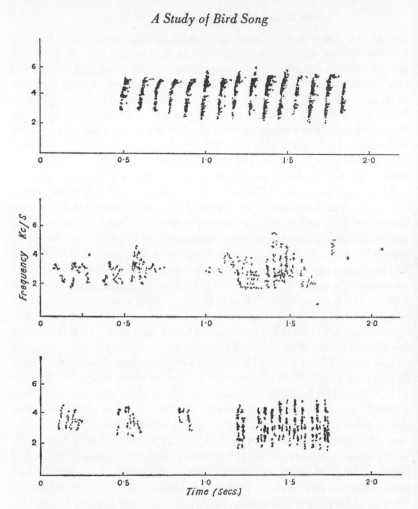

Fig. 10. Sound spectrograms of (top) innate song of Chaffinch reared in isolation from 6 days of age; (middle) sub-song of young male about a month old; (bottom) spring sub-song of an old male consisting of chirps and a rattle. (After Poulsen 1958)

late another Chaffinch to sing (R. Hinde pers. comm.). Similarly the crowing of young cockerels is hastened if they can hear adult cocks crowing (Katz 1937).* As the song development of a Chaffinch proceeds the approximation of song-versions to that of neighbours becomes complete. Thus learning advances by copying others. Copying is particularly ap-

---

* The influence of social stimulation on sexual development, first noted by Craig, has been demonstrated by Burger (1953). He found testis growth in Starlings caged with females was greater than in males caged with other males.

parent in the terminal flourish which consequently shows much variability in different regions.

I have known a male, still uttering imperfect song, engage in mild flirtation when another male was perched only two feet away. Thus a certain amount of courtship can precede the full attainment of song and territorial defence. Three days later (1 March) this bird, which was probably occupying territory for the first time, sang fairly loud sub-song with a rattle and a few soft, grating notes at the end of each song, near to where he had been courting. Now and then two songs were run together. Later he would break into one or two practically complete songs. During an outburst on an exceptionally mild and sunny day there was much variation in the perfection of his songs. Next day the songs frequently ended with three rattles and often followed close on one another. On 5 March he was still singing sub-song with rattles but the following day the song was apparently complete and the female was responding with *chinks*. Early in the season when the song was developing the songs were often uttered at intervals of only one to three seconds but later he sang bursts with intervals of three to five seconds. This bird, or his successor in the territory, sang at similar short intervals early the next year and neighbours tended to maintain intervals of this character. At the end of May, when his daily output decreased, his tempo accelerated and frequently averaged intervals of three seconds but on days when his songs were at intervals of two to three seconds early in the morning he averaged five seconds in the evening. At the beginning of June, when the nestlings were killed by a grey squirrel and his mate departed, he sang with great constancy at 4–6 second intervals for some weeks. Evidently there are seasonal and local variations. Barber (1959) concluded that the rate of singing varied with stimulation associated with the breeding cycle, but his generalization that Chaffinches in south-west England are more vigorous singers than birds in the eastern counties is open to question. Ardent competition seems to increase the rapidity of successive songs. These observations render it doubtful whether there is an innately determined interval-tendency of 10–20 seconds (Thorpe 1958), unless it be for a given hormonal state and a given environmental situation. Certainly any inborn tendency of this kind is subject to major modifications.

Older birds utter only a little sub-song in spring and their first songs are incomplete. Sub-song may be interspersed. The end-flourish, when it first appears, is occasional and tentative. Songs increase in volume, become more emphatic and the intervals more regular. Only a few days are necessary for the complete process and the song remains the same from year to year. Thus the song annually recapitulates rapidly some of the features of the original maturation. Such recapitulation is also characteristic of the Pied Flycatcher's song each spring (Curio 1959a).

That Chaffinches learn their song to some extent is not a recent discovery. Bechstein commented that fully fledged birds are not too old to
learn a good song. Promptoff (1930) noted that the finer details of the
song are acquired during the first breeding season when the bird takes up
territory and sings against neighbours. Falconer (1941) observed that
each of two Chaffinches acquired a song-version from the other. Further
details of the process were discovered by Poulsen (1951). A Chaffinch in
its first spring learned some of the notes of a Linnet kept near it, but
when it heard wild Chaffinches singing it discarded the alien notes and
imitated its own species only. Poulsen found that there is a period of susceptibility before and after which Chaffinches are unable to learn their
song. Thorpe's research (1958) has confirmed and added to the findings
of other workers. Much of this was appreciated by the bird fanciers, such
as Bechstein. He remarked that young Nightingales captured in August
brought their song to completion when they heard a good singer in spring.
There are parallels between the process of visual learning known as
'imprinting' and this auditory learning.* In both there is a susceptible
period, the potentiality of learning the 'wrong' thing (visual object or
sound) and the more or less permanent retention of that which has been
acquired. Probably the psychological processes at work are fundamentally the same, for in birds the kind of relationship which in human
beings would be called emotional facilitates learning (p. 56).

Thorpe considers that the Chaffinch's innate basis of song involves the
production of a song of about $2\frac{1}{2}$ seconds duration with pauses of approximately 10–20 seconds and of a particular tonal quality. The song of
isolates 'is about the right length and of about the right number of notes
and these notes are of fairly normal tonality in themselves, though of
abnormally uniform tonal quality and often too low a pitch' (Fig. 10).
He suggests that what is the 'right' kind of song to copy may be recognized through the bird's experience of the quality of its own voice. Some
characteristics of pitch, quality, intensity, and time relations are inborn
but all else is learned.

Comparison between hand-reared, isolated birds and individuals
caught in September and then kept where they could hear only each other
showed that the latter had learned that the song should be divided into
three sections and that the ending should be a flourish. Thus some characteristics of the normal song were learned before the birds themselves
could sing. The bird fanciers were aware that a bird might learn song
before it could sing and it has long been suspected that birds might
acquire song at the nestling stage. Further details, especially of the terminal flourish, are worked out by the juveniles early the next spring in

* The term 'imprinting' was coined to describe the attachment of a young bird's
following response to the parent, a man, or other moving object.

competition with other Chaffinches. Then they learn two, three, or more song-versions from their neighbours. There is a peak learning period towards the end of this phase and by the thirteenth month susceptibility of this kind comes abruptly to an end. Baron von Pernau appreciated something of this for he remarked that a Chaffinch which acquired an alien song between February and May would never learn its true song. The Meadowlark's critical period of song-learning is between the beginning of sub-song at about four weeks old and the bird's first winter (Lanyon 1957). Generalization is precarious, for the Canary reaches a susceptible stage when learning is possible each autumn during the phase of singing sub-song (Poulsen 1959), and a Blackbird at least six years old mimicked a Pekin Robin, *Leiothrix lutea*, which it could not have heard earlier than two years before (Thielcke-Poltz and Thielcke 1960).

Counter-singing, during which birds learn songs from their neighbours, may continue into May or June (p. 126). Outbursts consist of a series of songs of one version followed by a series of another version; this is characteristic of a number of other species with other song-similarities such as the Cirl Bunting and the Reed Bunting. A bird singing against a rival tends to reply with that version in his repertoire which is most like that of the bird with which he is competing (Thorpe 1958). Similar behaviour has been noted in Red-winged Starlings (Rowan 1955). Thus the frequency of utterance of the song-version tends to increase. As Hinde (1958) remarks, this 'supports the view that song-learning consists primarily in the acquisition of a selective responsiveness to a particular song-type (or range of types)'. Marler (1956c) noticed a young male which had acquired one version from a neighbour, then moved nearer another's territory and began to acquire his song, but this neighbour mated and ceased to sing. The young bird then dropped his song and learnt another song from his neighbours. Another male with three versions sang one of them, which was not in his neighbours' repertoires, only ten per cent of the time. It was evidently falling into disuse. Thus rivalry between birds with similar song-versions tends to maintain these in the community's repertoire. As any Chaffinch is likely to have neighbours it is to his advantage to have more than one song-version so that he can reply to each with the version which most resembles his. Perhaps there may be some relationship between the number of territory-holders within hearing range of the average Chaffinch and the average number of song-versions in this species. When a community is isolated, even by a few surrounding fields, this reciprocal reinforcement of versions would favour the perpetuation of a dialect (p. 101). Probably there is an inborn limit to the number of song-versions a bird can learn. Lanyon (1957) found that Eastern Meadowlarks could acquire more than twice as many versions as Western

Meadowlarks. Neighbouring birds tend to sing similar songs.† It is not known how general song-learning of the kind characteristic of Chaffinches may be. Kellogg and Stein (1953), studying Alder Flycatcher songs recorded in widely separated areas, found that the birds had two song-versions which were conspicuously different but the songs of birds singing the same versions were very similar. The extent to which learning was responsible was not apparent. (For later work see Stein 1958.) Rufous-sided Towhees do not change versions to match those of neighbours. They may alternate versions for minutes at a time. The type of song uttered by a bird does not depend on the versions used by birds within earshot (Davis 1958). The syllable structure of the trills of neighbouring Chipping Sparrows is sometimes very similar but may be strikingly different (Marler and Isaac 1960a). Whether similarities are due to learning is not known.

In considering song-learning some mention must be made of the mimicries which some species include in their sub-songs, although this is discussed in Chapter V. Chaffinches imitate other species in their sub-songs, but even having performed such copying a bird will exclude mimicries entirely from its territorial song (Thorpe 1955). On the other hand a Blackbird which had learned to imitate some flute-notes in sub-song introduced them into his full song (Thielcke-Poltz and Thielcke 1960). Only in exceptional circumstances will a bird of any species abandon its own song and acquire that of another species (Ivor 1944). For copying to occur in Chaffinches it seems to be prerequisite that the tonal quality should be similar to that of the bird's own species—as with the Tree Pipit's song, which Baron von Pernau observed was copied by Chaffinches. When Poulsen (1959) placed Canaries in an aviary with more than 300 other species the only birds they imitated were the Grey Singing Finch, *Serinus leucopygia*, and Goldfinch-Canary hybrids—birds whose songs resemble the Canary song. As has already been mentioned an artificial song devised to imitate Chaffinch song was not copied—apparently because the notes were too pure. This barrier against excessive readiness to mimic extraneous sounds is adaptive as it prevents confusion, though in some species the imitation of such sounds may have a special function (p. 76). In some circumstances birds may learn sounds very different from those of their own songs. A Blackbird learned to imitate the click of the tape-machine used in tutoring it. This sound was below the pitch of the bird's own song (Thielcke-Poltz and Thielcke 1960). The Spotted Bowerbird imitates noises differing greatly from its inborn utterances (p. 75) and Canaries can be taught to enunciate words (Thorpe pers. comm.).

The Oregon Junco sings a trill of 10–20 repetitions of the same note with equal emphasis. However, there are wide variations in the structure of the component notes in the songs of individuals in a given population

(Marler 1959a). In September young birds associated together after being reared in isolation sang a soft, rambling song incorporating imitations of each other. They also learnt the song of a wild Junco outside. One juvenile acquired the song of a House Finch and the others learned it from this bird. There was much apparent improvization in these sub-songs which resulted in the production of abnormal songs when the birds were about eight months old. In March all three birds developed normal song, except that one song had peculiar timing. Thus Juncos inherit their songs but also are able to copy songs of their own or other species. It seems that in some species there is a tendency to copy quality and in others rhythm. Juncos differ from Chaffinches in that the imitations produced in sub-song break into the full song and persist for at least eighteen months. Canaries which sing the specific song will also utter learned songs (Poulsen 1959). Analysis of the note structure in these Juncos' songs revealed that each is different. This indicates that the note structure is not learnt. Marler suggests that this may be due to genetic polymorphism or 'variable expressivity' of the genes concerned.†

The songs already discussed are territorial although the Blackbird's song seems to have a reduced rôle in this respect. The Bullfinch's song has no such function and in this it resembles the songs of some corvine species. Nicolai (1959) noticed that when young Bullfinches were reared in an aviary their social and sexual responses became 'imprinted' or fixated on other species—a Canary or even a human being so that they reacted to him as to the female. With this imprinting was associated the learning of utterances from an individual *in loco parentis*—particularly the father-substitute, as is described below.

A young male Bullfinch, reared by a Canary in a cage with other young Bullfinches, paid special attention to a male Canary and when he sang his first undifferentiated youthful song in the autumn similarities to Canary song were apparent.* In the winter this Bullfinch produced an exact imitation of the Canary's song. Although this bird's offspring could hear the normal Bullfinch song they learnt their father's Canary song. One of these birds, with its mate, reared a chick in another aviary with other species and this bird sang the same song as his ancestor had acquired. Moreover, a male offspring of this bird also sang his grandfather's Canary song. Thus it is certain that in the wild the Bullfinch normally acquires his father's song. A male Bullfinch, fixated on a person, sang loudly when he came with food to the cage, with the result that two young Bullfinches learnt his song. Apparently when there is an 'emotional' relationship inducing the appropriate mood a bird may learn

---

* Canaries and Meadowlarks also learn sounds latently before they can utter them (Poulsen 1959; Lanyon 1957). Heinroth had a Nightingale which imitated for the first time a Blackcap heard six to eight months earlier.

sounds contemporaneous with the approach or presence of the object of this relationship. A hand-reared Blue Tit, fixated on human beings, uttered normal calls but no song (Højgaard 1958).

The learning ability of female Bullfinches is less than the males' and they learn only a few motifs of the male parent's song, but when they become 'betrothed' they acquire elements of their partner's song so that the song is a mixture of elements from both. If a female pairs again after losing her mate she learns nothing from his song. As the female sings scarcely at all during and immediately after breeding the young do not learn her song.

Thus the learning of song in this species is dependent on an 'emotional' bond which may be established with other species. This is the basis of the capacity shown by parrots and some other birds to learn human speech and other sounds (p. 81). In spite of the negative results of Nice's researches the capacity to learn song from a parent may be inherent in some strongly territorial birds such as the Robin (Lack 1943). The Thielckes quote observations which suggest that young Blackbirds could recognize their father's song. Sotavalta (1956) found such similarities in the songs of two Sprosser Nightingales that he suspected them to be father and son. The Heinroths considered that the Nightingale and Sprosser acquire their songs almost entirely by imitation. As the males cease to sing when the young hatch these cannot learn the song until the following spring, as they are unlikely to learn it in winter quarters. It would therefore appear that it would be through father and son happening to occupy adjoining territories that the son could acquire his father's song. Not enough is known of these relationships for firm conclusions to be drawn.

Clearly, different species have different kinds of susceptibility in regard to the learning situation and what may be acquired. Thus auditory imprinting does not occur in Mallard ducklings in the absence of visual stimulation but it occurs in young Wood Ducks (Klopfer 1957) which, in contrast to Mallard ducklings, hatch in cavity nests, and are therefore more dependent on auditory stimuli as clues during their first activities. Visual imprinting to human beings and auditory learning from them normally occur only when a bird is isolated from others of its kind.

In this rapid survey it has not been possible to do more than mention some of the problems raised by the learning of sounds by birds. Later we shall notice indications that some are able to establish associations between environmental sounds and their significance (p. 82). It seems, too, that some birds may develop modifications or 'improvements' in their songs not only during a season but from one year to the next. It is difficult to think of any other form of bird behaviour in which there is comparable variability and plasticity. The capacity for learning and mimicry involves not only similarities between the songs of more or less closed communities or populations but, because on the whole genetic copying results in greater identity of inborn characteristics between individuals than environmental learning, it endows birds with the capacity to diverge in this respect from the ancestral pattern, and so dialects of songs and calls arise, which, if they become sufficiently distinctive may prevent the interbreeding of populations. Thus modifications of song have a significant bearing on evolutionary development. After a consideration of sub-song, which is so intimately associated with song-learning, we shall return to this topic (Chapter V).

IV

SUB-SONG

When first we hear the shy-come Nightingales,
They seem to mutter o'er their songs in fear, . . .
But when a day or two confirms her stay
Boldly she sings and loud for half the day.
JOHN CLARE. *The Early Nightingale.*

IT has long been recognized that some birds may sing a particularly
quiet form of song. Nearly a thousand years ago the Lady Murasaki,
in *The Tale of Genji*, commented on '. . . the first fragmentary song
of the Nightingale'.† Gilbert White contrasted the Blackcap's 'loud and
wild pipe' with its 'inward melody'. Meredith noted the Blackbird's 'swift
half-warble' and Cowper commented on the Robin, warbling in winter
'with slender notes and more than half suppressed'.

Significance of the term 'sub-song'

We have already remarked that bird fanciers referred to quiet and in-
completely developed songs as 'recording'. The term 'sub-song' as originally used in connexion with birds by Nicholson (1927), and Nicholson
and Koch (1936), signified 'all performances which are so inwardly or
faintly uttered that they do not carry to anywhere near the distance over
which the bird is physically capable of making itself heard'. Nicholson
points out that sub-song is non-territorial.

Thorpe and Pilcher (1958) have defined sub-song by its acoustic
characteristics. They remark :

'Sub-song differs from true song in the following respects :

(1) The main fundamental frequency of pitch of the notes is apt to be
lower than in the full song.

(2) The frequency (or pitch) range of the sub-song as a whole and of
the individual notes of which it is composed tends to be greater.

(3) The sub-song is much quieter.

(4) The overall pattern of note comprising the utterance is entirely
different.

(5) The length of the phrases of the song bursts is different and tends
to be longer'.

These writers also believe sub-song to be (6) characteristic of lower
sexual motivation 'being generally produced earlier in the breeding

58

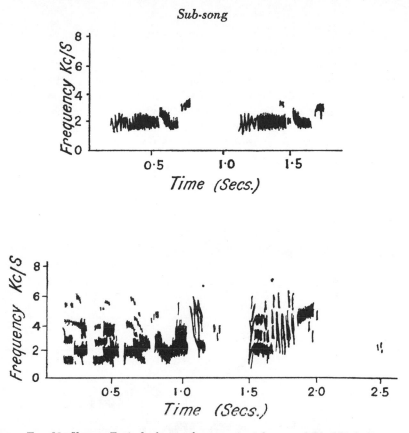

FIG. 11. *Upper:* Typical phrases from territorial song of Blackbird, N. London, April 1957. Phrases shown can be approximately rendered by the syllables *tll-ew*, *tll-ui*. Note fairly pure tone fundamental frequencies of the characteristic notes, restricted within a range of about 1·5 kcs. with little above 2·5 kcs. *Lower:* Typical phrases from sub-song of Blackbird, N. London, April 1957. Note very impure and therefore harsh-sounding notes as compared with upper sound spectrogram, with fundamental frequencies ranging between 0·5 and 5·0 kcs. (i.e. both higher and lower than those of territorial song). (After Thorpe and Pilcher 1958)

season', and suggest that (7) it may be practice for the 'true song'. They doubt whether the term can be usefully applied to the utterances of courting birds or sounds coordinating the activities of a mated pair.

Of the twelve species whose utterances are scrutinized, only three have sub-songs with all these characteristics. Thorpe and Pilcher are doubtful whether four of the species examined sing sub-song in the sense in which they use the term. In these circumstances one cannot feel confident that a satisfactory definition of sub-song has been achieved. Thielcke (1959b) points out, referring to the Blackbird's sub-song, which Thorpe and

59

Pilcher claim possesses all seven characteristics, that (4) does not apply, (5) is valid only in special circumstances, and (7) is not proven. However, (5) is true of most sub-songs and (7) is plausible (Figs. 11 and 12).

Attractive as it may be to use criteria which can be recorded by sound spectrograph in visual form to determine objectively whether or not an utterance should be called sub-song, yet, setting aside for the moment the question of the applicability of these criteria, the suggested restriction of the term to utterances shown to possess the characteristics indicated

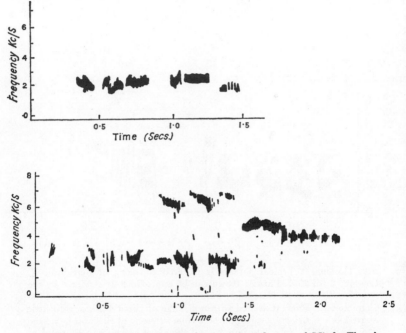

Fig. 12. *Upper:* Typical phrases from territorial song of Mistle Thrush, Kent, March 1954. The notes are characteristically pure. *Lower:* Typical phrases from sub-song of Mistle Thrush, Kent, March 1954. Notice harsh and impure notes with big frequency range and rambling, ill-defined phrases. (After Thorpe and Pilcher 1958)

would lead to confusion. In science it is seldom advisable to take a term which has always been used in a general sense and narrow its application stringently unless appropriate terms are proposed for the types of phenomenon left high and dry. If 'sub-song' were given the restricted connotation which has been suggested ornithologists would have to invent terms for other types of relatively quiet song. Moreover, dividing song thus into sub-song and 'true song' might suggest that sub-song is not really song. In practice it is desirable to use 'song' in the general sense in which it is employed in literature. It would be arbitrary and confusing to regard sub-song as other than one of the forms of song. Thus, if a form of song having all the acoustic characteristics enumerated by Thorpe and Pilcher is to be distinguished it should be given a name other than 'sub-song' or, if this term is used, it should be qualified in some way.

'Sub-song' is a useful general term to denote forms of quiet song. If we try to give it a restricted acoustically defined significance we encounter insuperable difficulties. Any listener to a Chaffinch in spring will notice a rapid transition from the type of song called sub-song by Thorpe and Pilcher to territorial song. Thorpe (1961) believes that the Chaffinch's sub-song has no communicatory value but at least the transitional stage to territorial song seems to be communicatory. The Hedgesparrow sings a sub-song which appears to be the utterance referred to by Thorpe. It is used in courtship. The Blackbird's sub-song, as heard in March, is so quiet that some notes are only just audible six feet away. It consists of very subdued renderings of normal motifs separated by still softer utterances which may include twittering as from a distant cageful of small birds; twanging notes, mimicries, and occasional alarm notes. The singing birds station themselves well apart and at this stage disputes between males and coition with females occur. The louder transitional form of this song is evidently communicatory.

Nicholson and Koch distinguished four levels of song above sub-song, expressing challenge, announcement, announcement and well-being, and well-being alone, but these categories are insufficiently defined. Lister (1953a) suggested a classification which has been adopted rather too readily by other authors. He divides song into two groups, Primary and Secondary, taking into consideration acoustics and function. Primary song, which is 'the normal loud specific song . . . seems to have most territorial significance'. Secondary song includes all other forms of song. It may be subdivided into 'whispering song', which is an ultra-quiet version of primary song, differing from sub-song, 'sub-song'—'the very quiet inward rendering of song which is intrinsically different from the primary song, and "rehearsed song"—the random utterance of song-notes by young, and sometimes old, birds before they have attained perfection in the "primary song".' 'Female song' is the singing of hen birds. Other songs, such as courtship songs, are included in secondary song as they 'are used so infrequently as not to justify their inclusion in the category of primary song'. This use of frequency as a criterion indicates that persistent utterance is considered to be the distinctive feature of 'primary song'.

There are difficulties in applying these categories. The vague reference to territory in the definition of primary song is unsatisfactory. To what extent sub-song is other than territorial is left obscure. If primary song is merely territorial song another term is not needed, but if the term includes the main song of such birds as estrildine finches, which are without a territorial song, this means that songs which differ in function and volume are included in one term. According to Lister's definition the loud territorial songs of the thrushes and the subdued social and courtship songs of these finches are alike primary song. The definition of 'sub-song' is also open to question. Some sub-songs, though relatively quiet as compared with the territorial songs of most song-birds, are not 'very quiet' and others apparently may not be 'intrinsically different' from the 'primary song', at least on some occasions. 'Whisper song' should be employed, as usually in the past, for the quietest form of song (or sub-song) uttered by a species (Pollard 1930; Laskey 1935). It may or may not differ substantially in pattern from the loudest form of song but often does so. For example, the Wren's whisper song is a most subdued twitter, very different from any of this bird's other forms of song (Armstrong 1955). Lanyon (1960) interprets 'rehearsed song' as the phase when to developmental sub-song are added 'vocal patterns suggestive of definitive primary song', these being interspersed within the framework of rambling warbling. This stage is difficult to define and it is doubtful whether it occurs generally. It would be absurd to deny this ultra-quiet song the title of whisper song merely because it is not a form of the territorial song. Apparently 'rehearsed song' is advanced or even transitional developmental sub-song for which the bird-fancier's term 'recording' should be retained. Recording, it should be noted, includes seasonally developmental song. Perhaps, if 'rehearsed song' is to be used at all it might be restricted to out-of-season low-intensity song. 'Female song', being identifiable by a non-acoustic criterion, should be classified on its merits.

The main criterion in this classification is volume. Although in practice this characteristic is useful in describing any song it does not, in isolation, provide an adequate basis for classification, nor does any other acoustic quality, or set of such qualities, though 'sub-song' may be used of any sustained and normally non-territorial (or meagrely territorial) utterance of a relatively subdued character in comparison with other utterances of the species or the songs in general of other comparable species. It must be stressed again that besides describing forms of song in acoustic terms we must, wherever possible, define them by their communicatory function—or lack of it.

Acknowledging this we are free to recognize the importance and interest of intensity differences and other acoustic peculiarities which may accompany them. Accepting sub-song as a general term, several types may be distinguished—developmental, which is usually non-communicatory in its earlier stages and with which we are mainly concerned here, apparently non-developmental non-communicatory sub-song, such as is sung by various corvids when incubating (p. 167) and was regarded by Nicholson as an expression of 'well-being', and communicatory forms which are best described in terms of their function, such as courtship or pair-maintenance. Possibly the regression to developmental sub-song by sick or senile Whitethroats noticed by Sauer (1955) may occur in other species. It should be considered regressive sub-song.

The characteristics which Thorpe and Pilcher regard as typical of 'sub-song' as they define it are those of the developmental sub-song of some species. We do not know to what extent in other species developing song may be expressed differently or whether there may be birds in which communicatory sub-song has several of the characteristics enumerated. Other common characteristics of developmental sub-song should be mentioned. Mimicries and call-notes often occur in these utterances and the singing bird usually keeps its beak closed and perches lower and in a less conspicuous position than when singing the territorial song. While territorial song tends to attain peaks in the early morning and to a lesser extent in the evening, non-communicatory sub-song may be uttered intermittently during the day. The subdued juvenile and courtship songs of the Red-backed Shrike may be heard at any time of day and even at night by artificial light (Blase 1960). Birds singing non-developmental sub-song may behave similarly in some or all of these respects.

Development and forms of sub-song

Amplifying what has already been said concerning the development of song (Chapter III), Blackbirds sing sub-song from August into November or early December—snatches of varied notes or a prolonged, rambling soliloquy of notes with a wide frequency range, including chatters, chirps, and abbreviated call-notes, and incorporating alarm calls as well as occasional fluting notes. They also sing softly early in the year as already mentioned. A Blackbird singing sub-song is like a shy amateur testing his talents, giving promise of ability but interjecting comments expressing vexation. Young birds seeking to occupy territory utter subdued song which is a rather louder form of sub-song. Such song may express some aggressiveness and may provoke attack, even from a female (Snow 1958). Thus we see that a precise demarcation between non-communicatory and communicatory sub-song is not always possible. Song Thrush and Robin sub-song are of substantially similar character. The Throstle's sub-song embodies Robin-like expressions. Blackbird and Song Thrush sub-songs conform to the characteristics enumerated above but the average main frequency of the Mistle Thrush's sub-song does not appear to be lower than in the territorial song (Thorpe and Pilcher 1958) (Fig. 12). I have heard a bird give a remarkable performance, switching from the bold, rather monotonous territorial song to a much more varied, rapid utterance, reminiscent of a Starling at times, and then continuing with the territorial song. The Redwing's sub-song has a much wider frequency range and less well-defined phrases than the territorial song, but uttered when the birds assemble at roosts it may be a form of advertising roosting sub-song or rallying song and may possess communicatory functions. Redwings moving north along the English coast in spring sing a sweet sub-song (Perry 1946) which may differ from the roosting sub-song. The territorial song of this species occurs in many dialects (p. 93). Woodlark sub-song is mainly heard before breeding but is uttered while nesting and in autumn. This species has a loud, repetitive song, used during courtship (C. Koffán *in litt.*).

Chaffinch developmental sub-song consists of a 'quiet rambling inconsequential series of notes, continuous or broken up into fragments lasting two or three seconds' (Marler 1956a). Most of the notes are very indefinite in pitch. This sub-song passes into territorial song through the elimination of extreme frequencies and imitations of the calls of other species. Call-notes appear in the sub-song and may be heard when a male seeks to copulate. It is not uncommon to hear a Chaffinch warbling sub-song and incorporating the territorial song very quietly. Smart (1943) refers to hearing the territorial song uttered so softly that it sounded as if the bird were in the distance.† Sub-songs of the kind described for the Chaffinch are uttered by the Hedgesparrow and American Goldfinch but it is rather doubtful whether the sub-songs of Brambling, Yellowhammer, Corn Bunting, and Crossbill conform to it (Thorpe and Pilcher 1958).

Many migrants utter sub-song in their winter quarters. Perhaps when sung in winter it may be considered to be regressive. In September the Blackcap's sub-song is subdued—a long, pleasant reiteration with little chatterings interspersed between a trickle of sweeter notes hinting at the full-throated notes of springtime. Chiffchaffs wintering in France south of the Loire sing 'softly, as if to themselves' (Delamain 1938). Blyth's Reed Warbler warbles during September and October in a quiet way and its song may swell from a whisper to a crescendo lasting several seconds. In India during October the Booted Warbler sings sub-song of varying volume while foraging (Lister 1953b). Probably comparison of the state of the gonads with behaviour would indicate parallel regression to conditions approximating to those which accompany developmental song in spring.

The Isabelline Wheatear utters sub-song in winter and Wheatears on migration sing while they occupy temporary territories (Conder 1956). As has already been remarked, when male Pied Flycatchers arrive at the breeding-ground their songs pass through stages characteristic of the young bird's developmental sub-song (Curio 1959a). The first song of young Dippers is an indefinite quiet warble and a beautiful sub-song is uttered in late autumn. Snatches of song may be sung by male or female when they meet (Heinroth and Heinroth 1924–33; Witherby *et al.* 1938; Rankin and Rankin 1940; Serle and Bryson 1935; Vogt 1944). During July and August adult male Starlings in Britain utter a great deal of very quiet song, which might be called whisper song, but later, as the gonads increase in size, song becomes loud. Adult females also sing in autumn but not so vigorously (Bullough 1942). An old female Mockingbird sang frequently 'a lovely whisper song' in October and first uttered the short territorial song two days later. Mimicries and subdued alarm notes were interspersed. Many other species, including some which do not include mimicries in the territorial song, mimic in sub-song. Male Mockingbirds also sing in this subdued way in autumn, incorporating many mimicries (Laskey 1936). The behaviour of Cardinals in these respects is rather similar.

The California Thrasher's forms of song have been classified into eight types, five of which are defined by their volume (Dyer 1943): '(1) Slumber song, softest of the sub-songs, bird drowsy or napping; (2) Quarter song, louder, more varied sub-song, from ground or digging; (3) Half-song, the "digging song" most often heard, long and varied, audible for fifty feet; (4) Three-quarter song audible at perhaps 120 feet, most varied of all the songs and with the most mimicry; (5) Full song, audibility 300 yards, extraordinarily rich and varied, sometimes responsive between the pair; (6) Courting, short, hysterical snatches of song, as the birds pursue each other, heard for several days as the nest nears completion; (7) Invitation to new mate, male climbed favourite tree, gave detached phrases of full song looking over the surrounding country; (8) Welcome to a new mate, different from all other songs heard'. This list is sufficient in itself to indicate that the character of song may be more varied and its functions wider than some definitions and discussions suggest. Although the first five types are separately designated it would appear that there is a gradual transition from very subdued to full song. The slumber song mentioned is not unique. Rand (1941b) noted that Curve-billed Thrashers on their 21st day sang half-asleep 'in an adult manner but faintly'. This observation and the instance quoted earlier, of a young Tree Pipit singing the adult song pattern in sub-song (p. 44), suggest that territorial song may not always crystallize from the sub-song in the manner described for the Chaffinch (p. 49). Robinson (1949), referring to the sub-song of Australian species, remarks : 'Occasionally I have seen a bird which seemed to be falling asleep as it sang.' Robins may close their eyes when uttering sub-song (Howard 1952) and there are records of birds singing thus while sun-bathing. Bechstein (1864) mentions parrots talking in their sleep.

Young Red-backed Shrikes, which begin to sing when six or seven weeks old, utter first a quiet, rambling twittering, with harsh notes interspersed. Captive juveniles sing throughout the winter and the song changes, without altering its structure, into the 'call-song'. Until the first spring the songs of wild, captive, and isolated birds are alike but then birds able to hear others enrich their utterances with imitations. Isolated birds retain the juvenile song all their lives.

The call-song which includes mimicries and is relatively subdued and unstereotyped is uttered until a female appears and then it soon ceases; but an unmated male may sing throughout the season. The loud call is more important than the song in defence of territory (Durango 1948). The courtship song reverts to simple constituents, and isolates also sing a soft, hurried, congested song in the presence of the female. Blase (1960) considers courtship song to be a displacement activity. It prepares the hen for mating. He believes that the call-song cannot be explained as a product of the aggression-escape-sex motivation complex, to which so much display and vocalization is attributed, as juvenile and call-song are both uttered in the same relaxed posture with feathers fluffed. Call-song, however, is sung from more prominent perches. Whether sexual motivation enters into juvenile song is unknown. However, juvenile song has the same attractive significance for the female as the call-song. When a seven-week cock twittered softly a ten-week female flew and perched beside him. He drove her away but when he sang again she returned. Another female begged from a male four days older when he sang. Adult females did not heed such song.

The Red-backed Shrike's song might be regarded as a song in a state of arrested development towards territorial song (Pl. IX). This is even more true of the Thick-billed Nutcracker's song. Swanberg (1951, 1956) calls it a 'mating song' but it is, rather, a connubial song, being uttered by permanently paired males. It appears to have no importance in the defence of territory but is probably useful in maintaining the pair-bond. The bird sings softly with bill closed and usually from a low perch (Pl. III). He distinguishes it from sub-song but apparently uses this term as applicable in a relative sense when a bird also has a louder territorial song. Even so, as the frequent loud calls of the Nutcracker have most of the functions of territorial song this subdued utterance is correctly considered sub-song. The Hawfinch's subdued song has little territorial significance (Mountford 1957). It is possible, of course, that some such songs are regressive.

Early in the season the song of the Rose-breasted Grosbeak is so faint that it is hardly audible beyond a distance of three feet. It is sustained for as long as three minutes. Many of the low, sweet notes of the courtship song run through it and it resembles this song much more than

the territorial song (p. 159). In mid-April the song has developed sufficiently to be heard at thirty feet, and about 1 May it has matured completely (Ivor 1944).

These examples, mainly of developmental non-communicatory sub-
song suggest that there may be considerable variation in its nature and
development in different species and also in the relationship to communicatory song and other utterances. Developmental sub-song may be regarded as containing material available, when required, to be elaborated
and put to practical use. Obviously the function, or lack of function, of a
song or sub-song should be included in defining it. Non-communicatory
non-developmental sub-song (self-expressive sub-song) appears to be
rather uncommon but, no doubt, in many species it is, as yet, unrecorded.
Isolated Jackdaws may sing all day in a very subdued, crackling way.
This sub-song can hardly be considered to have any signal function but
Jackdaws indulge in self-mimicry and their songs consist of meaningful
sounds (Lorenz 1952). A House Sparrow separated from its own kind
'would warble for over three minutes on end stimulated by running water
or the piano' (Kipps 1953). Bechstein (1864) remarks concerning Corncrakes : 'At pairing-time they make a purring noise like a cat; which, if
the bird be taken in the hand, will appear to proceed, not from the beak,
but the stomach'. When Yellow-eyed Penguins come ashore at their breeding grounds and engage in courtship the males sing a whisper song, 'a
very musical warbling sound' (Richdale 1941). A number of species
sing sub-song or whisper song while brooding (p. 167). According to
Amadon (1944) the subdued song of Canada Jays is a sign of alarm and
perplexity. Such song appears to be due to conflicting motivation and
may plausibly be considered displacement song (p. 132). Forms of communicatory sub-song are mentioned later (Chapter IX).

The division of sub-songs into communicatory and non-communicatory should not be regarded as rigid. Not only are these transitional
types but utterances which accompany or are part of the territorial song
may be uttered as subdued song. When a subdued phrase or series of
notes occurs in association with a louder phrase one might speculate as
to whether it is phylogenetically developmental or regressive but the
comparison between different species, which is sometimes useful where
other forms of behaviour are concerned, is of little help in this respect. To
assume that a part of a bird's song is a vestigial survival because it is of
low intensity would be precarious. Rather, we may ask what might be
the significance of pronounced differences in intensity or pattern in the
parts of a song. It would seem possible that in some instances one portion
might be of particular relevance to males, the other to females. There is
evidence that this is true of the Grasshopper Sparrow's song. According
to Smith (1959) this species has three primary forms of vocalization—

the Grasshopper Song and Sustained Song of the male, and the Trill, uttered by both male and female. The Grasshopper Song's main function is to proclaim and defend territory. The Sustained Song consists of a 'grasshopper' introduction and a series of melodious notes. Its primary function is to attract a mate but the 'grasshopper' introduction is hostile in character. This song also serves to maintain the pair-bond. The Trill also has this function. The female's Trill proclaims her as a potential mate and is also used as a signal to mate or young. Whatever their functions may be, double-character songs are fairly common and merit investigation. In April Blackbirds will sing typical song audible a hundred yards away but twitter sub-song with carrying power of about five yards between the normal motifs. When a Blackcap remains unmated late in the season he may sing vehemently before he abandons his territory in June but with markedly subdued warbling leading up to the loud mellow notes. Such song may be uttered when a male is out of hearing of other males. The Lesser Whitethroat's song consists of a quiet section, often including imitative notes, and much louder notes. At the beginning of July an unmated Lesser Whitethroat will tour an acre or more of ground alternating quiet and loud songs and occasionally singing in flight— evidently ardently requiring a mate. The subdued song or sub-song is usually uttered in April but it also occurs in September, sometimes with squealing notes also heard in spring. The Arctic Warbler's song, as one hears it a few days after the birds' arrival, includes intercalated *tzik* notes. The Chiffchaff does not really sing its name but utters a succession of notes at fairly regular intervals, alternating short series of loud and soft notes. This song may also be heard in July from unmated birds. This species has a warbling sub-song somewhat resembling the Willow Warbler's song. The song of the Wood Warbler is of double pattern, with plaintive notes occurring between shivering trills. The most remarkable song of this type which I have heard was uttered by a Blue Grosbeak at Panama. Six sweet deliberate notes are followed by a twittered sub-song. Other species of Grosbeak utter sub-song during courtship (p. 159). That parts of these songs may appeal more to the females than the males is, of course, speculative. Perhaps further plausibility is given to this suggestion by the evidence which is cited later indicating that the female Meadowlark identifies the male by his call rather than his song (p. 102). It should not be difficult with the aid of recordings to determine experimentally whether the valence of parts of songs such as have been mentioned is greater for one sex than the other. As courtship songs tend to be subdued one might expect that in songs with sections differing in volume the softer section would be more relevant to the female than the male.

Developmental sub-song may be regarded as a store-house of materials available, when necessary, to be elaborated and put to practical use. This view is supported by the nature of the songs sung by various shrikes. The male Red-backed Shrike usually arrives at the breeding ground before the female. He sings and calls from conspicuous perches but his loud call is of greater importance for the defence of territory than his song, which is relatively subdued and often includes mimicries (Durango 1948). Evidently the songs of these birds are not fully relevant to the defence of territory and the defiance of other males. The loud calls are more important in this respect, so the songs have not evolved the loudness and stereotyped pattern characteristic of full territorial song. The song is thus more advertising than territorial.

Female birds, both those which develop a territorial song, such as the Mockingbird, and others which do not normally produce a song of this kind, including the Chaffinch, may sing sub-song. Analysis of the hen Chaffinch's sub-song shows that it resembles the male's (Thorpe and Pilcher 1958). This supports other evidence that in non-communicatory sub-song there are potentialities for development into functional song (p. 67).

Generalizations in regard to the motivation of developmental sub-song must be made with diffidence but there are conspicuous resemblances or analogies between it and the play of young animals (p. 238). Both appear in developmental phases and contain elements which become incorporated later into functional behaviour patterns. Both also include imitative elements and there are analogies between the alarm calls incorporated into sub-song and the frequent moments of alertness of animals such as badger cubs during play. Furthermore, both play and developmental sub-song appear to be means of dissipating pent-up energy and in some sense seem to constitute practice for adult activities. There is in some species a sexual element underlying these forms of activity. Play may provide a means whereby through the elimination of some elements those most functional become prominent. Watching the play of young animals and listening to the sub-songs of birds are both pleasing, aesthetic experiences. Appreciation of the apparent spontaneity which they have in common may contribute to this enjoyment.

V

VOCAL MIMICRY

These birds [Magpies] get fond of uttering particular words, and not only learn them but love them, and secretly ponder them with careful reflexion, not concealing their engrossment. . . . It is an established fact that if the difficulty of a word beats them this causes their death.

PLINY. *Natural History*, X. ix

THE learning of sounds by birds is limited in various ways, as we have already noted (Chapter III). It is confined to certain periods and the quality of the sounds copied by particular species tends to be restricted. Copying behaviour is widespread in the animal world but it ranges from merely reproducing an instinctive activity seen or heard performed by another animal—mimetic or socially facilitated behaviour (Armstrong 1951a)—to true imitation, defined by Thorpe (1956) as 'the copying of a novel or otherwise improbable act or utterance, or some act for which there is clearly no instinctive tendency'. He considers that 'true visual imitation' has been proved to occur only in primates and cats. To obviate differences of opinion as to what is meant by an 'instinctive tendency' vocal imitation is here considered to be the vocal reproduction of sounds, not innately determined, as a consequence of hearing them. It has been shown that the character of the inborn proclivity to reproduce sounds varies immensely from species to species and even, to some extent, in different individuals. One species may be able to imitate sounds differing greatly from the specific song or calls, another may be unable to learn songs which differ more than slightly in quality from the specific song. For convenience in discussion 'imitation' is not always used here in a strict sense but mimicry is restricted to the copying of sounds other than those of the bird's own species.

Apart from the achievements of men and birds vocal imitation is extremely rare. Attempts to teach words to apes have met with very limited success. A siamang is said to have imitated the barking of a dog and the squeaking of a guinea pig (Yerkes and Yerkes 1929). Hartshorne (1958a) mentions a pet fox which learned to hum scales and a bulldog which could pronounce twenty words but without scientific authentication data of this kind are open to doubt. Even among primates vocal imitation hardly occurs. According to Iljin (1941) wolves learn to bark

70

like dogs but this writer was unaware that wolves have a latent tendency to bark.

Recognition of the imitative ability of birds goes back to food-gathering cultures. From time immemorial primitive South American peoples have domesticated parrots and taught them to 'talk'. Humboldt heard a parrot speak a dead language, all the people of the tribe in which it had been reared having been exterminated.* Aelian (xvi.2) and Pliny (x(42)58) refer to talking parrots. The latter's fantastically exaggerated notion of the Magpie's abilities is expressed in the quotation at the head of this chapter. Ctesias, in his *Indica* (iii), mentions a bird identifiable as the Blossom-headed Parakeet which could utter sentences in an Indian language. Talking mynahs and caged parrots are mentioned in the *Kama Sutra*. According to Chaucer Phoebus had a milk-white Crow,

> *Which in a cage he fostered many a day*
> *And taught to speken as men doe a Jay.*

And at the end of the seventeenth century Alessandro Magnasco painted a number of pictures showing a Jackdaw being taught to sing (Morassi 1958) (Pl. IV). Caged Magpies are shown in much earlier pictures, such as *The Prodigal Son* by Bosch. No doubt the tradition of teaching them was continuous from Roman times.

Baron von Pernau's Chaffinches learnt to sing like Tree Pipits and eighteenth-century bird fanciers taught their pets to whistle tunes by means of the 'bird flageolet'. Melodies to be taught to Woodlark, Skylark, House Sparrow, and other birds were published in 1717 (Godman 1954). In a poem which appeared in 1788 William Cowper wrote of a Bullfinch:

> *And though by nature mute*
> *Or only with a whistle blessed,*
> *Well-taught he all the sounds expressed*
> *Of flageolet or flute.*

Mozart bought a Starling which had been taught to sing. He left in his Commonplace Book the notation of the song and perhaps made use of the melody. Daines Barrington (1773) reported to the Royal Society that having listened to the songs of Linnets reared with Skylarks, Woodlarks, and Meadow Pipits, he had established that song was learned. He com-

---

* A German poet has rendered Humboldt's description of the bird into verse:
> *Kennt ihr die Mar, die Humboldt uns berichtet?*
> *Ein Indianerstamm ward ganz vernichtet*
> *Und seine Sprache sank mit ihm ins Grab,*
> *Ein Papagei nur, den die Sieger schonten,*
> *Sprach nach Jahrzehnten noch in der gewohnten*
> *Seltsamen Sprache, die kein Echo gab.*

mented on instances of mimicry, such as the reproduction by a Goldfinch of a Wren's song, but he generalized so widely that later observers were able to throw doubt on his findings. The discussion has continued at intervals until the present time (Kennedy 1797; Blackwall 1824; Altum 1868; Rennie 1883; Christoleit 1927; Feuerborn 1939).

Scott (1901, 1904) found that none of the seventy-eight birds of sixteen passerine species which he kept in aviaries within hearing of caged companions and birds out of doors sang the normal song but Sanborn (1932) queried some of his conclusions. His strictures went farther than was justified. Conradi's experiments (1905) should also be mentioned. The Heinroths (1924–33) showed that species varied greatly in the extent to which they learned their songs. More refined methods of study have established that some of their conclusions were incorrect and others only partly sound, but their work demonstrated that each species needs careful study and that generalization is unwise. They concluded that in some species song is inborn, in others it is learned and in yet others it is partly inborn and partly learned.

Notable mimics

Field naturalists all over the world have taken pleasure in noting mimicries by birds and have often been uncritical. Witchell (1896) was one of these rather imaginative observers but his book on bird song was the only serious attempt by a British writer to deal with the subject until quite recent times. He put forward the suggestion that some birds' songs imitate natural sounds, such as the trickling of streams and the rustling of leaves. Improbable as this may seem Blackbirds have been known to mimic crickets and other non-avian environmental sounds (Thielcke-Poltz and Thielcke 1960). Voigt (1901) discussed vocal mimicry and Sick (1935) drew up a list of wild birds in order of their imitative ability. Some thirty British species are reputed to be mimics (Witherby *et al.* 1938) though some of these are only occasional mimics and others mimic only in sub-song. The Marsh Warbler and the Jay are outstanding mockers. Walpole-Bond (1933) listed some thirty-nine species which he had heard mimicked by the Marsh Warbler. Conder (pers. comm.) has heard the calls of some thirty species reproduced by the Wheatear. The Sedge Warbler, Redstart, and Red-backed Shrike are also noted mimics. Some writers regard the Reed Warbler as imitative. Turner (1929) commented on its mimicry of the Bearded Tit but Brown and Davies (1949) only once noted mimicry during four seasons' study. Although Howard (1952) rates this bird as 'among the most wonderful of bird musicians' she does not mention mimicry. She includes the Chiffchaff among species which mimic but few ornithologists would agree. The Starling has a great reputation as a mimic, not only in Europe but also in Australia and New

Zealand where it mimics native and other introduced species (Thomson 1922; Saunders 1929; Chisholm 1946a). Observers have tended to exaggerate the imitative abilities of some birds to such an extent that it is wise to discount claims which have been made concerning this and many other species unless they are well authenticated. Very loquacious birds are apt to utter calls fortuitously resembling those of other species just as a silly person who talks incessantly will occasionally say something sensible. Edward Thomas, looking out on a November scene, may have been mistaken in thinking that a Starling had remembered the song of summering Swallows :

> *While the sweet last-left damsons from the bough*
> *With spangles of the morning's storm hung down*
> *Because the Starling shakes it, whistling what*
> *Once Swallows sang.*

Of the European species not breeding in Britain Blyth's Reed Warbler, the Calandra Lark, and the Icterine Warbler are probably the most remarkable mimics. Stadler (1930) gives a representative list of instances of birds imitating other species—Tree Pipit mimicking Great Tit, Black Redstart the Snowfinch and Bonelli's Warbler, Stonechats mimicking Alpine Choughs, and Song Thrushes uttering Redshank calls at Rossitten. On the Irish coast I have heard such mimicry incorporated in the Thrush's song.

Among Asian birds the Shama and mynahs are famous for their imitativeness. They have long been favourites with bird-fanciers in East and West, particularly because of their ability to reproduce human speech with great accuracy. Pepys mentions an 'East India Nightingale,' the name by which the Shama was then popularly known, which he heard in the Duke of York's rooms in St. James's in 1664: 'There is a bird comes from the East Indies . . . talks many things and neighs like the horse and other things, the best almost I ever heard in my life.' A man was recently fined £2 for keeping birds which, it was alleged, created a nuisance in the neighbourhood. His Indian Hill Mynah sang 'All the nice girls love a sailor' and uttered wolf whistles. This species surpasses parrots in the verisimilitude with which it imitates human speech, using its resonators to reproduce vowels faithfully—a feat at which parrots are much less expert (Thorpe 1959) (Fig. 13).

The only African species with a wide reputation for mimicry—apart from parrots—are the Robin Chats, especially the Noisy Robin Chat (Pakenham 1943; Roberts 1948). Benson (1946, 1948) comments that at Nairobi the repertoire of *Cossypha semirufa* is practically limited to mimicry whereas it is very unusual to hear mimicry in Nyasaland.

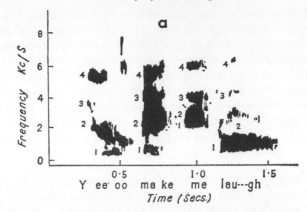

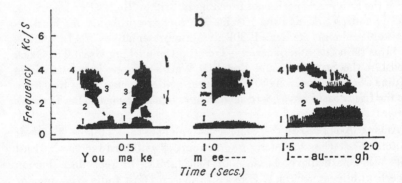

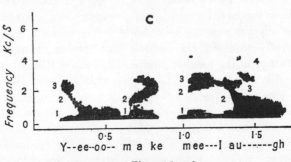

Fig. 13. The phrase 'You make me laugh' spoken by: (a) Indian Hill Mynah; (b) adult human male, New Jersey accent; (c) adult human female, New England accent. (After Thorpe 1959)

Apparently the extent of mimicry may vary locally. This seems to be true of the Fiscal Shrike as mimicry has not been noted in the northern subspecies (Moreau *in litt.*). Some drongos also mimic other species (Benson 1960). The South African Black-headed Oriole pours out a subdued 'tuneful babble' incorporating mimicries (Vincent 1936). In captivity the East African Glossy Starling imitates other birds (Falkner 1943). The Pied Wheatear is said to be a good mimic.

The Mockingbird is by far the most famous North American mimic. According to Townsend (1924) one imitated fifty-five species in an hour and Chapman (1904) mentions with some reserve a report that another imitated thirty-two species in ten minutes but Miller (1938) believes that only ten per cent of the song is imitative. Electronic recordings of bird songs show that mimicries may be more plentiful than is generally supposed. Although the Blue Jay, Rose-breasted Grosbeak, and some American shrikes are claimed to be mimics the only outstanding performers in the United States, apart from the Mockingbird, appear to be the Catbird, thrashers, and, perhaps, the Yellow-breasted Chat.

In Central and South America accomplished mimics are few. The most notable performer in Costa Rica is not the White-breasted Mockingbird but the Guatemalan Black Ousel (Skutch 1950). The Mockingbird of the Galapagos has a poor, feeble song. In South America the White-banded Mockingbird sings by the half-hour 'the songs of a score of species' and, according to Hudson (1892) its own song is such that other birds hearing it 'might well languish ever after in silent despair'. Wallace, in *Travels on the Amazon*, refers to the Yellow Troupial as having 'an extraordinary power of imitating the song of other birds, so as to render it worthy of the title of the South American Mockingbird'.

Chisholm (1946a) remarks that Australia 'appears to possess a greater number of mockingbirds of each class (major, minor and casual) than any other country'. He assesses the number at fifty-three (1951) but Marshall (1950b) considers that the proportion approximates to that in Britain. He remarks that 'it is quality and intensity of mimicry rather than the number of birds that are mimetic that makes the Australian avifauna especially notable in this respect'. He judges the Spotted Bowerbird to be 'probably the most gifted mockingbird known'. Chisholm (1946a) claims it to be 'the finest non-singing mocker in the world' and comments that the Superb Lyrebird is 'beyond doubt, the most accomplished of all vocalists among the large birds of the world'. In his opinion (1948) 'stolen notes' comprise at least seventy-five per cent of the vocabulary of Lyrebirds and some bowerbirds (Pl. V). None of the Australian relatives of the two New Zealand mimics, the Tui and Bellbird, is a mimic.†

A Study of Bird Song

THEORIES CONCERNING THE FUNCTION OF MIMICRY
Adaptation to habitat

Is mimicry an adaptation to particular types of habitat? Marshall, commenting on the fact that the Australian master mimics and many other mockers inhabit scrub, heath, thick forest, or rain forest, concludes that borrowing calls from other species is an aid to the continuous long-range advertisement which facilitates the breeding of birds in thick cover. However, habitats varying from scrub to rain forest have little in common and it has long been recognized that loud vocalizations, whether mimetic or not, serve this end in dense vegetation. Moreover, some mimetic species, such as the Calandra Lark in Europe, are birds of bare, open ground. This species and the Horsfield Bush Lark of Australia utter their mimicries in flight (Alexander 1927; Bourke 1947). Related birds of dense homogeneous habitats differ in their imitative ability. The Grasshopper Warbler and Savi's Warbler are not mimetic but other warblers of similar habitats are notable performers.

If any generalization concerning the relationship of mimicry to habitat be justified it might be that the principal natural mimics are mainly ground-frequenting species or birds which feed on or near the ground. Attention has been called to this by Chisholm (1946a). Such species tend to be good songsters, as Hartshorne (1958b) has pointed out. Apparently few birds which sing as they feed mimic. Perhaps birds which 'make an appointment' with singing not only tend to give a more polished and continuous performance but are more apt than other birds to pay attention to sounds around them and so notice, retain, and sometimes utter, reproductions of such sounds.

In theory mimicry of other species carried to extreme limits would make it practically impossible for birds to identify a song as being uttered by one of their own species. This would be dysgenic. But, because no two birds are likely to incorporate exactly the same imitations in their songs, a limited amount of vocal mimicry would be highly effective in proclaiming individual identity. There are, of course, other ways in which birds do this, such as by uttering a song with distinctive characteristics. Indeed this may well be the significance of the differences, sometimes only in the finer details, between the utterances of individual birds (p. 95).

Argus Pheasants in their isolated display courts in the jungle emit their loud call in such a manner that, although it is so simple and crude, even the human listener can distinguish the cry of one bird from that of another (Beebe 1918–22). Presumably it is advantageous for the females to be able thus to distinguish the different males; if so, other species, such as the lyrebirds and bowerbirds, with somewhat similar

76

mating procedures, may be suspected of announcing individual identity by incorporating mimicries of other species, or extraneous sounds, in their repertoires. There are some indications that among lek birds individual identification is important. Ruffs are very silent birds but females can identify males visually as the adornments of no two birds are exactly alike. At the lek of Great Birds of Paradise the male with the most brilliant and extravagant plumes is able to secure a particularly advantageous place in the display tree and probably other birds recognize him by his appearance. Sexual selection operates among lek birds and this is likely to render identification of individual males by the females important, especially as the recognition of the partner by minute individual peculiarities of appearance and movements, such as occurs among birds mated for at least the duration of a nesting cycle, is hardly possible in such species.

Mimicry as diversionary display

Excitement, especially when caused by intrusion at the nest may elicit mimicry. Miss Howard remarks of the Sedge Warbler: 'I think this species becomes more of a caricaturist under the excitement of territorial defence'. When Marsh Warblers are proclaiming territory against one another they are highly imitative. The Brown Thornbill and Heath Wren mimic when alarmed at the nest and there is a record of a Rock Warbler imitating seven species on being disturbed with the young (Chisholm 1946a; Gilbert 1937). A Lyrebird broke into mimicry when her nestling was handled, imitating, among other sounds, the panting and yelping of a dog (Hindwood 1955). A female Spotted Bowerbird uttered loud mimicry and then performed distraction display when an observer approached the nest (Gaukrodger 1922). Another broke into noisy mimetic outbursts after its mate had been shot (McLennan 1946). Bowerbirds may also counterfeit calls when disturbed at the bower. Bourke (1949b) mentions Black-backed Bellmagpies mimicking while two males fought and another looked on. A Satin Bowerbird may mimic during courtship song (Robinson 1949). Intruders at Jays' nests evoke remarkable imitative calls, including the cries of nest predators (p. 80).

The stimuli calling forth such mimicry seem to be the same as evoke song from other birds when alarmed at the nest or with young. The motivation may be to some extent defensive and territorial but these calls are evidently the outcome of conflicting impulses such as have given rise to distraction display, though unlike it they have not become ritualized (Armstrong 1949, 1954b). Whatever the motivation of seemingly incongruous utterances may be we need to consider whether, in fact, these are adaptive or may become so. The alarm calls uttered when a predator is near the nest may sometimes tend to deflect it and, if so, they may have survival value. Could this be true of mimicries also? There seems to be no evidence that mimicries, as such, are effective in this way. It might seem, for example, that the mimicry by a bird of the distress note of the young would be a means of attracting a predator away from the chicks, but such behaviour does not appear to have been recorded, except, possibly, in some species during distraction display when the visual performance is much more effective than any sounds uttered.

Mimicry as a means of alluring prey

From time to time it has been suggested that some birds attract others within reach by imitating their calls. The author of *The Boke of St. Albans*, usually assumed to be Dame Juliana Berners, called the Great Grey Shrike an 'ungratefull subtill fowle', believing that thus it lured small birds to where they could be seized. Audubon accused the Northern Shrike of the same subterfuge and more recently a naturalist has mentioned the possibility that the cries of the Australian Butcherbird are effective in this manner (Pollard 1930). In default of evidence this theory need not be taken seriously. Visual lures are employed by such organisms as the angler fish, *Lophius piscatorius*, and the Javanese spider, *Ornithiscatoides decipiens*, which simulates a bird-dropping and thus attracts butterflies (Hardy 1959; Bristowe 1958), but acoustic alluring deception appears to be confined to man. Hunters of many races attract birds by imitating their calls. Some prehistoric whistles and flutes made of bird bones may have been used for this purpose (Armstrong 1958b; Megaw 1960). Modern fowlers also attract birds by mimicking the call of a predator. André (1904) describes how plumage hunters in Trinidad attracted hummingbirds and other species within range of their guns by imitating the owl, *Glaucidium phalaenoides*. In Mexico collectors lure vireos by squeaking and mimicking a related species, *G. gnoma* (Schaldach 1960). Hartley (1950b) mentions seeing a number of Mistle Thrushes and Blackbirds summoned by an imitation of the *ke-wick* of the Tawny Owl.

Mobbing of owls and other predators by birds of various species is normally adaptive because, although occasionally a mobbed bird is able to seize one of its tormentors, or another predator, such as man, may profit by the situation to capture one of the mobbing birds, individuals alerted to the location of a predator are safer than if they were unaware of its presence. Experiments in which the recorded mobbing calls of crows were reproduced showed that birds were attracted from far away up to the loudspeaker (Frings and Frings 1957). It should be noted that by mobbing a predator birds further the survival of species other than their own just as by their visual and vocal signals sea-birds, such as gulls and terns, indicate a source of food to other species (p. 19). This behaviour persists because there are seldom consequences to the disadvantage of birds which alert others to the presence of enemies or sporadic supplies of food. Only where two sympatric species are in serious competition for food would it be to the advantage of one that the other should be more vulnerable than itself. Signalling a source of food usually occurs when it is locally and temporarily abundant so that a free-for-all is to the detriment of none.

The meagre evidence available suggests that when birds respond to predators' calls this is a learned rather than an inborn response. Experiments in which a hand-reared Song Sparrow was allowed to hear mimicries of the calls of the Great Horned, Barred, and Barn Owl evoked no response (Nice and ter Pelkwyk 1941) but Miller (1952) found that American Falconidae, jays and Magpie reacted to counterfeit owl calls. Small passerines responded particularly to the voices of the smaller owls but birds normally resident outside the range of an owl species usually showed no recognition of the call as a signal of danger. Reactions were found to be direct or a response to the behaviour of other alarmed birds. The location of the sounds was quickly discovered. Further experimentation along these lines would be profitable.

If it were to their advantage birds might have evolved vocal alluring calls since they may deceive each other accidentally by their mimicries. Bechstein (1864) owned a Lesser Grey Shrike which could imitate a Quail. This bird, 'however lively its song, always stopped in order to imitate the Quail's call, whenever it heard it; and the latter, before it became accustomed to the mimicry, would go furiously about the room, endeavouring to find its rival'. Certain notes in Robin songs cause Chaffinches to make escape responses (Marler 1956a). The Smooth-billed Ani has a distinctive cry which causes the flock to fly up. A Mockingbird included it in its song and unintentionally made the Anis take wing from time to time (Davis 1940). When a Great Grey Bowerbird whistled like a hawk a flock of doves dashed for cover (Selvage 1954) and a hen and her chicks did likewise when a Spotted Bowerbird imitated a Whistling Eagle (Campbell 1901; Chisholm 1948). A White-backed Bellmagpie which could bark like a dog or mew like a cat used to perch on a fence and call the fowls together (Thomson 1922). On the other hand, Song Thrushes are not deceived by Lyrebirds which reproduce their phrases (Chisholm 1948) nor do poultry heed the clucks of Starlings which have learned these calls while frequenting the hen-run.

Probably acoustic means of alluring prey have not evolved because they would involve dysgenic specialization.† The more effective they might become the more danger of the species allured being eliminated in the predator's range. Also, if the birds deceived and preyed upon were young or migratory the decoy calls would be of no avail during much of the year. Moreover, as happened with the Quail just mentioned, birds would learn to distinguish mimicries from genuine calls if they heard them repeatedly.

Although vocalizations are not used to lure prey they may, perhaps, become adapted to induce a bird to feed another of a different species. The Koel, which is reared with the brood of the Indian Crow, utters Crow calls only during the nestling and fledgling stages. In the only instance investigated of a Koel being reared by another species the chick did not call like a Crow (Hutson 1956). We have not enough data on which to base any conclusion but it would seem that young Koels may copy the calls of their nest-mates.

Mimicry as a device for frightening predators

Another theory concerning mimicry is that by uttering calls resembling those of predators birds are able to scare away potential marauders. There is no valid evidence to support this but incidents which have a bearing on it are worth quoting. When attacked by Tawny Owls or caught in a trap Jays may utter the Owl's hoot. A Lanceolated Jay barked like a dog when one approached. Male or female Jays disturbed with young may mimic Magpies and when a Jay was alarmed by a cat it uttered the Blackbird's alarm call and then its own raucous scream (Goodwin 1946, 1956). A tame Irish Jay mewed for food as it had heard the cat do (Ussher and Warren 1900). A Great Grey Bowerbird was heard mewing from a post below which a cat was sleeping. At last the cat got up, glared at the bird, and departed (Selvage 1954). A Mockingbird ceased imitating a Killdeer when an American Sparrowhawk, *Falco sparverius*, flew past and gave the Sparrowhawk's call. Perhaps coincidence cannot be excluded. Apparently the sight of a circling Red-shouldered Hawk caused a Blue Jay to imitate it (Townsend 1924). A Ringnecked Parakeet has been known to utter the call of Barraband's Parakeet while attacking it (Bedford 1954). An Indian shrike which preys on frogs is said to incorporate their screams in its song (Finn n.d.). No doubt other instances of this type could be quoted but there is no record of a predator being frightened away by an imitation of its threat call or attracted by an imitation of its own call or the call of another predator although, as we have noted, there is some evidence of birds recognizing predators' calls. Various explanations of this may be suggested. Normally, the appearance rather than the utterance of predators is frightening; birds seldom have the opportunity of learning to reproduce the threat calls of other species and sufficiently loud imitation may be difficult to attain. Eagles, falcons, and hawks preying on other birds may utter series of calls (Pl. VI) but do not utter continuous song.

V*a*.   Lyre Bird singing and displaying

V*b*.   Lyre Bird singing in his display court

VI.   Peregrine Falcon calling

Factors affecting the learning and reproduction of mimicries

The significance of such mimicries as those quoted lies, not in their effectiveness as defensive adaptations but in the light they throw on how mimicries are acquired and elicited. Some mimicries are learned and reproduced in situations in which a relationship which might be called 'emotional' is established (Nicolai 1959). That the bird fanciers were aware of this to some extent is suggested by their comments on some species as being both imitative and affectionate. Thus Bechstein (1864) remarked that the Bullfinch is 'highly affectionate'. We have already noted that this species learns its song in a relationship of 'emotional attachment' to another individual (p. 56). Bechstein calls the Purple-capped Lory 'the most docile and talkative, the tamest, most affectionate and most attractive of the parrots'. It has been suggested that the copying of speech is partly motivated by the effort to recall the teacher with whom an emotional bond has been established (Mowrer 1950). Certainly there is significance in the fact that a bird being taught by a person is receiving such undivided attention as it rarely receives even as a chick or from its mate.

Apparently birds may learn mimicries not only when in a state of emotional *rapport* but in the contrary emotional condition. Lorenz (1952) tells the story of a free-living tame Hooded Crow which reappeared with a broken toe after several weeks' absence. In the accent of a lower Austrian street urchin the bird said the equivalent of 'Got 'im in t'bloomin' trap !' He had apparently heard and learned this expression while in a distressed condition. A Blue-fronted Amazon Parrot belonging to Konrad Lorenz's brother was once frightened by a chimney-sweep and months later shrieked 'The chimney-sweep is coming' when he appeared. The bird had not heard the phrase uttered more than three times in its life. On the other hand, in some circumstances learning may be hindered by emotional disturbance (Bené 1945). This is a common problem in our schools.

Mimicries may also be acquired and associations established when there is no obvious 'emotional' stimulus, unless the novelty of some experience be considered to be of this kind. A captive Mockingbird uttered the Flicker call on two occasions when one appeared silently outside a window (Laskey 1944b). A Jay will utter the call of a Heron or Crow when one of these flies over (Goodwin 1956) and a Great Grey Shrike gave the characteristic call of a Pied Wagtail when one flew past (Sick 1935). The Micheners write thus of Mockingbirds : 'Their best imitation, if it is in fact imitation, is that of the squeaky begging notes of the baby Mockingbird. As soon as the female is incubating eggs and before any baby Mockingbird notes are heard in the vicinity, at least some of the males introduce a series of these baby squeaks into their songs and continue to do so until the babies are big enough to do their own squeaking'. Anticipatory behaviour is well known in birds. An unmated male Chaffinch will make courtship postures on hearing the call of a female looking for a mate without having seen her (Marler 1956a). I have seen a male Wren begin to display on hearing his mate with her brood out of sight behind the gable of a house (Armstrong 1955). Of particular interest is the bringing of food to the nest before the young have hatched (Armstrong 1947; Skutch 1953; Nolan 1958b) and the leading of ratels and human beings to bees' nests by honeyguides (Friedmann 1955).

Birds not only learn sounds but also establish associations between them and persons, animals, or contemporaneous events. Canaries which

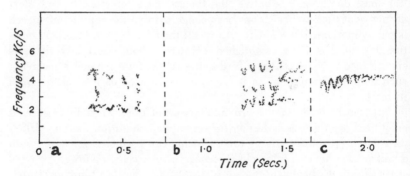

Fig. 14. Calls of Canaries. (a) Call-note of Roller Canary; (b) the Canary's imitation of the call-note of the Roller Canary; (c) the call-note of the Canary. These are contact calls. (After Poulsen 1959)

have learned the alarm call of the Roller Canary utter it on seeing an owl (Poulsen 1959) (Fig. 14). A Blackbird gave the warning call of the Pekin Robin in the appropriate situations. Where Great and Coal Tits breed together the Great Tits may acquire the alarm notes of the Coal Tits (Thielcke-Poltz and Thielcke 1960). My wife had a parrot at her home in Brazil which greeted the butcher, but never the milkman, with, 'Is the meat tender today?' The association had been formed through hearing the butcher greeted by members of the household with these words. A Budgerigar made gurgling noises when a bottle was lifted, uttered the Bee-eater call when one appeared, and said 'Come in' when there was a knock at the door (Heinroth and Heinroth 1959). Koehler (1951, 1954) kept a parrot which said 'Allo!' when the telephone receiver was picked up and 'Na, auf Wiedersehen' when he left the room. At first it said this when he opened the door, then when he went towards the door, and finally when he stood up to leave the room. Lucanus (1923, 1925) mentions a parrot which said 'Adieu' when a guest was departing and then acquired the trick of using this expression when someone it disliked was present. Another parrot used to say 'na' when it expected some action to take place. There is little difference between the use of acquired sounds by such birds and a human infant's early efforts at speech. When a Grey Parrot saw a Hoopoe some years after the death of a Hoopoe which had been his companion he uttered the bird's pet name (Lorenz 1952). Thus birds establish associations between sounds and events, remember them, and even establish anticipatory associations. There appears to be a connexion between birds' ability to learn sounds and manipulative ability—apart from highly stereotyped behaviour in nest-building. Parrots may use their beaks as a third foot and they also employ their feet adroitly to hold food. Corvids also use a foot to secure food while they peck and the Carrion Crow, Rook, Jackdaw, and Jay are among the few birds known to be able to pull up food suspended on a string. These birds are all mimics. The Greenfinch and Great Tit are also able to perform the string-pulling feat (Thorpe 1956). Remarkable manipulative skill is manifested by bowerbirds in painting their bowers and these birds are among the most exceptionally gifted mimics (p. 75). It is acknowledged that the ability of man's ancestors to coordinate eye and hand contributed greatly to the development of the brain, perception of relationships, abstract thought, and speech. Proto-man's cries may have come to express relationship between objects, thus eventually conveying items of information of an abstract character (De Laguna 1928). Birds have made some advance along the same road.

Combined vocal and visual mimicry

Valid evidence of the occurrence of combined vocal and visual mimicry in birds would be of much interest but most alleged instances are ill-substantiated. An Oxford Starling is said to have swayed and called like the bell it was imitating and another is reputed to have called and drummed like a Flicker. A juvenile Blackbird copied the movements of an older bird singing sub-song but merely opened its beak (Witchell 1896; Allard 1939; Howard 1952). There is an account of a Catbird which flew and called like a kingfisher (Townsend 1924). The only well-authenticated instance of double mimicry also concerns a Catbird. When a male Bobolink arrived on a Montana farm a Catbird followed it around for at least half an hour mimicking the entire Bobolink song. Seven weeks later a typical Bobolink flight-song was heard and the Catbird was seen descending from about thirty feet mimicking the movements as well as the notes of the Bobolink (Weydemeyer 1930). It should not be difficult to determine experimentally whether linked visual and vocal mimicry does indeed occur. For this purpose parrots would be suitable subjects as they are manipulative as well as imitative.†

The learning of mimicries

Supplementing what has been said already concerning the learning and development of song some comments may be made on the learning of the calls of other species and extraneous sounds. In all organisms learning ability is greatest in youth though there are differences between groups, species, and individuals in the rate at which it declines. The younger members of a monkey clan are the innovators (Miyadi 1959). Blase (1960) goes so far as to say that 'in their youth, practically all song birds tend to mimic'. Copying of sounds by birds usually occurs during the first two years though parrots retain the ability longer and an East African Glossy Starling learned to imitate vocally the drumming of a woodpecker at the age of nine years (Falkner 1943). The occurrence of mimicries in developmental sub-song has already been mentioned (p. 47). At least in some species it is correlated with an increasing production of sex hormone. Mimicry in such circumstances illustrates lability or versatility in behaviour which decreases with age. Although Chaffinches include mimicries in their developmental sub-song, not only do they eliminate these as the territorial song develops but they lose all imitative ability when rather more than a year old. Apparently the Regent Bowerbird, which mimics other birds in whisper song does not mimic in full voice although some other bowerbirds are such accomplished mockers (Chisholm 1951; Marshall 1954). Phases occur for some years in the life of the Canary when imitative ability recurs (p. 53). The Red-backed Shrike's song which has comparatively little territorial relevance remains subdued and imitative. The most vigorous birds are the most zealous singers and the best mimics. The more often they sing the more often they incorporate mimicries (Blase 1960). Such facts throw light on the procedure involved in learning. They suggest that the advantages of stereotyped behaviour are so great in many respects that the trend of development is to eliminate plasticity. In other words, loss of learning ability in many organisms, if not all, is due not merely to decay in versatility and originality but to positive processes which have evolved because of the advantages of stereotyped behaviour.

In most species mimicries are learned mainly in the first two years. This is what we might expect in view of what is known concerning song-learning in general (Chapter III). Also, like song-versions, they are apt to be acquired during particular periods of susceptibility (Blase 1960). None of the birds breeding in Europe which winter in Africa is known to reproduce call-notes of any African species. A Mistletoebird gave perfect imitations of other species in its first autumn (Ramsey 1946), and a Nightingale learned the call of a Crested Lark at the end of its second year (Heinroth 1910). Superb Lyrebirds begin to display and croon when a few months old. Some may possess a repertoire of mimicries when aged a year, others begin to mimic at about that age. According to Pratt (1937) the first mimicries are crude but each season they improve. This needs verification. A Lyrebird, caged when two years old, had acquired its full repertoire. It did not learn any calls from its companions in the aviary (Chisholm 1946a).

The best account of how a bird acquires its repertoire of mimicries concerns a Mockingbird (Laskey 1944b). A hand-reared male sang whisper song similar to adult song when twenty-nine days old but mimicries were first uttered at four and a half months. At nine months he began reciprocating with the call or song of another bird shortly after hearing it. In the spring of his second year he added more calls, including the squeak a washing machine had developed in the previous fortnight. Among other sounds acquired was the *caw* of distant crows. He also reproduced a Cowbird's song two days after hearing it.

Among birds noted as copying sounds immediately after hearing them are a number of Australian species, including the female Shrike-tit, Rufous Scrub-bird, and Grey Thrush—which is said to have promptly imitated an opossum's squeal. A Satin Bowerbird echoed a boy's laughing scream. Another, in captivity, readily copied the calls of other birds but soon forgot them if they were not repeated (Chisholm 1946a, 1950a). Similarly the Emerald Toucanet mimics with exactitude but apparently reproduces a call only so long as it hears it from time to time (Wagner 1944). The Brown Thornbill pays attention to novel sounds and is reputed to learn the notes of young birds and the dominant or newest songs around (Erickson 1953). The Red-backed Shrike mimics accurately on first uttering calls newly added to its repertoire (Blase 1960).

We have commented earlier on the delay which may occur in the reproduction of what is learnt (p. 55). A Grey Parrot may repeat a word accurately for the first time a week or more after hearing it (Baldwin 1914). An American Catbird reproduced in spring for the first time a whistled note which it had heard the previous summer (Townsend 1924) and a Brown Thrasher is said to have first sung a melody acquired from a captive Mockingbird four years after hearing it. Some songs were uttered for a time and then abandoned (Thomas 1952). This account and instances of other birds mimicking sounds soon after hearing them indicates that novel utterances are often acquired otherwise than by trial-and-error learning (Thorpe 1956).

As illustrations of the memory capacity of birds it may be mentioned that an Amazon Parrot has been known to acquire a vocabulary of between fifty and a hundred words (Lashley 1913). Probably some Budgerigars acquire a larger repertoire. A parrot, bought by a cardinal, is reputed to have been able to recite the Apostles' Creed correctly (Kircher 1650).

The abandonment or forgetting of sounds has received less attention than the learning of them. The bird fanciers noted that during the moult birds were apt to forget what they had learned but if their learning had been a slow process they were more likely to remember—as is true of human learning. House Sparrows placed with Canaries learned their song but forgot it when they could no longer hear the Canaries. Eight weeks later, when replaced with the Canaries, they regained it (Conradi 1905). Individual birds may differ in their capacity to retain sounds which have been learned. Poulsen (1959) found that four Canaries which had acquired alien songs lost these when placed with Canaries singing normally, whereas three others, in similar conditions, retained the acquired songs all their lives. Blackbirds 'forget' motifs (Thielcke-Poltz and Thielcke 1960). A Grey Parrot which had learned to count one, two, three in German ceased to do so but began again after two years. Another said 'Heil Hitler' in the tone of a previous owner three years after it had changed hands (Koehler 1951). Patterson (1904) had a bird of this species for nineteen years which 'sang Methodist ditties and swore desperately at passersby'. We may assume that the tastes of previous owners differed and that its repertoire had been retained for a long time.

Naturally wild birds may sometimes utter mimicries learnt far from where they acquired them. On the island of Skokholm, Wheatears mainly mimic species not resident there (Conder pers. comm.) and Redstarts utter notes borrowed from Robins, Nightingales, and other species in habitats from which these birds are absent (Buxton 1950). According to Hudson (1920) the White-banded Mockingbird imitates in its Patagonian breeding quarters notes heard in sub-tropical forests a thousand miles away. In the California Thrasher's winter song the calls of summer visitors are heard and in its summer song are reminiscences of winter visitors (Bent 1948). Also, during the winter, a Golden Whistler female or immature male was heard imitating a Variegated Wren and Striated Thornbill (Jack 1949b). Lyrebirds in Gippsland have been known to utter the notes of birds not heard in the district for fifteen years and one bird reproduced the whirring of a circular saw thirty years after the timber mill in the area had been dismantled (Chisholm 1948). It is hardly credible that the bird had survived more than thirty years, so, if the observation is reliable, it may have learned the sound from another bird or in another area. Robinson (1956) quotes W. H. Loaring on the Western Bellmagpie's mimicries : 'The repertoire includes the songs and calls or parts thereof of very many of the larger birds of the district down to the songs of the Whistlers. Members of No. 1 clan picked up the bark of a dog—three deep-voiced barks usually being given, apparently in mimicry of one particular dog—and although the animal has long since departed this particular item appears to have been handed down to later generations'. A Bellmagpie learned a flute melody of fifteen notes in two phrases. Some years later when another Bellmagpie acquired the melody they used to sing together antiphonally, the first bird singing the first phrase, the second adding the ending. When the younger bird died its mentor returned to singing the whole melody. Comparable behaviour has been recorded of a Canary which learnt to pipe 'God save the King' from a Bullfinch. If the Bullfinch paused too long before 'Send him victorious . . .' the Canary would complete the tune (Henschel 1903). I am reminded of hearing a kilted Scottish boy scout complete the verse of a Chinese song when a Chinese scout with whom he was marching abruptly stopped singing! †

Mimicry is most characteristic of male birds as they are, on the whole, the singing sex, but females of some species also have this capacity. Hen Blackbirds not only learn motifs but may utter an acquired call in the appropriate situation (Thielcke-Poltz and Thielcke 1960). Female parrots become good talkers and female Jays imitate other birds (Finn n.d.; Goodwin 1956). Other female mimics include the lyrebirds, Satin Bowerbird, and Yellow-throated Scrub Wren (Gilbert 1928; Chisholm 1946a).

In the wild mimicry is usually a seasonal phenomenon for song itself depends on the activity of the gonads. However, it will be remembered that Canaries mimic in autumn (p. 53). The mockeries of the Satin Bowerbird are normally heard only during the season of territory tenure and display, while spermatogenesis is taking place. Imitations of other birds are uttered by the male while displaying to the female. Removal of the gonads inhibits mimicry and injections of testosterone propionate re-establish it. Mimicry may occur to a minor extent during the postnuptial season but there is a certain amount of interstitial activity at this time (Marshall 1950b, 1954).

VI

SONG DIALECTS AND THE
RELATIONSHIP OF VOCALIZATION
TO SPECIATION

In accordance with regional differences birds of the same
species seem to differ not only in appearance but also in
their calls and behaviour.

LONGOLIUS. *Dialogus de avibus.* Cologne, 1544.

I T has long been known that the song-pattern of a species may vary in
different localities, the members of the community all tending to sing
a type of song, or a series of types, differing from the pattern characteristic of other communities. Bird fanciers, anxious to secure individual
birds or strains with notable songs, were much interested in these differences. Two and a half centuries ago Thomas Ward was aware that the
young should be closely associated with older birds if they were to
acquire the perfect song. In Germany also Chaffinches from certain
regions, such as the Thuringer Wald and the Harz mountains, were
specially prized for their fine songs. Such sums were given for an outstanding singer that there was a proverb, 'The finch is worth a cow'. The
bird-fanciers gave names to different song-versions. Tucker (1809) commented on local differences in Chaffinch song and Newton (1896), who
quoted some earlier references, remarked : 'A curious question, which has
as yet attracted but little attention, is whether the notes of the same
species of bird are in all countries alike. From my own observations I
am inclined to think that they are not, and that there exist "dialects", so
to speak of the song.' Howard (1900, 1902b) claimed that the songs of the
Whitethroat, Wren, and Cuckoo differed in various regions of the British
Isles. Voigt (1913), Stadler (1929, 1930), Sick (1939), Peitzmeier (1949),
Sauer (1955), and Thorpe (1961) are among the writers who have discussed bird dialects.

Given sufficient historical information one can trace the factors responsible for dialect differences in human populations, as, for example, in
Ulster, where present-day dialects are attributable to immigrations of
people from England and Scotland into an Irish-speaking area. Although,
in a sense, every version of a language characteristic of a community is a

dialect, yet in using the word either of human speech or of bird song it is possible, by taking into consideration the relative sizes of the areas in which particular variations are heard, to speak of a given variation as a widespread or restricted dialect. Thus, over the greater part of continental Europe the Chiffchaff intones its name in the familiar fashion but the song has distinctive peculiarities in the Iberian peninsula, where, in the absence of the Willow Warbler, there are resemblances to this bird's song. The utterance of this race may be said to be a restricted dialect in the sense that a dialect is a subordinate version of a language. We are accustomed to think crudely of dialects of speech as versions diverging from the 'correct' current norm but such ideas are out of place in considering bird dialects.

Cultural segregation, which often initiates and perpetuates differences in human dialects, cannot occur among birds, although differences in such characteristics as the nature of the pair-bond and the structure of the nest may arise in separated populations. Also, as we shall see, isolating mechanisms, including vocalizations, may prevent the inter-breeding of sympatric communities (p. 102). In such circumstances the status of the communities as taxonomic entities can be evaluated only after careful study.

Bird dialects differ from dialects of human speech in two important respects. Firstly, they always have a geographical basis, while dialect differences may exist within human groups, even to the extent of men and women speaking different dialects, as is recorded by Humboldt of the Caribs; and secondly, in birds, but not in man, there are hereditary predispositions to certain types of utterance.† Even in highly imitative birds and those in which there is great variation in the songs of individuals the song is usually characteristic to the extent that the practised human ear has little or no difficulty in recognizing the species (p. 6).

Subjectivity of interpretation has been an obstacle to the study of bird dialects. Haviland (1916b) dismissed the song of Lapland Buntings on the Yenesei as 'a loud, toneless gush of melody' while other observers in Lapland have rated the song highly (Armstrong and Westall 1953). Probably the birds sing the same song in both areas but until recordings are available we cannot be certain. Stanford (1945) states that in Burma the Cuckoo sings as it does in Britain but Popham (1891) thought that Siberian Cuckoos sing differently from British birds. He could hardly have confused the call of Blyth's Cuckoo, *Cuculus saturatus*, with that of *C. canorus*. The two species look alike in the field but the song of *C. saturatus* is reminiscent of the Hoopoe's call-note. Howard's inference (1900, 1902b) that dialect differences in the voices of British species are due to local differences in humidity has not been confirmed. A recording of the

Cuckoo made in Kenya by Myles North shows that the song has not the cadence characteristic of the utterance in Europe.

Electronic recordings are now making it possible not only to eliminate the subjectivity in the assessments of regional differences but provide data for the taxonomist. Sound spectrograms of the songs of the Brown-throated Wren of Mexico and the House Wren of North America show greater similarities than exist between the two North American races of the House Wren. Taken together with a cline in morphological characters the evidence shows that the birds are conspecific (Lanyon 1960c). Song recordings have also confirmed that the Rock Nuthatch, *Sitta neumayer*, is more closely related to *S. castanea* than to *S. europaea* (Löhrl 1960). On the evidence of the analysis of calls of North American crows a new species, the Sinaloa Crow, *Corvus sinaloae*, has been proposed (L. I. Davis 1958) but the differences could hardly justify more than sub-specific rank.

Lest selection of song dialects for special consideration should give a false impression it must be stressed that the calls and songs of some species remain so similar throughout vast areas that the ornithologist may be unable to detect differences between the vocalizations of individuals hundreds of miles apart. To my ear there is no appreciable difference between the song of the Willow Warbler in Lapland and in Switzerland nor between the music of the Nightingale in Nottinghamshire and in the Camargue—though the Nightingale's song is reputed to be of a more varied character in Europe than in Persia (Meiklejohn 1948). The Skylark is said to sing in Japan as it does in England (St. John 1880) and its song in Burma is 'almost indistinguishable from its Hampshire song' (Stanford 1945). The Mountain Leaf Warbler is widely distributed in the South Seas in definitely distinguishable races but the ear cannot detect any variation in song from New Guinea to the outermost Solomon Islands (Mayr 1942).

Smythies (1960) lists twenty non-migratory species whose voices in Burma and Borneo are sufficiently similar to be immediately recognizable to a naturalist familiar with them in one of these areas visiting the other. In Borneo, the birds being generally smaller in size, the notes tend to be less resonant. Blyth's Cuckoo sings four notes in Burma, three in Borneo. There is also a difference in the way the notes of the Indian Cuckoo are pitched, and the Striped Babbler has a much richer repertoire in Borneo. Differences of these magnitudes are exceptional.

A list of the songs and calls of birds heard in areas of Africa as far apart as Abyssinia and South Africa drawn up by Benson (1948) shows that he found 176 instances of no variation within the species or pairs of allopatric species—birds whose breeding ranges do not overlap—and only thirty-three in which differences, mostly slight, were detected. Where allied species were concerned there was generally a voice difference and also a difference in ecological preference, amounting to complete separation in some instances. In birds of two genera, however, no ecological separation was discernible. The isolating mechanisms in such circumstances must be morphological or behavioural (including vocal), or both.

The Wood Pewee is found from Manitoba to Texas and across the United States to the Great Plains but there is no difference between the songs of the eastern and western birds and the differences between the northern and southern populations are slight (Craig 1943).

In human speech there are many different characteristics by which dialects may be distinguished. An unusual word, a peculiarity of pronunciation or voice production, such as betrayed the Ephraimites (Judges XII, 5–6), or a characteristic rhythm, may indicate that the speaker hails from an identifiable region. As individuals hear themselves speak by bone conduction they may be incapable of hearing and altering some of their own speech peculiarities of diction apparent to others. Among birds dialects may be distinguished on the basis of a comparable variety of clues. There may be differences in the inflection of notes, in the quality and number of notes uttered or their order, in rhythm, length of phrase, the number and order of song-versions, or other characteristics, though there must be constancy of variation, or in the limits of variation in the community, for their utterances to constitute a dialect. All such variations are within the dictionary definition of dialect as possessing 'distinguishable vocabulary, pronunciation, or idioms'.

Call-notes tend to remain more constant than songs because as a general rule less learning is involved. In many species the call-notes, or most of them, are inborn (p. 102) but the vocalizations may differ in quality or other respects in separated areas of the range. In Denmark, where there are no pronounced geographical barriers, the *huit* alarm call of the Chaffinch occurs in a number of different dialects but observers agree that variations may be due to learning (Poulsen 1958). In southwestern Spain the local race of Green Woodpecker utters the notes of its 'yaffle' more slowly than the British race. If observations by Meinertzhagen (1943) are reliable Ravens in western Europe have a different call from the birds in Asia and the call of the Black Partridge in the Himalayas is not identifiable as the note of the same species in Persia and Iraq. Jackson's Francolin has a different type of call in the Aberdare Mountains at 4000 feet and on Mount Kenya. Chisholm (1948) claims that the calls of the Mud-lark and the Shrike-tit differ in Victoria and Queensland. The voice of the Willie Wagtail is of such a character in the Solomon Islands as compared with Australia that it is virtually unrecognizable as the utterance of the same bird. The sustained ringing call of the Satin Bowerbird differs greatly in two regions—around Sidney and in the McPherson range.

Song dialects may differ in many respects. The Whip Bird's melody in Queensland is more musical and elaborate than in the Danderongs of Victoria and the Olive Whistler's song in Victoria is poorer than on the Lamington Plateau of South Queensland where the forest is dense and prevailing mists often restrict visibility (Hartshorne 1953, pers. comm.). Communities of the Fox Sparrow sing different forms of song in different types of habitat (Linsdale 1928). The Rufous-naped Lark, *Mirafra africana tropicalis*, of the upland grasslands at 8000 feet in the Crater Highlands of Northern Tanganyika sings a varied song in hovering flight at a height of twenty feet instead of uttering a few mournful notes from a bush or termite hill as does the subspecies *athi* at lower elevations (Elliott and Fuggles-Couchman 1948). I formed the impression that in Iceland and Lapland Meadow Pipits fly higher in their song-flight and sing more elaborate songs than birds in Britain (Armstrong and Westall 1953). According to Saunders (1951) Song Sparrows utter songs of five types. The percentage of these varies geographically. The birds of the sea-coast region of Connecticut and south-eastern New York sing a phrase with a single introductory note whereas some individuals in central and western New York utter double introductory notes. There is great individual variation in the songs of the Rufous-sided Towhee—so much so that the listener can often identify individuals by their songs, but the songs of Florida birds can usually be readily distinguished from those of northern individuals. Analysis of the songs of Carolina Wrens in Florida and Ohio has shown that Florida birds have a higher singing rate, slightly longer songs, shorter phrases, and fewer notes to the phrase (Borror 1956, 1959b).†

We must take into consideration the possibility that observers may sometimes be mistaken in their estimates of differences between songs and call-notes in different regions. Memory of sounds is often unreliable and ability to hear certain frequencies may deteriorate but on the other hand differences apparent to the human ear may be much more evident to the birds themselves.

The examples cited show that separation of one community from another is a prime factor in permitting divergence in song and generating dialect variations. Separation is probably always initially topographical or geographical though ecological factors are sometimes potent in maintaining or increasing the isolation necessary for voice distinctions to develop. These may arise primarily or entirely through genetic variations, as with Border Canaries, or through learning, as with Chaffinches, or both may operate. When dialects occur in species known to be imitative there is a very strong presumption that learning is involved. The situation is then comparable to a considerable extent with a common type of dialect formation in human communities. Among people and birds alike isolation contributes to the formation and perpetuation of dialects. An extreme situation is reached in the mountainous jungle-clad area of New Guinea where distinct languages are spoken in neighbouring valleys. In such conditions cultural differences are accentuated, such as taboos on intermarriage, and antagonisms may become ritualized into forms of warfare or head-hunting, so that a whole complex of isolating 'mechanisms' arises. When dialects which are fairly similar come into contact, fusion and blurring of distinctions may occur but distinct languages tend to retain their autonomy, even though borrowing may occur, or else one exterminates the other. Human language, being a highly complex manipulation of meaningful sounds, is not subject to the over-riding requirements which the necessity for producing stereotyped signals with unmistakable significance imposes on birds. Nevertheless bird song variations, more than other evolutionary variations, seem to be influenced by principles approximating to those which govern human cultural evolution. Learning may occur and variation is free to operate within wider limits than is adaptive in many other spheres.

In Iceland Redwings sing differently in neighbouring valleys. The birds around Thingvellir utter songs distinguishable from those of birds over the mountain ridge in Hvalfjördur. Local variations have been noted in other areas of the Redwing's breeding range but they are most frequent and distinctive towards the Arctic Circle (Witherby *et al.* 1938; Russow 1940; Armstrong 1950a). The Snow Bunting, another bird of high latitudes, also readily forms dialects. Chapman (1958), travelling along the Greenland coast, noticed that his Eskimo companions identified headlands in foggy weather by the characteristic songs of the Buntings. The songs are individually variable but those of neighbours resemble each other (Tinbergen 1939)—a situation similar to that which holds of Chaffinches. Snow Buntings, and to a lesser extent, Iceland Redwings, occur in small nesting populations. In the Cairngorms, Lapland, and Iceland I have seen groups of a few Snow Buntings breeding in places well isolated from other groups, and farther north snow conditions tend to separate breeding communities. In some areas Snow Buntings sing where food competitors are absent and no other song-bird is to be heard. Sparsity of population may have a bearing on dialect formation in high latitudes. The density of species near the limits of their range is often low. The Wren in Iceland and the Chaffinch in Madeira are 'thin on the ground' (Armstrong 1950a, 1954a; Thorpe 1958). Probably the most important song divergence in such conditions is the loosening of stereotypy which tends to occur in the absence of related species. In Australia, which has no species closely related to the Magpie Lark, the songs of individuals differ considerably (Robinson 1946–47). Where birds breed near the limits of their geographical range or climatic tolerance the sparseness of individuals and reduction in vocal competition would tend towards the relaxation of the rigidity of song structure. At the limits of their range individuals of a species tend to form isolated communities in the most favourable habitats. In mountainous areas these may be sheltered valleys. Wherever high mountain ridges and ranges occur populations are liable to become isolated and evolve characteristics of voice and appearance distinct from other populations. Song and call dialects arise and a loosening-up of song-pattern and vocabulary may occur. Such developments take place in regions such as are found in the Arctic, where there may be only one or two species of song-bird in some areas, and on oceanic islands. In such circumstances a highly distinctive song is of less value than where competition is severe.†

The songs of the Willow Warbler and Chiffchaff are highly distinctive and diagnostic although the birds are very similar in appearance. The Chiffchaff's song is inborn according to the Heinroths as, indeed, the Willow Warbler's may be also, for the song does not vary over a huge area. The breeding ranges of the two species overlap in most of Europe but the Chiffchaff has the more southerly distribution and occurs in the Iberian peninsula where the Willow Warbler does not breed. There it approximates to the Willow Warbler in having paler legs, eggs with larger spots, and a song in which, instead of the *chaff* syllable, a series of descending notes is uttered (Ticehurst 1938). The Chiffchaffs of north-west Africa resemble British Chiffchaffs in every respect but song, which consists of a stereotyped pattern of about ten notes delivered with a halting rhythm and at least two changes of pitch (Snow 1952). The utterance is very similar to that of the Iberian Chiffchaff. On Gran Canaria and Tenerife the song differs from that of the Spanish birds though leg- and egg-colour are similar (Tristram 1889; Lack and Southern 1949). On Tenerife its song is harsher, shorter, and pitched slightly lower than that of the British bird, with less or no alteration between high and low notes. The call is like a House Sparrow's chirp. Evidently the Willow Warbler and Chiffchaff diverged from an ancestral form, the Chiffchaff evolving in and becoming adapted to a warmer breeding area than the Willow Warbler. Differentiation in song must have occurred during the separation of the lines of evolution and areas of distribution. Presumably at the time when the two populations came into secondary contact song was a primary isolating factor and further differentiation took place where the breeding areas of the two forms overlapped. The great climatic changes in northern Europe during the advance and recession of the ice may have been of importance in stimulating differentiation through isolating populations, as they were in initiating the divergence of the ancestors of the Carrion and Hooded Crow. They may also have been influential in stimulating the differentiation between the House Sparrow and the Spanish Sparrow. Differences of voice, plumage, and behaviour now prevent the House and Tree Sparrow interbreeding. Evidently when the Neolithic revolution in culture took place the House Sparrows of the Middle East were adapted to exploit the food and nesting niches provided by man but divergence must have taken place earlier than this. The Blackcap and Garden Warbler have quite similar habitat requirements and nesting behaviour, and there are resemblances in song (Raines 1945). Apparently when the birds became sympatric after a period of separation of the lines of descent plumage differences were a primary factor in preventing hybridization. Thus the Willow Warbler and Chiffchaff are kept apart primarily by song differences, the Garden Warbler and Blackcap by differences in plumage as well as song. No doubt the differences between these two birds' songs are much more apparent to the birds than to ourselves. If, however, these species tend to exclude each other from their territories song similarities may be advantageous (p. 118). Some warblers, such as the Willow and Wood, and Lesser Whitethroat, seem to have highly stereotyped songs but sound spectrograms reveal that each bird has several versions. Even jingles of individual Corn Buntings vary. So, also, do the songs of the Chipping Sparrow and Oregon Junco which, to the ear, sound very reiterative (Marler 1959a; Marler and Isaac 1960a). Apart from its song the Greenish Warbler closely resembles the Chiffchaff. The differences in song may have arisen when populations began to migrate to separate breeding areas. So far as is known highly distinctive types of song are the main or sole factors preventing interbreeding between two populations of the Nightingale-Wren in Costa Rica (Slud 1958). Some species are sparsely distributed in tropical forests so that circumstances might arise in which a population might divide and the two groups contract and only increase and overlap after song peculiarities had developed. Ecological preferences are sometimes so marked that a species is never found away from a particular limited type of habitat (Skutch 1951b). The Marsh Tit and Willow Tit are more easily distinguishable from each other by their utterances than by their appearance. They, too, apparently represent lines of development from a common stock which are now prevented from interbreeding in part by the differences in the vocalizations of the two species.

Some examples may be given illustrating the tendency for the songs and calls of birds isolated on islands to lose some of their specific distinctiveness. A comparison of Chaffinch dialects in Denmark revealed that the most divergent was that of the birds on the island of Bornholm. The

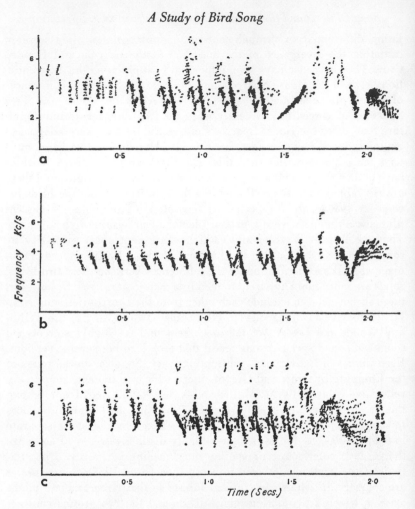

Fig. 15. Sound spectrograms of Chaffinch song-dialects. (a) Bird from Copenhagen; (b) bird from Bornholm. Note short end-phrase; (c) Scandinavian bird. A short note follows the end-flourish. (After Poulsen 1958)

song there has a simpler conclusion (Poulsen 1958) (Fig. 15).

The South Sea Island Warbler sings a beautiful song on some islands and an unmusical ditty on others. On Pitcairn no song has been noted (Mayr 1942). The Gough Island Bunting has a more rambling, variable song than is usual in buntings (Thorpe pers. comm.). The song of the bunting, *Zonotrichia capensis*, in Santo Domingo differs greatly from the songs of mainland races (Chapman 1940). Lack and Southern compared the voices of sixteen species of bird in Britain and Tenerife and found that the songs on Tenerife were apt to be 'shorter and simpler'

VII*a*. Broad-tailed Hummingbird in flight, showing sound-producing tip of first primary

VII*b*. Magnificent Riflebird displaying. The wing feathers produce a hissing rustle

VIIIa. King Bird of Paradise in display

VIIIb. King Bird of Paradise displaying green interior
of mouth. The beak is not opened so widely when the

though not infrequently louder and coarser, than those of their British counterparts'. There tends to be more variety and less distinctiveness in some songs on Tenerife, and the songs of birds in islands of the group only a few miles apart differ. The Robin on Tenerife utters three or four phrases in variable sequence, recalling the phrases of the Song Thrush, with Nightingale-like notes. In the absence of competition from related species uniformity of utterance is reduced. These observations confirm that on islands, as in the Arctic, where there is little or no competition from related species there is less uniformity of utterance than where such competition occurs. Moreover, species isolated from related species or other birds exploiting similar food-niches evolve more varied calls and songs. On Tenerife the Blue Tit has a wide range of call-notes and on Pico in the Azores the Goldcrest calls 'are of bewildering variety' (Marler and Boatman 1951). In other respects also birds on islands or otherwise isolated from competition may become less specific in their behaviour and more catholic in such matters as foraging and choice of nesting site (Svärdson 1949). For example, in Iceland Snipe nest among stunted birch. On the other hand where the Nightingale and Sprosser overlap, the ecological differences between them are found to be greater than elsewhere.

When the songs of Chaffinches on various islands are compared the amount of variation is found to be considerable. The Tenerife form of the Chaffinch has a song resembling fairly closely the poor type of utterance characteristic of the Blue Chaffinch, *Fringilla teydea*, on the same island. Its call differs from that of British birds. The Palma Chaffinch's phrase differs markedly. On Gran Canaria the song terminates in a sustained trill. In Libya the song is said to be shorter and to lack a terminal flourish (Stanford 1954).

It might be supposed that in species which learn their songs to a considerable extent song-divergence would occur more readily than in birds whose song is largely innate. This, however, does not follow. The song of the north European form of the Bullfinch is pitched much lower than the songs of the west European forms (Nicolai 1956). In this species the song is learned but is not used in the maintenance of territory. It plays a minor rôle in pair-formation. Blackbirds retain exactly the pitch and rhythms of the refrains they learn so song dialects are maintained in some areas (Messmer and Messmer 1956). On the whole it is remarkable that song-learning and dialect development have, apparently, played so small a part in speciation. Indeed, there are instances of two populations with common ancestry diverging much more, after separation, in appearance than in vocalizations (p. 105).

There are two classical examples of specialized adaptive radiation in birds of oceanic islands—Darwin's finches on the Galapagos Islands and the Honeycreepers of the Hawaiian chain (Lack 1947; Amadon 1950). Apparently only a small stock, or perhaps a single pair, reached these islands, and, finding a wide variety of ecological niches unexploited, their descendants, throughout the centuries, adapted themselves to occupy them and in so doing evolved into a number of genera and species. The songs of Darwin's finches are simple and unmelodious. There is considerable diversity in the songs of individuals of the same species, but the songs of different species, and even of different genera, have such similarities that it is often difficult to recognize species by ear. As we have noted, this tendency is apparent in other insular groups elsewhere. Vocal distinctiveness is not as adaptive on oceanic islands as where competition is more varied and severe.

The Galapagos archipelago is small and relatively compact but the Hawaiian islands are strung along the Pacific ocean for 1600 miles and possibly date from as late as the end of the Pliocene. Naturally Hawaii offers more varied niches than the Galapagos. There are arid areas but dense vegetation clothes many of the islands. On Kauai a rainfall of 51.56 feet in a year has been recorded. The Honeycreepers, adapting themselves to these varied conditions, have evolved rapidly. There are two subfamilies, Drepaniinae and Psittirostrinae, with songs and call-notes which are quite dissimilar. Indeed, differences in vocalization are among the considerations justifying this division into two major groups.* Even in species which differ greatly in the form of the bill—a very labile character—similarities in song indicate their affinity. The beak of the Akiapolaau, *Hemignathus wilsoni,* possesses a long, curved mandible, contrasting with the relatively much smaller beaks of related *Loxops* species but its song has complex elements indistinguishable from the songs of these birds. The males of the Drepaniinae utter trilling notes, but in the Psittirostrinae the songs may be harsh, monotonous, or gurgling. The different forms have call-notes which are very similar. This is in accordance with constancy of calls being in general greater than in songs. It is apparent, however, that the evolution of specific differences and the consequent accentuation of competition has increased the value of distinctive song. Moreover, the relatively dense habitats frequented by most honeycreepers may have promoted greater distinctiveness in song (p. 222).

Adaptive radiation is exemplified vividly by the birds of oceanic islands but it is, of course, among the great, pervasive, evolutionary phenomena. For example, the woodhewers or woodcreepers of Central and South America manifest variations in bill-length and shape, in-

---

* Delacour (1943) discussing the classification of the estrildine finches, points out that one of the features by which the waxbills (Estrildae) may be distinguished from the grass-finches (Erythrurae) is the sweetness of their calls and songs.

dicating adaptation to different types of feeding niche, comparable with the adaptation of Honeycreepers. Although they are not among the song-birds proper (Oscines) their vocalizations vary greatly from species to species. One species may be heard at a distance of two miles, others have quiet, insect-like calls (Hudson 1892).

It is common knowledge that the speed of evolutionary change can be immensely variable. This is as true of vocalization as of structure. Some forms, such as the mollusc *Lingula* have hardly changed in 500 million years, the Coelacanth fish is very similar to fishes which swam the Devonian seas, the reptile *Sphenodon* and the opossum have survived from the Jurassic and Cretaceous respectively. On the other hand, evolution can be rapid, especially when ability to exploit new niches has been achieved, as with the birds in the Pliocene. The speed with which bird utterances can be modified is also very variable. The acquisition of the power of flight, involving rapid movement in three planes, and the ability to nest and forage in high, concealing foliage, must have stimulated the evolution of sound signals, though some forms of utterance, such as the bill-snapping and hissing of some species may have remained practically unchanged since the birds evolved (p. 16). It is unlikely that the snake-like sounds and movements of the Wryneck and some tits (Armstrong 1947) evolved in Europe during the Pleistocene or in relation to man. This would imply that these deterrent calls and activities arose in a sub-tropical or tropical region where arboreal snakes took refuge in tree cavities, and predators, particularly small mammals, became conditioned to react warily to them. Presumably this type of behaviour evolved during the Pliocene. Although the thrush (*Turdus*) stock must have reached North America earlier than the Pleistocene the American turdines retain the technique of using mud to line their nests, and their songs have close affinities with the European, Asian, and African species.

The relevance of the environment to the speed at which songs change may be illustrated by comparing the songs of different races of the Wren. There are close similarities between the songs of the American Winter Wren and the European Wren. I have been mistaken in believing that the European Wren's song is about half the duration of the Winter Wren's (Armstrong 1955).† Although there is little variation noticeable from Scotland to the South of France—indeed, none at all appreciable to my ear—the insular races off Scotland and in the North Atlantic sing distinctive versions. This is all the more interesting as learning seems to play, at most, a minor part in the development of the song. In the Hebrides and Iceland one has the impression of a loosening of the song-pattern such as is characteristic of some of the birds of insular habitats already mentioned. Mayr (1956), quoting R. T. Peterson, is mistaken in stating that local variations in Wren dialects in different areas of continental Europe and in America are probably greater than between European and American birds. The Wren may be assumed to have reached Eurasia over Bering Strait during the Pleistocene (Mayr 1946). Its advent to such islands as Iceland, St. Kilda, and Shetland is likely to have been considerably later than its occupation of continental Europe so the song must have changed relatively quickly on these islands. Small, isolated populations of Wrens tend to diverge from a norm in song more rapidly than large, homogeneous populations. This is also true of the morphological characters of the species and is a general rule.

In isolation the songs of at least some species may, perhaps, tend to revert to an ancestral form, or to show ancestral characteristics. Populations of the Chaffinch on the Azores resemble other insular populations of many species in singing a simpler song approximating to that of birds reared in isolation (Poulsen 1951; Marler and Boatman 1951; Marler 1952). If this be so it may mean that where competition is reduced the rôle of learning decreases. Learning might thus be supposed to be an adaptation whereby, in the more competitive environments, song acquires additional distinctiveness. Accordingly, the songs of some isolated communities may be regressive. Probably the situation is more complicated than this would suggest. The song of the Hebridean Wren on Lewis and Harris seems to differ more from the songs of the mainland birds and those of St. Kilda than the St. Kilda Wren's song from the song of the mainland bird although Lewis and Harris are much nearer the mainland than St. Kilda. To what extent genetic variation, loosening of the stereotyped pattern, learning, regression, and individual variation are involved in such situations is a matter for future research.

According to evolutionary standards modification of song may sometimes be rapid, although as we have noted it may in some species lag far behind changes in plumage. As it is unlikely that the island races of Wren survived during the Ice Age the song-changes must have taken place during less than 10,000 years. Probably substantial alterations in song may occur in a much shorter period, especially in imitative species. The extent to which the young hear and copy the song of the males, and even of the male parent, is important in this respect (p. 55). Morphological changes, ranked as subspecific differences, may occur in birds during 5000 years or less (Moreau 1930). It has been claimed that the Faeroe house mouse, introduced little more than 250 years ago, is sufficiently distinct to be given specific status (Evans and Vevers 1938). Zimmerman (1960) shows that at least five species of insect have become differentiated on the banana since its introduction to Hawaii about 1000 years ago. Recent investigations of industrial melanism have demonstrated how speedily alterations in the pigmentation of moth populations may occur (Kettlewell 1956)—and also that adaptation of this kind may take place more rapidly than adaptive changes in behaviour, for there is no evidence that forms with lighter pigmentation in smoke-polluted areas seek resting-places more in accordance with their coloration and so reduce the danger from predators. Of course evolutionary changes may take place much more rapidly in insects than in birds as the generations succeed each other more quickly.

Information on the tenacity of song dialects, their advance or retreat, is meagre. Forms of the so-called 'rain-call' of the Chaffinch are recorded from areas which have apparently been song-isolated to a considerable extent for a long time.* There is disagreement as to whether it is inborn or learned, but probably, as is true of Chaffinch song, there is an inborn basis and an additional learned refinement (Sick 1950; Peitzmeier 1955). There are also local dialects of the alarm call (Poulsen 1958). Marler (1952) remarks: 'The suggested existence of song types confined to a particular region cannot be substantiated although this condition is approached in one case.' This is in the Thames area where a particular song-type or version is so characteristic that there would be a presumption that any bird singing it elsewhere hailed from there.

An excellent illustration of the way in which isolation promotes dialect formation has been noted in Stuttgart where, in three parks, the Chaffinches sing distinctive dialects. Sick (1939) has shown by studying the history of the parks that the distinctiveness of these dialects cannot be of longer duration than the establishment of these areas as parks some 300 years ago. A railway yard has apparently been sufficient barrier to promote dialect. On the basis of what is known concerning dialect-formation by Chaffinches it would be unjustifiable to assume that these dialects have remained unchanged all the time. The presumption is that they became and remained distinctive because of the isolation of the communities. Two factors have been important—learning of song-versions and the attachment of birds to a breeding site.

The constancy of a form of song in any area presupposes that birds which move away in winter return to it to breed. Many species, including the Chaffinch, possess this tendency but a mature bird with established song-versions settling among birds of an area other than where it had been bred the previous year would introduce new song-versions and they would be acquired by neighbouring birds in their first breeding season (p. 50). That this is likely to occur is shown by ringing returns. For example, a Chaffinch ringed as a nestling at Trondheim was recorded four months later in Holland and again in Derbyshire almost four years later.

The songs of Ruby-crowned Kinglets differ somewhat in the eastern

---

* This call is heard during the breeding season and may be elicited by misty weather or apprehension of danger.

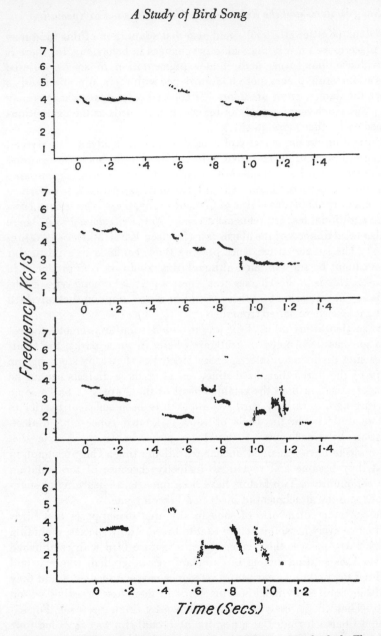

Fɪɢ. 16. Songs from the bivalent repertoire of a Western Meadowlark. The two upper sound spectrograms resemble the songs of the Eastern Meadowlark; the two lower are characteristic of the Western Meadowlark. This bird was paired with two females, one a Western female, the other Eastern. (After Lanyon 1957)

United States and the northern Rocky mountains. The eastern dialect was found to be extending westwards in Montana about 1929 (Saunders 1929) but there appears to be no up-to-date information as to whether this spread has continued. In Germany particulars have been collected of the alleged extension of a form of Blackcap song. It has been claimed that from 1920 to 1953 this dialect expanded at the rate of about five kilometres a year (Mörike 1953; Knecht 1955). Mörike thinks that the diffusion of the dialect may be correlated with the outward spread of young males but the validity of these findings has been questioned. Sauer (1955) has shown that the dialect was known to occur much earlier than other writers realized—in the Tyrol as long ago as ninety years. Therefore it did not spread into Germany from the Alps in thirty years as had been supposed. He suggests that population density may have a bearing on the utterance of this form of song and that it may be elicited by pugnacity. This example provides an indication of the pitfalls which await investigators of the spread of song dialects.

It should be noted that types of vocalization are not the only forms of bird behaviour which may be transmitted by tradition and disseminated by example. There is evidence that some feeding adaptations may also be perpetuated and spread by non-genetic transmission (Klopfer 1959).†

The extent to which differences in vocalization are important in evolution deserves consideration. The effectiveness of such differences as a reproductive barrier has been most closely studied in North America. The breeding ranges of Eastern and Western Meadowlarks overlap and their habitat preferences differ only slightly. Hybrids sometimes occur. In appearance the two species are similar but their calls and songs are distinctive. As in so many other species most of the calls are innate but it seems that the distinctive songs are learned. Hybridization could thus occur if a male had not learned the specific song correctly. This can happen. A Western Meadowlark, paired with two females, had a bivalent repertoire and sang the songs of both (Lanyon 1957) (Fig 16). Apparently, however, the female, at pair-formation, identifies the male of her species by his call-notes, which are inborn. Thus it might seem that the song plays a subordinate rôle in preventing inter-breeding and the major auditory isolating factors are the calls. Although the evidence points in this direction, song is so generally a means of attracting the female that one is reluctant to believe that it is not effective to some extent as a cue to the identification of the male. A Treecreeper may sing a composite song, embodying the song of the Short-toed Treecreeper (p. 104). In aviary conditions a Goldfinch × Greenfinch hybrid acquired a Chaffinch song (Figs. 17 and 18).

A Study of Bird Song

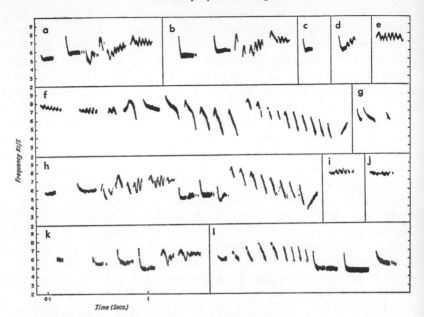

Fig. 17. Sound spectrograms of utterances of Short-toed Treecreeper and Treecreeper illustrating:
a. Song of Short-toed Treecreeper.
b. Song of another Short-toed Treecreeper.
c. Excitement call *tüt*.
d. Transition between two forms of call of Short-toed Treecreeper.
e. *Srih* call.
f. Song of Treecreeper.
g. Begging call of nestling Treecreeper.
h. Composite song of a Treecreeper beginning with elements of Short-toed Treecreeper song and ending with final Treecreeper motive.
i. *Srih* call of adult Treecreeper.
j. *Srih* call of fledged young Treecreeper.
k. Short-toed Treecreeper song sung by Treecreeper. There is a *tüt* call too many at the beginning and the ending is much simplified.
l. Composite song of the same bird.

(After Thielcke 1960)

Alder Flycatcher populations are of two kinds, most readily distinguishable by their songs, which have been named onomatopoeically the *fee-bee-o* and the *fitz-bew* songs (Fig. 19). They overlap in distribution and there are minor differences between the two populations in morphological characters, habitat preference, choice of nest-site, type of nest, and size of egg. Where both populations occur inter-breeding is unknown. Experiments in which the 'wrong' song was played from a recording indicated that song was effective in keeping the populations reproductively isolated. In the very few experiments in which there was any reaction it was feeble (McCabe 1951; Stein 1958). Thus it seems that song is the chief isolating mechanism. If the populations are thus isolated they might be considered distinct species but it remains to be established that the females do not respond, or respond negatively, to the 'wrong' songs.

The Red-bellied and Golden-fronted Woodpeckers closely resemble each other except in the coloration of the head and they are sympatric in an area of the United States. They hold mutually exclusive territories where their distribution overlaps and their foraging behaviour is similar. Selander and Giller (1959) state that the nature of the reproductive isolating mechanisms is unknown but head coloration is known to be an important feature in identification in many species and, as the sound spectrograms show, there are differences in vocalizations. In contrast,

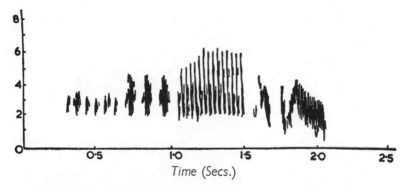
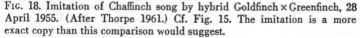

FIG. 18. Imitation of Chaffinch song by hybrid Goldfinch × Greenfinch, 28 April 1955. (After Thorpe 1961.) Cf. Fig. 15. The imitation is a more exact copy than this comparison would suggest.

hybrids between the Red-shafted and Yellow-shafted Flicker are frequent, there are few or no differences in call-notes and drumming although there are differences in plumage. These flickers must have diverged when the barrier of the glaciated Rockies separated populations. Forms of utterance and instrumental signalling have remained practically unchanged while conspicuous plumage differences have evolved. The Red-breasted and Black-headed Grosbeaks have also been regarded as distinct species, though now generally considered conspecific. Hybrids occur over a large area. There are conspicuous differences in plumage but differences in song and call-notes are not marked.

The effectiveness of differences in vocalization as a barrier has been closely studied mostly in North America but the problem is complicated

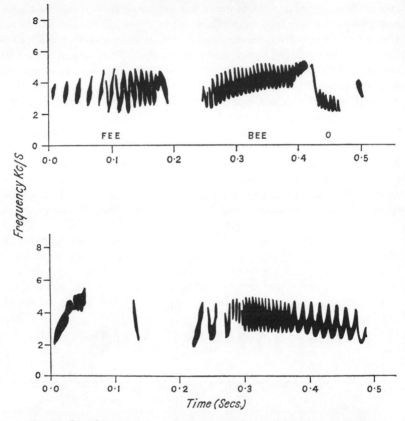

Fɪɢ. 19. Sound spectrograms of the territorial songs of two sympatric non-inter-breeding populations of Alder Flycatcher. (a) The 'fee-bee-o' advertising song; (b) the 'fitz-bew' advertising song. The 'fitz-bew' type singer has two other patterns of song but the 'fee-bee-o' song type apparently uses only one pattern. It is now suggested that the two song types may represent distinct species. (After Stein 1958)

by the difficulty of ascertaining the extent to which the songs and call-notes of a species are inborn or learned. Theoretically, it might seem that in species which learn much of their songs, such as the Chaffinch, circumstances might readily arise in which an isolated community could fairly quickly develop song-versions sufficiently distinctive to prevent inter-breeding when secondary contact took place so that other distinctions might appear and speciation occur. There are, however, strong forces at work to prevent the course of evolution taking this path. Divergence on the basis of auditory identification without corresponding habitat and other adaptations would not be adaptive, the strong tendency for birds to imitate only the song-versions of neighbouring birds would act as a conservative influence, and so far as birds with characteristics similar to those of the Chaffinch are concerned, the tendency to retain imitations only of those sounds within a particular range of characteristics (p. 54) and the importance of visual releasers in courtship, act to militate against such a process. In birds auditory identificatory clues appear to be usually the ancillaries of processes of evolutionary differentiation rather than its spear-points.

The ranges of the Red-winged Blackbird and Tricolored Redwing overlap extensively in North America. These birds are very similar in appearance but the latter's territorial song, fighting, and threat display are feebler. The former occurs in many races, the latter is monotypic. The stronger sociability of the Tricolored Redwing is the characteristic with which the differences between the two species may be correlated.

Mixed matings occur when forms have different utterances but this is uncommon, especially if the differences are considerable. The songs of Rufous-sided Towhees and Spotted Towhees are dissimilar in some respects but in some populations intermediate forms are found so that it is now suggested that these birds should all be considered Rufous-sided Towhees, *Pipilo eryopthalmus* (Sibley and West 1959). Similarly, although Brown Jay, *Psilorhinus morio*, and White-tipped Brown Jay, *P. mexicanus*, populations differ in colour, size of the birds, and call-notes; yet Selander (1959) advocates that they should be regarded as conspecific. A race of the Rufous-naped Wren which is confined to southwestern Mexico is distinctive in song, coloration, and nesting behaviour (Skutch 1958a).†

Signal sounds act as isolating mechanisms in other groups besides birds, including batrachians (Blair 1955a, b, 1956, 1958). Differences between species may sometimes be a by-product of body-size (Blair and Littlejohn 1960). We have seen that differences between the utterances of some birds occurring in Burma and Borneo may be thus explained (p. 90). Lanyon (1960a) has shown that the calls of some larger geographical forms of the Crested Flycatcher are pitched lower than the notes of smaller races (Fig. 1, top row). The mating calls of two species of spadefoot toad which hybridize to some extent differ more markedly in the zone of overlap than elsewhere. So, too, with the mating calls of two species of frog (Blair 1955a, b; Bogert 1960). This situation may be compared with that in Europe where the Chiffchaff and Willow Warbler are sympatric. As has been remarked (p. 94) the Chiffchaff's song is more distinctive where the species overlap than in the Iberian peninsula from which the Willow Warbler is absent. In such circumstances selective pressure promotes divergence in utterance.

In Orthoptera distinctive song is inborn. Fulton (1931, 1937) mated pairs of *Nemobius fasciatus* belonging to two physiological or ecological races, *socius* and *tinnulus*, with characteristic and easily recognized songs, and found that the song of the progeny was an intermediate type never detected in nature.† Where overlapping occurs in wild populations there is no interbreeding. Evidently the songs are important in keeping the races separate. Perdeck (1958), studying two species of grasshopper, found that reactions to song were almost entirely responsible for preventing hybridization. Hybrids had intermediate songs. Females were unresponsive to hybrid males' songs but hybrid females responded to the songs of hybrid males and to the males of both species. In some genera of frogs and toads hybrids have intermediate mating calls but in some characteristics they may resemble those of one or other parent species or they may be unlike both. Their calling habits apparently may resemble those of either parent (Bogert 1960). Isolating mechanisms commonly reinforce each other. This is true of amphibia. In grasshoppers song is a predominant isolating mechanism but not in hummingbirds (Banks and Johnson 1961).

A few instances may be given of the forms of vocalization and related behaviour observed in hybrids. The song as well as the plumage may be intermediate, as has been noted in Golden-winged × Blue-winged Warbler and Hermit × Townsend Warbler matings and also in crosses between some other American warblers (Jewett 1944; Bent 1953). In behaviour and vocalization the Golden-winged and Blue-winged Warblers are fairly similar. The former is a northern form, the latter southern, and the Golden-wing favours higher wooded slopes than the Blue-wing but in the geographical zone of overlap their habitat preferences are insufficient to keep them apart. The songs of hybrids may resemble the songs of either form or be a mixture of both. It is not known whether these birds learn their songs to any extent but probably they are inborn. The main difference is in the number of notes but the songs of the Golden-wing and Blue-wing differ from those of all other North American warblers. One writer (Bent 1953) considers that only some of the notes in the songs of the Hermit Warbler are similar but other observers find it so difficult to distinguish the songs that they think the birds themselves become confused (Jewett 1944). When secondary contact occurs the possibility of hybridization depends not only on habitat preferences and the degree of similarity in vocalizations and appearance but also on there being sufficient resemblance in the whole pair-formation and courtship procedure. Unfortunately such behaviour in these warblers has been insufficiently studied.

A drake Teal × Shoveler hybrid with morphological characters obviously derived from both parents uttered the hoarse croak of the Shoveler drake (Payn 1943) but a cross between a Stock Dove and a Woodpigeon called in a manner dissimilar to both parent species (Creutz 1961). Hybrid cardueline finches produce characteristic cardueline songs composed of elaborated call-notes, often those of both parent species (Hinde 1956b). A bird identical in appearance with a Chipping Sparrow but singing the song of a Clay-coloured Sparrow appeared two springs in succession at Toronto. However, it was not established that this was a hybrid (Tasker 1955). There is no such uncertainty concerning a hybrid between a Chestnut-collared Longspur and a McCown's Longspur as the bird was collected. The song was indistinguishable from that of the Chestnut-collared but the song-flight resembled McCown's. The song-flights are quite easily distinguishable; the former circles and descends with beating wings, the latter sails downwards with wings outstretched and raised (Sibley and Pettingill 1955). The 'booming' of a Prairie Chicken × Sharp-tailed Grouse hybrid was sufficiently similar to that of a Prairie Chicken to attract the nearest rival on the arena to challenge him but then, when the hybrid displayed and danced like a Sharp-tailed Grouse, the rival lost interest and went back to his display court (Allen 1961). The songs of dove hybrids have been studied at Cambridge.

The possibility that differences in courtship song and not only in territorial song may sometimes prevent interbreeding must also be borne in mind, but at the close range normal during this phase visual releasers would usually be of sufficient stimulatory importance to over-ride vocal characteristics in preventing mis-identification. Also, courtship songs seem to differ less than territorial songs. This aspect of song has received little attention but apparently the nest-invitation vocalizations of Finnish and German Pied Flycatchers differ (Curio 1959a). Possibly also the nest-invitation of the Hebridean Wren differs somewhat from that of mainland birds. Display at the nest with song by mated males appears to be more frequent (Armstrong 1953a). It has been argued that differences in song would tend to prevent Wrens arriving, as they do, on Fair Isle from Shetland or farther afield from breeding with the indigenous Wrens but this could hardly apply on such a small and open island where females from elsewhere would, in spring, be courted at sight, for the courtship songs of the various races are more alike than their territorial songs. Thus there may be some gene flow between Wrens arriving on Fair Isle and the resident population (Armstrong 1953b, c, 1959b; Williamson 1959).

The experience of aviculturists shows that differences in voice or appearance can often be over-ridden when a mate of the bird's own kind is not available. In wild bird populations cross-matings are rare as ecological and ethological adaptations tend to prevent them. Hinde (1959) cites a number of instances of artificial interference with habitat

distinctions resulting in hybridization. These indicate that habitat preferences contribute to reproductive isolation. As he points out, ethological
mechanisms are important in this respect. Among these, vocal characteristics play a larger part than he suggests. The success of bird fanciers in
obtaining hybrids must be due in considerable measure to reduction in
the effectiveness of auditory releasers when birds are confined in a small
area. The female is secluded from those sounds which, at the beginning
of the breeding cycle, normally attract her towards a mate of her own
species. Thus an important isolating mechanism effective in preventing
mis-matings is eliminated. Among ducks, some game birds, hummingbirds, and birds of paradise—species in which territorialism of the
standard type is reduced or absent and in which visual releasers are
highly important in the relationship of the sexes—natural hybrids are
comparatively common. Most of these birds utter calls rather than songs.
Thus in the absence of territorial song hybridization occurs more readily.
Some sixteen wild Goldfinch×Greenfinch hybrids have been noted
(Meise 1936). The Goldfinch is a species in which the song is only mildly
territorial. Cross-matings also occur between the Carrion Crow and
Hooded Crow in two belts of overlap in Europe and one in Asia. There
are no marked differences in voice, behaviour, or habitat preference.

The Herring Gull and Lesser Black-backed Gull will also breed together but they are probably conspecific. It would not be difficult to cite
further evidence to confirm the view that differences in appearance seem
to constitute a lesser barrier to hybridization than vocal differences.

There is no need to stress further here the importance of the corollary
that distinctive songs and calls are of the highest importance in bringing
the sexes together (pp. 14 and 118). Although there are sometimes similarities in certain respects in the vocalizations of members of a genus or
even of a family, there are normally crucial differences in other respects.
Thus turdines sing characteristically semi-continuous songs but distinctiveness is achieved by differences in timing, duration of notes, and relative changes of pitch (Dilger 1956a, b; Stein 1956; Marler 1959b). We
have already commented on the differences in the details of songs which
probably facilitate individual identification (p. 95).

Naturally, when birds differ noticeably in regard to morphological,
ethological, and vocal characteristics they are unlikely to be conspecific
but, as was indicated earlier, even when there are differences in all three
they are not always of such a magnitude as to constitute conclusive evidence of specific distinctions. The St. Kilda Wren differs to some extent in
all three respects from the European Wren but is rightly regarded as conspecific. Mayr (1956) points out that the Golden-crested Kinglet differs
in all three ways from the Goldcrest of Eurasia but if Nethersole-
Thompson (1944) is correct in stating that the Goldcrest's song in

Scotland is much weaker and thinner than in southern England it would seem that, if detectable differences of this kind can exist in Britain, where only one race of the Goldcrest is recognized, much greater vocal differences would not in themselves be good evidence for regarding the North American and Eurasian birds as belonging to separate species. The calls and songs of the Treecreeper of Europe and the American Treecreeper are very similar but, according to Mayr, they differ from those of the

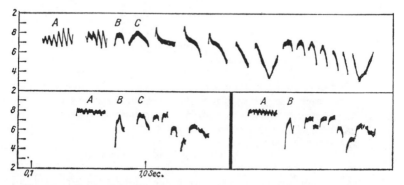

FIG. 20. *Above:* Song of Treecreeper (Freiburg). *Below:* Two songs of American Brown Creeper. Homologous and probably homologous elements are indicated by A, and B, C, respectively. The song of the Brown Creeper resembles that of the Treecreeper more than that of the Short-toed Treecreeper. (After Thielcke 1961)

Short-toed Treecreeper. Mayr regards this as evidence supporting the decision that *Certhia familiaris* and *C. americana* belong to one species and that *C. brachydactyla* is distinct (Fig. 20). However Stadler (1930) states that *C. brachydactyla ultramonte* sings in very different style from the mid-European *C. brachydactyla.*† Thus, again, it is evident that before vocalizations can be regarded as providing firm evidence for the use of taxonomists, sound spectrograms of the songs of a number of individuals in different areas should be compared.

VII

TERRITORIAL SONG AND
RELATED FORMS OF SONG

The song and mating call of the male birds has among
other functions not only the purpose of indicating from a
distance to the females, which react only to the voice of
their own species, their location—often somewhat concealed,
but it also serves in many species as a mutual signal, to fix
the distance of the nests, and thus the required size of the
territories, since males which happen to get too close to each
other fight until one of the combatants has retired to the
requisite distance.

BERNARD ALTUM. *Der Vogel und sein Leben* (1868).

T H E concept of an area occupied or defended by a bird occurs in
Aristotle (H.A.ix.32) and other classical writers (Lack 1944) but
the first allusion to the appropriation by a bird of an area in
which it sings and from which it excludes all birds of its own species except its mate is by Olina in *Uccelliera* (1622), referring to the Nightingale.
Baron von Pernau, writing in 1707, remarks on birds 'selecting a special
place . . . afterwards not allowing another male to show up there. They
sing fervently all day long from the top of such trees, to induce one of
the passing females (which always arrive last on migration) to come
down' (Stresemann 1947).

Some obscurity envelops the account of the Solitaire by Francis Leguat
which appeared in 1708 but it has a good claim to rank as the earliest
detailed description of a bird's territorial behaviour (Armstrong 1953d).†
The narrative, which describes the life of some Huguenot refugees on
Rodriguez, seems to have fictional elements but the details concerning
the Solitaire are evidently based on eye-witnesses' accounts. Both sexes
defended an area of about 200 yards radius and the instrumental 'song',
which carried this distance, was effective in attracting the female and
repelling males. For several minutes at a time the bird would pirouette
rapidly, whirling its wings with a clattering noise, created apparently
by the impact of knobs on the wing-joints 'the size of a musket ball'.

The relationship between song and territory was first described in
detail by Bernard Altum in 1868 (Mayr 1935). He pointed out that song
was a long-range warning, reducing fighting and delimiting the bound-

aries of a territory. Birds do not fight for the females but sing to maintain their breeding area. He stressed that this procedure enabled the fittest individuals to reproduce their kind.

Independently Moffat (1903) reached the conclusion that 'The chief and primary use of song is to advertise the presence in a certain area of an unvanquished cock-bird, who claims that area as his, and will allow no other cock-bird to enter it without a battle'. Craig in 1908 referred to the effectiveness of song when a bird is 'defending its own territory against invasion by a stranger'. Howard's part in developing the theory is too well known to need emphasis. Controversy concerning the function of territory still continues, as a symposium on the subject in *The Ibis* (1956) shows, but the principal facts in regard to the relationship between song and territory were known long ago. The writers quoted realized that song commonly proclaims (a) the bird's species, (b) sex, and (c) that it is in possession of a domain. Further, (d) the song is such as to attract females and repel males.

As we shall see, song may have a wide variety of functions besides serving to declare proprietorial rights (Chapter IX). Craig (1908) and Armstrong (1947, 1950d) have listed some of these functions. The items of information which may be communicated by territorial song have already been reviewed (Chapter I), and attention has been called to its importance as the most conspicuous and informative type of utterance. Here we may indicate briefly the information a male bird may acquire on hearing another male of his own species sing. Such information includes items concerning the three categories—Identity, Motivation, and Environment (p. 6).

TABLE VI

INFORMATION CONVEYED BY TERRITORIAL SONG

Identity	Species	The bird is of like species,
	Sex	a male,
	Individuality	with such-and-such characteristics,
	Status	an established (or new) neighbour,
Motivation	Aggressive	expressing defiance,
Environment	Territory	in that defended area,
	Location	singing now in that place.

In particular instances rather more or less information might be transmitted and, of course, the information acquired by a female differs considerably, partly because to her the territorial song is attractive rather than repellent, and partly because her attentiveness to the song and its effect upon her depend on whether she is already mated. Indeed, in all discussions of signals conveyed by sound we must bear in mind the state of the bird at the receiving end. A song may repel, attract, stimulate, or be a matter of indifference according to whether the receptor is of the same or opposite sex or a bird in or not in the appropriate condition.

To be effective, territorial song must have three primary characteristics. It must be loud, persistent, and distinctive. We shall deal with these briefly.

Volume

Loudness is essential to territorial song because it is basically advertisement effective at a distance and a means of avoiding bodily encounters. It is labour- and life-saving, substituting intimidation from a citadel for visual demonstrations of defiance or beak-and-claw conflicts on the periphery. The territorial song is usually loud enough to be heard well beyond the bounds of the holding. For example, the Reed Warbler's song, which has less volume than the Sedge Warbler's, may be heard 300 yards away although the average territory is of about 300 square yards (Brown and Davies 1949). The volume of a song is related to many factors (p. 33), but the relevance of song intensity to the nature of the habitat and the character of the pair-bond is exemplified by the relatively loud voices of such different species as the Bittern and the Wren, both of which are polygamous birds with far-carrying songs normally living in cover restricting visibility (p. 220). Experiments with recorded songs of the Hermit Thrush, Wood Thrush, and Veery show that at loud intensity males are strongly repelled but when the songs are played softly the birds become bold (Dilger 1956a). Would-be invaders of a domain may decamp without even glimpsing the owner if he is singing strongly (Lack 1943).

As a matrimonial advertisement and *cri de coeur* songs need to be far-carrying but the continuance or recrudescence of territorial song by many species after the formation of the pair-bond suggests that in such species the alluring function of song is less important than its defensive function. Maljchevsky (1959), whose studies were made mainly in the neighbourhood of Leningrad, has even argued that song does not serve in the defence of territory but operates to bring the sexes together. This particular opinion may, perhaps, be attributed partly to bias due to observation made in fairly high latitudes where birds of some passerine species are thin on the ground. Competition is reduced and the function of song in attracting a mate is increased (Armstrong 1950a). There is better experimental evidence that song repels males than there is to show that it attracts females but every field ornithologist could cite observations of the attractive power of male song.

The effect of a number of males in an area singing at the same time is to render the whole community conspicuous to a female passing within range so that probably the chances of all the males obtaining mates are increased, at least in some migratory species such as the Willow Warbler (May 1949). The evidence for the sexually stimulating effect of display has been reviewed elsewhere (Armstrong 1947). The pioneer work of Whitman (1919) and Craig disclosed the importance of vocalization in this respect and Darling (1952) stressed—some would say over-emphasized—the socially beneficent effects of territorial display activities. In some species, perhaps many, full song is more rapidly attained when a number of males sing against one another (p. 48). The songs of House Wrens attain perfection earlier in good seasons when there is a larger population and the females arrive earlier (Kendeigh 1941a). Territorial situations rapidly bring juvenile male Song Sparrows into a more advanced stage of song though this may be only temporary (Nice 1943). The utterances of other pairs enhance the development of the gonads of both sexes of Budgerigar (Ficken *et al.* 1960). This kind of situation differs from territorial situations but the experiments prove that vocalizations need not be those of a bird courting or mated to another to have a stimulating effect on the gonads (Craig 1908, 1913).

When a Chaffinch which had been stimulated by hormone injections to sing out of the normal season uttered its song a wild Chaffinch flew down and sang in reply (Hinde pers. comm.). Thus there is evidence, not only that singing may arouse other birds within hearing to break into song (p. 186), but that competition plays a part in the development of song. However, we can generalize too readily from one species to another. Curio (1959a) noticed that Pied Flycatchers sang more in areas where they were thinly distributed than in woods with a dense population; in such circumstances alarm calls took the place of song to a large extent. Unlike many species which utter songs shorter than the intervals between them Pied Flycatchers do not engage in counter-singing. There are grounds for believing that in some other species, such as the Great Tit (Gompertz 1961), certain calls may have much of the valence of territorial song. This may be true of the Chaffinch and Greenfinch (Hulme 1959), and possibly of the Wren and Blue Tit.

It will be remembered that the Thick-billed Nutcracker and Red-backed Shrike also utter loud, harsh calls which seem to be more important in proclaiming proprietary rights than their relatively subdued songs (p. 66). This consideration illustrates the difficulty of defining 'song' according to the complexity of its pattern or a 'call-note' on the basis of simplicity of function.

In most species the loudness of the song, together with the frequency of its repetition, declines with the waning of territorial defence and mounts when territorialism is at its height. Similarly, as territorial ardour wanes song is apt to be uttered from a lower perch or song-flight is abandoned for singing on a fixed stance (Sutton and Parmelee 1955). Moreover, song which has little or no relevance to the defence of territory tends to be relatively subdued (pp. 61 and 69). Rock Thrushes, which may possess two territories, one some kilometres from the other, have hunting perches where they sing a 'conversational' song, and specific perches on which the territorial song is uttered (Farkas 1955).† Together, these facts indicate by contrast the adaptive value of loud territorial utterance.

Persistence

Persistence is inseparably linked with loudness in territorial song because such song is essentially an expression of vigour (Armstrong 1956). The sustained character and repetitiveness of this type of vocalization is correlated with its association with the more or less prolonged occupation of an area. Utterances connected with transitory events, such as the movements of predators or companions, tend to be brief and are reiterated only so long as the stimulus object is present (p. 23). No other type of utterance—and in some species no other kind of activity— occupies so much of a bird's time when in a fully aroused state. A Red-eyed Vireo has been known to utter 22,197 songs in a day (de Kiriline 1954) and a Nightingale was silent for only one and a quarter hours in the twenty-four (Bond 1951).

It should be noted that persistence and reiteration are not a characteristic only of normal territorial song. The Violet-headed Hummingbird and various Violet-ears (*Colibri spp.*) sing mating songs tirelessly all day for months, pausing only occasionally to seek food or repel an intruder. The area from which such intruders are driven is a communal mating station or lek away from feeding sites to which the females resort (Skutch 1958b). Such assemblies, like other leks, may be maintained for years in the same place.

Many observers have published information showing how persistently birds sing (Chapter XI). Sustained song is adaptive as it informs a bird's neighbours that he is on the alert, vigorous, prepared to resist intrusion, and, it may be, on the look-out for a mate. Individuals trespassing in neighbours' territories are silent and secretive. They avoid the area where they hear the owner singing. Birds which sing feebly or seldom are at a disadvantage in gaining a territory or mate. Unmated cocks tend to sing more persistently than mated birds (p. 66) but unmated males of some species, such as Ovenbirds, hold small territories (Stenger and Falls 1959). Montagu (1802) proved by removing the mates respectively of a Redstart, Nightingale, and Goldcrest that in these circumstances song increased. The unmated Goldcrest remained in song until the end of August. When a Rufous-sided Towhee's mate was killed he became more vocal, singing and calling more frequently than when his mate was alive (Davis 1958). Similar behaviour has been recorded of many birds. Vigorous song and general efficiency go together, as the following observations show.

According to Conder (1948) the most songful Goldfinches hold the largest territories. A Song Sparrow which sang an exceptional amount was also exceptionally long-lived (Nice 1943). Bee-eaters defend perches rather than territories, ruffling their plumage and calling. The birds which do so most vigorously copulate most frequently (Swift 1959). Buxton (1950) mentions a Redstart which was the finest and most persistent singer he had ever heard and was also the most remarkable mimic. All four nests came to grief but the male's energetic song evidently had an influence in stimulating the female to renewed attempts. Buxton refers to the effectiveness of his 'crazy persistence' in singing and displaying in inducing 'the reluctant hen' to begin the fourth nest (Fig 36). Erickson (1950) gives the history of a Rufous Whistler which courted females but did not succeed in inducing one to breed with him during three seasons. She attributes his failure to his having occupied a territory offering few suitable nesting sites. During his first and only partnership with a female the nest was blown out of the tree by a gale. According to this account the male sang assiduously during one year but the previous year 'his "lonely" song quietened' and 'he seemed unperturbed by his mateless condition'. Normally a Rufous Whistler sings throughout the year apart from a brief respite during the moult (Jack 1949a). We may suspect that this bird lacked adequate vigour and that his holding a territory without suitable nest-sites was due to this. Such an interpretation would be in agreement with what is known of two Wrens. One of them was a very vigorous bird, as indicated by the size and nature of his territory, the number of nests he built and mates he secured each year. He also sang with outstanding energy and persistence. A neighbour, who sang weakly, built few nests, was nomadic for part of the time and held an unfavourable territory when he settled in one. He did not secure a mate until his third year (Kluijver *et al.* 1940). Wrens which sing vigorously may acquire the mates, potential mates, and territories of less assertive males (Armstrong 1955). Among House Wrens individual differences in reproductive vigour play a part in securing a territory and a mate. Timid singers—mainly young birds—do not breed and males which secure favourably placed nest-sites apparently have an advantage in obtaining mates (Kendeigh 1941a). A Reed Warbler is liable to lose his mate unless he replies vehemently to an intruder. Brown and Davies (1949) noted three instances of females deserting mates who responded weakly, or not at all, to the persistent singing of a trespasser. A Mockingbird which stopped singing because of an injury lost his territory and was unable to re-establish himself when he recovered (Laskey 1936). Instances may, indeed, be cited of birds deficient in song or with abnormal voices breeding successfully but these can usually be explained by the predominance of factors other than sound signals relevant to mating. 'Song-lazy' Blackbirds may breed successfully (Heyder 1931) but in this species the defence of territory depends, more than in most turdines, on visual display, as the sexual dimorphism would suggest (Armstrong 1958a; Snow 1958).†

The close relationship between persistent song and the possession of territory is also shown in the correlation between the maintenance of the domain and continuance of song throughout most of the year in such species as the Robin and Dipper. Furthermore, the prolongation of song and the extended maintenance of territory is associated with successive polygamy in some birds, such as the Wren and Corn Bunting. Obviously in species of this type the territorial song retains its function as a means of attracting females and does not serve merely as a warning to males.

Distinctiveness

The importance of distinctiveness in territorial song has already been stressed (p. 110). To be effective it must be unmistakable and carry precise information concerning the singer's identity. This accounts for much of the variety and complexity of passerine songs as, in general, such elaboration enables varied information to be transmitted without mistakes occurring. Errors are further guarded against by the different responses which are elicited in the mature male and female by the species song. Wild hybrids between birds with markedly different songs are very rare (p. 107). Treecreepers and Short-toed Treecreepers imitate each other's songs (Thielcke 1960b) (p. 104) but this does not seem to result in hybridization.

As Marler (1960) points out, there is an exception to the rule that specific distinctiveness in territorial song is adaptive. When two or more species are in competition for the resources of a habitat it may be advantageous for their utterances to have similarities so that they may maintain mutually exclusive territories. This situation occurs among some North American tits. In a Mexican valley Marler found the Brown Towhee, Cactus Wren, and Ladderback Woodpecker, all with rather similar songs, engaged in counter-singing. Takahe (*Notornis*) often answer Weka Rails, which have very similar calls (Williams 1960). As they are very aggressive against them during the breeding season this behaviour may be evidence of inter-specific rivalry. When the territories of Ringed Plover and Little Ringed Plover overlap the larger species resents the presence of the other and may take over its nests. There is much aggressive display and calling (Armstrong 1952b).

Few instances of birds making erroneous identifications of song are on record and these are rather inconclusive. A Rufous Whistler and White-winged Triller may engage in vocal duels which are discontinued when the birds come within sight of each other. Each bird then goes his own way (Robinson 1949). In such circumstances the birds merely waste some energy but Moffat's observations (1903) suggest that mistaken identification of song may occasionally lead to a bird killing a male of another species. He reports seeing a Mistle Thrush on two occasions carrying a Blackbird in its feet and dropping the carcass at a considerable distance. The most reasonable explanation of this strange behaviour, as he suggests, would seem to be that the Mistle Thrush mistook the Blackbird's song for the singing of a rival of its own species. So far as the attractive or sexually stimulating effect of the male's vocalizations are concerned there is evidence that abnormality or divergence may be dysgenic. Of two Jackson's Whydahs a bird with a voice markedly different from that of a neighbour was much less successful in attracting females to his 'court' or dancing ground (Van Someren 1946). Kortlandt (1940a) noticed that an abnormal voice interfered with the pair-formation of Cormorants.

Many considerations suggest that bird song has evolved from call-notes, particularly those concerned with contact, escape, aggression, and anxiety. Elaboration and stereotypy have been the hand-maids of distinctiveness. Courtship and other forms of song appear to be a secondary development from territorial song in many species.

The establishment of territory

The procedure by which territory is established varies considerably, especially according to whether the birds are resident or not, but commonly there is increasing loudness, persistence, and distinctiveness as the birds 'find their feet'. A few examples will illustrate this. Before a female appears the male Reed Bunting begins to sing instead of call from the roost and changes from flying direct to the foraging area to singing from a tree. As the days pass he sings more continuously and grows increasingly intolerant of other males (Howard 1929). Mature Chaffinches return to their previous territories, and rapidly come into full song. Other males utter *chinks*, sub-song, and then song as they begin to defend an area. The birds establish song stations and prospect possible nest-sites—as the females do later (Marler 1956a). Flocks of Great Tits break up into pairs, roaming beyond the flock range. Fighting occurs in defence of the female and the males sing haphazardly here and there. Next the pair concentrates on part of the original foraging area and song stations are established. Finally, the preferred area becomes delimited as the males measure their strength against each other and the song stations diminish in importance (Hinde 1952). Wrens generally try to maintain their territories throughout the year. During the summer, birds of the year edge their way into established territories singing a quiet, irregular, jingly song. In spring there is vigorous rivalry, expressed in song. At almost any time of year determined intruders may evict birds from part or all of their holdings (Armstrong 1955).

Probably the value of territorial song in proclaiming individuality as well as specific identity has been underestimated. As detailed investigation proceeds it becomes increasingly probable that the significance of differences in songs or repertoires of song-versions may be in the clues they provide to the identity of the singer. In some species there is good reason to believe that birds established in adjoining territories recognize each other's utterances (p. 10). Thus Ovenbirds, *Seiurus auro-capillus*, are able to distinguish the songs of different individuals, recognize those of birds in neighbouring territories, and react most strongly to the songs of strangers (Weeden and Falls 1959). Magpie Larks which have a sustained pair-bond sing duets. They are brought to full synchronization each breeding season. Each pair's duet is distinctive enough to be recognized by a human observer. When the pairs are established the duets are uttered in such a way that the birds maintain their domains without serious dissension but if a stranger intrudes his singing provokes violent resentment. When serious territorial altercations arise in this way the normal course of events may be disrupted so much that females neglect broods and the chicks die (Robinson 1946–47, pers. comm.). Evidently in this species the territorial song-duets play an important part in maintaining the *status quo* and integrating the territory-owners into a unit without serious dissensions. American warblers with individually distinctive songs become vocal all over the woods on the song of one bird being heard (Kendeigh 1945a). Probably they are registering that the established relationship is intact more than defying each other. No doubt the measure of defiance in territorial song varies greatly from species to species according to circumstances and at different seasons. Where there is a shortage of nesting sites or a species is in exceptionally great numbers territorial song may be particularly belligerent but nevertheless territorialism is an integrative and stimulating influence as well as a system of defence.

Among birds of passage, territory establishment tends to be a speedy process. House Wrens and birds of many other species sing increasingly as they approach their destination. When the males settle down they sing imperfect, incomplete songs in an intermittent way and may not reach vigorous song for a week or longer (Kendeigh 1941a). Warblers tend to sing infrequently and tentatively on first reaching their breeding haunts, growing bolder in song and activities as they roam around the chosen area. There may be chasing and sparring during the main influx. Among Reed Warblers there is a dramatic change from tolerance to animosity. Willow Warblers defend territory after pair-formation but with decreasing vigour as the season advances. A Whitethroat or Redstart may delimit his domain within a few hours. Birds, especially cavity-nesting species, usually desert an area if, after a short exploratory period, they find it to be deficient in nest-sites (Howard 1907–14; Brown and Davies 1949; May 1949; Buxton 1950).

The relative importance of song in pair-formation and defence of territory varies in different species and to some extent in different habitats. Great Tits form pairs weeks prior to the development of full song and many retain their mates from year to year (Kluijver 1951). The Great Tit does not easily find suitable nesting cavities, so the accentuation of song in April, coinciding with egg-laying, may be of special importance at this time in protecting the nesting area. The advertising song of the Blackbird may have little function in pair-formation but the defence of territory in this species involves defence of the mate. According to Snow (1956, 1958) the serious fights which occur are usually between females competing for a mate but I have seen daily skirmishing and displaying between females in which the ownership of ground was at stake (Armstrong 1958a). The Phainopepla advertises his territory by conspicuous perching and display rather than by song but birds long unmated begin to sing, thus indicating the relevance of song to pairing (Rand and Rand 1943). Cactus Wrens remain mated and sing throughout the year. Such song is defensive, for both sexes sing in territorial quarrels, but although the male's song remains attractive to the female, singing in these circumstances is obviously not concerned with pair-formation (Anderson and Anderson 1957).

Species which act in an exceptional way illustrate by contrast the significance of territorial song. The female Costa Rican Tityra prospects for a territory while several males follow her around, awaiting her choice both of territory and mate. These birds have a very limited vocabulary consisting of a grunt and some dry, insect-like notes (Skutch 1946a). Swanberg (1951) shows that Thick-billed Nutcrackers, which remain mated for life, hold, rather than defend territories—for pairs respect the domains of others. The position and boundaries of the areas occupied are proclaimed by means of harsh cries. The subdued song, as already mentioned (p. 66), maintains the pair-bond, but does not constitute an announcement of the possession of a territory or advertisement for a mate.

The recrudescence of the gonads which evokes breeding behaviour may occur to a limited extent in autumn, manifesting itself in song and territorial activity. Starlings associate in pairs, occupy small areas around nesting cavities, and sing in autumn (Bullough 1942). Song Sparrows sing, fight, and hold temporary territories then. A young bird which establishes such a domain tends to return to it in spring (Nice 1937). Tits of various species sing in autumn and juvenile Marsh Tits warble then in 'preferred areas' (Hinde 1952). The Marsh Tit, Plain Tit, and some Willow Tits retain territory in winter and pair after occupying territory. Other species which abandon their breeding territories and flock in winter form pairs before they establish territory (Gibb 1956a). I have noticed that in August Corn Buntings will occupy song stations, and probably territories, on heaths where they have not bred, within ear-shot of one another. Robins visiting Italy in winter sing and hold territories until December (Alexander 1917). The Mourning Chat migrates from breeding quarters between the Nile and the Red Sea to winter in the fringes of the Lower Egyptian desert. The birds defend separate territories and sing from July to October, and less frequently from November to February. Individuals of several species of chat repel birds of other species as well as of their own from winter territories in North Africa. White Wagtails also sing in winter quarters (Hartley 1946, 1949, 1950a; Simmons 1951) (Fig. 21). Dippers sing constantly in autumn and winter. They hold larger territories then than they do in summer (Serle and Bryson 1935; Eggebrecht 1937; Vogt 1944). Female Robins and Mockingbirds sing and maintain territory in autumn when there is some gonadal activity (Marshall 1952b). At this season Black Grouse display and crow at the lek but the activities are belligerent and not concerned with courtship (Lack 1939b).

The extent to which autumnal song is connected with territory or incipient breeding activities must be ascertained for each species separately. The songs of Willow Warblers as the birds drift southwards in passage seem without communicatory function. Snipe drum out of the breeding season in areas where they nest but not in regions to which they migrate outside the breeding range (Lynes 1913). This suggests a correlation between retention of territory, non-vocal song, and the activity of the gonads.

There is strong circumstantial evidence that defended winter territories are valuable as foraging areas at a season when food is relatively scarce to birds of such contrasting habitat preferences as the Dipper, Mourning Chat, and Whooping Crane (Allen 1960). The winter fighting of tits and Rock Pipits is 'in effect food fighting' (Gibb 1954, 1956b). Robinson (1949) believes that for Australian Bellmagpies, which hold group territories throughout the year, food is really the fundamental reason for the defence of territory. Pairs of Thick-billed Nutcrackers

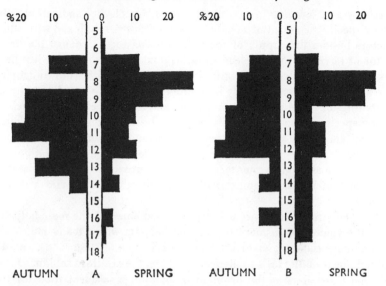

Fig. 21. Comparison of the distribution of song throughout the day in the 'Autumn' and 'Spring' song-periods of the White Wagtail in Egypt: (a) 1941–42; (b) 1943–44. The 'Autumn' song-period ends early in January and the 'Spring' song-period begins about a fortnight later. In the 'Autumn' periods the bulk of the song is in the late forenoon while in the 'Spring' periods the major output comes in the hours 8–9 a.m. 'Spring' song continues longer throughout the day than 'Autumn' song. (After Hartley 1946)

hold their domains for life. Within them they hide stores of nuts which are vital for their survival in winter (Swanberg 1951, 1956). There are similarities in the behaviour of Jays (Goodwin 1956). In view of such facts we should not accept too readily the view that spring territories, being often highly compressible, are seldom of much significance as feeding areas (Lack 1954). If pairs of any species are suitably distributed over their breeding area at the beginning of the season defence of the territories as foraging areas later is unimportant (Armstrong 1956). It is significant that the size of Ovenbird territories increases with increasing height and density of the canopy and with decreasing vegetation near the ground (Stenger and Falls 1959). This suggests a correlation between foraging niches and size of territory. Study of birds on islets where they breed in areas much smaller than their normal territories but in which they find sufficient food to rear young suggests that some birds may normally occupy territories larger than necessary from the point of view of the food supply in an average season (Beer *et al.* 1956).

Similarly denser breeding populations of tits than are usually found may be created by providing nest-boxes. Such facts do not show that territory as a foraging area is unimportant though they indicate that in many species the potential variability in territory size is linked with other factors besides the supply of food. Arguments for or against the 'food value of territory' may mislead those who take part in them unless they take into account that food availability, foraging, and territorial activity are among a number of closely integrated factors in the breeding pattern, including the character of the pair-bond and nesting behaviour, which in many species are modifiable to greater or lesser extent to accommodate circumstances. Not only are territories elastic but there is plasticity in the relationship of territorialism to other adaptations. The relationship between at least some winter territories and foraging is apparent because the situation is less complex than where breeding territories are concerned.

In bleak areas Wrens are usually monogamous and the male helps to feed the young but in more favourable habitats where many males are polygamous the male gives little help with some of the broods, yet, although the foraging falls to the female alone, the nestlings seldom starve. We must assume that the problem of obtaining sufficient food for the nestlings in bleak areas is resolved by the male collaborating actively rather than by the establishment of correspondingly larger territories as foraging areas, because journeys beyond a certain distance from the nest would be uneconomic. Since one bird can feed a brood in a favourable habitat the assumption is that this is due to the greater availability of food there. Less time and effort has to be expended in obtaining it and bringing it to the nest. Thus the proximity of food to the nest is vital and so the territory, being the area in which food is nearest to the nest, is of prime importance as a foraging area but any discussion of the function of the Wren's territory which did not take into account its facultative polygamy would be futile. The shape of the nest, the persistence of the song, the bird's small size, enabling it to forage in crevices, and the size of the territory are closely related to the nature of the pair-bond.†

Hinde (1956c) summarizing the arguments for and against territory as a foraging ground remarks: 'The key question is not whether the territory contains approximately the food needed, but whether the available food would be reduced sufficiently to affect ultimate reproductive success if territories were compressed beyond the usual (admittedly imprecise) limit in the habitat in question. The effect could be felt by partial starvation of the young, undue exhaustion of the parents in their efforts to find food, or even in over-depletion of the food stocks'. He states that there is absolutely no evidence for this. This may be queried. In bleak habitats two Wrens are needed to rear a family which could be reared by one in a richer habitat. In such habitats the food may be so indigestible that some of it is disgorged and when there is an unusually high population in a restricted area, such as St. Kilda, young perish in the nest (Armstrong and Thorpe 1952; Armstrong 1959b). There is also evidence that birds feeding young may lose weight and become debilitated, and that when a female Wren's energies are over-taxed or she disappears or dies the male comes to the rescue, even to the extent of undertaking all the duties at the nest (Whitehouse and Armstrong 1953; Armstrong 1955).

Enquiry into the reasons for the absence of territorial behaviour in some species may help to illustrate, by contrast, the function of territory. The polygamous, communal-nesting Buffalo Weaver has no territorial song and the only defended area is the immediate vicinity of the nest. The birds forage in flocks and, apparently, feed the young mainly on grasshoppers although, significantly, polygamous weavers, in contrast to their monogamous relatives, are mainly seed-eaters. Where three or four young are present in the nest at least one is commonly found to be sickly. Crook (1958) believes the mortality to be due to lack of nourishment. It would seem that this species is adapted to exploit sporadic abundant supplies of insect food during the breeding season but that these may sometimes be insufficient for the colony's needs. Young terns of several species may perish similarly when fish shoals fail. Defence of ground as a foraging territory would be dysgenic in an area where the supply of food is liable to be abundant here and there for short spells. Thus territorialism is weak in most species which are aerial and marine foragers. The Wattled Starling follows locust swarms and settles to breed near them, nesting communally with two or three nests adjoining and as many as a dozen such nests in one small tree. In Europe and Asia the Rosy Pastor also breeds in colonies where locusts are plentiful. Neither of these birds is territorial.

Thus there is cumulative evidence concerning at least one of the most territorial species, the Wren, suggesting that the character of the food supply is very important in relation to the whole integrated pattern of its behaviour, including pair-bond, territorial defence, and song, and from others that the absence of territorial defence by song or display is connected with such behaviour being ineffective as a means of safeguarding the supply of food for the young. Doubtless there are many forms of behaviour between these extremes but these considerations suggest that it is unduly sceptical to deny the likelihood that in many species territorial behaviour is, to some extent, the safeguarding of a foraging area and that song may thus be related indirectly to the availability of food.

It has been suggested that the dispersal of nests of species in which the nests, eggs, or incubating female are cryptic is effective in foiling predators (Tinbergen 1953) and that territory, in some species, ensures that nests are widely separated and therefore in less danger of being plundered. While it has long been recognized that wide nest-dispersal augments the difficulties of nest-finding it is questionable whether territorial behaviour is of major importance in this respect. Several writers have pointed out that such dispersion occurs in the absence of territorial behaviour (Jenkins 1961). The nests of the cryptic females of lek species are scattered although the females do not defend territories. If the principle were of general application we should expect that vividly hued birds, without a powerful song, would exemplify it, for it is doubtful whether a bird's vocalizations, as such, apart from its behaviour while singing, appreciably increase its vulnerability. There are many birds with bright coloration and weak territorialism, such as, in Europe, the Rosy Pastor, Goldfinch, Hawfinch, Mealy Redpoll, Swallow, and Bee-eater which nest to some extent in colonies and therefore are doubly conspicuous. Granted that some of them are protected in some measure by unpalatability, the comparative inaccessibility of their nests, or corporate defence, yet it remains true that just those passerine birds which, in theory, might benefit most from dispersed nesting do not exemplify it. Probably, apart from a few exceptional species, the foiling of predators through nest-dispersal is merely a by-product of territorialism which integrates with other associated adaptations. Wide nest-dispersal is a consequence of a behaviour complex in which strong territorialism, powerful song, and cryptic coloration are commonly associated (p. 227; Table XIII).†

Counter-singing

Male birds singing in their territories attend to the singing of neighbouring birds of their own species. The learning of song-versions by Chaffinches and the answering of versions with those most similar in a bird's repertoire (p. 50) reveal the attention which birds pay to each other's songs and provide additional evidence that birds can recognize songs as those of particular individuals (p. 53). This is probably fairly general. Such behaviour is adaptive as it is more important to come to terms with a stranger than to spend energy on neighbours with whom a *modus vivendi* has already been established. Moreover, birds become habituated to some extent to the songs normally heard around them. Indeed, behavioural adaptation to the environment by any organism consists largely of inattentiveness to the irrelevant. Abnormal repetition of a stimulus tends to weaken response. Thus recordings of the Turnstone's aggressive call played repeatedly induced displacement-sleeping, and exhaustion of territorial defence (Bergman 1958).

Many species with clearly marked and fairly regular intervals between songs engage in counter-singing (Armstrong 1944a) and as the pauses are usually longer than the songs the birds tend to alternate, though, where territorial song is concerned, as distinct from duetting by paired birds (p. 180), exact co-ordinated alternation seldom occurs (Sauer 1954; Armstrong 1955). Four hundred years ago Thomas Tusser in his *Five Hundred Good Pointes of Husbandrie* remarked:

> *Cock croweth at midnight few times above six*
> *With pause to his fellow to answer betwixt.*

When one cock crows another answers after about ten seconds and so on for about a quarter of an hour (Katz and Revesz 1921). A Blonde Ring-dove hearing another cooing far away utters his perch coo three or more times, then listens, coos again, and so on (Craig 1943). Probably the duration of the pauses between the songs of some species is an adaptation enabling the birds to listen to, and sometimes learn from, one another (pp. 43 and 242). The songs of many buntings, some finches, and various other birds are among those which are shorter than the intervals between, but the songs and pauses of the Wren are approximately the same length —five to six seconds—so that the birds get 'out of step'. The Hedgespar-row commonly sings at rather irregular intervals. The *Phylloscopus* warblers and buntings tend to have discontinuous songs of the sentence or utterance-interval type although the patterns of the songs may differ very greatly, but it is difficult to discover any correlation with habitat, except to the extent that the buntings which have become adapted to high lati-tudes utter their songs in flight (p. 140). While there is evidently an innate basis for the song-intervals the factors which modify the individual's pauses are complex and various. One or more of the following factors may have a bearing on this in some species—the age and condition of the bird, the season, phase of the breeding cycle, time of day, weather, stimuli from other individuals; and probably, in at least some species, danger from predators.

Threat and belligerent song

As Altum observed, territorial song is sung in accentuated style by many species when disputes between two males occur. At close quarters visual threat display accompanies it. Lack (1943) quotes an anonymous versifier of 1834:

> *O blind to Nature's all-accordant plan,*
> *Think not the war-song is confined to man;*
> *In shrill defiance, ere they join the fray*
> *Robin to Robin chaunts the martial lay.*

In many species chases take place at the boundary of the territory or back and forth across it, with or without song. Song duels occasionally culminate in fighting. Species vary immensely in the extent to which they have developed intimidation techniques employing visual or acoustic signals though, in general, when birds are face to face visual displays are much more important than song, and threat sounds tend to replace elaborate vocalization. Just as, in a review of forms of visual display, gradations may be noted between almost normal maintenance movements, such as occur when a bird intends to fly, to extravagant, ritualized elaborations of these movements (Daanje 1950), so in some species there occur types of song varying from the normal territorial utterance to a much distorted form characteristic of fierce quarrelling and culminating sometimes in actual fighting. Although there is no point at which a definite distinction can be made between territorial song and this extreme form, as all territorial song probably has some element of threat, it may be called 'threat', 'belligerent', or 'fighting' song. In unrelated species it tends to be generated in like situations and to possess basic similarities. The higher the aggressive motivation and the greater the imminence of combat the greater the distortion. In the accentuated form it becomes congested, rapid, and even frenzied. At an early phase of an altercation it may be hurled forth coherently but later it tends to be sung in a stifled, subdued manner as if the bird were choking with rage. While territorial song tends to be uttered more vigorously as song duels warm up, fighting song is relatively subdued when birds are almost at grips with each other. Also, unlike territorial song, which may be uttered when out of sight and hearing of other males of the species, belligerent song is sung when rivals can see each other. It is usually distorted territorial song and correlated with aggressive visual demonstrations against a rival but in some species it may be evoked by fright or great stress. The precise motivation of such singing is unexplored. In a single species various gradations in vehemence and forms of expression may be noted. Extremes can be labelled but intermediate forms must be treated on their merits. Thus the threat song of the Rufous-sided Towhee is a rapid, subdued form—sometimes barely audible—uttered when males are in close proximity, but heightened excitement due to the menacing visit of a Scrub Jay was observed to accentuate greatly the output of territorial song by one of these birds for some hours afterwards (Davis 1958).†

A few examples will illustrate some of the many types of fighting song. Song Thrushes engage in song duels and sometimes try 'to sing each other down' (Siivonen 1939). Such duels, which occur among Robins, Wrens and many other birds, have a parallel among the Eskimo. Two rivals will sing at each other until one gives in through sheer exhaustion (Gray 1912). Shrews also may settle territorial quarrels by vocal duelling (Crowcroft 1957). Between Song Thrushes pugnacity may mount until one bird hotly chases the other, the pursued bird sometimes uttering rapid, stifled, and jumbled song. After one chase involving three birds they all plunged into a bush and fighting song was heard. Then a bird flew out with feathers adhering to its open bill. Related species may differ in the extent to which they use belligerent song. American Robins sing 'whisper song' during fights (Young 1951) and perhaps during courtship. Snow (1958) states that Blackbirds utter the same subdued, hurried, confused kind of song when courting as during intense threat display. If this is so it would indicate that the accepted theory of sexual display as a complex of attack, escape, and sexual motivation may need reconsideration, but another observer noted that when a young male Blackbird intruded an older male sang softly a Song Thrush type of song for five minutes (Brooks-King 1942). European Robins flaunt their ruddy breasts at rivals, and sing in a strangled or congested way. The intensity of the song and its coherence may change very quickly.

Perhaps fighting song is rather more characteristic of temperate-region birds which retain territory most of the year, than of migrants or tropical species. I have referred elsewhere (1955) to the Wren's 'challenge song'. It is heard when a male suddenly finds himself close to an unidentified bird of his own species but is the threat song uttered in specific circumstances. If an intruder flees after one or two of these songs have been sung at him the other bird may sing in flight as he joins in the chase. Wrens sometimes scuffle in the air after hurling snatches of song at one another. Howard (1935) observed one singing while standing on his conquered adversary's body. Dippers sing incoherently while fighting. Two were seen battering each other with wings and beaks on the surface of a pool for some minutes. Then one seized his opponent and ducked him repeatedly. The dominated bird burst into song each time his head appeared above the surface (Carter 1883). The Redstart, perching below the bird to be attacked, emits a harsh Whitethroat-like warble which Buxton (1950) calls the 'challenging song'. The Woodlark's challenge song is subdued, stifled, and hissing (C. Koffán *in litt.*). Song Sparrows may sing after grappling on the ground and there may be prolonged singing in flight when Indigo Buntings chase each other (Saunders 1929). Squabbles often accentuate the amount and vehemence of song and sometimes evoke song from females. Great and Blue Tits sing during lulls in skirmishes and female Blue Tits utter song when involved in fighting (Hinde 1952). A Blue Tit mated to a male in very poor condition uttered an unusual amount of song. It seemed as if she was compensating for his deficiencies (R. Jellis pers. comm.). While a Wren-tit was fighting another male his mate sang (Erickson 1938). Goldfinches sing during aggressive as well as courtship posturings and male Hawfinches threaten each other with their huge bills almost in contact, breaking off singing when one snaps at the other (Conder 1948; Mountfort 1957). Wheatears warble quietly as well as sing during territorial disputes. Song Sparrows seeking to secure territories near established birds also sing in a quiet, rapid way (Nice 1937). In species with reduced territorialism, song during altercations seems to undergo less modification than in highly territorial birds. The 'pendulum flights' with song of some species mainly breeding in open habitats are a special form of territorial song rather than belligerent song (p. 139).

If territorial song evolved as a substitute for fighting and visual threat, as seems highly probable, we may assume with some plausibility that it developed from contact, alarm, threat and, possibly, escape notes and became elaborated as the defence distance around males increased. We must qualify this by remembering that defiance calls, especially when uttered by a male associating with a female, may, up to a point, have the effect of attracting and stimulating other males. As birds succeeded in settling their differences at a distance in the course of evolutionary development we may further suppose that the spheres of influence became accepted as proprietorial areas—and so territory came into being. According to these postulates fighting song is a secondary adaptation whereby the elaborated utterance reverts to the function of the archaic threat calls. At all events it is probable that elaboration of song and consolidation of territory proceeded *pari passu* as a procedure eliminating dysgenic fighting. Thus territorialism is dominance with topographical reference (Armstrong 1947). It enables birds to mate and breed in close proximity in spite of differences in dominance and pugnacity (Castoro and Guhl 1959; Davis 1959). Such a ritualization of aggressiveness is of special importance as beaks and claws used by such agile creatures could inflict severe wounds if disputes were carried *à l'outrance*. Economy of effort is also achieved through the elaborated defiance sounds acquiring attractiveness for the females. With development along these lines many birds have been able to dispense with bright adornments and so reduce jeopardy from predators. If evolution has followed this path we may suppose that song, like visual display, is the product of conflicting impulses. Song and display may be regarded as resultants of the transference of conflict to some extent from the environment to within the organism. They represent the outcome of its resolution there in the form of visual and vocal signals, which are the by-product of inhibitory mechanisms acting to restrain the direct expression of pugnacity or submissiveness. Ritualization reduces fighting, and territorialism is a ritualization of behaviour related to space.†

Incongruous song, excitement song, hostility song, and displacement song

Commonly birds sing in incongruous situations but the motivations involved are little understood. The time, place, or general situation in which song is uttered may be incongruous. The factor common to most of these songs is that the bird appears to be in a state of excitement. A Mockingbird may sing at night, presumably when disturbed (Laskey 1936). A Song Thrush, bewildered by my accidentally frightening the young from the nest, immediately sang a frenzied, congested song while standing on a branch lying on the ground—a most unusual perch. A White-crowned Sparrow, carried in a car, broke into song at any jolt (Blanchard 1941). Any loud noise will evoke song from a Rufous Whistler (Jack 1949). Birds flying into the beam of a lighthouse may sing. Especially in the breeding season the threshold of song production in many species is low and song is one of the types of response which is most readily elicited by excitement of almost any kind. Even wounded and dying birds have been known to sing (Armstrong 1947). Such utterances may be designated responses to sub-optimal stimuli but this does not go far towards explaining their motivation.

In many situations, including the instances cited, we may plausibly assume that hostility is an element in the motivation. Much song is mainly defensive or defiant, as we have noted (p. 113) and sudden excitement being frequently due to a potentially menacing situation, defence mechanisms, even if inappropriate, are apt to be elicited when a bird is surprised. In some species such utterances, associated with correlated activities, may have become adaptive as diversionary display (Armstrong 1949). A few examples of song which might be regarded as 'hostility song' follow. This term is chosen to distinguish intra-specific song— 'fighting song'—from song elicited by an intruder of another species.

A human intruder near the nest of a Fantail Warbler, *Cisticola juncides*, becomes the centre, or even the target, of its song-flights (Givens and Hitchcock 1953) and a Red-spotted Bluethroat may swoop in song-flight close to an observer as if in threat (Armstrong and Westall 1953). When a White-eyed Vireo was lifted by its bill from the nest it promptly returned to it and sang (Saunders 1929). A Skylark will sing after escaping from a Sparrowhawk and I have induced one to rise singing again and again by repeatedly approaching and withdrawing from the nest. A Dunlin, concerned for the chicks, utters its trilling song while fluttering over a man or a dog. Stints too, both Little and Temminck's, behave similarly (p. 139). Birds as various as Wrens and Sandpipers sing on being released after ringing.

In some species certain forms of song other than the bi-valent territorial song appear to be dual-purpose so that it is hardly appropriate to consider the song as incongruous in either of the situations in which it may be uttered. Thus Pied Flycatchers usually sing their congested song (*gepresste Gesang*) during the inspection of the nest-hole but it may also be sung when a raptor or other large bird flies over (von Haartman and

Löhrl 1950). This is probably an instance of an utterance appropriate to another situation elicited as a reaction to a sub-optimal or sub-relevant object, becoming ritualized as a response to it. If we suppose the utterance of the nest-inspection song to be an outcome of the conflict to flee or to remain it may be considered displacement song.

This type of adaptation is comparable with the ritualization into display of transference or displacement activities. A variety of forms of utterance have been called displacement song but in some instances it is not certain that the cases cited are motivated in the manner accepted as typical of displacement activity—that is, through the disinhibition of the next available activity when thwarting occurs.† According to Sauer (1954) one of the characteristic calls in the Whitethroat's vocabulary is frequently uttered as a displacement activity when the bird is in a conflict situation and Blase (1960) considers the Red-backed Shrike's courtship song to be displacement song. This may be mistaken, for although such courtship song appears to be due, like so much song, to conflicting motivation, it does not come into the category of displacement activity unless we consider it to be a substitute for copulatory activity. Similarly, when birds sing quietly while incubating (p. 167) this might be considered a consequence of the conflict between the incubation impulse and the impulse to leave the nest. Such a possibility would be confirmed if it were proved that in these circumstances the impulse to sing becomes accentuated as each incubation session draws to a close. The Canary-like whisper song uttered by Canada Jays when frustrated is described as displacement song by de Kiriline (1957). Florida Jays also sing in a subdued manner when alarmed (Amadon 1944). Jays emit soft mimicries when disturbed at the nest, and bowerbirds utter louder mimicries when disturbed at the bower. In all such situations there is thwarted activity and conflicting motivation. We may therefore refer to these utterances with some justification as displacement song or calls. I have heard two Wrens, engaged in a territorial dispute, sing a twittery whisper song between vehement fighting songs. Apart from this incident I have never noticed this whisper song except in 'domestic' situations when a Wren is on or near the nest or roost (p. 169). The Nightingale-Thrush also sings whisper song while expostulating with intruders as well as in 'domestic situations' (Skutch 1960) and apparently Kirtland's Warbler repels intruders with a whisper song (Borror 1961). Such whisper song during altercations seems entitled to be called displacement song. The utterance of congested song by Pied Flycatchers when a raptor flies over, mentioned above, may have originated from a comparable inappropriate utterance. It should not be forgotten that some inappropriate predator alarm calls may be due to mistaken identity. Excited Avocets may utter the 'gull-warning' cry when a bird of another species approaches, or give the normal alarm when a gull appears (Makkink 1936). House Sparrows engaged in a 'social song' assembly may utter the airborne predator warning when surprised by a person (Daanje 1941).

The interest of the type of behaviour first called 'displacement activity' by Armstrong (1947) was realized by Selous as long ago as 1914. Commenting on the odd bathing antics of the Red-throated Diver—which would now be called ritualized 'displacement-bathing'—when excited by the approach of a third bird, he remarked : 'Nevertheless, they have not, in my opinion, had a sexual origin but, by what I call the "law of inter-changeability of energies"—or more strictly, of their mode of expression —have been deflected into this channel . . . excitement of any kind, if sufficiently strong, demands motion to carry it off, and where no special routine of movements appropriate to the special excitement exists, another one belonging to some other class of emotion is apt to be fallen into, since it is easier for any stream to run in any channel that has already been made than to cut out a new one for itself'. Later, he says : 'Antics . . . are ever ready (so to express it) to multiply or interchange their exciting causes, so that their origin may often have little to do with the use, or some of the uses, to which they are subsequently put.' Thus Selous not only noticed the peculiarities of these activities, which he mentions in other contexts, but formulated a theory to explain them which has similarities to that accepted today. Kirkman (1937) devotes several pages to the discussion of 'substitute reactions' as he called displacement activities. He observed them and elicited them experimentally during his work in nesting colonies of Black-headed Gulls which began in 1905 and continued for many years. Tinbergen (1957) refers to 'the discovery of displacement by Tinbergen (1940) and Kortlandt (1940a)', but Kortlandt (1959a) states that 'the notion of displacement activities was explicitly suggested by Craig (1918)'. Apart from the work of Craig and Kirkman a number of other writers had published details of these activities in various species prior to 1940 (References in Armstrong 1942). Kirkman, for example, called attention to Adams's paper (1931) describing displacement activities evoked in cats during experimental work.

Tinbergen's earlier view that the character of a displacement activity owed little or nothing to objects in the environment has been modified. The realization that the presence of such environmental stimuli may determine the evocation of one kind of displacement activity rather than another adds a complication to the interpretation of some of these puzzling forms of behaviour in which the normal relationship between object and activity is dislocated (Armstrong 1950b; Baerends 1958).

Various definitions of displacement activity have been given (Armstrong 1950; Tinbergen 1952; Van Iersel and Bol 1958) and a considerable literature on it has been published. Some of the problems have been clarified by Von Holst and St. Paul (1960) who have explored the relationship of behaviour-patterns to one another by inserting electrodes into the brain stems of birds. In practice, they are identifiable as irrelevant activities performed in situations of frustration or thwarting but, as has been sufficiently indicated, certain utterances of some birds are elicited in such varied circumstances that it is often difficult to determine when a given utterance is uttered 'out of context'.

The extent to which transference song occurs is debatable. Transference activities were identified and defined as follows : 'The drive issues in a consummatory act in which a substitute for the normal object is involved. When such a transference of the drive to a substitute object occurs . . . the activity would be called a "transference activity"' (Armstrong 1952). Subsequently the term 're-direction activity' was coined, and it has been construed in a variety of senses overlapping with the significance of 'transference activity' (Bastock *et al.* 1953; Moynihan 1955b; Ficken and Dilger 1960).

To eliminate confusion it is proposed that 're-direction activity' be abandoned and 'transference activity' be re-defined as follows: An activity normally activated but subjected to thwarting causing deflection from the initiating object, animal, or situation to a substitute, sub-relevant goal (Armstrong 1961). Thus defined there seem to be few, if any, instances of transference song on record. Song may be elicited by or uttered at an incongruous animal or object but activated song is seldom or never deflected to another, substitute object. Activities, including song, may be inappropriately orientated without being deflected, after activation, to a substitute object.†

VIII

SONG-FLIGHT AND NON-VOCAL SONG

> It certainly was a remarkable provision of Nature to assign
> to the same species of animal both song and flight; so that
> those which had to cheer other living things with the voice
> should be usually aloft; whence the sound could spread
> around through a greater space, and reach a greater number
> of hearers; and so that the air, which is the element destined
> for sound, should be populous with vocal and musical
> creatures.
>
> GIACOMO LEOPARDI. *Elogio degli uccelli.*

BIRDS, more than any other living creatures, make the heavens their
stage. Many combine aerial expertise with their musical performance. Thus they make themselves visually conspicuous and enable
their songs, vocal or instrumental, to be heard over a wide area. Display-
flight need not be accompanied by song but silent display-flight is comparatively rare. Probably acoustic conspicuousness adds little to the
already considerable vulnerability of display-flighting birds while increasing the effectiveness of the display. The hazards incurred by display-
flighting birds explain why this form of display has not been adopted by
more birds. I have seen a Whimbrel outfly a Gyrfalcon by ascending
higher and higher but a Fieldfare which I glimpsed being chased by one
of these falcons was captured. The Whimbrel's plangent cries ring down
from a height as it performs its very conspicuous display-flight but the
Fieldfare's song-flight is a rapid dash from tree to tree as if vulnerability
limited its performance. The rarity of song-flights among forest-dwelling
birds must be due, in large part, to the danger of being seized by a
raptor swerving around the tree-tops (p. 221). Bicknell's Grey-cheeked
Thrush is apparently unique among thrushes in rising on rapidly beating
wings and executing a circling song-flight, but it does so just before
darkness (Dilger 1956a). The Streaked Saltator flies up in song at dusk
when other birds have ceased singing (Skutch 1954a). Similarly the
Woodcock, less agile in the air than many other waders, starts 'roding'
at dusk. Only by unusual misadventure would a Sparrowhawk be able
to seize a Wren performing its brief display-flight from twig to twig or a
Whitethroat springing up a few feet in song from the briars, but the Tree
Pipit, circling above the tree-tops, takes greater risks. Very few Wrens
are captured by Sparrowhawks and the percentage of a Whitethroat

135

population captured—two and a half—was half that of Tree Pipits (Tinbergen 1946). The Skylark ranks fourth in the Sparrowhawk's prey (Uttendörfer 1939, 1952). Aerial song-flighting must pay high dividends in some respects to outweigh the jeopardy it entails. However, we do not know what proportion of the birds were in song-flight when captured (Pl. XII).

Types of song-flight

Song-flighting birds may be loosely classified according to the importance of the performances in the repertoire of display activities. Firstly, there are the species which at peaks of ardour sing snatches of their normal song in flight; secondly, there are those which sing from a perch or while moving about in cover but, at some phases of the breeding cycle, utter a form of song in flight which may diverge somewhat from the usual pattern; thirdly, there are species whose song is normally uttered on the wing, and fourthly, there are the birds which spend most of their time on the wing and sing as they fly.

To the first category belong the Wren, Blackbird, Mockingbird, and Cuckoo. Perhaps, when mere snatches of song are uttered occasionally during flight this might be called flight-song to distinguish it from stereotyped territorial or courtship display-flight. Unfortunately in American usage flight-song is equivalent to song-flight in British terminology. To the second category belong a number of Palaearctic warblers, the Rock Thrush, and Wheatear, and, in North America, a varied selection including the Ovenbird, Song and Swamp Sparrows, Indigo Bunting, Meadowlark, and Townsend's Solitaire (Saunders 1929), and a wide range of species elsewhere. The third class includes the larks and some pipits, in America the Bobolink, and especially in the Holarctic, many waders. The fourth group consists of swallows, some nightjars, and hummingbirds with instrumental song and a few other highly aerial species. The songs of birds of this group tend to be relevant to the pair-bond rather than effective in defending territory.

These categories serve to denote different types of song-flight rather than constitute a system of classification. There are various intermediate forms and in many species the performance varies according to the phase of the breeding cycle. Birds which normally sing perched may utter snatches of song on the wing when in a stimulated state. Even a highly aerial species, such as the Skylark, may utter its first song of the day and its late-season songs on the ground. The Blue Grouse performs its first morning drumming flight as it descends from the roosting tree but thereafter springs up from the ground to drum (Wing 1946). In a number of species the male sings as he flies toward, around, or with the female but not while performing a territorial song-flight. Birds of the third category which normally sing in flight vary from species like the Glossy Grassquit in the West Indies, which merely utters a wheezing note as it bobs up, a twinkling red and black speck, a foot or two above the herbage, to African species of Cisticolae with song-flights which take them to a moderate height (Lynes 1930) and birds such as the Horned Lark and Sprague's Pipit in North America which rise to 800 feet. Rather than discuss these categories separately some comments will be made on various characteristics, such as the pattern described in the air, function, relationship to habitat adaptations (p. 227), and structural modifications connected with the non-vocal sounds which many birds make during display.

Flight Patterns

Except in the simplest forms of flight-song or song-flight the bird as a rule performs some unusual type of wing-beat or describes a distinctive pattern in the air. Among the waders, for example, the Golden Plover's wing-beat falters, the Oystercatcher flaps in slow motion, the Redshank hovers with quivering wings. In areas where several related species breed sympatrically the flight pattern as well as the songs are usually distinctive—indeed, a human observer may sometimes identify species more readily by the figures described in flight than by the song. The Skylark mounts vertically, the Woodlark spirals, the Calandra Lark flies in wide circles and 'rotates and flutters in one place with what appear to be alternate strokes of the wings' (Mountfort 1954), the Lesser Short-toed switchbacks less obviously and the Hoopoe Lark utters a long drawn-out note, then flings itself into the air with closed wings, turns, and dives to the ground with rapid wing-strokes and a medley of notes (Stanford 1954). The designs woven in the air by different species of hummingbird vary greatly (Figs. 22 and 23). Only two out of seven North American hummingbirds perform similar flight displays and each species makes a distinctive sound with wings or tail (Banks and Johnson 1961) (Pl. VII).†

Function

The relative importance of intimidating males or attracting the female in some song-flights is not always easy to ascertain. According to Hale (1956) the main function of the Redshank's display-flight is to facilitate pair-formation as this species does not maintain territory, but other observers disagree (Grosskopf 1959). Whatever territorial significance the Spotted Redshank's display may have, it seems to be relevant to the female. The male rises with the characteristic *chueet* call, then crying *chup, chup, chup* . . . repeatedly flies to a height of about fifty feet, dives steeply, and zig-zags close to the ground. During the swerving zig-zags the pale under-surface of the wings and the white rump contrast strongly with the black underparts. The display bears some similarity to that of the Lapwing. As these aerobatics would be most effective viewed from the ground we may assume that the display is mainly to attract or stimulate the female (Armstrong 1950c; 1951b; Armstrong and Westall 1953). The dark breast and belly coloration of a number of other species, the reverse of the usual pattern of concealing coloration, must be functional in display. In some passerines and bustards such coloration has an epigamic function. Probably, therefore, in the display-flights of waders, and some other birds, such as the Shoveler, especially when male and female join in flight close together, the female is stimulated. The American Woodcock's song-flight is a territorial advertisement. The wings make a melodious sound (Pitelka 1943). The song-flight of the Golden Plover, one of the species with this type of coloration, may be ambivalent or function differently in different phases of the display. High flights with slow wing-beats during which the male utters a plaintive call are mainly territorial but other aerial manoeuvres in which the female takes part belong to the courtship procedure. In some of these flights the wings make a humming noise (Brown 1938). The Pectoral Sandpiper performs a spectacular song-flight in which the birds look like bobbing yellow balloons but when they establish territories away from breeding grounds this display does not occur (Hamilton 1959). This suggests that the display is largely to attract the female. The Greenshank's song-flight is a proclamation of territory and warning to rivals but when the tempo of excited performance is high it indicates that the male is anxious for a mate, or, if mated, for coition. It can express various forms of excitement, particularly when in the company of the female, as when she is escorted to the nest or the feeding ground (Nethersole-Thompson 1951). This applies to the song-flights of a number of waders which may be elicited by different types of stimulus. It has been suggested that such displays might more appropriately be called 'excitement flights' than 'courtship flights' (von Frisch 1960).

The Goldfinch performs a territorial song-flight with slowly beating wings and fanned tail, rather similar to the Greenfinch's display-flight. Another form of flight in which the wings are rapidly quivered and the tail is raised precedes coition (Conder 1948). The American Goldfinch's song-flight is hovering and hesitant (Stokes 1950). In many species the presence of the female stimulates the male to display. Sauer (1954) states that the Whitethroat's song-flight attracts the female but it is difficult to believe that it does not serve also to deter rivals.

We may assume that the types of song-flight in which the female participates with the male are stimulatory and synchronize the sexual rhythms of the pair. The display-flight of the Lapwing apparently has a stimulating effect on males and females—like the ground display and scrape-making. The bird twists and turns low down with the air whistling through its rounded wings. The performance seems adapted to impress the female below, but as Lapwings sometimes appear paired on the breeding ground and males will song-flight together it may be concluded that both sexes are stimulated by these song-flights (Laven 1941). Self-stimulation as well as reciprocal stimulation may occur.

Aggressive flights with song or calls are made by many species and a hostile component is evident in some song-flights. The 'pendulum' flights by rival males back and forth over an invisible boundary are a means of settling the limits of territories. They are most characteristic of birds of open terrain, such as the Prairie Horned Lark and Snow Bunting (Pickwell 1931; Tinbergen 1939). The Lapwing makes swishing stoops at intruders, Temminck's Stints hover trilling above a predator (Haviland 1916a), and a male will perform a 'butterfly flight' and display with quivering wings, trilling, at an intruding male (Armstrong and Westall 1953). Such behaviour probably indicates that there is an aggressive element in the normal song-flight. The Little Ringed Plover's song-flight in which the male flies with butterfly-beats back and forth is territorial advertisement which decreases during incubation and practically ceases later—like the Lapland Bunting's song-flight. A flying intruder is opposed by the owner advancing and stalling before it, uttering a buzzing version of the usual note (Simmons 1956). A Turnstone, after driving away an intruder may go into display-flight on returning to his territory, moving with slower wing-beats than usual. He then displays to his mate —so long as there is no strange Turnstone about (Bergman 1946). As the male dominates his mate when in his territory there is apparently an aggressive element in this display-flight also. According to von Frisch (1956, 1959) the song-flights of the Curlew and many other waders appear to be relevant to territorial defence rather than courtship. This may be true, in the main, of most high and wide song-flights.

Relation to the breeding cycle

Among passerines the phase of song-flighting varies in different species. Wheatears at first warble softly and defend territory but when the females arrive and pairs are formed warbling practically ceases and the cocks sing loudly, frequently flying up to twenty feet, highly conspicuous, fluttering black and white minstrels. Neighbouring males carry on song-flight contests (Conder 1956). Thus the display-flight is in defence of the territory containing the female. Territory is maintained until the young are independent or even until the adults migrate.

The elaborate song-flight of the Cypriot race of the Pied Wheatear is a courtship procedure. The cock, pouring out a continuous stream of song, darts rapidly back and forth past the female and then flies off, still singing. The Isabelline Wheatear flutters before the female, flies up performing aerobatics and spirals back again. The Black Wheatear mounts singing, then sinks in song to the hen (Witherby *et al.* 1938).

Lapland Buntings carol high in air over the territories but song ceases abruptly when the males take charge of the oldest chicks—which leave the nest in a flightless condition. Thus on Baffin Island song was at its height in the last week of June but had ceased altogether on 6 July (Sutton and Parmelee 1955). Similarly, in Siberia territory is maintained strictly, with fighting, until the young leave the nest (Milkeiv 1939). Some observers who have studied the birds in Lapland late in the season have been puzzled at the apparent absence of song and territorialism (Rowell 1957) but, in common with many other species, Lapland Buntings vehemently defend territory during the earlier phases of breeding so that any given area is parcelled into lots such that the number of pairs in it is economic. The birds are single-brooded so that song-flighting is apparently in defence of territory and mate, as in the Wheatear. The cessation of such flights occurs when the help of the male is needed to rear the young.

Snow Buntings fly in a ritualized song-flight demonstrating against neighbours. The song is a jingle without the sweet, detached notes of the Lapland Bunting. The male takes charge of some of the young when they leave the nest, the female of the others (Tinbergen 1939).

Among birds of our second group song-flighting is usually a manifestation of high ardour or excitement, as it is in species of our first category. This may be caused by the presence of the female but, in so far as we can generalize, this behaviour does not seem to be due to one type of stimulation. When a female is in his territory a male Wren, although he may have already courted a female and installed her in a nest, will break out into song-flights again but he will also sing when chasing an intruder or on being released after ringing. Meadowlarks are also polygamous and may be heard song-flighting for three or four months in the year. Lanyon (1957) remarks: 'The stimuli commonly arose in situations involving territorial defence or association with sexually responsive females.' He notes that the whistled call-note of both Eastern and Western Meadowlark, restricted otherwise to times of excitement, is incorporated into the flight-song. Western Meadowlarks sing from March to October with a few weeks' respite during the moult in August. As with some other polygamous song-birds preoccupation with song and courtship limits the attention given by the males to the young. The Scarlet-breasted Troupial, which is related to the Meadowlark, flies up singing, performing a kind of somersault from time to time with a vocal flourish (Hudson 1892).

Song-flight with non-vocal song

Birds beating their wings in flight naturally make a certain amount of noise, though, in some species, particularly owls, which have special 'silencer' adaptations, this is reduced to a minimum. In widely separated groups behaviour has been evolved in which the wings are employed as sound-producing instruments. Among flight-displaying species the noise made by some is merely ancillary to their passage through the air but there are others which produce a mechanical sound as an integral constituent of the display, and yet others in which the instrumental sound is the *raison d'être* of the flight. In many species the noise made by a companion taking off serves to alert others on the ground. Some passerine nestlings begin to beg when they hear the fluttering of the returning parent's wings. The wing-music of the Mute Swan takes the place of the contact calls which other species of swan utter in flight. The Goldeneye is sometimes called 'Whistler' because of the noise of the wing beats. The sound made by the drake's wings is louder than that made by the adult female's and the wings of the young females do not make this 'ringing' noise. Many species of dove are noisy in flight. In some these wing-made sounds probably serve as alarm or contact signals, and in a few, such as the Woodpigeon which claps its wings in flight, these sounds are part of the display. As Blue-eared Starlings fly their wings make an amazingly loud noise (Vincent 1936). The guans *Penelope cristata* and *Chamaepetes unicolor* make a drumming with their wings as they glide. In the dense forests where they live this drumming must indicate the location of individuals to one another. Hornbills are also noisy in flight. The humming which gives their name to hummingbirds is, of course, a by-product of their rapid wing-movements though it must also signal the presence of a bird to others. In some species sounds made in this way are exaggerated to serve as display sounds. A hissing noise is made by the wings of the courting male Costa's Hummingbird as he dives through the air. Structural modifications, enabling loud and distinctive noises to be made have taken place. As the Broad-tailed Hummingbird plunges downward forty to fifty feet in display a rattling whistle is heard. The noise is created by the air rushing through slots at the tips of the primaries (Pl. VII, Fig. 22). Related sound-producing structures are found in at least two other members of the same genus. Normally the wing-beats are seventy-five per second but during the dive they accelerate to 200 per second (Edgerton *et al.* 1951). While display-flighting the male Lucifer Hummingbird makes a loud humming with his wings. The male of this species has no other song apart from three 'flups' with the tail made at the end of the dive (Fig. 23) (Wagner 1946; Banks and Johnson 1961). The oddly curved and stiffened feathers of the Singing Hummingbird, *Campylopteris*

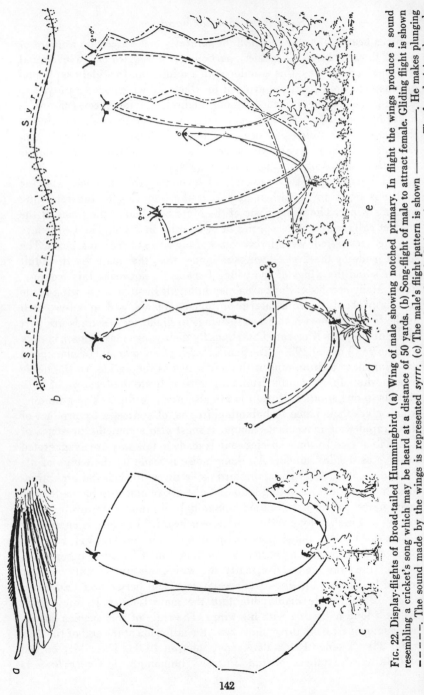

FIG. 22. Display-flights of Broad-tailed Hummingbird. (a) Wing of male showing notched primary. In flight the wings produce a sound resembling a cricket's song which may be heard at a distance of 50 yards. (b) Song-flight of male to attract female. Gliding flight is shown – – – –. The sound made by the wings is represented *syrr*. (c) The male's flight pattern is shown ———. He makes plunging swoops while the female perches on a twig. (d) Second phase. The route of the female flight is shown – – – –. The female joins the male

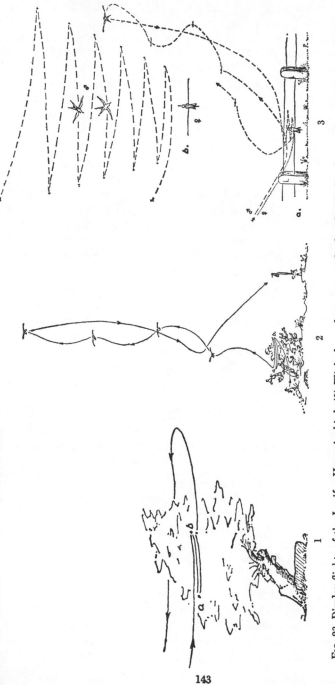

Fig. 23. Display-flights of the Lucifer Hummingbird. (1) Flight by male to attract the female. He flies from side to side in a pendulum flight about ten times. The wings make a loud burring noise. Unlike most hummingbirds the males of this species have no vocal song. (2) Flight of higher intensity to attract the female. He mounts and then dives to perform a pendulum flight in front of her. (3) Courtship flight of the male to attract the female during highly stimulated phase. (a) Display-flight of the male in the presence of the female. He mounts and swoops to perform a diminishing pendulum-swing flight in front of the female. This is sexually stimulating. (b) Detail of the pendulum flight. (After Wagner 1946)

curvipennis, produce 'an almost frightening roar' as the bird flies (Sutton 1945). A structural modification of the fourth primary of the Little Bustard is thought to be responsible for a whistling sound during the nuptial flight (Ingram 1956).

The Chimney Swift leaps backwards and snaps its wings together in flight up to six times in succession to deter an intruder (Fischer 1958). The male Nightjar claps his wings—apparently over his back—to call the female and also, late in the season, when a third bird is in the territory. The female claps when sexually excited. The cock Red-necked Nightjar makes a series of claps when chasing the female. The 'boom' of the Nighthawk is caused by the air passing through the wing feathers as it checks its aerial dive. Short-eared Owls clap their wings in display-flight over the nesting area and when the nest is threatened (Dubois 1924; Armstrong and Phillips 1925). The Fantail Warbler, *Cisticola juncidis*, makes display-claps at a human intruder and the female performs thus when concerned for the safety of the young (Givens and Hitchcock 1953). Many other species of this group make noises in flight. The Kalahari Swift Warbler swoops, clapping, at a person approaching the nest, the male Shortwing Grass Warbler whirrs up and then nose-dives, the Pale-crowned Cloud Warbler cruises at a great height and wing-snaps (Lynes 1930; Roberts 1948). Warblers of the genus *Prinia*, such as the Graceful Warbler, perform wing-snapping aerial dances which seem to be primarily aggressive though similar behaviour may occur in sexual situations. The bird dives or flits around making a triple snapping, presumably caused by the wings brushing against the upward-flicked tail (Simmons 1954). Contact between wings and tail also occurs in the Long-tailed Sugarbird's display flight, giving rise to clapping noises (Vincent 1947–49). The cock Mozambique Chin-spot Flycatcher chases the female, flicking his wings to create a thudding sound (Sclater and Moreau 1933). The 'twanging' heard as the Golden-crowned Spadebill flies back and forth is apparently caused by the wings (Skutch 1958a).

Among New World birds with non-vocal song-flights may, perhaps, be included Gould's Manakin although the snapping sound made with thickened wing-quills is made during leaps rather than flights from twig to twig in the bird's 'court' (Chapman 1935; Armstrong 1947). The female Long-tailed Manakin attracts the male's attention by swooping close to him with loud wing-clapping (Wagner 1945b). The Blue-backed Manakin also apparently makes mechanical noises during display (Gilliard 1959; Sick 1959).† Pairs of Scissor-tailed Flycatcher in La Plata may join others in corporate flight, mounting rocket-like to a great height and then zooming downwards in wild zig-zags, opening and closing the long tail feathers, and so creating loud whirring or rattling sounds. The

IX*a*.   Red-backed Shrike singing sub-song to the incubating female

X*b*.   Male Wren singing sub-song and displaying to the female in front of the nest

Xa. Male Bronze Mannikin singing the courtship song to the female

Xb. Male Rufous Song Lark singing at the nest

wings may also contribute to the noise (Hudson 1892; Fitch 1950). During courtship flights the wings of Wagler's Oropendola make 'a rushing roar' (Chapman 1928). According to Hudson (1892) Chiloe Wigeon sailing aloft in a flock approach and clap one another's wings— a procedure so remarkable as to call for further confirmation. When the drake Pintail passes close below the duck during the display flight a loud clattering is heard but it is uncertain whether this is caused by contact or 'braking' (Witherby *et al.* 1939).

As we have already noted, there are waders, such as the Golden Plover, Lapwing, and Black-tailed Godwit (Huxley and Montague 1926), with displays the effectiveness of which is increased, to greater or lesser extent, by wing-noises. There are others such as the Snipe and Jack Snipe, whose display flight is adapted primarily for the production of instrumental sound. Apparently both sexes perform. The Australian Snipe makes a 'winnowing hum' during its sailing flight and power dive (Wolfe 1954). The tail feathers of the Pin-tailed Snipe have become modified for sound production. Thus it is apparent that in a number of groups selection has worked in favour of noise-production during the display-flight until in some species structural modification has followed the trend to make loud, distinctive sounds during the display. Snipe drum when a human intruder approaches the nest so the motivation is probably primarily aggressive.

The behaviour of African honeyguides is remarkable in many respects. The Greater Honeyguide frequents a tree favoured also by other males and there calls to attract females. From time to time one appears and the bird in occupation copulates without ceremony. Thus males do not defend territory but occupy 'stud-posts'. After coition a drumming or rustling flight is heard. This sound is produced by the movements of the wings. Probably it also serves to call the females. The Lyre-tailed Honeyguide reiterates a 'tin-horn' note which is heard when the bird has spiralled up and then dives with the wind rushing through the peculiarly shaped tail feathers. As the sexes have specialized rectrices the sound may be made by both (Friedmann 1955–58; Ranger 1955). The Lesser Honeyguide flies around in an undulating course, the wing-beats making loud claps (Brown 1948).†

Bagshawe (1939) heard a Giant Petrel clap its feet together in flight 'making quite a loud noise' but it is doubtful whether this action had any display significance.

Non-vocal song

Non-vocal acoustic means of communication have been evolved by animals ranging from spiders and insects to primates (Appendix). Among birds practically all such signalling devices are refinements of maintenance activities, elaborated and ritualized. We may review these adaptations in relation to the maintenance activities from which they probably developed, or to which they seem most closely related :

LOCOMOTION

Aerial. All the species mentioned in the previous section come under this heading. Here we may comment on various derivative types of wing or feather movement. This division is somewhat artificial as there are groups in which some species make their sound-signals from a perch while others issue signals of a similar type in flight. The Ruffed Grouse drums with his wings as he stands on a log or other perch. Samuel Hearne, who made a journey north from Hudson Bay from 1769 to 1772 wrote that the noise could be heard at a distance of half a mile. The Blue Grouse drums on the wing, while related American tetraonids *Tympanuchus, Centrocercus*, and *Pedioceles* posture communally but do not drum (Wing 1946). According to Blackford (1958) the Blue Grouse makes three kinds of wing note—a wing flutter, which may be performed by male or female, wing drumming performed by an individual or enacted during communal display, and the wing clap in response to the flight of a female from the cock's courting ground. Sharp-tailed Grouse displaying in their territories boom and click their tail quills (O'Gara 1946). Among Old World species the Black Grouse displays socially and leaps into the air. When flying the wings make a rushing noise which may serve as a signal. Black Grouse will crow and Blue Grouse drum on hearing one of their species take flight (Höhn 1953; Wing 1946). The Capercaillie leaps up in display flapping noisily. The Red Grouse and Ptarmigan spring up calling and beating their wings. The Pheasant makes a dull thudding or roaring noise with his wings while standing on the ground. Medieval writers regarded the Domestic Cock as an exemplar of the good Christian. As it beats its body with its wings before crowing so the Christian offers penitence before praise.

When the displaying Rifle Bird raises his wings like a great iridescent blue-black butterfly a loud swishing is caused by special structures on the feathers rubbing against each other. As the feathers have become broadened, rendering the visual display more effective, we may presume that the sound-production modifications took place *pari passu* (Pl. VII). The Peacock, strutting with his train fanned, deliberately agitates the quills, making a rustling clatter. He may do this when alarmed, as well as when displaying to the female, so probably some aggressive motivation is involved. A frightened Blue-fronted Amazon Parrot spreads its wings and tail, the wings making a hissing noise as when a red hot iron is plunged into water (Cott 1940). Exactly the same type of sound is made in the same way by both sexes of the Painted Snipe as a threat and apparently also during courtship (Finn 1902).† Reference has already been made to the clattering of the wing-joints in the Solitaire's display (p. 112).

Terrestrial. The strutting Turkeycock makes clicking sounds by catching a foot on the quills of the drooped wing feathers. This practice may have evolved through the bird's feet tripping in the wing during his mincing steps or while scratching the ground with wings pendant during display—originally a feeding movement. The Kiwi stamps its feet when annoyed—perhaps an alarm signal like the rabbit's drumming on the ground with its feet.

Aquatic. A male Coot will stand on a raft of weed or the nest slapping the water with a foot, producing a loud noise. This may have the function of song, repelling males and attracting females (Turner 1924; Grimeyer 1943).

Feeding. Signalling by mechanical means has reached its highest development in the woodpeckers. No doubt the practice originated from pecking at insects in crevices. The sound is created by the bird's bill

Fig. 24. Sheldrake making a rippling courtship call by scraping the bill along the wing quills. (After Makkink 1936 and Tinbergen 1940)

rapidly striking a branch which acts as a resonator. Northern Flickers may choose odd resonators such as an ash-bin lid. Different species have recognizable techniques differing in (1) duration, (2) number of taps, (3) rhythm—uniform or varying, and (4) intensity (Géroudet 1946). The Black Woodpecker makes two, or perhaps three, kinds of signal by the impact of its bill (Blume 1958), but the chicks drum with their tongues (Sielmann 1959). The Pileated Woodpecker has similar techniques but tongue-drumming has not been noted. Pairs of Red-bellied and Red-headed Woodpecker signal to each other by mutual tapping. Both tap at the rate of two to three per second in bursts of five to fifteen taps each (Kilham 1958a, b) (Fig. 27). Tits also tap on the outside (or inside) of the nesting-hole to attract the female (p. 163).

During the 'klappering' which White Storks perform as a mutual display the neck is bent down until the bill is near the nest and then the head is raised over the back while the mandibles are clattered together. As the action of lowering the bill also occurs in the display of herons and may be derived from the posture of seizing fish, klappering may have originated in the same way. Boat-billed Herons and some related species also rattle their mandibles. On the other hand the clashing of bills in the mutual display of paired Gannets and Puffins may be a ritualization of aggressive movements into appeasement display. Albatrosses snap their mandibles during courtship (Pl. XVI).

Birds of many species snap their mandibles, usually aggressively and sometimes in flight. Owls make such clicking noises but apparently in some species they are caused by contacts between the tongue and palate (Gooch 1940; Pakenham 1943; Hill 1955). The tapping of chicks inside the egg acts as a signal to the parent. There is some evidence that unhatched chicks may make clicking signal sounds in other ways.

Preening. The drakes of a number of duck species displacement-preen during courtship but the displaying Sheldrake rubs his bill along the wing-quills (Fig. 24), producing a 'rippling' noise and the Mallard behaves in a rather similar manner (Makkink 1931; Lorenz 1941).

IX

SONG AND THE ANNUAL CYCLE

The males of song-birds, and many others, do not in
general search for the female, but, on the contrary, their
business in the spring is to perch on some conspicuous spot,
breathing out their full and amorous notes, which, by instinct,
the female knows and repairs to the spot to choose her mate.

G. MONTAGU. *Ornithological Dictionary* (1802).

TERRITORIAL song being so conspicuous naturalists have given
it great prominence and often written as if there were no other
kind of song. Also, in field work and the discussions on the function of territory carried on since the appearance of Howard's *Territory
in Bird Life* consideration of such song has naturally received much
emphasis. Recently, indeed, call-notes have been studied more seriously
than the various types of non-territorial song. Because these forms have
been neglected we know comparatively little about their nature and functions. Undoubtedly they are uttered by many more species than is at
present realized.

In a number of species of song-bird the females respond to more intimate utterances by males as the birds get to know each other and establish
rapport. There is an increase in sexual motivation, culminating in
many species, in utterances which immediately precede or accompany
copulation. From the standpoint of the bird receiving the auditory signals
they are increasingly effective as sexual stimulation.

We must not forget that song which for convenience we style 'territorial' may have wider functions than defending ground against males
and attracting females. The songs of Magpie Larks are believed to coordinate the sexual cycles, stimulate the birds sexually, and strengthen
the pair-bond (Robinson 1946–47). As we have already noted, territorial
songs may become modified so that they acquire an additional, or a
different, function (Chapter VII). The significance of the Woodlark's song
varies according to circumstances and the mode of utterance. The nearer
the nest and the female the softer the song. A modified form—the 'warning song'—signals danger (C. Koffán *in litt.*). Although the Chiffchaff's
song might seem simple and stereotyped Homann (1960) classifies five
forms : territorial, rivalry, excitement, display, and courtship. In addition he lists seven call-notes uttered by the adult and eight by the young.

149

A number of North American warblers utter a modified 'nesting' song after the territorial song has decreased or ceased (Bent 1953). In many situations song aids in maintaining contact between the male and female. In mated birds the absence of the female often elicits song.

Pair-formation song when male and female hold territory

A necessary preliminary to the chain of events which results in breeding is the allaying of the tendency of birds to flee from one another—especially the female from the male. Thus, in those species in which both sexes sing and hold territory, reduction or cessation of territorial song by the female precedes pair-formation. We must remember that reduction in song or abstention from it may exercise a positive communicatory function. In many species the silence of the female is a signal to the male and an element in the courtship sequence. The Robin's procedure illustrates the importance of reducing song in a species in which pair-formation and nesting are separated by more than three months. Early one mid-December morning the hen flies to the cock, who either retreats or takes up a threatening posture as if she were a rival male. If he does the latter she may square up to him. The cock sings vigorously—the challenge song—and the hen may also sing. This behaviour continues for some time with intervals while the birds displacement-feed—an indication of tension. Eventually the cock begins to follow the hen in short flights, singing subdued phrases. After a day or two pair-formation is completed (Lack 1943). In spring, when coition occurs, there is usually no preliminary display. The birds have grown to know each other individually and their sexual cycles have become synchronized so that the songs and posturings which in many species precede copulation are omitted.

Pair-formation or courtship song preceding territorial song

As we noted earlier in reference to the Great Tit (p. 119) full territorial song does not always precede pair-formation. The Yellow Fieldfinch of La Plata lives in flocks but the birds take up territories in the breeding season. According to Hudson (1892) the courtship song is 'feeble, sketchy music' accompanying circlings and short flights above the female, culminating in the male's prostrating himself with outspread wings and whisper song, but when pair-formation and nest-building have been accomplished he spirals up 150 feet, singing melodiously, and still singing, parachutes down while the song dwindles 'to the finest threads of sound and faintest tinklings, as if from a cithern touched by fairy fingers'.

Unmated Wheatears warble quietly and display at intruders, calling *tuc, tuc* until the bird flies away. After pair-formation this warbling ceases almost entirely, giving place to the loud, conspicuous song-flights (Conder 1956). Two factors may have a bearing on this procedure : The Wheatear's habitat is such that a female can locate a male visually much more readily than a bird in woodland could do so, and apparently the birds mate for life.

American Goldfinches form pairs while in the flock, engaging in courtship song and song-flights. The couples leave the flock but do not take up territories until just before nesting begins. The pair-bond is maintained by the male feeding his mate as well as by song (Stokes 1950). There are similarities in the pair-formation behaviour of other carduelines (Hinde 1956b).

Pair-formation song and call-song with little or no territorial significance

Dominance is aggression related to other individuals; territorialism is 'a spatial expression of intolerance and a topographical function of the self-determination impulse' (Armstrong 1942, 1947). Davies (1959), discussing Starling behaviour, comes to a similar conclusion. This bird's song seems to have a function intermediate between that of a typical territorial bird and of species, such as the estrildine finches, in which song is sexual and social. Bronze Mannikins never court without singing but they sing at other times (Pl. X). The songs of Zebra and Spice Finches have sexual and social, but not territorial, functions (Delacour 1943; Morris 1954, 1957; Moynihan and Hall 1954). To differentiate between pair-formation song and courtship song in such species would be to make an artificial distinction.

A Starling will sing to woo a female, or to recall her if she moves away, and the song defends the area close around the nest rather than a territory (Morley 1941). The Bearded Tit defends only a small area adjacent to the nest. Little song is uttered but a widowed male sings assiduously (Koenig 1951). The song is more a call-song than a pair-formation song. So, too, is the song of the Brown Towhee. The cock sings until a female joins him and then sings no more. The birds remain permanently mated (Quaintance 1938). The Red-backed Shrike ceases his call-song soon after a female appears and also reduces the frequency of his harsh call-note (Durango 1948, 1956; Blase 1960).

The male Sierra Nevada Rosy Finch defends a moving territory around the female (Twining 1938, 1940). So does the Black Rosy Finch. One is reminded of the bitterling and its defence of the perambulating mussel in which the eggs have been laid. The main utterance of the Black Rosy Finch is a continuous chirping. This chirping, together with a display in which the tail is cocked and the wings vibrated, attracts the female and is equivalent to a song (French 1959).

Call-song in lek or mating-station birds

The utterances whereby male lek birds attract the females may be mentioned here although they cannot be considered pair-formation songs because these birds do not form a sustained pair-bond. Nor can they be considered non-territorial as the males' 'courts' are territories of an exceptional kind, constituting mating territories. Black Grouse crow, Prairie Chickens boom, and Gould's Manakins make snapping noises (p. 144) to attract the females. Other species of manakin, the Cock of the Rock, and Jackson's Whydah, utter vocal calls. Lyrebirds are highly gifted singers and mockers. The male establishes several courts or singing stances, thus advertising the ownership of the area in which they are situated. A few species issue an invitation to a mating-station or copulation site rather than a mating territory (p. 145). This is true of some honeyguides and bellbirds, probably of some hummingbirds, and possibly also of some manakins (Friedmann 1955; Wagner 1945a, b).

Modification in the output of song during and after pair-formation

In most fully territorial birds, especially migratory species, the period of pair-formation is a time of reduced or suppressed song; not many utter much courtship or nuptial song and energy is devoted to courting and other related activities. Territorial defence involving the protection of the female is apt to be strong in many species from the time when the females arrive to egg-laying (Hinde 1956c). As Nice (1943) points out, referring to the Song Sparrow, cessation of song around the time of arrival of the hens is an indication that a cock is dead or mated. Reduction of song on pair-formation is characteristic of many warblers, finches, buntings, and other species. A Pied Flycatcher reduced his songs from 3620 to 1000 per day on the arrival of the female (von Haartman 1956). In this species there is maximum song before nest-building, then when this begins song almost ceases, but, later, it increases until an output of 200 songs per hour is reached. This is maintained until the eggs hatch and then singing virtually comes to an end (Curio 1959a). The Redstart stops singing during nest-building (Fig. 36) (Buxton 1950) but the American Redstart sings constantly until the nest is built and then ceases (Baker 1944). A number of species, including the Skylark not only reduce song drastically during nest-building and incubation but definitely increase it when feeding young (Fig. 25) (Clark 1947). As the males of these species do not normally build or incubate but help to feed the young the temporary reduction in song is not due to concentration on other activities. The contrasts between different species in this matter are striking and unexplained. An unmated Great Spotted Woodpecker drummed 598 times in one day before pairing but only five times during a day's observation after this, and not at all when nest-hacking—but not all birds of this species reduce their drumming so abruptly (Pynnönen 1939). Song may be greatly reduced or abandoned altogether when the male begins to feed the young, as in the Chaffinch. When a brood is destroyed shortly before the young are ready to fledge the cock may at once begin to sing persistently and continue to do so for weeks. Barrett (1947) noted that a Chaffinch sang most during the two weeks when the first and second nests were being built but that when a third nest was constructed there was

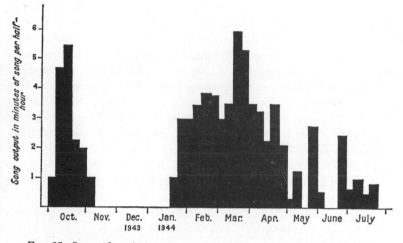

Fig. 25. Seasonal variations in song output of a Skylark measured in weekly sample periods, each of thirty minutes. Adverse weather conditions affect song output during the autumn, winter, and first weeks of the spring song period, but during the breeding season song output is closely related to the male's activities. The reduction of song during periods in May and June is correlated with nest-building and incubation by the female. Song is resumed when the young are being fed. (After Clark 1947)

no such outburst of song. However, I have known there to be little song during the building of the first nest. In some species the cock may continue to sing strongly after the young hatch but usually the daily output tends to decrease. When a bird's song is not fully territorial the reduction of song may follow changes in the breeding cycle less closely. The Starling builds less and sings more one or two days before the beginning of egg-laying (Wallraff 1953).

During and after pair-formation defence of territory may be relaxed together with vocal defiance. A Reed Warbler preoccupied with courting and his intended mate were forced out of his territory (Brown and Davies 1949). When Western Meadowlarks form pairs the territories are hardly defended at all and there are only occasional outbursts of song (Kendeigh

1941b). On securing a mate the female Red-necked Phalarope no longer makes her territorial wing-burring.

The Brown Thrasher sometimes selects the nesting territory after mating. The male usually ceases to sing then but may do so regularly near the future nest-site (Saunders 1942). Song is uttered by the Nuthatch from the second half of November onwards and even during severe cold in January. It is normal after pair-formation when at least part of the territory has already been occupied so it does not serve to attract the female except when a bereaved male sings (Löhrl 1958). The Blackbird, whose song is rather ineffective in deterring trespassers, often maintains a high output after pairing. Song increases while the female is incubating, then it decreases and remains scanty until the young are nearing independence, about three weeks after leaving the nest, by which time the female is busy with a new nest (Snow 1958), for in this species and a good many other passerines overlapping broods occur (Armstrong 1955). This adaptation which involves the male taking responsibility for the young, partially or entirely, has the effect of reducing his songfulness, but commonly when a second brood is initiated a second song-peak occurs, as is shown for the Wren, Hedgesparrow, and Song Thrush by Cox (1944) (Fig. 26).In many species there is less song during the second brood. The Wheatear sings so little then that it is difficult for an observer to ascertain the boundaries of territories but there is much less competition as only some sixty-four per cent of first broods are followed by a second brood (Conder 1956). The connexion between attention to the young and output of song is sometimes vividly illustrated when a bird loses his mate. In such circumstances a male Wren will cease singing completely and devote himself entirely to tending the nestlings.

Some species which practise successive polygamy, such as the Wren and Corn Bunting, tend to have a prolonged song-season because energy which might otherwise be devoted to tending the young goes into attracting females. The weavers with this type of pair-bond utter call-notes, but not songs, to lure females to their conspicuous pensile nests (Armstrong 1955).

Some types of song do not fit neatly into any category. For example, the Cliff Swallow's song attracts other individuals and augments pugnacity but does not repel (Emlen 1954). Thus it has aggressive content like territorial song but also, apparently, a social function. In some species territorial song may also stimulate other males sexually (p. 115). Further development along such lines could result in vocalizations of the kind characteristic of estrildine finches and Budgerigars which have a social and sexually stimulatory value, but more probably these may have developed from contact notes.

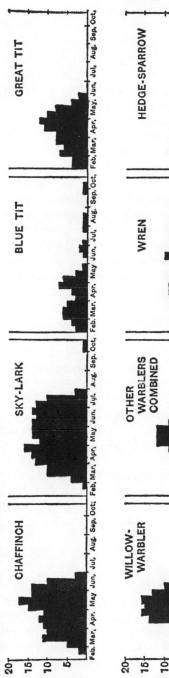

FIG. 26. Histograms showing the variation in the numbers of individuals of eleven species singing during daily morning and evening transects from February to October. (After Cox 1944.)

Modification of the character of territorial song during pair-formation

We have been considering, in the main, alterations in output of song correlated with pair-formation and the nesting cycle but there are species in which the territorial song becomes modified in intensity and pattern when the female appears in the male's domain or when active courtship begins. Pair-formation song and courtship song may then be one and the same. At this phase the melodious utterances of the Blackcap give place, to a large extent, to mimicries and high-pitched squealing (Howard 1907–14). The House Wren reiterates his song until a female arrives. Then he sings more energetically and intersperses a 'mating song' of high-pitched, squeaky notes which apparently stimulate her sexually. When the pair-bond is formed the song tends to alter to a 'nesting song' which is softer, of lower pitch, and slower. There may be two or three variations in pitch level and the singing may be lively or listless (Kendeigh 1941a). The song coordinates the activities of the pair—as does the song of many species when continued through the breeding cycle (p. 169). Laskey (1936) makes a distinction between the Mockingbird's territorial defence song and a modified form, for she mentions a male 'singing gaily in the mate-calling manner'—a song including mimicries. Similarly Erickson (1950) refers to a repetition of short phrases as the 'lonely' song of a deserted Rufous Whistler. A courting Wren modifies his utterance to a subdued, melodious warble but may suddenly break out into a louder sustained song or fly off and reiterate his territorial song.

Courtship and nuptial song

In many species to distinguish between pair-formation and courtship song would be artificial, though the latter tends to be softer, but the distinction is sometimes useful because in some species pair-formation and courtship—in the sense of sexual stimulation—are separated in time. Similarly no rigid distinction can be made between courtship and nuptial song but for descriptive purposes it is sometimes useful to differentiate between courtship song, signifying song leading up to copulation, and nuptial song—song closely associated with copulation, either immediately pre-copulatory, copulatory, or post-copulatory. As all these forms of song are uttered at close quarters they tend to be softer and less specifically distinctive and stereotyped than territorial song.

Snow (1958) regards the Blackbird's courtship display, which is associated with pair-formation, as 'comparatively infrequent' but in my experience it is common, though song accompanying it is rare (Armstrong 1958a). The cock, assuming an odd, strained appearance with beak open, neck low, rump feathers raised, and tail depressed, moves in an inhibited, stilted way back and forth. He may utter a congested or 'strangled' song composed of 'chattering alarm notes, rough warbles, and subdued snatches of what sounds like true song'. This is similar to forms of sub-song heard in autumn from solitary birds. The Messmers (1956) refer to a courtship trill as well as a courtship song and state that soliciting females utter a strained, half-suppressed song. They classify Blackbird song into territorial, nest-building, incubation, and rearing song but state that these forms are characterized only by degrees of frequency of utterance.

The courtship of the Dipper includes song and bears sufficient resemblance to the Wren's courtship to suggest, taken together with other similarities, that the dippers are related to the wrens and not to the thrushes, as has so often been suggested. Harvie-Brown (1861) gives a description of a courting pair, standing on a stone in a stream. The male pointed his bill upwards, uttering 'a small but pleasing song', while the female, flirting her tail and drooping her wings, hopped around him. He kept turning to face her while she kept uttering 'her usual note'. The Wren's courtship sub-song, in common with many such sub-songs, may be uttered as a prolonged warbling (Pl. IX). Thus in this respect it conforms to one of Thorpe and Pilcher's criteria but differs from another by expressing strong sexual motivation.

The Lapland Bunting utters a territorial song in flight (p. 140). His courtship posturing is accompanied by melody. He approaches the female, holding himself bolt upright, showing off his black bib and snowy under-surface, and the birds touch bills. Flying to a bush he utters his call-note, then descends to perform his dance. Again standing upright he sings and spreads his wings, directed downwards, one drawn across his breast, the other turned to the rear. Vibrating them and still singing he advances obliquely towards the crouching female so that the rufous nape feathers and, to some extent, those of the back, are displayed as well as his wings and black throat (Homeyer 1897). McCown's Longspur, a related species, elevates one wing and sings softly while courting (Mickey 1942).

Another Arctic species with a song-flight and courting song is the Red-spotted Bluethroat (Armstrong and Westall 1953). Aplin (1896) describes the courtship: 'Presently the male of the pair sang in an ecstasy for his plain-coloured mate, which I could see, was creeping and hopping among the growth of arctic birch close to where he settled, and he was performing like a Robin. His head and neck were stretched up, and his bill pointed upwards; his tail was flirted up and down, or held at less than a right angle with his body, and his wings were drooped. So he sang until she moved away and he darted after her.' This display has similarities to the threat display of the related Robin.

Much has been written concerning the Lyrebird's display. It combines

157

the territorial song of typical song-birds with the display of lek species. The bird establishes a series of 'courts' in his territory where he displays his strikingly developed tail plumes and sings a loud, elaborate, and pleasing song, which serves to defy males and attract females (Armstrong 1947) (Pl. V). The display behaviour of the King Bird of Paradise is similar to the extent that song and the exhibition of magnificent plumes are combined and the performance is a form of court or lek display. The behaviour of both species is adapted to impress and stimulate the female. No doubt sexual selection operates. The King Bird's performance is probably unsurpassed among birds so Ingram's description (1907) merits quotation in full:

'He always commences his display by giving forth several notes and squeaks, sometimes resembling the call of a quail, sometimes the whine of a pet dog. Next he spreads out his wings, occasionally quite hiding his head; at times stretched upright, he flaps them, as if he intended to take flight, and then, with a sudden movement, gives himself a half turn, so that he faces the spectators, puffing out his silky-white lower feathers; now he bursts into his beautiful melodious warbling song, so enchanting to hear but so difficult to describe. Some weeks ago I was crossing a meadow and heard the song of a skylark high up in the heavens, and I exclaimed at once: "That is the love-chant of my King-bird". He sings a low bubbling note, displaying all the while his beautiful fan-like side-plumes, which he opens and closes in time with the variations of his song. These fan-plumes can only be expanded when his wings are closed and during this part of his display he closes his wings and spreads out his short tail, pressing it close over his back, so as to throw the long tail-wires over his head, while he gently swings his body from side to side. The spiral tips of the wires look like small balls of burnished green metal, and the swaying movements give them the effect of being tossed from one side to the other, so that I have named this part of the display the "Juggling". The swaying of the body seems to keep time with the song, and at intervals, with a swallowing movement of his throat, the bird raises and lowers his head. Then comes the finale, which lasts only a few seconds. He suddenly turns right round and shows his back, the white fluffy feathers under the tail bristling in his excitement; he bends down on the perch in the attitude of a fighting cock, his widely-opened bill showing distinctly the extraordinary apple-green colour of the inside of the mouth, and sings the same gurgling notes without once closing his bill, and with a slow dying-away movement of his tail and body. A single drawn-out note is then uttered, the tail and wires are lowered, and the song and dance are over' (Pl. VIII).

Courtship or nuptial song occurs as normal procedure in a wide variety of species and at least occasionally in many more. Among the latter the

Grasshopper Warbler, Water Pipit (Bailly 1853–55), Tree Sparrow (Boyd 1949), Chaffinch, and Starling may be mentioned. In Australia many birds, both permanent territory-holders and others, utter mating and pre-copulatory songs (Robinson 1949).

The nuptial song of the Rose-breasted Grosbeak is particularly beautiful. According to Ivor (1944) as a cock crouched before the hen 'the mating song poured forth from his open beak as he moved toward the female, weaving his head and body in an erratic dance in which he resembled some magnificent butterfly rather than a bird. The downward and forward sweep of his wings revealed in striking contrast the blacks and whites of the separated flight feathers, the vivid rose of the underwing coverts and the white of the rump. The song, quite different from the territorial song was soft, low and continuous, with a great variety of notes; some of the sweetest notes were so faint that I had to listen intently to hear them though the bird was only two feet away; for pure rapture I cannot recall any song which equals the courtship song of the Rose-breasted (and Black-headed) Grosbeak'. As the song ended the male caught hold of the female's primaries three times. Then she crouched and coition followed. The cock then flew to a branch and sang the territorial song. Such singing of the territorial song may be an 'overflow activity' (Armstrong 1950b) 'after-discharge' or expression of dominance. The early song of the Rose-breasted Grosbeak is very faint and continuous. It is much more like courtship song than territorial singing. By mid-April it is still uttered with the bill closed but by the end of the month the bird is in full song.

Courtship song in some species may culminate in copulatory or coitional song. The Hedgesparrow's courtship song, which is sweeter than the territorial utterance, may be heard from February to July. It is a ripple of quiet warbling reminiscent of a Garden Warbler and is sometimes sustained for nearly a minute (Lister 1953a). Song of this kind can sound like a Skylark's distant song with the high notes omitted. The warbling varies in volume and may be uttered in short phrases. The cock may even sing thus while briefly hovering and engaged in a mêlée with the female. I have heard a bird uttering this slender warble while copulating with the female in the grass at the foot of a bush. The Woodlark also sings an odd little song while copulating on the ground (*Camb. Bird Cl. Rep.* 1945). Before coition and perhaps during it, the Swallow and Sand Martin sing. While copulating a Blackbird may emit a 'chirruping twitter' (König 1938). A Mockingbird sang during the flight and 'dance' prior to coition until the act (Bent 1948). The Blue Jay utters a precoitional song (Kilham 1956). Many species emit specific call-notes soliciting copulation (p. 13).

After coition or attempted coition some birds sing. Wrens do so. The song sounds like an excited territorial or challenge song (p. 128). We have noted that after treading the female the Rose-breasted Grosbeak sings the territorial song but the Scarlet Grosbeak twitters sub-song after the act. In similar circumstances a female Greenfinch may utter a scrap of song (Richardson 1947). A Satin Bowerbird uttered mimicries and other calls while displaying to the female and after copulating. He appeared to be trying to attract her thus to the bower (Chaffer 1959). Two White-backed Bellmagpies tried to copulate with a female and when they flew up a carolling sub-song was heard (Sicker 1946).†

Not many female birds utter courtship or nuptial songs. The hen Cardinal sings early in the year when being courted and may attract and invite the cock by singing when she desires coition (Laskey 1944a). The female Blue Wren sings an invitation to the male to mount. He may do so without coitus taking place—an indication that her ardour is greater than his (Robinson 1949). A female Chaffinch, injected with male hormone, sang sub-song as she tried to copulate with a stuffed and mounted male. As the cock may sing a soft phrase before treading the female we may assume that the injection produced this condition in the female (Perry 1948; Poulsen 1958; Thorpe 1958).

Mutual courtship song is characteristic of some highly social species. Australian Magpie Larks of both sexes sing a mating song and after pair-formation they join in duets and seek out a territory (Robinson 1949). Male and female Bluebird engage in a frenzy of warbling during courtship (Thomas 1946a). Possibly there is mutual song during Dipper courtship but the sound of the streams frequented by the birds often makes it difficult to determine whether the female contributes notes when the birds are together.

SONG DURING NESTING PRELIMINARIES

In some species the male selects the nest-site and may build part or all of the nest, though he does not line it; in others the female selects and builds. The male may indicate a site to the female, which she may or may not choose. This occurs most often in species which breed in a cavity or use a covered nest constructed by the cock. In very few species the female indicates proposed sites to the male. Sometimes male and female prospect together. In all these procedures song may be used. Examples follow of nest-prospecting when no nest or nest-cavity already exists, when such a cavity has been located by the male and, perhaps to a minor extent, been prepared or made attractive to the female, and when a nest or substructure has been built by the male. Clear-cut lines of distinction between these procedures cannot be drawn.

XI. Nightingale singing and displaying to his mate
brooding newly hatched chicks

XII*a*. Skylark singing in flight

XII*b*. Whooper Swans calling and displaying after their migratory flight
from the north in October

Nest-site prospecting and selection song

In some species mated birds sing sub-song while prospecting for a nest-site. Mated Cardinals thus engaged utter 'almost inaudible trills' (Laskey 1944a). Scottish Crossbills sing as they look for a suitable place to nest. A male was seen to place a twig in a crotch, but the female, singing softly, did not accept the invitation. The cock Twite guides the female and sings while she examines the proposed site. After the male Linnet has selected a site he displays to the hen, singing rather like a Violet-eared Waxbill (Nethersole-Thompson and Nethersole-Thompson 1943; Wharton-Tigar 1946). Prospecting Brown Thrashers sing whisper song and various Central American flycatchers sing while examining possible sites. Such songs may elicit songs from neighbouring pairs of related species (Skutch 1951a).

The motivation of such muted songs is little understood. 'Low-intensity' song, unlike low-intensity activities of other kinds, cannot be assumed to be due to low motivation, indeed it may be uttered when birds appear to be in a state of suppressed excitement and may well be subject to conflicting motivation. The semi-repressed type of utterance characteristic of many sexual contexts may be an expression of escape-attack-attraction motivation such as is believed to be responsible for much epigamic display. It may thus be a form of 'compromise activity' (Armstrong 1949). Blackbirds, when disturbed while singing sub-song, will perform displacement bill-wiping, suggestive of a tense state. If we may argue from what is known of the Red-backed Shrike's song development some such songs may be, in structure, a reversion to a form of developmental, juvenile song. At least some of these songs manifest several of the characteristics of sub-song as defined by Thorpe and Pilcher (1958) (p. 58). Some of them appear to be communicatory, others not. Nearly everybody is familiar with the subdued snatches of song uttered by Robins while perched watching a person engaged in digging. There are similarities to the types of song mentioned and both appear to be due to a 'damping' of song due to incipient action, nest-building, or seizing prey as the case may be. It would not be difficult for song originating in some such way to become ritualized and acquire signal functions.

In general ground-nesting birds select the site without much ceremonial, except when 'scrape-making' forms part of the display (Armstrong 1947). Such birds have a wider choice of sites than cavity-nesting species and conspicuous songs or calls during site selection might increase the vulnerability of some species unduly. Some male ground-nesting buntings merely utter a nest-site call similar to the solicitation note (Andrew 1956–57). In contrast to the procedure of birds belonging to the genus *Sylvia* the female in the phylloscopid warblers builds the nest and is not attracted to a partly-built structure. In the first-named group the nest is usually in bushes, in the second the domed nest is usually on or very near the ground. The most that the male does seems to be occasionally to 'suggest' a site. The cock Crested Lark walks around and calls loudly at suitable sites, crouches, and bows to the hen (Barrett *et al.* 1948).

Greenshanks seeking a site for the nest visit different parts of the cock's territory, the female uttering a sobbing cry, the male singing his wild notes. He leads the female from one likely spot to another and the decision rests with her (Nethersole-Thompson 1951). The hen Red-necked Phalarope selects the site. From time to time she makes the wing-burring again—for it ceases when the male joins the female. She then flies off with him to one of the scrapes she has made. Thus he knows where the eggs are laid and is able to take charge in due course (Tinbergen 1935). Although the Nightjar makes no nest the male repeatedly attracts the female to the site proposed for egg-laying, uttering a soft, continuous, rolling note and scraping vigorously with both feet (Heinroth 1909).

Nest-cavity invitation songs

Nocturnal birds which nest in cavities use nest-invitation calls. The Little Owl 'sings' while flying around the nesting-place and the male Tengmalm's Owl calls continuously from a hole in a tree. He also courtship-feeds the female at the proposed site, carrying prey for her to eat and so stimulates her to take up residence (Haverschmidt 1946; Stadler 1932; Kuhk 1943, 1949). Leach's Fork-tailed Petrels call at night from the burrows they have excavated or occupied. Thus the females are attracted. The procedure of some other petrels is similar.

Green Woodpeckers call to one another from trees as much as 500 metres apart. Apparently the tree from which the female calls is usually chosen as the site for excavating the nest (Blume 1955, 1957, 1958). Female Red-bellied and Red-headed Woodpeckers join in mutual tapping with the male, apparently to indicate approval of the site for nesting. Pileated Woodpeckers have an analogous procedure (Kilham 1958, 1959a, b, 1960) (Fig. 27).† Pair-formation among Rock Doves depends on the securing of a suitable site by the male. Nearby he utters an alluring call but like some other birds which call for a female, such as the Heron, he is apt to attack her when she first approaches (Heinroth 1948). An Australian species, the Spotted Pardalote, uses a distinctive call to attract the female to the nest-site, which is in a burrow (Roberts 1953). While the female Snow Finch perches or moves about close at hand the cock investigates crevices among boulders. A male was seen to enter many holes until at last he found one which appeared to be satisfactory. He sang inside. Then the female joined him and spent a long time within (Lang 1946).

Male House Sparrows perch near crevices, chirping incessantly, thus advertising nest-sites which they have appropriated, and to which they are anxious to introduce a female (Daanje 1941; Summers-Smith 1955). The Great Tit's display is more elaborate. Accompanied by a female the cock approaches the entrance to his cavity or nest-box. He may look inside and tap the sides or twist his head so that the hen, feeding close by, is able to see the contrasting markings. This pecking, which is sometimes quite loud, may, perhaps, be the survival of an ancestral impulse to hack

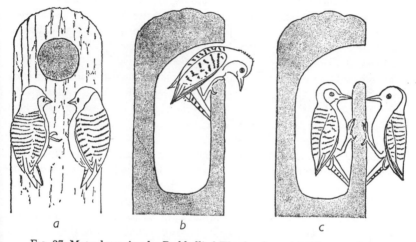

a   *b*   *c*

FIG. 27. Mutual tapping by Red-bellied Woodpeckers. (a) When starting a new nesting-hole the pair tap together outside; (b) the mate calls from his roost in the nesting cavity at dawn; (c) he begins to tap inside as his mate alights and she joins in the tapping. (After Kilham 1958)

out a cavity, as is the practice of the Willow Tit. As usually performed it has display significance. If the female does not approach he may fly out and back again. As she draws closer to the entrance she quivers her wings with increasing vigour. The male song, uttered outside the box while waiting for the female, differs from the form characteristic of territorial altercations (Hinde 1952). The male Nuthatch shows the nest-hole to the female and becomes mated should she accept (Löhrl 1958).

There are similarities between the nest-indication displays of the Redstart, Pied, Collared, and Semi-collared Flycatchers. The plumage of the males presents strong contrasts. In particular, the colour patterns on the head and breast are conspicuous as the bird looks out of a hole. The cock flies back and forth ostentatiously, clings to the outside of the proposed nesting-site, or goes in and out. Their singing adds to their conspicuousness. A cock Redstart, accompanied by a female, will sing loudly while flying to the nest-site or even while hovering in front of it with tail fanned. At intervals, when he emerges from the hole, or before entering, he utters a stanza (Buxton 1950). Similarly, Pied Flycatchers take possession of holes and defend them. They enter and emerge from time to time and the male may lay the foundation of the nest. When a female appears the proprietor leads the way ostentatiously, clings with quivering wings at the entrance, and utters sharp squeaks and quiet, stifled songs (von Haartman 1949, 1951). Such songs indicate high stimulation. They may be heard from inside the cavity and when the female indicates her readiness for coition; also as transference song during fights with rivals or other birds and when raptors fly over (Creutz 1955; Curio 1959a) (p. 132). The nest-invitation displays of the Collared and Semi-collared Flycatchers are of the same type (Löhrl 1951; Curio 1959b). In contrast the Spotted Flycatcher nests on a ledge or recess rather than inside a hole. The male may build 'cock's nests'. He makes little aerial sallies, visible a long way off, uttering a call-note until a female appears and then sings softly (Gooch 1938). In the flycatchers contrasting plumage, hole-nesting, nest-indication, and a tendency to polygamy are associated. It would seem that resort to cavities for nesting has resulted in convergence in an integrated group of adaptations with some divergence in the associated adornments. The Spotted Flycatcher is exceptional in having dull coloration and in possessing these other characteristics to a minor extent.

The Black Wheatear creates a breastwork of pebbles in front of the nest. It is doubtful whether this is effective in concealing the nest and sitting bird but the carrying of the stones appears to be part of a nest-invitation display which is preceded and followed by a song-flight (Ferguson-Lees 1960b). Possibly the pebble-paving at the entrance to the Rock Wren's nest may be explained similarly (Bent 1948).

Nest-invitation songs

In the species mentioned the males invite the females to an already existent cavity but some cock birds sing to guide a potential mate to the already constructed foundation of nest. Among these are the Blackcap, Garden Warbler, Whitethroat, Lesser Whitethroat, and Dartford Warbler. There is little difference between the procedures of the two first-named. The cock arrives about a fortnight before the female, secures a territory, and sings vigorously. He builds frail platforms in bushes near to his favourite song-perches—sometimes as many as seven and even building another after one has been chosen. The longer he remains unmated the more work he may do on his nests and the larger they become. When a female joins a male she flies to where he is singing near a nest-platform and he begins displaying, drooping and flapping his wings and spreading his tail. His song changes to sub-song and he flies to the actual nest-site and utters a few phrases of the normal territorial song. The female follows and stays to inspect his handiwork while he returns to his song-perch and sings a variant of the usual song which may last as long as half a minute. The cock may also utter a plaintive call-note to induce the hen to follow. When she is at the site she fidgets with some of the material and perhaps adds one or more scraps if she approves of it. A Garden Warbler may sit on the structure and do some building. A female has been observed to inspect two cocks' nests and reject them both. She departed, and the cock, unable to attract another, went away after a fortnight. On choosing a platform the hen does practically all the work in completing it. She may remove some of the material provided by the cock. When the nest has been approved the male's out-lying song-stations are abandoned and the territory contracts to a smaller area around the nest (Raines 1945). Sexual selection operates to some extent in these nest-indicating and -preparing species as males in less favourable habitats with second-rate nests or nest-sites are less successful in mating (Armstrong 1955).

Many species have a nest-site call. A number of Australian species sing and posture at the nest—White-faced Herons, Magpie-Larks, and Willie Wagtails. The latter will sing and display at the site for weeks without building more than a platform (Robinson 1949). Darwin's finches utter crude songs as they fly to and from nesting-sites. The males carry material ostentatiously to these sites and there vibrate or flap their wings but they may borrow the nests of other individuals, or even of other species, for their display (Lack 1947). This undiscriminating behaviour and lack of obvious distinctiveness in the songs are an outcome of living in an environment where there was no competition from other avian groups and practically no predation. Conspicuous, prolonged display, song, or calling at a nest-site are most characteristic of birds which for one reason or another are not thereby exposed to great hazards from predators—island- and cliff-nesting birds, large species nesting in tall trees and, perhaps, to some extent, Australian species exempt from the attacks of predatory placental mammals.

In comparatively few species does the male complete the nest structure before obtaining a mate. Most such species are polygamous to some extent. A number of the weavers build several nests to which the male invites females in turn by singing, displaying, and calling. The polygamous Penduline Tit builds more than one nest but behaviour is variable and I have seen a female helping with the work. The cock perches, singing, close to or inside the nest (Burckhardt 1948). The Wren tends to be monogamous in bleak areas but polygamous and apt to build as many

as ten or a dozen nests in favourable habitats. Usually the cock builds
and attracts females to his nests—in the first instance by his territorial
song. Singing strophes of varying length, intensity, and pattern he goes
from twig to twig enticing the hen towards one of his nests. The song is
sweet, subdued, and sometimes sustained into a long ripple of melody
but now and then it breaks out loudly, approximating to the territorial
song. The female follows demurely, apparently taking little interest.
When the male reaches the nest he perches on a twig outside, pouring
forth a delightfully sweet shadow-song as he stands with vibrating wings
like a cloak around him and widely fanned tail (Pl. IX). He pops inside,
then out again to sing and display. Eventually the hen creeps in while he
performs excitedly outside. He may even accompany her inside. If the
nest is to her liking she lines it with feathers. She may inspect more than
one nest before her choice is made (Armstrong 1955). Her decision to
stay in a territory is apparently determined to a considerable extent by
the suitability of the nests available. We have already noted that a
Garden Warbler may leave a male, apparently because of his unsatisfactory nest-platforms. A related form of sexual selection has been
recorded in Jackson's Whydah. Van Someren (1946) found that if the
central tuft of grass were removed from the male's dancing ground
females would not alight. He concluded that 'the tuft possessed more significance to the hen than the cock'. Thus in some species the male's success
in leaving progeny depends on his nest-building efficiency and in others
on his selection and preparation of an appropriate display court.

The House Wren's nest-invitation is of a somewhat similar type to that
of the Wren (Kendeigh 1941a) though in this species the male prepares
a foundation in a cavity. There are parallels in the Cactus Wren's behaviour but nest-invitation is less pronounced as the pair occupy a territory together throughout the winter. At least sometimes the female
lays eggs in her mate's roosting nest. The male sings and utters a whining
call outside the nest, and sometimes inside (Anderson and Anderson
1957, 1959).

Nest-building song

Nest-building song is unusual as in very many species only the female
builds, and song by females is relatively rare (p. 175). Also, song in
such circumstances dissipates energy and might betray the nest to predators. Australian Willie Wagtails visit nest-sites with material for about
a month and their carolling then is without the aggressive quality of
territorial song (Robinson 1949). At intervals while working on the nest
the male East Coast Grosbeak Weaver perches close by and trills on two
notes (Sclater and Moreau 1933). Females of the American and Lawrence
Goldfinch warble while busy on the nest (Berger 1953; Linsdale 1950);

but the hen Chaffinch merely utters a faint *chink* as she brings material. While the cock King Quail gathers grass to form a hood over the nest he gives a vibrant ventriloquial call similar to that which, later on, he uses to attract the chicks to take caterpillars (Tarr 1948a). Skutch (1948a, b) remarks that the construction of the nest calls forth song or calls from trogons, jacamars, and other birds. A cock Nuthatch sings vigorously near where his mate is building and thus renders it easy for a naturalist to locate the nest (Löhrl 1958). The male Wren sings in an intermittent way while building. A human observer, or a female Wren, may thus discover what he is doing. I have known a female creep close to a singing male while he worked and distract him from building. It may be advantageous for female Wrens thus to discover where nests are situated, for not only may they make a better choice of which nest of several to select for the first clutch, but probably they are able to remember such nests as potential dormitories for the fledged young or suitable sites for a later brood. In a wide variety of species the male perches singing as he watches the female build. His song seems to express pent-up excitement but it may also stimulate her and strengthen the *rapport* between them.

Incubation song

In spite of the danger of drawing attention to the nest by singing during incubation birds of a number of species do so—though usually quietly. Indeed, the song uttered on the nest may often be called 'whisper song'. Although some strongly territorial birds sing thus the practice seems to be more characteristic of passerines without a loud, elaborate territorial song, such as various birds of the Crow family. The incubating female Carrion Crow emits a very subdued 'crackling' song sustained for several minutes, and the Hooded Crow, Jackdaw, and Jay warble in a somewhat similar way. The Jackdaw's song ripples quietly along and includes mimicries. The Rook's has been compared to a 'bass or guttural reproduction of the varied and spluttering song of the Starling' (Witherby *et al.* 1938). Female Wrens occasionally utter an extremely quiet whisper song while sitting (Armstrong 1955) and House Martins sing in the nest at first light. The Blackcap sometimes warbles in the nest. Exceptionally a Reed Warbler will sing loudly on the nest (Hosking and Smith 1943). A number of Australian passerines sing nest-songs (Wolstenholme 1926). The female of some species, such as wrens and trogons, answers her mate with a low note from the nest (Skutch 1942, 1953). Probably this is more characteristic of birds in the tropics and other regions with mild winters where many species maintain the pair-bond for more than one season.

Nests of the American Goldfinch may be found by listening for the bird singing while building or incubating. The Warbling Vireo may also betray the nest by singing on it (Berger 1953). The cock Catbird sings on the nest for minutes at a time and the incubating female replies with a beautiful sub-song (Whittle 1923; Palmer 1949). The Cardinal also carols on the nest in answer to her mate (Laskey 1944a), and the Orange-billed Sparrow sings on the eggs (Skutch 1954). Rose-breasted and Black-headed Grosbeaks sing while incubating or brooding young (Ivor 1944; Weston 1947). The Brown Thrasher sings softly and sweetly on the nest as a signal to the male to incubate (Thomas 1952). Moreau (1949) noticed that an incubating female Paradise Flycatcher sang a much thinner song than her mate when another male approached. A strange male approaching an incubating Greenshank may elicit 'song' (Nethersole-Thompson 1951).

These instances show that singing on the eggs has signal significance in some species but not in others. Thus generalization as to its motivation would be out of place. It may sometimes be due to tension when the impulses to leave the nest and to continue incubating are in conflict but the only evidence indicating that such song is apt to be sung when tension is liable to be strongest concerns the species in which it operates as a signal to the bird's mate that it is time to be relieved. On the other hand many of these sub-songs are uttered at times when the bird appears to be in a state of contentment. In regard to pattern some incubation songs are more or less modified forms of the territorial song of the species but others bear little or no resemblance to it and, as we have seen, incubation songs are uttered by some species not possessing a territorial song.*

Song during nest-relief

Some of the songs mentioned might be considered nest-relief songs but this type of utterance, which often has communicatory significance, is heard from other species besides those which sing an incubation song. A cock Reed Warbler uttered 'a very low inward warbling' near the nest when he came to take the place of his mate (Brown and Davies 1949). Male and female Rose-breasted Grosbeaks sing signal songs, shorter and fainter than territorial song, on such occasions (Allen 1916; Ivor 1944). When the male Nightjar changes places with the incubating female he flies in with a strange *quaw-ee* call and she replies with soft churring. They squat side by side swaying and churring. Suddenly the female departs, leaving her mate on the eggs (Selous 1905). Many birds also engage in mutual calling or posturing when they meet at the nest (p. 181). A Common Sandpiper sang sub-song during nest-relief (Morrison 1949).

* It has been suggested that perhaps the reduction of song during incubation is due to an increased rate of prolactin secretion and a corresponding reduction of androgen output (Eisner 1960) but the Rufous-sided Towhee's song decreases after the young hatch without any testis regression (Davis 1958) and the sudden accentuation of song by the males of many species when the nest comes to grief (Fig. 36) shows that in such circumstances environmental stimuli are of paramount importance.

Terek Sandpipers make a 'soft and sweet warbling noise' during the change-over, while the young are being brooded and also during threat display at other species (Ferguson-Lees 1959). For variety of circumstances in which such song may be evoked comparison may be made with the Wren which sings whisper song when brooding, feeding young, or leading them from the nest or to a roost; also when going to roost and occasionally when fighting (p. 62). In both species whisper song while threatening might be considered displacement song (p. 132). Displacement activities due to conflicting impulses are common at the change-over and probably in some species the motivation of song on such occasions is somewhat similar.

Species too numerous to mention utter a signal song or call which indicates the arrival of the male near the nest. The Song Sparrow sings a specialized form of song on these occasions but the Rufous-sided Towhee does not. The call of the latter is more important than the song in attracting the female from the nest (Nice 1937; Davis 1960).

Song while tending young

The female Grey-capped Flycatcher frequently hums a churring nest-song or calls to her mate while she incubates but when the young hatch she sings no more for a time. A little later she sings a version of the male's dawn song when feeding the nestlings. Sometimes this feeding-song may convey to the male that the young have emerged from the eggs. He also utters a feeding-song when attending to their needs (Skutch 1953). A Rufous Song Lark has been photographed singing at the nest (Pl. X). The two mates of a Hick's Seedeater increased the frequency and intensity of their song when the young hatched (Gross 1952). Polyandry of this kind is unusual in birds (Armstrong 1964) as is also the increase of song at this phase. The Madagascar Magpie-Robin utters song on arriving at the nest (Van Someren 1947) and a female Greenfinch has been heard warbling as she stood over the young (Ferguson-Lees 1943). Various birds sing snatches as they approach or leave the nest (p. 168).† The Song Sparrow sings after carrying away the faeces. Sometimes song at the nest is evoked by the presence of the female rather than the young. Turner (1929) wrote : 'I have never seen a bird so brimful of emotion as a male Nightingale that I watched at close quarters for a week. On the day the young were hatched the male only brought food. Each time he visited his brooding mate he sang such a song as I had never heard before. His beak was full of juicy grubs for the family but this did not hinder him from pouring out a stream of liquid bubbling notes so soft and sweet that they were inaudible six feet away' (Pl. XI). A cock Wren, ready to initiate another brood, sings and quivers his wings near the nest while holding food, as this Nightingale did, so we may assume that the bird's motivation was sexual rather than parental. The female Wren was engaged in feeding the young (Pl. IX).

Song when tending young may be communicatory in some species and circumstances and not in others. Probably the medley of low notes uttered by a female Greenshank and the soft whistle of a Stone Curlew as the young hatch convey information to them (Simms 1958). Such sounds may stimulate the chicks and facilitate the establishment of *rapport*. The very subdued twittering of the female Wren as she stands with food over the nestlings before their eyes open may be assumed to alert them to beg, and later, when similar notes are uttered as a gush of twittering sub-song as the parent arrives at the nest, this would seem to be their function. The Nuthatch emits similar soft chirps while feeding the nestlings (Löhrl 1958). Probably sub-calls or sub-song of this kind are characteristic of many birds which rear young where visibility is poor. Unless one can put an ear to the nest they may pass unnoticed.

Saunders (1929) refers to young House Wrens being stimulated to open their bills by the male's song. Some young birds may be conditioned to beg by the repetition of sounds quite different from those made by the parents. The very subdued song of the Grey-capped Flycatcher when beginning to bring larger morsels to the nest probably serves as a signal to the nestlings (Skutch 1953).

Song when young leave nest

A female Wren sometimes leads the young into the wider world uttering the whisper song. In some species the male becomes stimulated by the departure of the young and expresses himself in song. While I watched young Redwings fledging at midnight in Lapland the male sang from time to time in a small tree overhead. A cock Partridge 'went wild with excitement' on peeping into the nest and seeing the newly-hatched young (Hosking and Newberry 1940).

Roosting song

Male Wrens leading young to the roost utter snatches of song which provide clues enabling them to follow. This procedure is very similar to the male's behaviour in leading a prospective mate to the nest. Females utter the whisper song when inducing the newly-fledged birds to enter the roost. Wrens also sing at dusk in winter when they gather to seek a communal roost. This constitutes a rallying song with significance for males and females. It sounds like a rather weak and imperfect territorial song though it resembles the full song fairly closely. Thus on such occasions song differing little from the territorial song has the effect of attracting males and not, as one might expect, repelling them. Their response approximates to that of females. There is a similar functional change in the aggressive call of the Chukar Partridge which serves to repel intruders during the breeding season but later becomes a rallying call (Stokes 1961).

One of the most familiar rallying calls to be heard in some parts of the English countryside is the creaking of Partridges at dusk. Those acquainted with Asian hillsides will recall the rather similar calls of Francolin. The mellow, fluting dusk song of the Chestnut-headed Tinamou in the forest of Central America is of heart-stirring beauty—perhaps the loveliest curfew in the animal world (Armstrong 1940).

The most striking examples of roosting song are those in which large flocks are concerned. Starlings not only make a chattering hub-bub at the sleeping quarters but also sing and call on trees *en route* to the roost. With some such species it is difficult to decide where the difference lies between songs and calls.

Autumnal song

It need not be stressed further that some birds utter song practically all the year round. Usually there is a cessation or great diminution during the moult. Autumnal song may be of regular occurrence, as in the Robin and Song Thrush, or exceptional, as in the Chaffinch. Of course autumn and winter song may be more frequent in the milder regions of a bird's range than where conditions are more severe. Autumnal song is usually less vigorous than spring song though a few North American species sing the full song in the 'fall' (Saunders 1929). When the output of autumnal or winter song by resident species reaches an amount approximating to the output of spring song it is usually territorial but there are quite a number of birds whose autumnal song has not been shown to have territorial significance. Whether it is effectively functional as communication is doubtful. At least in some species it appears to be non-communicatory and a by-product of gonadal activity. When the Red-backed Shrike sings the call-song at the end of the breeding season it has lost its attractive function for the female does not respond to it (Blase 1960). As long ago as 1802 Montagu realized that there was a connexion between the development of song and the state of the sexual organs. He wrote: 'Birds in song are generally found to have the *testes* somewhat dilated.'

In general, autumnal and winter song seem to be expressions of a physiological condition giving rise to behaviour including the belligerent component but usually without the courtship motivation of spring song. They are forms of low-intensity breeding-season behaviour. Probably the autumn display of Blackcock (Lack 1939b) and the late-season defence of territory by Pectoral Sandpipers (Hamilton 1959) are visual expressions of comparable states. Aggressive display occurs without courtship posturing. Similarly, outside the breeding season semi-territorial threat behaviour is exhibited by Black-headed Gulls. It can be considered incipient territorial pair-formation (Franck 1959).

As Bullough (1942) pointed out, it is significant that not only do male Starlings and Robins sing and hold territories in autumn but females also do so to some extent. When the amount of male sex hormone in the male Starling's blood rises above a certain point his beak begins to turn yellow, he sings loudly, and behaves in other respects as is appropriate before breeding. Apparently when the content of male sex hormone in the female's blood exceeds that of female sex hormone she also sings. In Rooks there is a post-nuptial period of testis reorganization with interstitial development which precedes the autumnal sexual flights and the refurbishing of nests. Similar development is correlated with the singing of the Robin in autumn. Commenting on these facts Marshall (1952b) remarks that the new generation of endocrine Leydig cells 'appear to secrete sufficiently to stimulate the late summer and autumn display of many species'. Stieve (1950) found spermatocytes in the gonads of Black Grouse displaying in autumn and also in the undeveloped gonads of some species of autumn-singing birds.

The relationship between the state of the gonads and behaviour, including song, is complex because of the reciprocity between physiological and psychological factors. The work of Lehrman (1959) has elucidated this relationship in the breeding cycle of doves. Davis (1958) discussing the Rufous-sided Towhee, remarks that 'the appearance and disappearance of song, height of singing perch, complexity of song, amount of singing, time of awakening song, and times of first and last vocalizing of the day relative to sunrise and sunset all show variation which correlates either with the onset and progression of the gonad cycle, or with a given individual's status in the breeding season'. Independently of gonadal development the amount of singing varies as between mated and unmated males. Events during the breeding cycle may have a marked influence on song (Fig. 36). Out of the breeding season the song of a Chaffinch, artificially induced by injections, may stimulate a wild bird to sing (p. 49). When a male of this species in my garden came into song again immediately after he had lost his brood a neighbour who had also abandoned song began to sing against him.

The diminution and cessation of song in Rufous-sided Towhees, as in other species, is correlated with gonadal regression and the moult, but autumn song by individual Towhees is not linked with gonadal recrudescence in adults although there is evidence that in a few first-year males the gonads may become slightly active in autumn. On examination of some of these birds' gonads a number of Leydig cells were found. Perhaps these birds were hatched early in the season. In some other species, such as the White-crowned Sparrow (Blanchard 1941) no gonadal activity has been detected. Similarly the decrease in song by Rufous-sided Towhees in April does not seem to be correlated with changes in the gonads but with environmental stimuli.

Migratory song

No hard and fast distinction can be drawn between autumnal song and autumnal migratory song. In Hungary Starlings assemble in large flocks to roost communally prior to migrating, but before setting out they return to their nesting-places to sing 'a short good-bye song' (Pátkai 1939). It seems that at this season there is a slight recrudescence of the physiological state attained in spring. Skylarks, Reed Warblers, Willow Warblers, Chiffchaffs, and White-throated Sparrows are among the species which sing as they move southwards after breeding.

As the time for the spring migration approaches birds in their winter quarters tend to begin singing or to do so more persistently and vigorously. Probably the gonads are already active and there is hormonal discharge during this phase. Before departing Redwings burst into subsong (Perry 1946). According to Chapman (1942) Trumpeter Swans utter a special song prior to starting for the north. They sing all night with a peculiar cadence to rhyme with the words 'going over the river' which they repeat over and over again. The next morning they start in a body leaving only the weaker individuals behind to build up strength to follow (Pl. XII).†

The Blackcap, Chiffchaff, Icterine, and Melodious Warblers are among species which sing before leaving winter quarters in Africa. In the two first-mentioned species this is not associated with pairing or territory (Rooke 1947). Many Palaearctic migrants sing in Egypt, though typical territorial song hardly occurs and only three species are known certainly to pair before proceeding northwards (Moreau and Moreau 1928). Various passerines sing passing through Malta and Heligoland (Gätke 1896; Gibb 1951). Greenland Wheatears perform their display-flight on Lundy (Perry 1940) and Willow Warblers, Chiffchaffs, and Nightingales sing as they filter northwards or loiter for a day in a coppice. Sand Martins twitter freely on spring passage and some northing American warblers, such as the Myrtle Warbler, sing a 'characterless song' (Saunders 1929). Many Palaearctic species are silent for a short time when they arrive where they will establish territory. This may occur when there are cold spells but a bird about to settle in a territory tends to act in a quiet, secretive way at first. What has been observed of House Wrens may be generally true—there is more song as the birds approach nearer to their destination. When they first arrive mature House Wrens sing imperfect and incomplete songs, loud but of untypical pattern (Kendeigh 1941a). Purple Finches utter rambling songs before they move to the nesting areas.

When actually flying on the migratory journey characteristic call-notes are uttered (Tyler 1916).† During the phase of migratory restlessness a Baltimore Oriole perched with whirring wings uttering a note not heard in other circumstances, her eyes wide open but unconscious of persons near her (Pugsley 1946). In similar circumstances a Cuckoo 'became lost in a kind of trance with eyes open and wings ceaselessly moving. The bird became, as it were, locked in the passion of that sense by which the movements of flying were simulated' (Kidd 1921). Birds flying up to lighthouses on misty nights are apt to utter snatches which may, perhaps, be regarded as 'excitement' or 'hostility' song.

Winter song

Singing in winter by resident birds of temperate regions, such as the Tawny Owl, Robin, Dipper, and Wren, usually indicates the retention of territory (p. 122). In some species, including the three former, the Mockingbird, and Nuttall (White-crowned) Sparrow, the female also sings. The fact that when a common winter territory is held both sexes tend to defend it with song supports the view that there is a connexion between song and the availability of food in the territory, for we may assume it to be adaptive that ground necessary for subsistence should be defended. Contact song is important in winter.

There is a good deal of desultory song by Palaearctic migrants in Africa (Bannerman 1930–51). The Nightingale sings persistently in Nigeria though not exuberantly as in the breeding season (Serle 1957). It also sings well in the southern Congo. There the Whitethroat sings in a lively way, the Icterine Warbler finely, and the Great Reed Warbler in snatches (Lynes 1938). The Lesser Whitethroat sings regularly in Egypt (Nicoll 1930). Verheyen (1953) maintains that most migrants to Africa establish territories for a short period, defending them with vocalizations, though the songs may be subdued or fragmentary. The domains of these birds are believed to be smaller than spring territories. During the moult song ceases but afterwards the birds begin to sing again as their testes increase in size.

As has already been mentioned (p. 123) some chats maintain territories in arid areas in winter and the White Wagtail sings at that season in Egypt (Hartley 1946, 1949, 1950a). In rare instances birds normally nesting in the north may breed in their winter quarters as Swallows and White Storks have done in South Africa. The Hermit Thrush is in full voice for about a week in its winter quarters but sings only rarely and crudely during the migration (Saunders 1929).

X

FEMALE SONG, DUETTING, AND
CORPORATE SONG

The hen did walk in a four-fold method towards her
chickens: 1. She had a common call, and that she hath all
day long. 2. She had a special call, and that she had but
sometimes. 3. She had a brooding note. And, 4. She had an
outcry.
                                JOHN BUNYAN. *Pilgrim's Progress.*

THE traditional poetic fancy that the female bird sings has been
so thoroughly discredited that it is now necessary to emphasize
that many female birds do sing. Indeed, there is so much evidence
of regular, occasional, exceptional, and artificially induced song by
females that we may assume that at least a tendency to sing is latent in
hen song-birds of very many species. The potential songfulness of the
female has been suppressed because among birds, as in human society,
division of labour is advantageous. In particular, when the male establishes and defends territory with song his mate is left free to concentrate
on egg-laying and incubation—and also, in many species, nest-building
and much of the foraging for the young. There is a general tendency for
the male to cooperate with the female as the nesting cycle proceeds and
to reduce activities, such as territorial singing, which in the earlier
phases differentiate his activities from those of the female. Thus the
responsibilities of each are more efficiently performed than if all duties
were shared. Territorial song is a dominant element in the pattern of
breeding activities which renders division of labour advantageous in
many song-birds.

Although differentiation of rôles has been carried so far among birds
—as, for example, to an extreme in the feeding of the female on the nest
by hornbills—plasticity of behaviour has been retained by many species
to such an extent that one sex may, if necessity should arise, undertake
the rôle of the other. There are species in which responsibilities are determined inflexibly to an extent that can be disadvantageous. For example,
male Pigeons will not brood when it is the female's turn to do so, while,
on the other hand, in some other species in which the male normally
gives little attention to the chicks he may succeed in rearing them if his
mate disappears. Females which do not normally build nests and males

175

which do not usually incubate may, on occasion, do so (Armstrong 1955; Snow 1958). In view of such facts it is not surprising that, in species in which the male usually does all the singing, exceptional females may also develop this capacity. Superstitions concerning crowing hens show that country folk have long realized that masculinization may occur in domestic fowl.

> Poule qui chante, Prêtre qui danse,
> Et Femme qui parle latin,
> N'arrivent jamais à bon fin.

Female song may be divided into four categories with respect to territory—though, of course, non-territorial song occurs : (1) The female, but not the male, normally sings and in some instances defends territory (Red-necked Phalarope and perhaps the Painted Snipe and a few other species); (2) the female sings and defends territory alone (for part of the year) or with the male (Robin, Mockingbird, Loggerhead Shrike, California Shrike, White-crowned Sparrow); (3) the female sings as well, or nearly as well, as the male but the song is concerned as much or more with the relationship between the sexes than the defence of territory (Bullfinch, Crossbill, Swallow, some vireos. In many non-songbirds both sexes are equally vocal); (4) the female sings exceptionally, as in old age, when isolated, injected with male hormones, or suffering from some physiological peculiarity (Chaffinch, Canary, Song Sparrow, Blackbird, Domestic Fowl, Jackdaw) (cf. Nice 1943).

The species in which the female sings and the male does not are all birds with the normal rôles of the sexes reversed to greater or lesser extent—the Coucal, Red-necked Phalarope, Painted Snipe, Variegated Tinamou, button quails, and Emu, but song in most of these tends to be comparatively simple and in some territorialism is weak (Armstrong 1961). The Red-necked Phalarope is the most extreme of a number of waders in which the male occupies himself to a very considerable extent with domestic duties. A review of the behaviour and ecology of species in which sex-rôles are reversed suggests that this may be an adaptation to lack of availability of food or intermittent supplies. In theory, where food is not readily obtainable females debilitated by egg-laying would be best able to replenish their energy by feeding actively if the males were to undertake incubation.

The advantages consequent upon the female defending a territory of her own for part of the year, as the Robin does, are not easily discerned and it has been argued that autumn and winter territories serve no useful end. As has already been indicated, this is difficult to believe. Perhaps female territorialism of this kind introduces a competitive element into the spacing of the birds and is a factor in a selective process eliminating the less vigorous or tending to extend distribution into marginal areas.

In some species, particularly the dippers, territories which are defended with song and threat displays by both sexes must be essential to the pairs as foraging areas (Eggebrecht 1937; Vogt 1944; Bakus 1959a, b). Male and female Mockingbird maintain the winter territory with song, calls, and aggressive activities. The male's mate of the early part of the year may or may not remain with him to defend the territory. Both sexes of Loggerhead Shrike, Wren-tit, and Robin sing or give similar calls in defending winter territory—areas which may be of importance as sources of food.

A female may share the song-defence of the territory to some extent with her mate (Lack 1939a) but usually hen birds which hold territory in autumn and winter do not sing much when breeding. The female Mockingbird seldom helps to maintain the breeding territory. The two mates of a White-crowned Sparrow will each utter strong territorial song and defend her ground against the other (Blanchard 1941). Usually when both birds of a pair defend territory each fights the opponent of its own sex. For example, when a mated hen Cardinal noticed an intruding female singing she drove her away (Laskey 1944a). In this species song is as closely associated with courtship and connubiality as with territory —perhaps more so—and the birds often sing antiphonally.

Female song is relatively common among Australian birds. This may be correlated with climatic conditions which facilitate the maintenance of the pair-bond. The female is active in defending territory with song and the sexes are equally vocal in such species as Bellmagpies, Butcher-birds, and Willie Wagtails. These species are usually permanent territory holders (Robinson 1949). Male and female Rufous Whistler engage in songful territorial disputes, two or three birds contributing threads of melody which mingle into a web of sound. This singing breaks out only when a female participates (Erickson 1951).

Not all female birds which sing use their song in defending territory. An exceptional female Wood Thrush sang not only from the nest rim but from outside the breeding territory 'by mistake' (Brackbill 1948). The male Nuttall White-crowned Sparrow defends his domain with song but when he fights another male his mate postures but does not sing (Blanchard 1941). On the other hand a fight between two male Wren-tits elicited song from the mate of one of them (Erickson 1938).

Subdued female song tends to be characteristic of species with weak territorialism, such as crossbills, cardueline, and estrildine finches. When song acquires high advertising and territorial significance its social importance tends to decrease. Both sexes of Bullfinch sing—as is true of many other species with a long-sustained or permanent pair-bond—but the song is not of great value either in pair-formation or defending terri-tory (Nicolai 1956). The female Baltimore Oriole is a fine songster with a softer voice than the male (Pugsley 1946) but the territorial responses of orioles are apt to be weak and, in the Orchard Oriole, are almost non-existent.

When female song is uttered only by exceptional females it practically always differs to some extent from the male's song but in other species in which female song is usual, such as the Cardinal and Poorwill, the songs of the sexes are indistinguishable (Laskey 1944a; Brauner 1953). In some species in which both sexes are good singers the song may be effective in courtship or connubial situations as well as during territorial or other quarrels. The main distinction between categories (2) and (3) is that in the latter sexual motivation tends to be more prominent.

The interest of category (4) lies in the evidence which exceptional female song provides of latent possibilities of song. Song of this kind is often the expression of endocrine imbalance such as may occur in aged birds. Hens may crow in old age and aviculturists have long been aware that old female Canaries sometimes sing. Very few observations have been made of the development of song by exceptional females in the wild but Snow (1958) was able to follow the fortunes of an aged and particularly dark hen Blackbird. In 1954 her eggs were infertile, in 1955 she built only half a nest and the next year she did not try to nest. In May of that year her mate was killed. Two days later she began to sing in a simple, monotonous way. During the autumn she uttered typical subsong. Apparently while she had a mate the physiological peculiarity which had developed remained suppressed to some extent, and then, on losing him her maleness expressed itself in song. Such instances in which physiological and psychological factors may have influenced one another are of great interest.

In typically territorial birds occasional females may sing a little and yet be sufficiently normal to rear a brood. Several instances of wild hen Chaffinches singing have been recorded. Males sometimes approach singing females, apparently puzzled by their behaviour (Lack 1941b). The mate of such a bird may become confused and attack her. One such female stopped singing after laying the third egg and started again in a desultory way when the nest was robbed (England 1945). At this nest the cock undertook major responsibility for feeding the young and sanitation. He spent much time chevying his mate to her duties but the lives of the chicks were in jeopardy owing to the lack of coordinated activity by the parents in caring for them. In so far as exceptional female song is communicatory it tends to be misleading. Usually it differs from normal territorial song in pattern or intensity, or both. The final flourish was missing from a female Chaffinch's song and instead a few guttural, thrush-like notes were added (Warburg 1941). Another female sometimes attempted ineffectively to sing the final notes (Tucker 1944).

Female Song, Duetting, and Corporate Song

When female Song Sparrows sing it is usually in the period before nest-building. They utter short unmusical songs from higher perches than females normally choose. One such female wandered from male to male and was unduly long in laying the first egg after nest-building. Birds of this type, like hormone-injected females of other species, are unusually aggressive. According to Nice (1943) the song may be 'very loud' and is like the adult male's 'with all the music and variety omitted'. Juvenile females sometimes warble harshly in autumn. A female House Wren defended territory against birds of her own, and even of other, species. She built a nest, laid sterile eggs, but was not observed to sing (Norton 1929). When an exceptional female Wren builds a nest her mate acts as if bewildered (Armstrong 1955).

Ephemeral female song tends to occur early in the breeding cycle but there are exceptions. During their first few days in the breeding area female Marsh Warblers may sing brief, feeble songs (Walpole-Bond 1933). A female Willow Warbler, engaged in pair-formation, stammered a few notes resembling the first attempts at song by young males (Brock 1910). Abnormal, unmusical songs by female Indigo Buntings and Rufous-sided Towhees are confined to the period before nest-building (Nolan 1958a). A female Meadowlark occasionally sang subdued, incomplete songs when preening early in the morning at the peak of the courtship period (Lanyon 1957). In contrast a hen Bicknell's Thrush uttered a frail, hoarse song in response to her mate's song-flight but sang loudly when the eggs hatched (Wallace 1939). The song of a female Wood Thrush was also often elicited by her mate's song. She sang frequently during the laying and incubation periods of two matings but her song declined from brood to brood. The protesting squeaks of young American Robins being ringed also stimulated her to sing (Brackbill 1948). Female Nightingale-Thrushes 'deliver little ghosts of song while approaching or leaving the nest, contemplating the nestlings or in the midst of scolding intruders with a churring note' (Skutch 1960). We are reminded of the Wren's whisper song.

Among the species in which isolated females have been known to sing are the Jackdaw, Cedar Waxwing, Violet-eared Waxbill, Baltimore Oriole, Northern Shrike, and Serin (Nice 1943). Exceptional instances such as these remind us of the delicate inter-relationship of internal and environmental factors which govern the production of song. It would seem that sometimes lack of normal sexual activity may evoke exceptional song from female birds (Gerber 1956).

It is well known that excess male hormone will cause female birds to break into song but we have noted that strong psychological stimuli may elicit song when the physiological condition is not such as would otherwise result in song (p. 49). At the peak of breeding condition

179

suboptimal stimuli will elicit song. Male American Dippers may be induced to sing during the incubation period, when they are normally silent,
by human whistling (Bakus 1959b). The history of the hen Blackbird
already mentioned suggests that psychological factors may inhibit song
for a time in a female with masculine tendencies.

Duetting

Although counter-singing (p. 126)₊ and duetting may bear some
resemblance acoustically the circumstances in which they are uttered are
quite different. Counter-singing is more or less alternate territorial song
by rivals; duetting is mutual or reciprocal song by paired birds. It is a
means whereby contact, *rapport*, and the social bond are maintained.
In counter-singing the songs tend to get 'out of step' whereas in duetting
there is often very precise coordination as there is in the courtship dance
movements of some species of manakin. Again, in counter-singing the
birds sing the same or very similar songs whereas in duetting the utterances may, and commonly do, differ. Probably duetting in many species
has arisen through the elaboration and coordination of the contact notes
uttered by male and female rather than from territorial song. It might be
argued that some duetting consists of reciprocal call-notes rather than
songs but it would be pedantic to deny duetting to be song because of
this.

Duetting may be unison or antiphonal. It has been suggested by Haverschmidt (1947) and Van Tyne and Berger (1959), who list a number of
species in which pairs sing together, that antiphonal singing is not
properly duetting but to regard it as a separate category would be
impractical. In human music, among primitive and sophisticated communities alike, there is antiphonal singing and instrumental music. In
New Guinea natives play flutes antiphonally, one a tone higher than the
other (Bateson 1936). Antiphonal or responsive duetting among birds
may be one of three types : (1) The male's song calls forth a response,
imperfectly coordinated, from the female. (Initiation by the female
is uncommon); (2) the birds sing in regular alternation; (3) the female
adds her utterance so promptly that the utterance sounds like a single
stereotyped song. Her contribution often differs from the male's notes.
Duetting is communicatory and is commonly a form of contact con-
versation. By definition, it is restricted to mated birds, or, in special
circumstances, birds engaged in pair-formation. Instances of learned
song uttered antiphonally are a special case (p. 87). Other utterances
in which birds respond to one another, as in territorial rivalry, parent-
young relationship, or other social relationships are readily distinguishable and may be regarded as dual or corporate utterances of one character
or another according to circumstances.

Mutual displays often include duetting though the sounds made by some birds which display thus, including some storks, gannets and boobies, albatrosses, and other aquatic species, are crude. These mutual ceremonies have an appeasement function. They maintain and consolidate the pair-bond (Armstrong 1947). They are evidently a ritualized compromise between aggressive and fleeing tendencies and are performed mainly by large, well-armed, conspicuous species nesting in exposed or isolated places, such as islands, cliffs, or tall trees—birds in little jeopardy from predators (p. 227) (Pls. XIII, XIV and XVI). Mutual display, with or without duetting, is performed by some diving birds, notably loons (divers) and grebes.

In the courtship displays of some species, particularly the manakins, reciprocal movements and calls amount to a dance with vocal accompaniment. Two male Blue-backed Manakins dance and call in a beautifully coordinated display before the female (Snow 1956b). Among other large birds which perform mutual posturing with each bird contributing vocal accompaniment are Crested Screamers and various cranes. Here only a few species which sing duets can be mentioned.

I have described the mutual ceremonial of Whooper Swans elsewhere (1940): 'Suddenly, for no apparent reason, there is a commotion and one bird of a pair starts in pursuit of an intruder and they flog the water with threshing wings and splattering feet. The partner of the angry bird flaps after him. He desists from the chase, and now the two stately birds swim face to face with tail-feathers erected. A wild clangour rings over the lake as both swans, with beaks raised and gleaming wings uplifted, co-operate in a resonant duet, the pen replying to the quick "honking" of the cob with repeated notes half a tone lower. How wild and glorious is the song of the swans with their exultant throats. They flap their wings and repeatedly dip their necks in sinuous simultaneity, then both rear up in the water. Now they swim together with necks and heads keeping time in a rhythmic forward motion. Sometimes, so perfectly coordinated are the movements, it seems as if there were but one bird, reflected in a mirror. All this time the clamour resounds over the water and away to the ragged hills, but as the activities gradually subside the trumpet-notes lose their rapidity and excited urgency, and soon the birds are swimming placidly some distance apart, the male uttering occasional calls which are immediately answered by the female.'

Hudson (1892) thus describes the greeting display of Red Ovenbirds: 'The first bird, on the appearance of its mate flying to join it, begins to emit loud, measured notes, and sometimes a continuous trill, somewhat metallic in sound; but immediately on the other bird striking in this introductory passage is changed to triplets, strongly accented on the first note, in a *tempo vivace*; while the second bird utters loud single notes in the same time. While thus singing they are facing each other, necks outstretched and tails expanded, the wings of the first bird vibrating rapidly to the rapid utterance, while those of the second bird beat measured time. The finale consists of three or four notes, uttered by the second bird alone, strong and clear in an ascending scale, the last very piercing'. Probably, among British birds, the Dipper's display most nearly approximates to this, though it is not nearly so elaborate. When the female approaches the male his song becomes louder and clearer. Her song is less sweet. One of a pair will snatch at food in the other's bill while both sing (Rankin and Rankin 1940). There are similarities in the display at the nest by Hebridean Wrens but the female is silent and undemonstrative (Armstrong 1953a).

Duetting is commonest in the tropics. Skutch (1946b) writes of Buff-rumped Warblers: 'The male sang a ringing crescendo, loud, mellow and jubilant, and from time to time his mate replied in a full-toned warble so beautiful that, no less than the music of Orpheus, it seemed to possess the power to "draw iron tears down Pluto's cheek". This responsive singing seems to be an example of the forms which lie between the exchange of simple contact notes and stereotyped duetting.

Male and female Ahanta Francolins duet together—usually on moonlit nights—uttering dissimilar calls. Newly-formed pairs are rather inefficient in coordinating their calls but when the birds have been mated some time they synchronize perfectly. During the early phase 'they show acute consciousness of their inability to sing together' (Holman 1947). Skutch (1945b) describes the unison duetting of Blue-throated Green Motmots at dawn. Sometimes one responds from the nesting burrow to the mellow piping of the other already in the open but usually the male waits for his mate and then 'the two sing in unison a single fluid harmony'. Another species which duets in harmony is the Bush Shrike, *Laniarius erythrogaster*. The birds keep time as perfectly as to a conductor's baton. The phrase, uttered as by a single bird, is a harmonious male and female concert. Niethammer (1955) states that only when the sound film of a Bush Shrike performance was run through was it possible to detect that the male began a fraction of a second before the female. She reacted with lightning rapidity even when unable to see her mate.† Other bush shrikes, including the Bokmakierie, are good duettists. The male Zanzibar Boubou gives a powerful fluting call to which the female 'with perfect synchronization replies with a deep groan' (Sclater and Moreau 1933). Madagascar Coucals, *Centropus t. toulou*, duet in perfect unison and the male Madagascar Broad-billed Roller gives a cackling laugh with its companion joining in (Van Someren 1947). Some other rollers, ant-shrikes, Australian butcherbirds and barbets duet. The Great Himalayan Barbet sings *pi-yoo* every two seconds while the female adds her single notes in perfect time but four times as rapidly (Osmaston 1941). In the duetting of butcherbirds and also Magpie Larks male and female are equally vocal. The antiphonal song of the Magpie Lark is uttered with raised wings and spread tail. One calls *te-he* and the other follows with *pee-o-wit* so quickly that it sounds like the utterance of a single bird (Robinson 1946–47). Some species of Australian frogs are also reputed to sing duets (Cobb 1897) but better evidence is needed.

The duets of the Whippoorwill Wren, *Thryothorous mystacalis ruficaudatus*, in Venezuela continue steadily during at least six months of the year. One bird sings the first phrase and the other, even when far distant, answers immediately. The pairs remain for several seasons, and perhaps indefinitely, in the same area and tend to be sparsely distributed—a state of affairs which is not unusual in tropical species (Davis 1941b; Beebe 1950). In such circumstances contact songs or calls are advantageous and attain precise coordination. Rufous-naped Cactus Wrens sing together in such an expert way that it is difficult to believe that two birds are involved but the cock Bicoloured Cactus Wren gurgles 'Keep your feet wet' and his mate close by sings 'What d'you care?' (Fuertes 1916). Many other tropical wrens duet with greater or lesser degrees of co-ordination (Armstrong 1955; Skutch 1958a).

It may well be that duetting is important in pair-formation as well as pair-maintenance in these and other species. Marshall (1960) found that 'squeal duets' served this function in Abert and Brown (Canyon) Towhees. A bird gives a *seee* call from a territory and engages in a duet with a responding bird and 'if the new bird is single, and of the opposite sex, a pair is in the making'. Duetting does not seem to be recorded of any species with a brief pair-bond—another indication of its significance in pair-maintenance. Its absence in small migratory passerines is correlated with their pair-bond being of comparatively short duration. By contrast, the Bullfinch which remains paired from season to season is adapted visually and vocally for the maintenance of the bond, having a conspicuous white rump and responsive call-notes. These are hardly sufficiently coordinated to be called duetting but indicate how it might develop from contact calls.

Birds which duet, and particularly those which sing antiphonally, are often similar in appearance, but there are exceptions. The male *Thamnophilus doliatus* of Surinam is barred black and white, while the female is chestnut. The performance is not so stereotyped as some. They may sing a few rhythmical notes simultaneously or the female may respond to the male with similar or somewhat higher-pitched notes. As they sing the birds erect the crown feathers and quiver the partly-fanned tail (Haverschmidt 1947).

Antiphonal duetting is performed by nocturnal as well as diurnal species and indeed is particularly effective in keeping birds in touch with one another at night. Among owls it varies from ragged responsive utterances to exact antiphonal singing. Barred Owls chant 'Who, who, who, who cooks for you all?'—one in a hooting tone, the other as a burst of laughter (Huxley 1919). Spectacled Owls call *woof-woof-woof*, answering each other with perfect regularity as if they were striking the heads of different-sized barrels with wooden mallets (Chapman 1930). Eagle Owls reciprocate, the male standing upright, the female bowing at each call. Little Owls also respond to each other in a kind of duet. The birds heard by a non-ornithologist in Burma were probably owls. One would call out the first note of Offenbach's 'O Night of Love' to be answered by the other with the two ensuing notes. This continued with a maddening regularity (Rodger 1943).

Pairs of Marbled Wood Quail sing their duet, which is of the most perfectly coordinated type, as they run together at dusk through the Central American forest. Their hurried whistles sound as if some musical boy were trying to attract a friend's attention. The ringing, urgent *oo-oo-oo⁻ᵒᵒ-oo* is repeated again and again as the birds trip away through the tree trunks. The *⁻ᵒᵒ-oo* response of the second bird comes so quickly that, without prior knowledge, one would never suspect that two birds were involved (Armstrong 1940). Wood Rails keep time in their unison duets but one sings at least thrice as many notes as the other. They sound like 'an aged couple singing in shaky, quavering voices a song of their youth' (Chapman 1930; Skutch 1959).

Non-vocal duetting is rare but mutual klappering is performed by White Storks and mutual drumming occurs in mated pairs of Red-bellied Woodpeckers (Fig. 27).

In regions where the rainfall is irregular or uncertain it is advantageous for birds to initiate breeding promptly as soon as the rains break. This commonly involves being paired beforehand. The rainy season in Mexico may begin at a variable time and a number of species there, including the Black Phoebe and Scarlet Flycatcher, form pairs three or four months before nesting (Wagner 1941). Similarly in Australia, climatic conditions, and particularly the rainfall which in the north is unpredictable, determine the onset of breeding. Much of the bird song is related to the preservation of the pair-bond rather than the defence of territory (Robinson 1945, 1949). Female song and duetting are relatively common and such species seem to hold territory throughout the year. In equatorial Africa there is also a close correlation between the rains and nesting. Duetting birds are found in all these regions so there can be no doubt concerning the relationship between duetting, a sustained pair-bond, and climatic conditions. Many of the best duettists are insectivorous species. For them the weather has a very definite bearing on the availability of food and consequently on the optimum time to rear the brood. Thus duetting illustrates the intricate integration between the nature of a bird's activities and its habitat. At first glance it might not be apparent that rainfall could determine the type of song sung by birds, but clearly this is so.

Corporate song and calling

If the term 'chorus' be regarded, as is usual, as connoting a form of coordinated common utterance, it is only by a kind of picturesque licence that we can use it of birds. They often stimulate one another to utter sounds but there is seldom coordination of simultaneous utterance except in such situations as have already been mentioned. There is no co-ordination during the so-called 'dawn chorus'. The corporate calling of such birds as nesting Sandwich Terns, roosting Starlings, or passerines mobbing an owl is no more a true chorus than the clamour made by a rioting crowd. It need hardly be mentioned that there is no evidence of birds in a group adapting their notes to constitute harmony, and accounts of birds timing their calling or activities under the guidance of an individual acting as a 'conductor' may be attributed to inaccurate observation.

Social utterances involving more than two birds—omitting occasions when simultaneous calling is fortuitous or merely due to a common environmental stimulus—may be graded from situations in which the calling or singing of one bird stimulates others to do the same, through forms of activity in which calls are associated with corporate movements, such as more or less coordinated flock flights, to highly ritualized social displays in which the utterances are integrated into the whole coordinated patterns of activity.

When corporate calling occurs and the birds are not responding individually to some environmental stimulus, such as an advancing predator, or merely squabbling, we may assume that they are stimulating each other. Related mimetic or socially facilitated behaviour is a normal feature of the life of many animals (Armstrong 1951a). Occasionally a bird may even trigger off behaviour in another species in this way, as when a Shoveler went into distraction display on seeing a Mallard doing so (Hickling 1950) or a flight-displaying Bishop Bird, *Euplectes macroura*, stimulated neighbouring *E. orix* males to perform their equivalent displays (Emlen 1957). Sometimes birds may be stimulated to sing on hearing other species (Lack 1943). Apparently the singing of a Black Redstart may evoke song from a Redstart (Buxton 1950) and Marler (1960a) has noticed three species in Mexico apparently counter-singing.†

The most familiar type of corporate calling is the babel of sound made by gatherings of birds at the roost or other assembly point, as by Starlings on city buildings. Aggression and mutual stimulation are involved. The clamour of Glossy Starlings at their roost may be heard a quarter of a mile away (Serle 1957). In the breeding season Starlings have communal perches (Schuz 1942; Kessel 1957) indicating that the birds find singing together congenial. Indeed, it seems that sociability tends to supersede competitive impulses in a number of species. In their breeding quarters in Europe Corn Buntings sing competitively and they do so even when breeding is over (p. 122) but in North Africa they assemble in flocks of up to 300 birds and all sing together (Stanford 1954). For many years Pied Wagtails have assembled to roost in some trees in the heart of Dublin, apparently attracting each other by their calls as well as their movements. Hudson (1892) speaks of 10,000 Fieldfinches assembled in trees : 'They sing in a concert of innumerable voices, producing a great volume of sound, as of a high wind heard at a distance. Heard near, it is a great mass of melody; not a confused tangle of musical sounds as when a host of Troupials sing in concert, but the notes, although numberless, seem to flow smoothly and separately, producing an effect on the ear similar to that which rain does on the sight, when the sun shines on and lightens up the myriads of drops falling all one way'.

As we shall see presently light values are important in initiating morning song but in some species the birds apparently influence each other so that corporate song occurs. The Bearded or Rufous-breasted Ground Robin utters a whistling song at dawn, dusk, or on cloudy days. One bird begins, others start to vie with it until a large number are singing together (Roberts 1948). Flocks of Evening Grosbreaks sing together, the volume rising and falling. Excitable individuals stimulate their neighbours to sing (Parks 1947). Laysan Rails—now extinct—used to sing together. Frohawk (1892) wrote : 'Soon after dusk they all, as if by a given signal, strike up a most peculiar chorus, which lasts for a few seconds, and then all remain silent. I can only compare the sound to a handful of marbles being thrown on a glass roof and then descending in a succession of bounds'. In New Zealand Weka Rails similarly join in an outcry and then fall silent (Wilson 1937). Tuis also behave in this way but in this species and many others corporate calling is mimetically initiated and apparently not linked with light intensity.

Such calling is characteristic of strongly social species on their breeding grounds, such as gulls, terns, and some species of penguin (Armstrong 1947; Sladen 1958). Where birds occupy territories of a considerable size a bird's song may arouse its neighbours to sing. In such circumstances we may assume that the proprietorial significance of the song is greater than its mimetic content. Thus the more pairs of Eastern Bluebirds in an area the more warbling there is (Thomas 1946a) and when a

Magnolia Warbler sings in resenting the invasion of his territory other individuals all over the woods burst into song (Kendeigh 1945a). Not only do Least Flycatcher's stimulate one another's singing but the quality of the song depends to some extent on the number of males singing in adjoining territories (Macqueen 1950). Australian Bellmagpies employ group calling as corporate defence and all the birds are incited to vigorous utterance but Butcherbirds and Kookaburras, which also hold permanent territories, will sing in them with others without quarrelling (Robinson 1949).

It will be evident from these examples that corporate utterances vary immensely in their motivation. They may be mainly aggressive, social, or sexual, and in most or all such utterances there is mingled motivation. A few further examples may be given, illustrating various types of motivation. Great Snipe gather at dusk to display and utter whirring, hissing, and other calls. Collett (1876) wrote: 'At a short distance the sound of the notes of the different birds is by no means unpleasant; for it may be compared with the song of the Willow-wren whilst a strong wind is sighing amongst the branches of the forest trees'. The motivation at these gatherings is primarily sexual but probably to some extent aggressive, as they may be regarded as a form of lek display. Probably the communal dances of *Myrmecochila aethiops cryptoleuca* are of a somewhat similar character. The birds elongate their necks, emitting squawks. Gatherings of up to eight Black-chinned Antcreepers assemble to sing and display excitedly (Davis 1949). When four or five Guimet's or Violet-eared Hummingbirds consort the females are attracted (Skutch 1946b). It would seem that the screaming parties of Cachalotes are partly aggressive but primarily social, for old and young gather to participate in an uproar initiated by a single bird which ends with the birds pursuing each other in the bushes (Hudson 1892). The piping parties of Oyster-catchers appear to be stimulated by mingled aggressive, sexual, and social impulses (Armstrong 1947).

It need hardly be pointed out that mimetic activity is of much wider interest than in its relationship to bird song. In human affairs it influences behaviour by contributing to the coherence of society and, to a large extent, suppressing divergence from standard behaviour. The future of humanity would seem to depend on a constructive compromise between individual originality and the tyranny of motivation derived from tendencies to behave mimetically inherited from our animal ancestry.

XI

THE INFLUENCE OF LIGHT, WEATHER, AND TEMPERATURE ON SONG

Cock croweth at Midnight times few above six,
With pause to his Fellow to answer betwixt;
At three a Clock thicker, and then as you know,
Like all into Mattins, nere Day they do crow.
At Midnight, at three, and an Hour yet Day,
They utter their language as well as they may.

THOMAS TUSSER
Five Hundred good Pointes of Husbandrie
(1580).

ALTHOUGH since very early times the activities of birds served, to some extent, as calendars and clocks for primitive people, yet only quite recently has there been serious study of the connexion between such activities, particularly song, and changes in light intensity, temperature, and other meteorological factors. This is not surprising as the relationship between a bird's utterances and its environment is highly complex. As we have noted, song may serve many functions and be uttered by some species at any time of the year but the association of territorial and sexually motivated song with the breeding season is so close that the factors which exercise a favourable influence on the breeding cycle are relevant to most song-production. These have been summarized elsewhere (Armstrong 1947).

TABLE VII

FACTORS FAVOURABLY INFLUENCING THE BREEDING CYCLE OF BIRDS

Internal factors

1. The growth of the gonads, the secretion of sex hormones, and the state of the reproductive system.
2. General metabolism and health.

Environmental factors

3. The effect of light.
4. Favourable weather.
5. Adequate food supply.
6. The availability of a suitable nesting site and nesting material.

Psychological factors

7. The possession of a territory.
8. The presence and appropriate behaviour, including vocalization, of a mate or potential mate.
9. Social stimulation.
10. Social rank.
11. Self-stimulation.

The integrated relationship of all or most of these brings about the initiation of breeding and associated song. We shall review briefly the major environmental factors which have a bearing on song production.

The influence of light intensity and day-length

Observational and experimental evidence indicating the importance of light in helping to bring birds into breeding (and singing) condition has been summarized in the review already mentioned, and more recently by Farner (1959) and Marshall (1959). Bird fanciers in Holland and Japan have long been aware that birds can be brought into song by altering the duration of light to which they are exposed. It has been shown experimentally that in some species testis progression and increase in song are concomitant. In the tropics, where there is little or no variation in day-length, alterations in ultra-violet light and intensity of illumination may regulate the twice-yearly breeding of some species though work on the birds of Ascension Island has shown that the adjustment is a highly complex matter. In very many species increasing light, by stimulating the development of the gonads, elicits song and territorial behaviour. Birds which migrate from the tropics in spring thereby increase the duration of light to which they are subjected and are consequently active for longer periods each day than in their winter quarters (Fig. 28).

Besides affecting the seasonal production of song light influences the beginning, ending, and amount of diurnal song because of its bearing on diurnal activity in general. This is equally true, conversely, of nocturnal birds, though of course, when Nightingales or Corncrakes sing much of the night as well as during the day this does not mean that they have emancipated themselves from the controlling effect of light on their songfulness. When a bird prolongs its activity to an unusual extent we can usually point to factors governing such behaviour. The Nightingale is particularly vocal at night because it is then that females may fly in and Barn Owls hunt in daylight when prey is scarce. Even the Guacharo, living in dark caverns, and flying by night, is subject to the diurnal rhythm (Armstrong 1959a). The output of song by birds is governed to a great extent by rhythm, and even changes in the order of phrases in continuous and semi-continuous songs may be mainly cyclic (p. 40).

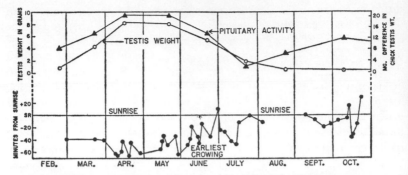

Fig. 28. Earliest daybreak crowing by the Ring-necked Pheasant (*Phasianus colchicus*) on clear mornings, 1944 to 1947, as recorded by A. Leopold, in relation to sunrise and to the annual cycle of testis and pituitary activity as determined by Greeley and Meyer (1953) for Poynette, Wisconsin. The crowing curve is correlated with the gonadotropic activity of the pituitary. Presumably this is also true of passerines which sing progressively earlier as the season advances. (After Leopold and Eynon 1961)

There is abundant evidence for the existence of innate rhythms in a wide range of organisms, vertebrate and invertebrate, including birds, but apart from the behaviour of some creatures with very specialized habitats, such as internal parasites and creatures of the ocean depths, about whose behaviour we know little, many of these rhythms are obviously geared directly or indirectly to alterations in light.

It has been suggested from time to time that not only day-length and its increase influence the development of the gonads and the production of song but that sunshine exerts a significant influence (Marshall 1949, 1952b, 1959). Evidence to this effect has been produced by Threadgold (1960) who compared testis volumes of House Sparrows from different latitudes in the British Isles and the United States. He concluded that the differences which he found in the testis cycle were mainly a matter of the timing of the phases within the annual cycle and that 'there was no orderly progressive retardation of the phases with north latitude, as would be expected if day-length were the environmental factor with over-riding influence in the timing of the cycle'. The differences are explicable on the basis of the influence of the temperature and sunshine cycles as well as different configurations of day-length at the localities in the United States, Canada, southern England, and Northern Ireland from which the material examined was obtained. No doubt further investigations along these lines would explain some anomalies which have been noted in the latitudinal incidence of breeding and song.

Light intensity is the most important environmental factor determining the beginning and ending of a bird's day and therefore it has a direct influence on the beginning and, to a lesser extent, the ending of diurnal song. Most birds sing early in the morning but they are awake for some time before they sing (Lehtonen 1947; Scheer 1952c). They usually withdraw the beak from the scapulars, yawn, stretch, shake, sleek the feathers, and look around before flying elsewhere to sing. A Chaffinch becomes increasingly restless during about three hours before entering on the day's activity and a House Wren fidgets before flying out of the nest (Baldwin and Kendeigh 1927; Bergman 1950). Steinfatt (1940) found that a Yellowhammer was awake 5–10 minutes before he sang. In captivity Lapland Buntings are restless at night (Homeyer 1897), probably due to their activities being normally geared to the prolonged summer daylight of high latitudes. On three mornings a Great Tit was observed to sing six, seven, and two minutes after arriving at the nesting box from the roost which he had probably left about five minutes earlier (Hinde 1952). The cock Short-toed Treecreeper sings from the roosting hollow or a few seconds after leaving it but the hen preens in the roost for some time (Thielcke 1959a). Scheer (1950, 1951, 1952a, c) found that in spring the average delay between awakening and singing was three minutes for a Robin, five to six minutes for a Blackbird, fifteen to twenty minutes for a Chaffinch, and up to half an hour for a Greenfinch. He concluded—perhaps on too slender evidence—that the later the song the greater the period between awakening and singing.

The table below shows that there is a tendency for Wrens to sing more promptly after leaving the roost as they come into full breeding ardour:

TABLE VIII

RELATIONSHIP OF FIRST SONG TO DEPARTURE FROM ROOST

Date	Interval in seconds before song	Temperature (°F.)	Weather
10.2.44	120	39	Windy
10.2.44	60	29	Cloudy
4.3.44	30	23	Clear
6.3.44	5	28	Clear
9.3.44	5	32	Overcast
10.3.44	120	29	Misty
9.2.45	180	37	Overcast
27.2.45	30	47	Clear
21.3.45	9	37	Clear
28.4.45	10	40	Sleet
17.5.45	16	57	Clear

(*After Armstrong 1955*)

Late in the breeding season, and afterwards, the delay in singing may be considerably greater.

Probably increasing light seldom awakens birds roosting in dark places among bushes and in cavities. Birds placed in continual darkness rise and roost for some time at approximately the same time as they would have done normally (Palmgren 1949). It is quite unusual for the voices of early risers to arouse other birds from their roosts. A sleepy bird will respond to its mate's call (p. 10) but it is doubtful whether the songs of a rival stimulate a bird to leave the roost. Birds sleep through loud noises, such as trains drawing up close to them, but the breaking of a twig, or other sound already associated with danger, alerts them.

The order of bird song

The order in which different species sing in the morning remains remarkably constant, in spite of some variations and anomalies. Tusser's rhyme quoted at the head of this chapter and H. C. St. John's comment show that the time-keeping abilities of the Domestic Cock have long been appreciated in East and West. St. John (1880), writing about Japan, remarked : 'The common Domestic Cock in these regions crows with wonderful regularity at twelve at night, two and four. In China they are equally valuable and even more used for the purpose of time-keeping. Every fishing-junk carries a bird in a small cage, hung over the high-perched stern, for this purpose alone.' In Ireland the Cock was kept where the family slept to serve as an alarm clock.

The sequence of song is sufficiently constant for writers to have adopted the term 'bird clock' to indicate this sequence just as others have devised 'flower-clock gardens' stocked with plants whose blossoms open and close at various hours of the day. Marples (1939) prepared a table showing the average period before sunrise during several months when various birds were first heard.

TABLE IX

SEQUENCE OF MORNING SONG AND VOCALIZATION

Species	Minutes before sunrise
Blackbird	43·76
Song Thrush	42·73
Woodpigeon	42·35
Robin	34·04
Mistle Thrush	32·47
Turtle Dove	27·00
Pheasant	23·36
Willow Warbler	22·46
Wren	21·55
Great Tit	17·44
House Sparrow	16·62
Bullfinch	12·50

Species	Minutes before sunrise
Green Woodpecker	12·30
Blue Tit	9·50
Chaffinch	8·69
Whitethroat	6·66

On 12 May, when dawn was at 4.46 Middle European Time, Scheer (1950) in Darmstadt listed the birds he heard in this order:

TABLE X

Species	Time
Redstart	3.25
Black Redstart	3.48
Blackbird	3.52
Robin	3.56
Blackcap	3.59
Great Tit	4.05
Wren	4.07
Chiffchaff	4.09
Chaffinch	4.13
Serin	4.19
Swift	4.32

For comparison, the following data, obtained by Rollin (1953) in Northumberland and from correspondents in India and Africa, are of interest. They concern observations of the first birds to sing on 13 April 1952. The times are given in Local Apparent Time, the time by the sun at the place of observation:

TABLE XI

Glanton, Northumberland. 55° 30′N., 1° 53′W.

Species	Time
Pheasant	3.11
Woodpigeon	3.42
Skylark	3.58
Blackbird	4.12
Song Thrush	4.17
Wren	4.25
Yellowhammer	4.36
Chaffinch	4.57

Coonoor, Nilgiris, South India, 11° 20′N., 76° 50′E.

Species	Time
Indian Robin	4.18
Pied Bush Chat	4.52
Red-whiskered Bulbul	5.07
Tickell's Blue Flycatcher	5.12
Nilgiri Blackbird	5.17
Nilgiri Blue Flycatcher	5.17
House Sparrow	5.37
Spotted Munia	5.47

A Study of Bird Song

Darwendale, Southern Rhodesia. 17° 50'S., 30° 32'E.

Species	Time
Red-eyed Turtle Dove	4.56
Cape Turtle Dove	5.31
Laughing Dove	5.32
Striped Kingfisher	5.40
Black-eyed Bulbul	5.43
Kurrichane Thrush	5.44
Jardine's Babbler	5.45
Groundscraper Thrush	5.53

Such comparisons are approximate, for no account is taken of cloud cover, altitude, and stage of the breeding cycle, which may affect arising time (Nice 1943; Scheer 1952a), but it will be noted that vermivorous and insectivorous species are high on the lists, and grain-eaters, apart from the Columbidae, tend to be late-risers in temperate regions and tropics alike. This is valid of birds in high northern latitudes also (Armstrong 1954a). The explanation is complex and involves acuity of vision (p. 202) and the behaviour of prey organisms, some of which are more readily available early in the morning. There are exceptions, such as woodpeckers, which are tardy risers. The Swift modifies its aerial feeding according to the weather. It is sometimes stated that there is no 'dawn chorus' in the tropics but this is misleading. The volume of sound is not so great because, apart from strongly social species, there tend to be more species but fewer individuals in tropical forests and not many birds utter sustained sequences comparable with the songs of common northern turdines. Where such birds occur in the tropics their songs may constitute a delightful chorus. Cocoa Thrushes sing thus in some localities in Trinidad.

Writers such as Allard (1930) claim that some species are better 'time-keepers' than others—that is, they keep more definitely to a specific 'singing-light'. The American Robin, Wood Thrush, and House Wren are said to be noteworthy in this respect but although some species are more sensitive than others to slight changes in light intensity this view needs further investigation. The weather and the inclination of the sun below the horizon at the time of first song must be taken into consideration. Probably the earliest risers tend to be the best time-keepers but this may be related to the rate at which light intensity increases in the morning. We must not suppose that there is always a direct correlation between light intensity and song. Groebbels (1956) noticed that on cloudy mornings some birds wait to sing until the light intensity is much brighter than that at which they start to sing on clear, favourable mornings.

Birds near their peak of sexual ardour tend to sing earlier than those not so advanced, and parents feeding nestlings usually are active longer hours than birds not so engaged. In captivity, and perhaps also in the wild, a dominant bird arises earlier than a subordinate (Dunnett and Hinde 1953). It has been shown for various temperate region species, including the Blackbird, Wren, and Great Tit, for the House Wren and Song Sparrow in the United States, and a Friar Bird in the tropics that individuals within a species have their own singing or calling light (Trebesius 1930–32; Armstrong 1955; Dunnett and Hinde 1953; Paatela 1934, 1938; Allard 1930; Nice 1943; Meyer 1929). Individual Swifts consistently differ from others in their roosting times (Lack 1956). Such individual differences have been noted in many species.

The intensity of light at which birds begin to call or sing varies according to the season and stage of the breeding cycle as is shown in Scheer's Table (1952a) reproduced here.

TABLE XII

SINGING OR CALLING BRIGHTNESS OF SOME SPECIES IN LUX

Species	Minimum at beginning of breeding cycle		Maximum during moult		Winter		Early Spring	
Blackbird	Mar./Apr.	0·1	Aug.	4	Dec./Jan.	0·5	Feb./Mar.	0·4
Chaffinch	Apr./May	4	Aug./Sept.	500	Dec./Jan.	4	Feb./Mar.	500
Serin	Apr./May	17	Sept.	200	—		—	
Greenfinch	Apr.	40	Aug./Sept.	450	Dec./Jan.	40	Feb./Mar.	300
Redstart	May	0·03	July/Aug.	3	—		—	
Black Redstart	Apr./May	0·15	Aug.	6	—		—	
Great Tit	Apr.	1·2	July	450	Dec./Jan.	7	Feb./Mar.	4·5
Wren	Mar./Apr.	0·4	Aug./Sept.	18	Nov.	1	Jan.	3·5
Chiffchaff	May/June	2·5	Aug.	1000	—		—	

The table shows that birds are vocal at weaker light intensities during the breeding season than later on, with the exception of the Greenfinch which is heard during winter at the same light intensity as at the beginning of the breeding cycle.

Although observers, when recording the first vocalizations of birds, often do so in relation to sunrise it is preferable to plot them in relation to Civil Twilight, when the sun is 6° below the horizon. This is the time when, for human beings, and apparently many birds, visibility becomes good enough for activity involving distinguishing objects out of doors. It is also important for navigation, being the time when the brighter stars cease, or begin, to be visible and the horizon is clearly enough defined to be favourable for observations. When bird songs throughout the year are plotted on a graph showing sunrise and Civil Twilight it is at once apparent that the period between the two reaches a maximum at the solstices. This is because the duration of twilight increases as we go north until at the summer solstice north of the Arctic Circle daylight prevails throughout the twenty-four hours. Thus a bird which sings earlier in relation to sunrise in March than it does in June is not necessarily singing at a weaker light value. In fact, birds tend to sing earlier relative to Civil Twilight and at lower light values as Table XII indicates. Mourning Doves change from calling at or after Civil Twilight in March to averaging seven minutes before in April and May. American Robins sing a few minutes before the beginning of Civil Twilight during the first part of March and then alter to singing considerably before Civil Twilight and as much as 73 minutes before sunrise (Nice 1943). The time when the Blackbird is first heard is somewhat before Civil Twilight from March until June and a little after it during August and September (Scheer 1952a) (Figs. 29 and 30). Early in the year Blackbirds tend to sing late in the day and progressively extend their singing into the afternoon but in mid-March they may suddenly begin singing even earlier than the Song Thrush and Robin. The dawn chorus of Song Thrushes in Northern Ireland precedes sunrise by 40 minutes in February and gets earlier until at the end of May it is 84 minutes before (Burkitt 1935). As Civil Twilight becomes earlier by less than 15 minutes in this period the birds sing at increasingly lower light values. They sing later into the darkness in the evening, changing from singing 45 minutes after sunset to 76 minutes after. In the autumn of 1960 and into the winter Song Thrushes sang vigorously in the morning but after a period of silence in January they sang only in the afternoon and evening until the third week of February. Blackbirds and Thrushes both tend to sing more into the middle of the day as the season advances. There are many anomalies and variations. The weather, age of the birds, sexual maturity, amount of competition, and other factors have a bearing on the daily incidence of song. In June the Wood Pewee sings close to Nautical Twilight (when the sun is 12° below the horizon) but by August is singing about Civil Twilight (Craig 1943). Earlier beginning of song relative to sunrise has been recorded of the Robin, Chaffinch, and other birds (Clark 1938). Great Tits emerge from their roosts on the average 26 minutes before sunrise in winter but some 37 minutes before sunrise in April and May. They sing in spring at 1 Lux (Kluijver 1950). As they roost at 250 Lux in midwinter when they presumably remain feeding as long as there is sufficient visibility, it is evident that their rising in spring is earlier than would be possible for profitable foraging, and is therefore due to a drive other than hunger. Graphs showing the arising or first song times of the Wren (Armstrong 1955) (Fig. 31) and Song Sparrow (Nice 1943) from midwinter to midsummer reveal a tendency to earlier rising relative to Civil Twilight. Nice divides this period into three phases, the first beginning in January and February when song occurs four minutes after Civil Twilight, the second from February to 4 March when it is close to it,

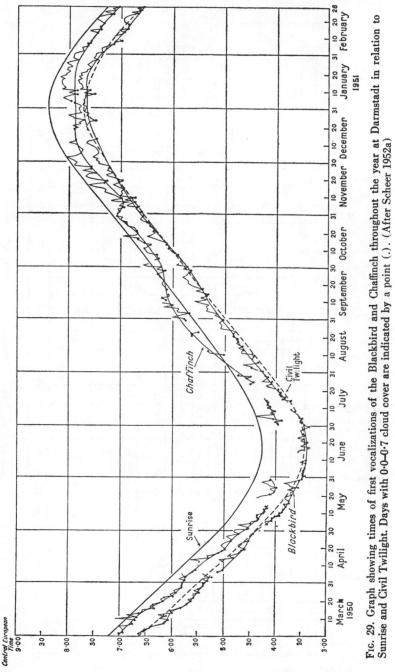

FIG. 29. Graph showing times of first vocalizations of the Blackbird and Chaffinch throughout the year at Darmstadt in relation to Sunrise and Civil Twilight. Days with 0·0–0·7 cloud cover are indicated by a point (.). (After Scheer 1952a)

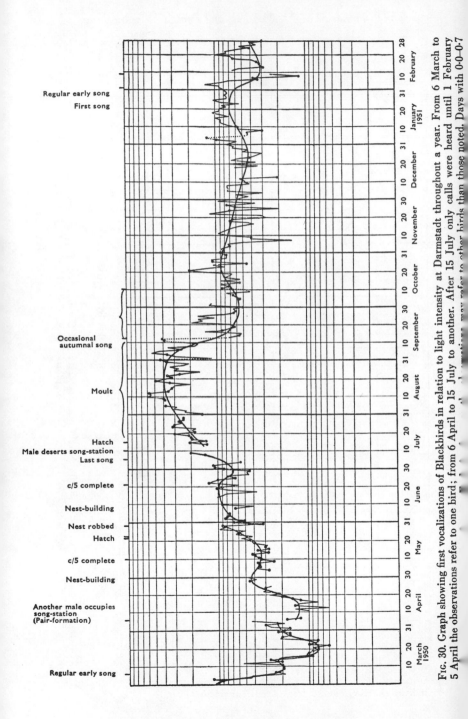

FIG. 30. Graph showing first vocalizations of Blackbirds in relation to light intensity at Darmstadt throughout a year. From 6 March to 5 April the observations refer to one bird; from 6 April to 15 July to another. After 15 July only calls were heard until 1 February 1951. Regular early song. First song. Occasional autumnal song. Moult. Hatch. Male deserts song-station. Last song. c/5 complete. Nest-building. Nest robbed. Hatch. c/5 complete. Nest-building. Another male occupies song-station (Pair-formation). Regular early song.

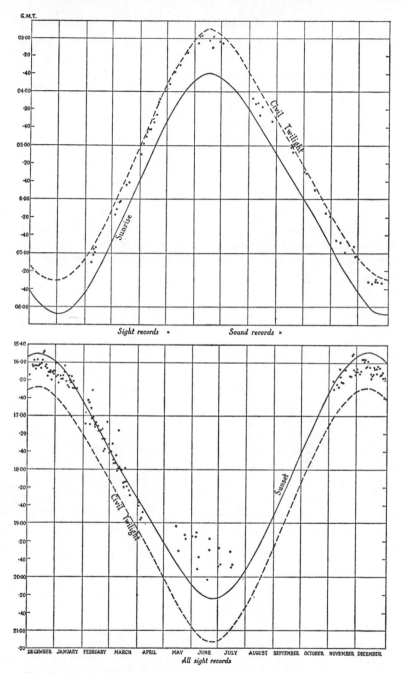

FIG. 31. Graphs showing the arising and roosting times of a Wren from December 1943 to December 1944. Most of the data refer to one identifiable individual. (Reproduced from Armstrong 1955)

and the third three to fourteen days later. The second period coincides with the occupation of territory and the third with full song, which continues until the weather becomes bleak. There are no abrupt changes corresponding to the great alterations in the way the bird's time is occupied.†

There are few principles of bird behaviour to which some species do not conform and we should expect to find exceptions to the rule that at the peak of sexual activity a bird's song is apt to be uttered in the dimmest light. Thus the Yellowhammer sings at lowest light intensity in June and July when there is little evidence of late nesting (Rollin 1958a). Reproductive activity can be geared to a wide variety of environmental conditions, and decreasing light may operate to induce breeding in some mammals. For example, the Emperor Penguin comes into breeding condition during decreasing light intensities and a period of low temperatures; but this does not necessarily imply that breeding is activated by decreasing light.

The influence of light on the cessation of song

Apart from some exceptions, such as nocturnal species, but not excluding Arctic passerines, the activities of most birds are at their maximum in the morning. There is a tendency for these activities to decrease and reach a minimum after midday and increase again towards evening. This has been found to apply to such different activities as copulation (in woodpeckers), the cooing display of Eider Ducks (Rollin 1958b), feeding nestlings and song. Also a considerable number of resident birds, such as the Great Tit, sing in the morning and evening when they first come into song and later extend their singing to the hours in between (Lehtonen 1947). Little is known concerning the factors responsible for this pattern of behaviour. Haecker (1916, 1924) argued that the ending of morning song and the cessation of song in the evening are due to fatigue but, at best, this can only be a partial explanation. The nature of fatigue in this context is obscure. The problem is complicated by the abundant evidence that there may be exhaustion of one kind of activity concerned without diminution in the energy with which other activities are performed. More than muscular fatigue is concerned. Yellowhammers sing less in high latitudes late in the season than in Britain (Fig. 32). It has been suggested by Rollin (1958) that this is due to the curtailment of sleep during long daylight and consequent exhaustion of energy, but this kind of problem needs further investigation. The times when birds arise and roost, and consequently are first heard in the morning and last heard in the evening, are related to their foraging behaviour as well as to light intensity. In the Arctic winter Great Tits are later to roost, relative to light intensity

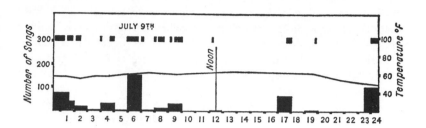

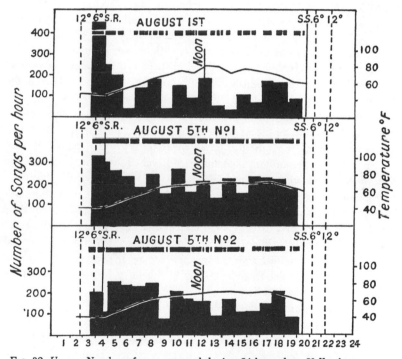

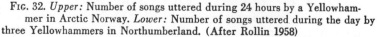

FIG. 32. *Upper:* Number of songs uttered during 24 hours by a Yellowhammer in Arctic Norway. *Lower:* Number of songs uttered during the day by three Yellowhammers in Northumberland. (After Rollin 1958)

and earlier in emerging than in temperate regions—indicating that they forage as long as possible (Palmgren 1944; Franz 1949, 1950). So closely related is the relative size of some birds' eyes to the length of daily activity that in some instances one might make a fair estimate by looking at its eyes as to whether a bird sings early or late in the dawn chorus. The early-rising Redstart, Black Redstart, and Robin have larger eyes than the late-rising House Sparrow. These birds are insectivorous and adapted for foraging in dim light (p. 194).

In some species, such as the Redstart, there are song-peaks morning and evening and also around midday or somewhat later (Fig. 36).

Decreasing light intensity is probably the most important factor in relation to the ending of evening song—and possibly, in those species which sing a definite evening song, its beginning. But the significant light intensities affecting the bird in the evening may differ from those affecting it in the morning. Thus the Wood Pewee's first phrase in the morning averages twenty-six minutes before Civil Twilight but the last phrase of the evening song averages eight and a half minutes before Civil Twilight—thirty-four minutes earlier than we might expect. Craig concluded that the bird was able to 'anticipate' the lower light values but his argument is unconvincing (Armstrong 1955). The Blue Honeycreeper and Red Ant Tanager cease singing before sunrise (Skutch 1954) and the morning song of the Boat-billed Flycatcher seldom continues until sunrise. The Alder Flycatcher's morning song is apparently determined by light intensities but, as the evening song ceases in darkness, if its cessation is determined by light the effect must be indirect (Skutch 1951a; McCabe 1951). A number of American Flycatchers sing a distinctive form of daybreak song (Borror 1961).

In general birds arise at lower light values than they go to roost but there is greater variation in the times birds go to roost than when they emerge. Starlings and Bronzed Grackles during October reached the roost at approximately three times the light values at which they departed (Nice 1943). The earliest rising birds tend to be the latest to roost and the last songs of species in the evening are usually in the reverse order of the first morning utterances.

In the tropics some birds which sing relatively early, such as doves and bulbuls, do so before leaving their roosts, and some owls, including the Spotted Eagle Owl, 'sing' before departing in the evening (Holman 1947). The Wood Pewee may sing from the roost but the practice of most birds of leaving the sleeping place before singing probably reduces their jeopardy from predators.

Song in relation to latitude

Various turdines in Britain, North America, Southern Rhodesia, South India, and New Zealand begin to sing when the sun is between 12° and 6° below the horizon. The observations cited earlier showed that thrushes in the northern hemisphere sang on an April day in dimmer light than thrushes in the southern hemisphere but this may mean no more than that the birds sing earlier the nearer they are to breeding condition. Miller (1958), investigating the song of the American Robin noted that between 38°N and 61°N in the latter half of June the morning song begins progressively earlier and ends progressively earlier with increase in latitude. He found some evidence that the duration of morning song increases with latitude and that the evening song tends to become earlier at higher latitudes. It may disappear completely as a distinct entity north of 58°. In regions of continual daylight there tends to be a lull in passerine song about 21.00 though some observers in different regions of the Arctic estimate that it occurs somewhat earlier or later (Fig. 32) (Armstrong 1954a). At 68°N I noticed a Fieldfare song-flighting at 23.30 on 2 July, a Redwing singing occasionally from 19.45 until 22.15 as the young left the nest, and a Red-spotted Bluethroat display-flighting between midnight and 01.20 as well as later in the morning. Birds which feed late tend to sing and display relatively late.†

Song in relation to solar eclipses

It has long been known that during total eclipses of the sun birds are apt to become silent or even to go to roost. During the total eclipse in the Canary Islands on 2 October 1959, which lasted for a minute and three-quarters, the Chaffinch was silent for twenty-three minutes from before until after totality. The minutes of silence of other species were respectively: Blue Tit 17, Blackbird 10, Canary 4, Chiffchaff 3. The Robin sang all through the eclipse. The crowing of Domestic Cocks was unaffected. Flocks of Canaries flew about excitedly and Chiffchaffs were constantly on the move when it was getting dark (Rollin 1959). There is some relationship between these data and the light values at which the birds normally sing. The Chaffinch is a much later riser and sings in a brighter light than the Robin and Blackbird. The Serin is also a late riser and the Chiffchaff is fairly late in beginning activity. (The converse may also be true to some extent—exceptionally bright light may awaken birds. During war-time blitzes when buildings were blazing House Sparrows flew around chirping, but noise as well as light may have disturbed them. Robins perched near bright street lamps sometimes sing when it is quite dark.) In southern Sweden the Robin sang freely during the 1954 eclipse and was then silent, the Blackbird sang most vigorously during the onset of the eclipse and then ceased. The Song Thrush came into fullest song after the eclipse (Kullenberg 1955).† Lehtonen (1959) in Finland, during the same eclipse which was eighty-nine per cent at its maximum, also noted that birds ceased to sing in the order usual at sunset. He found that most birds did not stay quite still as they did during the total eclipse of 9 July 1945 in Helsinki. Starling flocks behaved as they normally do at dusk. During maximum darkness for ten to fifteen minutes there were no flights. Where the sky was overcast the effect of the eclipse on bird life was greater than in areas where it was clear. There was an eclipse on 15 February 1961, which was ninety per cent at 7.45 a.m. at Cambridge. Sunrise was at 7.16 a.m. It was a misty morning. The eclipse had no noticeable effect on bird song.

Song in relation to earthquakes

A few comments may be interpolated here on the relation between bird song and another unusual phenomenon—the earthquake. Not unnaturally observations concerning the behaviour of birds during severe earthquakes are few although such disasters give rise to beliefs that birds have presentiments of them, as at Agadir, where it was rumoured that White Storks threw their young out of the nests before the earthquake. In the *Observer* of 12 June 1960, Patrick O'Donovan reported that immediately after the earthquake in Chile birds burst out singing 'loudly and discordantly'. As we have noted (p. 131) shock of various kinds may evoke songs or calls so this report may be accurate.†

Nocturnal song and the influence of moonlight

The mean time after sunset when the Tawny Owl utters its first call is nine minutes in August and September but in December and January it is 35–46 minutes after sunset. Between the last call and sunrise the mean time is 26–27 minutes in August and September but 55–66 in December and January (Hansen 1952). Thus this bird shortens its activities relative to the dark hours as diurnal birds tend to curtail their active day relative to light when there are most daylight hours. Birds, whether diurnal or nocturnal, tend to extend their foraging hours when the optimum conditions are shortest.

From 19 March to 19 May a pair of Screech Owls left the roost about eight minutes after sunset on clear or hazy evenings but about 7.4 minutes before sunset on very overcast evenings. From 23 March to 21 May they returned at times varying from a mean of fifteen minutes before sunrise to an average of two minutes before, according as the morning was clear or very cloudy (Allard 1937). The general principles governing the activities of diurnal and nocturnal birds are similar, apart from the reversal of behaviour in relation to increasing and decreasing light on the part of the latter.

Some waders song-flight in the evening and may be particularly noisy at night when they first occupy territory. The Sanderling's 'pairing flight' occurs most actively then and the Curlew performs its display-flight especially in the evening (Manniche 1910; Farren 1912). The Woodcock begins roding about five minutes later each evening, irrespective of the weather and as the days pass the number of flights decreases (Warwick and van Someren 1936). An American Woodcock called in the evening on 22 March with light at 28 foot-candles but on 28 March at 1·5 foot-candles. Of two males the bird living in the more densely foliaged territory appeared consistently earlier than the other, suggesting that the amount of light at the roosting place influences the beginning of activity (Pitelka 1943) (Fig. 33). In passerines there is little evidence that this applies.

The effect of moonlight on bird activities is often difficult to assess. It is surprising that Bussmann (1935) could find no evidence of the influence of moonlight or weather on the comings and goings of Barn Owls, but this species sometimes extends its hunting into daylight. Gilbert White commented on the Nightjar: 'This bird is most punctual in beginning its song exactly at the close of day; so exactly that I have known it strike up more than once at the report of the Portsmouth evening gun'. He was correct only in so far as he appreciated that there was a close relationship between light intensity and the bird's first song. With moonlight it sings 51 minutes after sunset but on other nights 35 minutes after. A Nightjar's last morning song averaged 78 minutes before sunrise with moonlight and 40 without it (Ashmore 1935). Moonlight would most influence the behaviour of diurnal birds which rise and roost at low light intensities—such as, possibly, Skylarks. On the Central Asian steppe they sing two to three hours before dawn (Ludlow 1928). It may affect the rising of the Wren (Armstrong 1955), thrushes, the Song Sparrow, and Kingbird (Ball 1945) and certainly influences the display of the Sage Grouse (Scott 1942). The American Robin sings earlier on moonlit mornings (Fig. 34) (Leopold and Eynon 1961).† The feeding of some birds, including Herons, can be extended after sunset when there is moonlight (Armstrong 1940).

Some birds which display and sing at night appear to be particularly stimulated by moonlight. Thus Collett (1876) remarked that the Great Snipe seemed to prefer bright nights for displaying and Pycraft (1912) and Turner (1924) noted numbers of Snipe bleating in the moonlight. In the Solomon Islands the Golden Whistler sings long before dawn on moonlight nights (Cain and Galbraith 1956) but Horsfield's Bush Lark

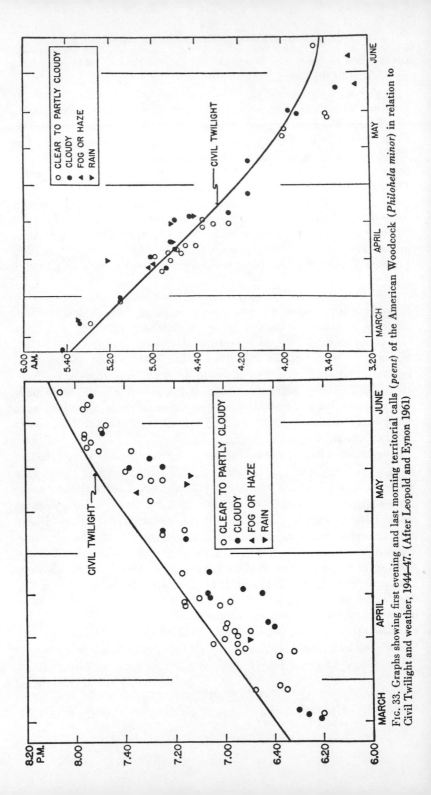

FIG. 33. Graphs showing first evening and last morning territorial calls (*peent*) of the American Woodcock (*Philohela minor*) in relation to Civil Twilight and weather, 1944–47. (After Leopold and Eynon 1961)

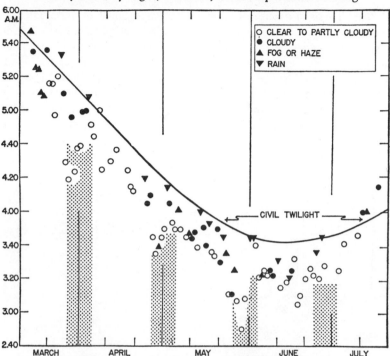

FIG. 34. First daybreak song of the American Robin (*Turdus migratorius*) in a suburban area at Madison, Wisconsin, during 1945 showing relationship to the beginning of Civil Twilight, weather, and moonlight. Stippling indicates periods from day before full moon to last quarter. (After Leopold and Eynon 1961)

sings just as much on dark as on moonlight nights (Bourke 1947) (Fig. 35). Its peaks of song are shortly after sunrise with a lower peak at sunset. At least twenty-four Australian species sing to some extent at night (Boehm 1950; Sedgwick 1951; Robinson 1946–47, 1949, 1956) and quite a number of European birds are also nocturnal singers, though some are only heard in exceptional circumstances. The Sprosser Nightingale in Finland at 61° 4′N sings steadily from midnight to 4.00 a.m., with a song-peak from 1.00 to 2.00 a.m. It also sings intermittently during the day (Piiparinen and Toivari 1958). A Nightingale sang at night for five hours and twenty-five minutes without a minute's pause (Bond 1951). Great Bustards sometimes display by the light of the full moon—'an almost spectral sight' (Gewalt 1959).

Influence on song of clouds, rain, and humidity

Graphs showing the singing- or calling-times of birds on successive days show that they are active later on dark mornings than when the sky is clear. These observations confirm the importance of light intensity among external factors influencing morning activity, including song. The awakening notes of Song Sparrows are heard from three to six minutes later in cloudy weather than on clear days. This is not due to cloudiness as such but to the reduction in light. Scheer (1952a) analysed data concerning the Blackbird and found that the bird's lateness on cloudy days was correlated with the light values so that it sang or called at the same brightness on heavily clouded mornings as on mornings of light cloud.

The American thrushes of the genera *Catharus* and *Hylocichla* sing

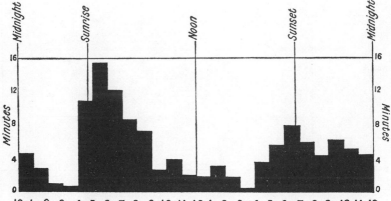

Histogram of hourly song-periods of a nesting pair of Horsfield's Bush-Larks

FIG. 35. The histogram was obtained by means of observations from 5 to 27 November. All records are averages of at least two listening periods lasting an hour or longer. No distinction has been made between dark and moon-lit nights but outbursts of song were as frequent on dark nights as when the moon was shining. (After Bourke 1947)

more actively in the evening than in the morning. Both morning and evening they sing for a longer period in cloudy weather (Dilger 1956a). All these species sing and call to some extent at night. The Nightingale-Thrush, *Catharus occidentalis*, is a 'true storm-thrush' according to Skutch (1960). It is very vocal in misty and rainy weather. As one might expect cloudiness tends to delay first song in the tropics as in temperate regions (Lutz 1931). As already mentioned, some birds delay singing on cloudy mornings until the light is brighter than would evoke song on clear mornings (p. 194).

Mist affects birds' activities, but to what extent reduction of visibility is effective rather than humidity or temperature is unknown. Fog de-

XIIIa. Greeting ceremony of Rockhopper Penguins

XIIIb. Trumpeting ceremony of the King Penguin

XIV. Cocoi Herons displaying

presses the amount of Skylark song and the singing which occurs tends to be from the ground (Clark 1947). Perhaps mist retards the singing of Wrens after they leave the roost (p. 191). In Lapland the song pauses of the Arctic Warbler are longer when mist descends (Lundevall 1952). Sustained heavy rain quenches the singing of Pied Flycatchers (Curio 1959a) and many other birds, but a Nightingale will continue in full song through a thunderstorm or be stimulated to sing by gun-fire (Bond 1951). Approaching thunderstorms evoke strange aerial antics from birds as various as White Pelicans and Bee-eaters (Armstrong 1947). In bad weather the amount of song by the Swallow is usually reduced but the output was specially high on a very inclement day—suggesting that above a certain threshold of stimulation song is not inhibited by unfavourable weather (Purchon 1948). This may well be true of other species.†

Where there are marked seasonal differences in rainfall and the breeding season of many species coincides with the rains there is an increase in song coinciding with them. Even when such birds are kept in captivity they may sing when rain falls as Darwin's finches did during showers when removed to California (Orr 1945). Rain can have an indirect effect on song. Wrens build when rain renders nesting material particularly pliable and they sing less when thus engaged. Robinson (1949) comments that in Australia 'moisture in the form of rain, heavy dew, or even an extensive storm hundreds of miles away may affect the volume of song during the non-breeding season'. According to Humboldt howler monkeys are vocal before rain.

In exceptional circumstances dew may influence the rising time of birds and thus the times of their first utterances. The terrain of the Tres Marias islands off the coast of Mexico is so arid that birds are compelled to rise early enough to drink the dew before it evaporates. Some, such as the Cardinal, drink from the small pools which accumulate at the base of the agave leaves. Ground doves bestir themselves later and drink from grass stalks (Heilfurth 1938). It is possible that the periods when food is available may influence the incidence of song, not merely to the extent that for many species their methods of feeding preclude song while they are thus engaged—but in more subtle ways. For example Blase (1960) noted a closer correlation between the singing of captive isolated Red-backed Shrikes and feeding times than alterations in lighting.

Influence of wind on song

Scheer (1952a) found a definite but slight correlation between wind and retarded song. The first vocalizations are later on windy or rainy days independently of light intensity. The effect of wind is to reduce the

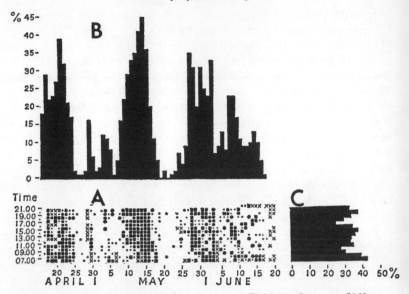

Fɪɢ. 36. The frequency of a Redstart's song at Eichstätt, Germany, 1943, throughout the breeding season.

In diagram A is shown the hourly record of song throughout the season, i.e. from assertion to abandonment of territory. To the symbols used numerical values have been allotted for the purpose of calculating the data of diagrams B and C.

    × =no observation : in these hours an average value is assumed.

    · =little song—numerical value assigned=1.

    ● =intermittent song—numerical value assigned=2.

    ■ =full song—numerical value assigned=3.

Diagram B is derived from A and shows the relative progress of song, day by day.

Diagram C, also derived from A, gives the relative frequency of song, hour by hour.

    Nest-building: 1st nest 26 April–3 May.

                  2nd nest 5 May–7 May

                  3rd nest 16 May–19 May.

                  4th nest 2 June–5 June.

The marked reduction in song while the female is building the nest is apparant. (After Buxton 1953)

output of song though this may vary with different species. During strong winds Skylarks sing on the ground and the output of song is much reduced (Rollin 1943; Clark 1947). In Lapland strong winds tend to shorten a bird's active day (Franz 1949). The Mistle Thrush is sometimes called the Storm Cock because it pipes during gales but the Greenshank sings less on windy days (Nethersole-Thompson 1951). The rate of calling of Tawny Owls is said to be in inverse relation to the velocity of the wind. Calling is greatly reduced when the weather is both windy and cold (Hansen 1952). On windy evenings Blackbirds at a winter roost are much quieter than on calm evenings (Colquhoun 1939) and Pied Flycatchers cease singing earlier on windy evenings (Curio 1959a). When a male bird is highly stimulated sexually the weather may have very little influence on his output of song. A Redstart sang in excellent style on a blustery day (21 April) but even more the next day which was still and sunny. There was much less song two days later when it was wet and windy (Buxton 1950). It might seem that this bird's output was much influenced by the weather but inspection of the daily histograms suggests that the sequence of courtship and nesting behaviour was much more important (Fig. 36). So, too, with Wrens. The male's interest in the female appears to have greater relevance to the output of song than the weather (Armstrong 1955) (Fig. 37). Sub-song is greatly increased.

Influence of temperature on song

Probably each species is adapted to a particular temperature range. Severe and sudden cold may inhibit ovulation and gametogenesis (Marshall 1959) but early breeding is encouraged by mild weather. Extreme weather, whether hot or cold, tends to inhibit song (Alexander 1931) but by artificially raising the temperature in winter Song Thrushes may be brought into song (Tinbergen 1939). Some tropical species sing during the heat of midday but the main outbursts of vocalization tend to be in the morning. Davis (1941c) noticed that in Cuba birds were nearly as active at midday as in the early morning but the temperature variation between dawn and 2.00 p.m. was only 14°. Seppä (1938) found that in Finland temperatures above 18°C or below 10°C are unfavourable to bird activities but noted that the Chaffinch's behaviour is more affected by temperature changes than the Great Tit's. Palmgren (1935) basing his inferences on the waxing and waning of song during the twenty-four hours of perpetual daylight north of the Arctic Circle came to the conclusion that temperature is crucial in determining the rest period. This is doubtful. The lull in passerine song which occurs about 21.00 occurs when humidity is sometimes low and temperature relatively high. The period of maximum song is more difficult to assess but according to my observations (1954a) it falls between midnight and 04.30. This suggests that increasing light rather than temperature is the important factor and agrees with what is known of bird song in general. Rollin's graphs (1958) show that the output of song by a Yellowhammer in Arctic Norway was mainly delivered from 22.30 until 9.00. This contrasts with the greater and more even spread of song during the shorter day in northern England. Rollin does not mention this bird's strong tendency to sing before dusk in the early part of the year (Fig. 32).

Nice (1937, 1943) has pointed out that as the season advances there

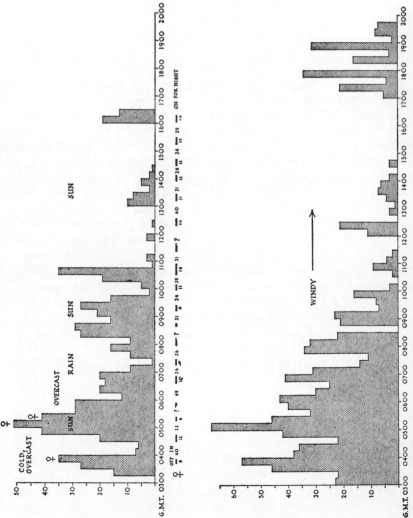

FIG. 37. Histograms showing song output of a Wren (*above*) on 26 May and (*below*) 4 June 1947. The vertical scale shows the number of songs per quarter-hour and the broken horizontal lines show the incubation rhythm of the female. The sign ♀ indicates the presence of a female near the male. As the season advances the output of song tends to be more concentrated in the early forenoon. Possibly the shower on 26 May reduced song but it is unlikely that the wind on 4 June affected song output appreciably. (After Armstrong 1955)

are decreasing temperature thresholds for singing, migration, and the beginning of egg-laying. Thus the first Song Sparrows coming in to breed arrive at higher temperatures (average 10·6°C, 51°F) than later birds (6°C, 54°F). The threshold of singing was 13·3°C, 54·2°F on 7 January and decreased about three-quarters of a degree Fahrenheit each day. The main immigration of males takes place at 43°F when singing and territorial behaviour are well established. Nice remarks that for a century 43°F has been recognized as the threshold for growth in wheat and other plants and is a base commonly used by meteorologists (Fig. 38).

One must qualify acceptance of these and other observations made in the field by the consideration that variables, such as light intensity, were

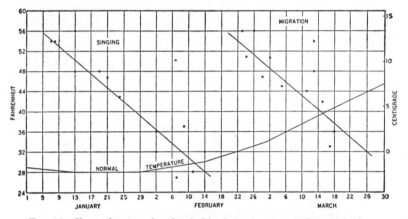

FIG. 38. Chart showing the threshold of singing in resident male Song Sparrows and the migration of males. The dates show that the threshold for singing was 54·2 degrees F. on 7 January and decreased 0·7 of a degree F. each day. This is similar to the threshold for migration but occurs a month and a half earlier. (After Nice 1937)

also operating. Thus von Haartman (1952) noticed that in Finland during years of higher spring temperatures the Chaffinch's morning song began earlier but Scheer (1952b) pointed out that the situation was complicated by the possibility that the temperature in Belgium, where Finnish Chaffinches spend the winter, might have a bearing on the physiological development of the birds, the date of their spring migration, and the beginning of song in spring. It has been argued that the Blackbird's commencement of song is influenced by the weather but the Chaffinch's is not. My own observations suggest that the Blackbird's beginning of song is more subject to the influence of weather than the Chaffinch's. However, very severe weather after the Chaffinch has come into song tends to silence it, while bright sunshine has a stimulating effect (Barrett 1947; Poulsen 1958). Saunders (1947) kept records of the first songs during the season of several species over many years and came to the conclusion that the influence of weather on the inception of song was the same for species which begin song at about the same time.

Curio's graph shows that Pied Flycatchers sing more readily in high than in low temperatures. Also in frosty or otherwise cold weather they sing in the tree-tops but when it is warmer nearer the nesting holes.

The effect of temperature on reproductive behaviour has been

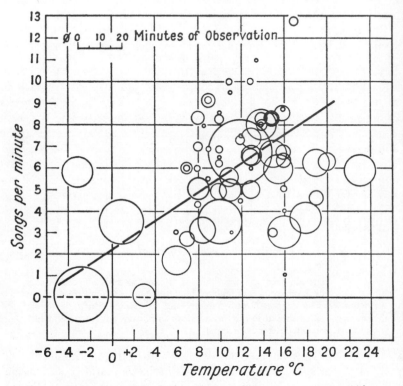

FIG. 39. Song output of Pied Flycatcher in relation to temperature. (After Curio 1959a)

repeatedly demonstrated (Kluijver 1951; Lack 1954; Goodacre and Lack 1959). Seasonal temperature variations modify the time of egg-laying in many species and it is a commonplace that in exceptionally mild winters pairs of birds may try to breed. In unusually warm December weather in England Blackbirds sing, Great Tits sing and fight, Dabchicks trill, and Blackcock display. A sharp rise in temperature may be more important than the actual temperature attained.

The influence of a rapid fall in temperature in checking or retarding breeding is also apparent. Birds which have occupied territory may abandon it temporarily during a cold spell in spring and on an unusually chilly morning there is a decrease in song. A Chaffinch in that state when the song has not yet reached maturity will sing less on such a morning but there is a tendency with all reproductive behaviour for birds at their peak of ardour to show less modification in behaviour with changes of weather than birds coming into breeding condition. An untimely fall of snow may silence a Song Sparrow or Nightingale (Nice 1937; Bond 1951) but the weather tends to have increasingly less capacity to inhibit song as birds attain the state of greatest stimulation. Snowfalls about the first week of March only slightly check the seasonal increase in Skylark song and birds may then sing during snowstorms. Discussing Skylark song Clark (1947) remarks : 'When the breeding cycle is begun adverse weather conditions do not appreciably affect song; they may do so to a greater extent during the autumn song period and the first weeks of the spring period. During the winter song is probably entirely dependent upon favourable weather conditions'. He notes, however, that the autumnal song period occurs so regularly and unanimously that it cannot be attributed to weather conditions, especially as these can be unfavourable when such song is uttered. During breeding there is a close relationship between the activities of the male and the amount of song.

The temperatures of starting seasonal singing are not those at which birds sing after coming into song. Song Sparrows in this early phase may sing at quite low temperatures for a day or two, but as late as 6 March a drop in temperature with wind will cause song to cease temporarily. When the autumn migration is delayed until October because of exceptionally mild weather Song Sparrows may sing.

Blanchard (1941), studying White-crowned Sparrows, found that the weather, especially temperature, has most influence in the period between the beginning of spermatogenesis and the first maturation of spermatocytes in the male gonads. Thus it may be that temperatures earlier than those when a bird begins its seasonal song have an influence not only on the date this begins but also on its earliness relative to light intensity. Experiments by Kendeigh with House Sparrows have shown that in summer, as compared with winter, there is an increase of 4·22 calories, there being less energy required for resistance to the cold. This increased energy is available for the activities of migration and reproduction.

Shaver and Walker (1930) observed that the cessation of the Mockingbird's diurnal song in winter and spring was not dependent on temperature and Emlen (1937) considered light intensity the only environmental factor with a direct bearing on the Mockingbird's awakening song. The beginning of song by the Alder Flycatcher is independent of temperature changes but when the minimum temperature is plotted against the duration of song there is a positive correlation (McCabe 1951). No correlation between temperature and the crepuscular roding of the American Woodcock has been detected. Light is the important factor (Pitelka 1943). Undoubtedly the influence of various external factors on the organism is so delicately balanced that in nature the effectiveness of some factors in governing behaviour is only observable in extreme conditions. Thus extremes of temperature, either high or low, reduce or inhibit the song of the Grasshopper Sparrow (Smith 1959). Probably this is true of many species. In general temperature changes are a less refined triggering mechanism for song than alterations in light. Laboratory experiments to supplement field observations are necessary to disentangle the importance at various phases of the different climatic and other factors we have been considering. Some generalizations may be made in regard to these as, for example, that female song and duetting are commoner where comparatively mild winters prevail but the necessary preliminary to the formulation of rules of general application must be the analysis of the particular factors involved.

To discuss the relationship between climate and bird song in further detail would involve the consideration of ecological factors outside our present scope, though some will be considered in the next chapter, but it must be emphasized that song should be interpreted as an element integrating the bird with its environment, a highly complex evolutionary adaptation whereby the internal world of the bird and the external world in which it is active and which activates it are kept *en rapport*.

XII

SONG AND ADAPTATIONS TO HABITAT

> It is also curious to note that with a few exceptions the
> resident birds are comparatively very silent, even those be-
> longing to groups which elsewhere are highly loquacious.
> The reason of this is not far to seek. In woods and thickets,
> where birds abound most, they are continually losing sight of
> each other, and are only prevented from scattering by call-
> ing often; while the muffling effect on sound of the close
> foliage, to which may be added a spirit of emulation where
> many voices are heard, incites most species, especially those
> that are social, to exert their voices to the utmost pitch in
> singing, calling and screaming. On the open pampas, birds,
> which are not compelled to live concealed on the surface,
> can see each other at long distances, and perpetual calling
> is not needful: moreover, in that still atmosphere sound
> travels far.
>
> W. H. HUDSON (1892)

As the structure of a bird is the end-product of progressive adaptation
to its habitat its morphology determines to greater or lesser extent
the posture adopted while singing but we must not assume that this
is exclusively necessitated by adaptations determined by its manner of
feeding and other maintenance activities. In discussing the singing of
birds in flight (Chapter VIII) we noted that birds differing widely in
structure sing on the wing. While the aerial instrumental song of some
species of nightjar may be assumed to be a subordinate adaptation
correlated with foraging on the wing this is certainly not true of other
species such as larks and waders. In these and many other species the
evolution of song-flight, correlated with habitat preference, has determined structural modifications, particularly in the wings and tail. Probably in most species which sing while perched this influence has been
slight or even negligible.

Posture during song

The relationship between a bird's general build and its posture during
song is obvious. The Nuthatch and Treecreeper, adapted to explore tree-
trunks, and some penguins, with legs set far back on the body to enable
them to swim swiftly, sing or call with their beaks held almost vertically.
The Nightjar may rattle out his song squatting low along, rather than

217

FIG. 40. Postures of some North American species during song. (a) Worm-eating Warbler in song; (b) the Winter Wren cocks up his tail as he sings; (c) front view of a singing Song Sparrow; (d) Chickadee singing the 'Phoebe' call; (e) Rose-breasted Grosbeak singing; (f) Meadowlark singing on a post. (After Saunders 1929)

FIG. 41. Posture of Bee-eater calling from perch and in normal stance. As the bird calls the black neck-band is rendered more conspicuous. (After Swift 1959)

across, a branch. In this posture the bird is less conspicuous to predators but often Nightjars perch across a branch or a stump while singing. Some species, including birds as different as the Violet-headed Humming-bird (Skutch 1958), Nightjar, and Wren, frequently turn their heads as they sing, thus sometimes creating a ventriloquial effect, others, such as the Rufous-sided Towhee (Davis 1948), face forward consistently. Some birds intercalate singing and preening. A Chaffinch will continue to maintain its regular rate of song while preening, lifting its head to sing every few seconds. The impulse to utter song appears to recur in a rhythm, dominating preening and other activities.

Some birds have peculiar mannerisms while singing. The Wren, when sexually excited, cocks his tail as he sings (Fig. 40). Utterances may be accompanied by raising the crown feathers or crest, inflating air-sacs, or the exposure of coloured adornments in or near the bill. The interior of the mouth may be vividly coloured (Armstrong 1947) (p. 158) or the movements of the mandibles may cause certain feathers to become highly conspicuous. As the Bee-eater calls its black neck-band becomes conspicuous (Fig. 41). When the Stagemaker sings the yellowish bases of the throat feathers are revealed so that the bird becomes more conspicuous in the shadowy rain-forest (Marshall 1954). During the Cut-throat Finch's display it sings in an erect posture exhibiting a crescent-shaped red marking on its throat and fluffing out the feathers of the lower breast to show a chestnut patch. When the Malachite Sunbird utters its courtship song it exposes the bright green pectoral tufts (Beven 1946). Some South American bellbirds erect remarkable fleshy adornments around the bill as they call and display (Pl. XV).† We can usually assume that song which is accompanied by the exhibition of detailed, but not necessarily vivid or strongly contrasting, adornments is stimulating to the female.

Height at which song is uttered

The height at which birds sing, whether in the air or vegetation, is often so characteristic as to be useful in identification though it varies with relation to the breeding cycle and the state of the gonads. Generally speaking the greater a bird's ardour the nearer it sings to the maximum height for the species. Developmental sub-song is practically never sung at the height normal for full song. The male Rufous-sided Towhee sings nearer the ground as the incubation period progresses, with a pronounced reduction in height shortly before the young hatch, and unmated males sing progressively lower as the season advances (Davis 1958). Thus birds make themselves particularly conspicuous when this is advantageous in relation to the propagation of the species, but tend to remain in cover while singing non-territorial song and so reduce their jeopardy from predators (p. 63).‡

Song and density of habitat

Dense habitats offer concealment alike to singing birds and their predators. Intra-specific acoustic advertisement is important in enabling birds of such habitats to locate each other (p. 76). Moreover, birds of dense, homogeneous habitats are usually cryptically coloured though a number of species of the Siberian forest, the taiga, wear bright adornments. Reed-beds constitute a particularly homogeneous concealing habitat. The Palaearctic warblers inhabiting them utter continuous songs. The Short-billed and Long-billed Marsh Wrens of North America which occupy habitats corresponding to those of our marsh-frequenting warblers have frequently-uttered discontinuous songs but, like these Old World warblers, sing much at night as they do (Welter 1935). The Swamp Sparrow also sings at night. The Long-billed Wren and Sedge Warbler both bob up from the herbage in short song-flights. The Bittern is also a nocturnal as well as diurnal singer. The Nightjar finds concealment in darkness rather than dense vegetation but it can hardly be coincidence that it utters a continuous, repetitive song similar to the songs of Savi's Warbler and the Grasshopper Warbler, though pitched much lower (p. 31) (Pl. II).

In contrast to the Palaearctic marsh warblers the Reed Bunting sings a comparatively slow phrase song but many of this bird's characteristics, including its coloration, type of nest, and preference for the fringes of reed-beds, indicate that it is much less specialized for life in this kind of habitat than the reed-frequenting warblers. Pairs sometimes nest away from water in Yellowhammer habitats.

Birds of tropical forest tend to utter conspicuous, loud frequent contact notes and some have penetrating songs. Species of dense forest in South America have louder call-notes than birds of the clearings and forest edge (Beebe 1917). We have already noted that the Olive Whistler's song is finest where it inhabits thick, misty forest (p. 92). A number of rain-forest birds sing duets but very few perform song-flights (p. 135). Skutch remarks that the Quetzal is the only bird of the tropical forest known to him which displays thus. My impression of the voices of New World rain-forest birds and jungle species in Indo-China was that continuous and semi-continuous songs are rare but raucous and repetitive calls are common and some species utter pure-toned notes.† Few noises can compete in harshness with the screams of parrots or in clarity of tone with the notes of tinamous and some tropical species of wren. In Europe these extremes are represented by the Jay and the Golden Oriole—both rather secretive frequenters of woodland. The Tawny Owl, which favours denser habitats than other British owls, has the clearest voice and is the most vocal. In Costa Rica the two species of tanager which inhabit undergrowth in the dense forests are more soberly coloured than most of the other representatives of the family but are the best singers (Skutch 1954). A noticeable proportion of tropical birds utter rather deep-toned resonant hoots, moans, or high-pitched whistles. Both extremes are far-carrying, distinctive, and thus adapted to facilitate the maintenance of contact. Marshall (1954) comments that birds of the Australian rain-forest floor utter far-carrying calls but this is also true of many canopy-frequenting birds. It may be remarked that among insects there are interesting correlations between habitats and singing behaviour. Thus, for example, in the eastern United States only those species of cricket which live in trees or tall shrubs sing at night and synchronize their songs (Alexander 1960). Among frogs, too, many species have characteristic preferences in regard to calling sites and sympatric species tend to use sites which differ from species to species. Even populations may differ. One population of *Leptodactylus nitidus* calls exclusively from bushes, another on walls, rocks, or cliffs (Bogert 1960).

Song in open habitats

Mention has already been made of the correlation between song-flights and open environments (p. 138). Almost every bird of the tundra performs a song-flight. So close is this correlation that the more monotonous the terrain the more tendency there is for birds to perform high or prolonged song-flights. Species which breed among boulders, such as the Wheatear and Snow Bunting, mount to lower altitudes than larks, pipits, and longspurs, which nest in low vegetation on the ground. Self-advertisement is particularly important among tundra birds as even a fortnight's delay in initiating breeding may entail disaster for the brood (Freuchen and Salomonsen 1959). The songs of several species are reported to be louder in the open, comparatively level regions of the western United States than in the mountains and many birds of the non-mountainous areas perform song-flights (Linsdale 1938a, b). Among related species those breeding in open tree-less habitats tend to sing the most prolonged songs. The species of bunting breeding in open habitats all differ from other members of the family in singing lark-like songs including sweet notes with good carrying power. The resemblance to lark song must be due to convergence accompanying adaptation to open country (Thorpe and Lade 1961). Marler's observation of three species with rather similar songs counter-singing in a Mexican valley (p. 185) raises the question whether in habitats where several species compete for a limited food supply the songs of some species tend to acquire common characteristics and to serve to repel food competitors.

Continuity of song in relation to habitat

It is remarkable that birds of completely contrasting song-habitats sing highly continuous songs—species which haunt marsh vegetation and birds which carol high in the air. Apart from the greater effectiveness of continuous song as advertisement it may be that this characteristic is to be explained in both types of singer by the comparative invulnerability of birds in these situations. Alike in reed-beds or in the sky a predator cannot easily approach near enough to seize a bird without betraying its presence. Movements and sounds made in parting reeds indicate the approach of any mammal and it is therefore at a disadvantage in making a spring. Some birds of prey, notably the Merlin, can catch Meadow Pipits and Skylarks in flight, but it is doubtful if they are often able to seize song-flighting birds. A number of species which frequent broad-leaved trees or thick bushes, such as thrushes, nightingales, and some warblers, also utter continuous or semi-continuous songs. In some this may be correlated with ground-foraging but it is also an adaptation associated with the concealment provided by foliage. The Ring Ouzel, which frequents bare hill-sides and has conspicuously contrasting plumage, utters one of the crudest of turdine songs. This interrupted type of song would enable it to keep a look-out for predators, as buntings, Chaffinches, and other discontinuous singers are able to do. Discontinuous songs are characteristic of numerous birds, mainly rather small, such as many buntings, the Wren, Hedgesparrow, and Chaffinch. Thus attention is frequently called to the singer without the expenditure of energy involved in uttering continuous song while the pauses provide opportunity for listening for the voices of other birds, and, in some birds like the Chaffinch during certain phases, of learning song-versions (p. 53). Moreover, these pauses enable the singer to listen and watch for approaching predators. The Hedgesparrow which usually forages, and often sings near the ground, frequently moves its perch and sings at irregular intervals, thus reducing its jeopardy from ground predators. Not only does the noise of a bird's own voice affect its hearing but some birds, perhaps many, become partially deaf while singing. The Capercaillie is said to be regardless of loud noises during its crowing performance and it has been proved that the hearing sensitivity of the Pigeon sinks to one-tenth when the beak is wide open (Bray and Thurlow 1942). Many discontinuous singers, such as buntings, occupy perches where they are conspicuous but from which, if alerted in time, they can find refuge in cover from aerial predators. Two species which suffer severely from the attacks of the Sparrowhawk are the House Sparrow and Redstart (Tinbergen 1946). Both make themselves conspicuous visually and vocally on dwellings around the gables of which Sparrowhawks can sweep unexpectedly. Few birds can afford to make themselves highly conspicuous in both respects. Thus among the American Tetraonidae the species which dance do not drum and those which drum do not dance (Wing 1946).

Song requirements in relation to choice of territory, adornments, and pair-bond

Not only may adaptations to the environment involve associated song adaptations but song requirements may affect the choice of territory. As the Tree Pipit normally sings flying up from the branch of a tree the presence of suitable song-perches is probably a factor in rendering an area attractive as a territory. The female Boat-billed Flycatcher frequently chooses to nest in the tree used as song-perch by the male (Skutch 1951a). Thus the presence of a suitable song-perch may not only influence the male's choice of territory but also the female's choice of a nest-site.

In some species the exploitation of visual conspicuousness appears to have resulted in the suppression of song—confirming that combined visual and vocal conspicuousness may, in some environments, render a bird highly vulnerable to predators. The Brown Towhee has no territorial song but the male makes himself highly conspicuous. The Phainopepla is another species in which sight advertisement is more important than song. Apparently reduction in song has followed adaptation to arid country dotted with small trees on the tops of which birds are easily seen. Quaintance (1938) has argued that the Brown Towhee's remote ancestor possessed a more elaborate song which degenerated as sight advertisement became dominant but the song may have more territorial importance than he realized.

Species with a long-sustained pair-bond, such as the Bullfinch, tend to develop contact notes rather than elaborate and continuous song but a number sing duets (p. 181). Small migratory species which pair-up anew each spring usually have relatively loud, distinctive songs—an adaptation accelerating formation of the pair-bond. Some highly aerial species constitute exceptions but their activities render them conspicuous.

Song in relation to foraging

The greatest suppression of vocalization or reduction to a rudimentary form is characteristic of some large aquatic and aerial species such as the Mute Swan and various Old and New World vultures, although there are a few comparatively silent birds, such as the Kiwi and the Ruff, in which comparatively silent behaviour is associated with other peculiarities in their way of life. Most song-less or relatively song-less species are birds with small nest-territories, social nesting, and wide-ranging foraging activities—many dependent on types of food sporadically, transiently, or intermittently available, such as carrion, shoals of fish or aggregations of other aquatic animals, concentrations of free-flying insects, or other aerial prey. Practically all these birds are highly conspicuous visually, either because of their outline in flight or by reason of their coloration, or both. By their calls and conspicuous coloration some species of gull and tern attract other birds to sources of food, especially shoaling fish, and as exploitation of such an abundant but transient supply is advantageous to the community and entails little or no deprivation of food for the individual these adaptations persist (Armstrong 1944b, 1946a; Frings *et al.* 1955).

Such species have no feeding territory around the nest and their conspicuous episematic coloration (Cott 1947) would attract predators if they nested in accessible situations. Many of them breed socially on islands, cliffs, or in tall trees. Their vocabulary tends to be unmusical, adapted to maintain contact with the mate and other birds in the colony. Among birds of this type sustained song is characteristic only of those marine species which display at night, and aerial foragers, such as hirundines. Alarm calls are more frequently uttered by gulls nesting on the ground than by the Kittiwake, breeding in the comparative safety of cliff ledges (Cullen 1957). Species differ greatly in the extent to which they sing as they feed. The Chiffchaff utters its simple song as it moves about the branches and the Wood Warbler sings sibilantly as it seeks cater-

XV.   Bearded or Mossy-throated Bellbird calling

XVI. Wandering Albatrosses courting. The birds bill, and the male brays and bows to the female

pillars in the canopy whereas ground-feeding birds such as the Song Thrush seldom sing while foraging. The Blackbird may warble sub-song in such circumstances (Snow 1958) and I have heard a male utter snatches of full song while seeking food on the ground—but this is unusual. The Wren sings from time to time while feeding but when in a state of strong stimulation may sing for minutes at a time from a perch. The Coal Tit sings as it feeds, the larger Blue Tit sometimes ceases foraging to sing, while the Great Tit, the largest of the three, normally concentrates on singing (Gibb 1954). The tiny Goldcrest is constantly on the move while singing. Thus there is a rough correlation between body size and rapidity of the metabolic processes with the tendency to sing on the move. Such insectivorous birds are more active than grain-eaters and are more prone to sing while feeding.

The relationship between habitat, feeding behaviour, and song may be illustrated by comparing the behaviour of some European woodpeckers. The Greater Spotted is much given to drumming and only rarely feeds on the ground; the Middle Spotted drums rather infrequently but utters a loud courtship call, while the Green 'yaffles' loudly and frequently but drums very rarely. It often flies out into wide heaths away from trees to feed on ants. No doubt this species diverged in song and appearance as it became increasingly adapted to foraging on the ground.

Song in relation to predation

Several writers have suggested a correlation between types of vocalization and feeding on the ground. Hartshorne (1958b) remarks that the 'ground-feeding members of the Parulidae (American wood warblers) include nearly all the loudest and most musical songsters in this family'. Species which feed on or near the ground are usually in particular jeopardy from ground predators and therefore selection has operated in favour of their being cryptically coloured. Their visual inconspicuousness tends to be compensated for by vocal conspicuousness. Few ground-foraging birds sing on the ground. The lyrebirds are notable exceptions with special peculiarities in their behaviour. Probably the absence from Australia of placental mammals in the past has rendered their song-display less hazardous than where such marauders occur. It is significant that the Ostrich, living where there are large beasts of prey, sleeps very fitfully, waking at intervals of not longer than fifteen minutes whereas the Emu sleeps for an hour or two on end (Immelmann 1960). Some passerine birds, such as the Blue Rock Thrush and Wall Creeper, sport bright adornments and both feed and sing on the ground but they run less danger from predators in their rocky or craggy habitats than birds which haunt less rugged terrain.

Turning to the adaptations reducing hazards in tropical forest it might seem that the coloration of canopy-frequenting birds conflicts with the principle that species making themselves conspicuous vocally tend to be cryptically coloured, for some such birds have loud call-notes. Many brightly hued birds of the canopy, such as parrots and toucans, are not as conspicuous in their natural environment as might be supposed. Vivid greens and yellows merge into sunlit foliage and many rain-forest trees carry brightly coloured blossoms on their summits. Where there are strong contrasts of light and shade, contrasting plumage tends to conceal the wearer. On or near the forest floor, where the light is dim and uniform, contrasting plumage is uncommon. Moreover, the flesh of vividly coloured birds is usually unpalatable (Cott 1947). Probably the adornments borne by some birds of the taiga can be worn with comparative impunity because conifers offer a safer retreat from flying predators than broad-leaved trees. The rarity of the turdine type of song in tropical forest may be partly due to the jeopardy from fast-flying raptors incurred by birds singing for minutes on end from one perch and partly to the usefulness of contact calls and songs in such habitats. The vulnerability of many gaily adorned species is reduced by their utterances consisting of brief but sometimes harsh and loud cries. Such a cry is easily locatable by other members of the species. Perhaps there is also a relationship to foraging behaviour and availability of food, for, as we have noted, long-sustained song presupposes that food is abundant enough to permit of long periods spent otherwise than foraging.

In contrast to tropical rain-forests with their great variety of trees huge stands of a single species are found in the forests of high latitudes. Territorialism and correlated song tend to be reduced in such birds as nutcrackers, waxwings, crossbills, and redpolls. In some areas both intraspecific and interspecific competition seem to be mild. It would seem that the birch and conifer forests of the north could support greater populations of the species represented than they do. Climatic factors may be more important than predation in limiting the numbers of some of these song-birds.

The periods when song is uttered during the twenty-four hours may be governed by hazards from predators. Leach's Petrel indulges in the song-flight at the breeding colony after dark. At other times these birds would be at the mercy of gulls. The communal displays of the Great Snipe, in which the birds stretch their necks and spread their tails while making varied noises, take place under cover of darkness when danger from predators is reduced. A number of species perform their song-flight at dusk. Probably in dull light they are not so liable to be seized by birds of prey. The Paraguayan Snipe, which flies more slowly than the Snipe, only drums at dusk or after dark (Cawkell and Hamilton 1961).

The relationship between adaptations to habitat and acoustic and visual self-advertisement

Although practically every bird advertises its presence to some extent both visually and vocally the close relationship between acoustic self-advertisement and a bird's total adaptation to its environment may be illustrated by setting the extremes in opposition.

TABLE XIII

FACTORS CORRELATED RESPECTIVELY WITH ACOUSTIC AND VISUAL SELF-ADVERTISEMENT

	Acoustic	*Visual*
Structural	Small size and weak armament	Large size and strong armament
Plumage	Inconspicuous	Conspicuous
Display	Simple	Elaborate
Habitat	Dense	Open
Territorialism	Strong	Weak
Pair-bond	Short	Prolonged
Nesting	Isolated	Social
Foraging	Competitive	Specialized
Feeding area	Fixed	Varied
Predation	Vulnerable	Relatively invulnerable
Palatability	High	Low

In general the importance of song for any species may be reckoned by evaluating the extent to which its characteristics are to be found in one column or the other. Although species may be thought of which are not obviously of either the acoustic or visual type, the table shows that the vocalizations of any bird must be understood in the context of its other adaptations. They are all closely integrated. The characteristics of some rather divergent species, such as some lek birds, must be interpreted in relation to their aberrant behaviour, particularly the vagueness or brevity of the pair-bond. It is recognized also that some birds with a prolonged pair-bond sing duets and may be highly vocal, but divergences of this and other kinds can be explained by taking into consideration climatic and ecological factors.

Elaborate and distinctive acoustic and/or visual releasers facilitate (a) rapid and efficient pair-formation and (b) effective territorialism, but double self-advertisement must be offset by one or more of the following adaptations in relation to predators:

(a) Agility.

(b) Defensive power.

(c) Habitat favourable to escape or immunity.

(d) Short period of vulnerability.

(e) Low density of predators in relation to prey.

(f) Distastefulness.

As examples of species in which these adaptations occur one might mention, (a) the Whimbrel which displays conspicuously and noisily in the air but can outfly its aerial enemy the Gyrfalcon (p. 135); (b) the Capercaillie which crows from a branch but is a match for almost any predator; (c) the Golden Oriole which calls loudly and clearly in dense vegetation; (d) small passerines whose song-flight is performed for a brief period and whose nesting cycle is short; (e) the Red-necked Phalarope in some areas, such as· Iceland; (f) the Bee-eater—a bird which Cott (1947) has shown to have highly distasteful flesh. Of course these and other birds in the various categories possess more than one protective adaptation.

The relationship of song to vulnerability is illustrated by comparing the adaptations of the Little Grebe and the Great Crested Grebe. The Little Grebe is very vocal in the breeding season and is one of the few aquatic species which perform musical duets, whereas the Great Crested Grebe is a rather silent bird. Its bill can be used in self-defence or aggression but the defenceless Little Grebe relies on its ability to escape under water—which provides immediately available 'cover'. There are similarities in appearance between the Pintail and the Long-tailed Duck and their habitat preferences are fairly alike. Of the two, the Long-tailed Duck is the noisier and the most conspicuous visually, in both sexes, but, in contrast to the Pintail it is an expert diver.

Another illustration of the relationship between the mode of self-advertisement, adornment, and habitat may be taken from a very different group. Hummingbirds with brilliant gorgets or other extravagant adornments such as birds of the genera *Calypte* and *Selasphorus* display in the open and perform remarkable song-flights, while in *Phaethornis* species the sexes tend to be isomorphic, their plumage is not so highly specific, and they perch to sing for long periods in thick cover (Sibley 1957).

Although habitats and the birds living in them are so extremely various yet a tabulation of some of the outstanding vocal characteristics correlated with habitats in climatic extremes may serve to call attention to principles of adaptation which have a broad application. The table is designed to show only that in certain habitats there is a tendency for some birds to possess song and plumage characteristics which are exceptional in others.

Underlying the data on which this table is based are principles applying to vocal signals which have been mentioned already, such as that in general the higher birds ascend in the trees and the denser the foliage the brighter their plumage tends to be, and conversely, the more birds frequent the ground or are nocturnal the more cryptic they become. It need not be stressed further that pair-bond and territorial behaviour are closely bound up with the characteristics mentioned.

TABLE XIV

ACOUSTIC AND VISUAL CHARACTERISTICS OF
BIRDS OF EXTREME BIOTOPES

Habitat	Acoustic signals	Coloration
Tundra (Homogeneous open)	Song-flight	Cryptic
Taiga (Homogeneous dense)	Contact notes Weak territorial song	Tendency to bright plumage
Rain-forest (Heterogeneous dense)	Loud contact notes Duetting *	Tendency to vivid plumage

* Duetting also occurs among birds of drier tropical habitats such as the Boubou Shrike which frequents dense thorny thickets.

Courtship at close quarters with a diminution in the importance of distinctive vocalizations may involve sexual selection and pronounced sexual dimorphism with the accentuation of morphological releasers, such as long plumes and bright colours, and a tendency to promiscuity. Plumage coloration is, generally speaking, a compromise between the conspicuousness advantageous in social and sexual relations and the cryptic characteristics which have survival value in relation to predators. In turn, the nature of a bird's song is related to these adaptations. It has long been a matter for comment that birds with exaggerated adornments and brilliant colours, such as the Peacock and Macaw, tend to have raucous voices. The short explanation is that most brilliantly coloured birds perform close-up courtship in which visual releasers are important and have so adapted themselves to their environment, by such expedients as nesting in cavities or dispensing with the help of the colourful male at the nest, that their visual conspicuousness to predators is offset. In those species in which the male has bright adornments which he loses with the post-nuptial moult, song also usually ceases then (Bicknell 1884). Persistent song throughout much of the year is mainly confined to iso-morphic species. As examples in the British Isles one might mention the Song Thrush, Dipper, Wren, Robin, and Skylark. In such species the voice is highly important in sexual recognition. Another consideration is that vividly plumaged birds in temperate regions would be in special danger during winter among leafless trees where they could be readily seen by predators. Although the Robin is hardly in this category it should be noted that its flesh, in common with that of many brilliantly adorned birds, is unpalatable. Of course many northern species retain vivid plumage throughout the year but they tend to be very agile or secretive. Some of them, such as the Goldfinch, are sociable in winter, and indeed at other times. Probably such gregarious birds are better able to avoid the attacks of predators than comparable solitary and duller-plumaged species as any one bird noticing a marauder is able to give prompt warning to its companions. This type of adaptation is another example of the integration between adornment, behaviour and utterances.

XIII

BIRD SONG AS ART AND PLAY

Imitating with the mouth the liquid notes of birds came
long before men were able to repeat smooth songs in melody
and please the ear.

LUCRETIUS. *De rerum natura*, v. 1380.

Suppose the singing birds musicians.

Richard II, I. iii. 288.

ESTHETIC pleasure in listening to bird songs may not be as ancient
as we are apt to assume. The Turtle Dove's cooing pleased the
Hebrew swain because of its associations rather than its intrinsic
beauty. There are a few appreciative incidental references in Greek and
Roman literature, notably a surprising little rhapsody on the Nightingale's song by Pliny, and some dainty expressions of enjoyment by Irish
scribes and Chinese poets but aesthetic appreciation of bird song appears
to be mainly confined to post-Renaissance times. The poems of Walther
von der Vogelweide—the poet who, according to tradition, asked that the
birds might be fed at his tomb—foreshadowed the sensitivity to nature's
moods and the songs of birds expressed by the troubadours, Dante, David
ap Gwylym, Chaucer, and many a writer since (Fig. 42). Nowadays when
the critical study of bird utterances has become almost an independent
science it is not surprising that as the intricacies of bird song are disclosed we find ourselves confronted by philosophical problems. Does all
this complexity serve merely utilitarian ends? Are birds insensitive to
the beauty which we find in their songs? Is our delight in bird voices
merely subjective? If we ask whether bird songs conform to aesthetic principles, the answer depends on how these principles are formulated and
our success in bringing them to bear on the observed characteristics of
such songs, but nobody need be taken seriously who would deny that bird
songs have some aesthetic qualities as, for example, rhythm and pattern.
It has been argued, of course, that the approximations in bird songs to
human aesthetic standards are fortuitous but this contention will be
shown to be unsound. The further question, whether birds have aesthetic
taste, is more difficult to answer and the best we can expect to do is to
clarify the issues a little.†

It must be accepted that the debate as to whether beauty is subjective,
as Kant maintained, or objective, still continues, and one of the few
opinions on aesthetics which would be generally accepted is that there

FIG. 42. One of the earliest attempts to record bird song in musical notation. (*Above*) The song of the Nightingale. (*Below*) Domestic Cock crowing; Domestic Hen clucking after laying; Hen calling chicks; Cuckoo
calling; Quail calling; Parrot talking Greek. (After Kircher 1650)

is no single criterion of beauty. In considering the aesthetic appreciation of bird song, whether by human beings or birds, to restrict ourselves to purely musical criteria would be to narrow our viewpoint unduly. The most practical approach to the question of whether birds' songs conform to aesthetic principles is to consider to what extent bird song conforms to the artistic principles enumerated by a working artist, William Hogarth, the painter. Naturally we must bear in mind the distinction, emphasized by Lessing, between the arts concerned with the coexistent in space, such as painting and sculpture, and those in which succession in time is important—poetry and music—but the basic aesthetic criteria are common to all artistic achievements, Hogarth's criteria, considered for convenience in reverse order, are : (1) Quantity or magnitude; (2) intricacy; (3) simplicity or distinctness; (4) uniformity, regularity, or symmetry; (5) variety in as many ways as possible, and (6) fitness of the parts to some design. He points out that these correct and restrain each other. This list could be simplified by regarding (2), (3), and (5) as all concerned with degrees of complexity. The list would then become : Magnitude, Complexity, Proportion, and Integration.

We might approach the problem by asking to what extent do bird songs conform to these criteria and it could be shown that most bird songs do so to a considerable extent but there is a more realistic procedure which enables us, for our immediate purpose, to by-pass the controversy concerning the subjectivity of aesthetic judgments. If these criteria are a product of the refinement of animal adaptations and discriminatory processes we should expect to find similarities between birds and men in their apprehension of aesthetic qualities, however much human appreciation has reached a higher plane than that attained by birds. This is, in fact, what we do find, though the evidence can only be sketched here.

Magnitude in bird communication has been sufficiently stressed (Chapter II and p. 114). According to their signal functions and other factors vocalizations may be loud or subdued, brief or prolonged. Alike with birds and men increase in magnitude tends to be attention-provoking or intimidating, reduction in magnitude, especially in volume of sound, to assuage disquiet or be reassuring. *Intricacy* in the animal world is primarily utilitarian. To what extent it goes beyond or emancipates itself from utility is the nub of our problem, but complexity, such as the patterns on a Peacock's train or the elaboration of the Nightingale's song, is primarily functional and if it exceeds this, however slightly, such gratuitous patterning could hardly be denied aesthetic value. It would then be entitled to be considered decorative. But in so far as any organism has an appreciation of functional intricacy there is at least the germ of aesthetic taste, unless 'appreciation' be regarded as employed in a purely mechanistic sense. Intricacy is challenging, evoking interest and ever nicer discrimination as it becomes more elaborate. In man this is an essential element in the development of aesthetic judgment.

Simplicity is the opposite of intricacy. In general, a simple signal is less mistakable and more effective than a complex signal but competition compels the development of intricacy. Traffic signals illustrate an effective compromise. Three circles of contrasting colours arranged vertically constitute an arrangement combining simplicity and complexity so effectively that error in identification is almost impossible. Similarly, urgent human signals indicating danger or calling for help tend to be as simple as is practicable. The warning notes of birds tend to be simple (p. 21). In nature purity of tone is unusual and so the pure tones in some birds' songs may be assumed to be useful in enabling these sounds to be distinguished from all others and so facilitate specific identification. Here we have a hint that symmetry which is biologically advantageous may be aesthetically satisfying—as it is, within limits, in our experience. It may not be coincidence that gibbons and Swiss yodellers use clear long-distance calls with rather similar characteristics.

Uniformity is an outstanding characteristic of animal behaviour. One need only mention the conformity to pattern of birds' nests and call attention to the frequent—perhaps over-frequent—use of the term 'mechanism' by ethologists in describing animal activities. Uniformity in the calls and songs of birds is essential to their signal functions. Even those species which vary their phrases or sequences most, or which are highly imitative, maintain a degree of uniformity such that an attentive human ear is seldom more than momentarily deceived. Uniformity of rhythm is particularly prominent in bird songs. Of all the characteristics of human music rhythm has the most widespread and fundamental appeal. This is not surprising in view of the huge extent to which animal life is governed by internal rhythms.

Variety is the counterpart to uniformity as complexity is to simplicity. The existence, and still more the reproduction, of higher animals depends on distinctive signals, given and received. Distinctiveness involves variety. It is requisite to proclaiming identity and preventing confusion. As has already been illustrated sound signals are of particular value to this end. In the course of evolution and the development of human culture alike divergence from uniformity has been a growing-point of progress. It is the gamble with safety which, if it succeeds, may initiate a rapid advance. Aesthetically and biologically variety and intricacy are important—primarily because in both spheres they are attention-provoking and stimulating.

Fitness of the parts to some design, involving as it does symmetry and harmony, implies all the preceding principles—appropriate magnitude, order, proportion, and integration. Our aesthetic judgments are built on

the apprehension of these constituents of the natural world and the correlation of our modes of apprehension with such principles through our
evolutionary inheritance. Integrative appreciation is much more intricate
than the appreciation of magnitude so far as sound is concerned. Birds
and some other animals can perceive relationships and configurations.
This is implied in a bird's recognition of the song of its species. Insight,
which is primarily the perception of relations, is a characteristic of many
groups (Thorpe 1956). Stereotyped releasing mechanisms of the lock
and key type play no great part in human behaviour but animal adaptations for summating or discriminating parts and whole adumbrate not
only our perception of relations but also the sense of appropriate relationship which is so important an element in aesthetic appreciation. If we
consider the calls of birds as language (Chapter I), or the mimetic
abilities with which so many birds are endowed as indicated by their
powers of mimicry, it is hard to resist the impression that human powers
of speech and capacity to apprehend information are fundamentally
similar to theirs.

Reference has already been made to rhythm as a fundamental aspect,
not only of music but of all experience and to the rôle of what musicians
have called 'instinct' in the formulation of scales (p. 30). Scientific
analysis is continually revealing further details of how reality is inter-
penetrated with or, we may even say, founded on rhythm. Pattern and
rhythm distinguish reality from the void. No integration is possible
without them—and even if it be argued that human experience 'projects'
them on what is apprehended their basic character remains. Cooke
(1959), discussing the composer's creative imagination, shown in producing 'vital and significant new rhythms out of the elements of old ones',
remarks : 'Although the composer's rhythmic sense is undoubtedly connected with the whole rhythm of nature (through his senses, bloodstream
and glands), with the speed and rhythm of the life he leads, and with the
rhythm and cadence of his native tongue, it remains inaccessible to our
understanding—until, perhaps, the musicians, physiologists and psychologists of the future explain its functioning for us.'

Thus, whatever else our aesthetic taste may be, it is an extension and
refinement of animal abilities. Paracelsus long ago realized something of
the natural affinity between man's capacities and those of the 'lower creation'. He wrote : 'Man need not be surprised that animals have animal
instincts that are so much like his own . . . Man may learn from the
animals, for they are his parents'. Therefore we are justified in postulating
the existence of aesthetic appreciation on a lower level among animals.
As we have seen, observation confirms this postulate. Aesthetic appreciation, like other forms of human apprehension, has a biological foundation
and evolutionary antecedents.†

235

If our aesthetic judgments are an extension of animal discrimination this does not undermine the thesis that aesthetic judgments have objectivity. The philosophical problem involved has to be argued on its merits. Principles, such as proportion and integration, are so basic to a rational view of the world that they are at least part of reality to the extent of being a framework of apprehension without which the world would be unintelligible.

We are handicapped in considering the capacity of animals for aesthetic experience because, by common consent, such experience is in part emotional. Ethological theory tends to avoid this concept though some psychologists working on animal behaviour find it useful.

Darwin, in *The Expression of the Emotions in Man and Animals* (1872), rejected psychological for mechanistic and biological methods of explanation. Following him Weismann (1899) claimed human music to be an accidental by-product of the development of voice and ear to serve utilitarian ends. Ethologists adopt mechanistic and biological, rather than psychological, methods of research. They have not met Craig's (1921–22) challenge. He showed that Darwin's principal thesis was that no characteristics have been evolved for 'expression', and claimed that 'expressive behaviour' is of great importance because of its meaning to the agent himself and its effect on his own behaviour. What this amounts to in terms of our present problem is that during communication an affective state is generated in both agent and receptor and there is 'appreciation' in some measure of each other's intentions. To deny that this is so and that evolution has proceeded in the direction of increased sensitivity of this type is gratuitously to create difficulties in conceiving how man's capacities evolved. Admit the two-way traffic of empathy or appreciation and we perceive how, through refinements of sensitivity within the organism, and in the course of increasingly complex social contacts and the evolution of more elaborate forms of communication, often acoustic, potentialities for more refined modes of apprehension and the organization of experience increased. Signals from the outside world could become more meaningful and response to them better integrated. Thus we may postulate that the capacity for proto-aesthetic or aesthetic experience evolved with the development of more highly refined capacities to interpret selectively and appreciatively, rather than mechanistically, signals of increasing elaboration and significance.

Alike during the courtship display and song of birds and in our own appreciation of music there is 'an affective state generated in both agent and receptor'. Cooke (1959), considering musical appreciation, reminds us that it involves 'transforming the heard sound of the music into emotional experience' and points out that we can never know how closely one person's emotions resemble those of another. Consequently it is a supposition that when we hear the music of Beethoven we are experiencing the feelings which inspired it. Nevertheless we feel quite definitely that there is this kind of communication, and that Beethoven's hope, written on the manuscript of the *Missa Solennis* and quoted by Cooke, finds fulfilment: 'Von Herzen—möge es wieder—zu Herzen gehn!'—'From the heart—may it go back—to the heart!' Indeed, it is apparent that the fullest communication between human beings involves such an emotional nexus. In short, human communication is of an incomplete character unless it involves *rapport* below the level of full consciousness. It presupposes susceptibilities based on ancestral experience going back to pre-human modes of apprehension.

Returning to an aspect of the matter already mentioned, we must ask whether in their singing birds have emancipated themselves at all from the utilitarian, for although the utilitarian can be, and often is, beautiful, elaboration which is not functionally necessitated must either be aesthetic or fortuitous. Where human activity is concerned decoration is only explicable as a manifestation of aesthetic taste—though sometimes bad taste. Palaeolithic man's implements would have been effective without the engravings on them, though, doubtless, he did not believe this. In decorating them his motives were magico-religious (Armstrong 1958). That does not alter the fact that some of these artifacts are true works of art in the sense that their workmanship and ornamentation go beyond necessity. It is impossible to believe that these craftsmen derived no aesthetic satisfaction from their craftsmanship. If we could find indications, however meagre, among birds, of the gratuitous in expression or apprehension this would support an affirmative answer to our second question—whether birds have aesthetic taste.

If the gratuitous decorative be accepted as an element in art we may make some comparisons with that form of activity in men and animals which most closely bears the marks of freedom from necessity—play. Schiller, Spencer, Groos, and more recently Bally (1945), have commented on the similarities between aesthetic activity and play. It is difficult to formulate a definition of the one which would exclude the other. We speak of playing games as well as music. Neither is strictly utilitarian. Both have been claimed to be expressions of superfluous or superabundant energy. Such an explanation has additional force if we interpret 'energy' as including motivation induced by sexual hormones. Over sixty years ago Groos suggested that the song of birds could be regarded as play and recently Sauer (1954) and Thorpe (1956) have accepted this view as a possible explanation of sub-song and vocal mimicry respectively.

There is no general agreement concerning the definition and function of play as a biological phenomenon. As usually understood play is practically confined to higher vertebrates and is best known in young mammals, though many of the observations cited as play among birds refer to adults (Armstrong 1947). Since play, apart from the activities of primates, is mainly a characteristic of mammals incapable of expressing themselves acoustically in a sufficiently elaborate and informative way to be called song, and song is almost restricted to birds, a group in which play is rather rare, there is some reason to suppose that play and song may be different and alternative ways of manifesting vitality and the impulse towards self-expression.

In young mammals, such as badgers and kittens, according to my own observations and those of others (Eibl-Eibesfeldt 1950) play consists of movements concerned with hunting, fighting, and, to some extent, sex. That badgers should be most playful when they issue from the set after being cooped up for hours and kittens play most actively at dusk suggests that environmental and internal factors may both be involved in the expression of 'bottled-up' energy in this way. Play has been considered a rehearsal of activities to be put to practical use later. This concept may explain the manipulative activities of children but is less applicable to bird activities such as flight, and to a lesser extent song, when the activity is such as to mature without practice. None the less it is probable that, for example, singing imperfect songs in youth may facilitate the production of the full song later. Play has also been regarded as a pleasurable and not directly functional activity (Beach 1945). This does little to advance our understanding. Bally describes play as a learned activity which has become loosely connected with its appetitive goal. This is rather unsatisfactory as play movements in many species seem to be innate, even if their coordination is such as to improve by practice, and sometimes the goal is attained (Sauer 1954). However, play activities are normally ranged in a loosely connected hierarchy and the consummatory act is not reached; that is, they are performed for their own sake.† This being so, a rigid distinction between play and art seems to be precluded. Vigorous defenders of 'art for art's sake' would not deny that among primitive people music is functional, as when it accompanies dancing or fertility ritual, but they would point out that in higher cultures it can become increasingly dissociated from utility. We may believe that developmental sub-song and mimicry are uttered to some extent 'for their own sake' but proof is difficult. In this respect the situation is the same in regard to the relationship between human music and play and bird music and play.

Some support for considering that there is an affinity between play and aesthetic activity is provided by their association in animal behaviour. Koehler (1921) describes parties of chimpanzees performing a round dance, stamping with their feet, their bodies bedecked with vines, rags, and other dangling objects. The activities of bowerbirds in choosing and manipulating objects of a preferred colour, together with their utterance of mimicry, hint that perhaps both types of behaviour share a common impulse. Over sixty years ago Romanes wrote of these birds : 'It is impossible to deny that an aesthetic element is displayed'. Marshall (1954) speaks of the Satin Bowerbird's display as involving 'astonishingly complex and, to some degree, aesthetic reproductive mechanisms' though as much might be said of the displays of many birds. There is hardly any activity performed by an animal which seems to embody an element of the gratuitous more than the painting of the bower by the Satin, Spotted and Regent Bowerbirds. All three are gifted mimics (Chaffer 1945; Goddard 1947). Reference has already been made to the possibility that in these birds great manipulative ability has facilitated the development of vocal mimicry (p. 83). A step or two has been taken along the road which man took towards speech and abstract thought. Play, art, and thought all imply a canalization of energy into behaviour determined to a reduced extent by biological necessity. A measure of indeterminism is characteristic of both. We may conclude that proof of the merely gratuitous or the purely decorative in bird music cannot be adduced but they provide evidence of a degree of freedom of expression which is one of the prerequisites of artistic expression.

In human aesthetic creation and enjoyment there is a degree of detachment. This principle of 'psychical distance' was emphasized by Bullough (1919). Too great emotional involvement spoils enjoyment, while, on the other hand, that which is too remote from our experience leaves us unmoved. Saunders (1929) claimed that 'the most beautiful and perfect songs are not those sung under stress of great excitement'. Craig (1943) endorsed this, commenting that isolation by distance or darkness is conducive to most pleasing song. Lorenz (1943b), Sauer (1955), Hartshorne (1955), and others have noted that a certain amount of relaxation is favourable to good song. Many American flycatchers are most melodious when they sing their twilight songs (Skutch 1951a). The argument is, in effect, that if psychical distance is common to bird and human experience we may regard this as indicating that aesthetic experience, as we know it, is, in some degree, shared by birds. This inference is not as convincing as some have maintained. Craig thought that spatial isolation could be equated with psychical distance, quoting the singing Skylark as isolated in space and the Nightingale by darkness ; but several Skylarks can often be heard singing together, the Nightingale sings by day as well as by night, and the Nightjar, isolated by distance and darkness, is not a good singer. Moreover, many courtship songs are sung under the stress of emotional excitement and yet, to our ears, are among the most beautiful of bird utterances. This is not contradicted by observations of male birds interrupting or altering their songs when a female appears, as, for example, when a Pallid Cuckoo's song became irregular and abbreviated when a female replied to him (Robinson 1956). Belligerent song is usually congested and distorted (p. 128). The song of a Sprosser Nightingale deteriorates when a bird is keyed up to singing against a rival (Sotavalta 1956). Song expressing strong aggressive impulses tends to lose the qualities which we consider beautiful. Thus we cannot generalize concerning 'emotional excitement' in this respect. Courtship utterances tend to be beautiful and aggressive utterances to be unaesthetic.† Craig makes a more cogent point when he remarks that 'long-range songs are formal and classical, short-range songs romantic'. He expresses the truth embodied in this statement more clearly when he says that 'songs at short range appeal to the intelligence of the hearer; for example, they serve to announce the location and species of the singer and sometimes his individual identity; songs at short range appeal to the emotions of the hearer, stimulating fear in an enemy, sexual emotion in the female'. Expressed more accurately long-range signals are primarily identificatory, short-range primarily stimulatory. We have noted that long-range, territorial song is the most informative of bird utterances. In terms of human appreciation music which is clear in tone and construction, formal and symmetrical, embodies the basic characteristics of long-range bird signals, while that which is extreme in volume or, in some instances, tempo, whether exceptionally loud and rapid threat song or very soft, slow courtship song is of the short-range type. One tends to be classical, the other romantic. Thus, again our aesthetic responses to music are seen to be a refinement of animal reactions. This is confirmed when we scrutinize short-range songs in more detail. As we have noted, defiant territorial song where rivals are fairly close tends to be exceptionally loud though somewhat distorted in pattern, song tends to be turbulent, harsh, and rapid, and courtship song becomes meditative, sweet, and subdued, and sometimes in slow tempo. In every opera we hear music of these contrasting types.

In connexion with 'psychical distance', which involves a measure of freedom from determination, the utterance of mimicry by birds is evidence that they possess some capacity for detachment. Artistic expression by human beings is normally preceded by a period of copying. Imitation is a stage towards freedom of expression. In birds it is a manifestation of interest in and attention to the activities of other individuals going beyond the merely utilitarian. Assimilated and transmuted imitation is the process whereby a creative artist climbs on the shoulders of his predecessors. Mimicry not only indicates some freedom from stereotyped mechanisms but suggests that the bird is at least on the threshold of combining utterances or motifs by free choice (p. 82). Craig holds that imitative birds are much superior to the Wood Pewee, the bird whose musical abilities he champions, 'because they exhibit a more intelligent appreciation of what they are doing when they sing'.

We have seen that some birds, such as the Canary, reach a phase in autumn when they sing sub-song and become capable again, as they were in youth, of acquiring new sounds (p. 53). Thus when the biological struggle is relaxed the birds become more receptive and associative. There are similarities between this state of affairs and the relaxation of the mind for the 'incubation' of ideas which is important in creative work (Armstrong 1946b). Song with low motivation tends to be pleasing to our ears. Hence the breeders of Roller Canaries used to keep them in darkened cages and bird fanciers sometimes barbarously blinded Gold-finches and other birds to improve their song. Experiments with rats show that sexual motivation is reduced if they are blinded at an early age (Greenbaum and Gunberg 1960). Perhaps these results suggest a connexion between reduction of visual activity in birds, decreased sexual motivation, and reduced stereotypy in song. In general when motivation is low, whether in the autumnal song, or the twilight song of some species, the song tends to seem more musical to our ears.

Apart from vocal mimicry the degree to which a bird chooses one motif rather than another to succeed an earlier motif must be taken into consideration in assessing its status as an artiste. This aspect of song can be most easily studied in turdines which utter a relatively slow succession of differing phrases. Among the most famous of these songsters is the Hermit Thrush. It sings with leisurely deliberation. Wing (1951) found that 'there was a continual change in the order in which the songs were sung, the song to be heard next being unpredictable'. Whether this be considered evidence of aesthetic choice or not it suggests such freedom to choose as is essential to artistic expression. Unfortunately, other studies suggest that the order of motifs in the songs of some birds with a larger repertoire may be, to some extent, predictable (p. 40). Attentive listening to other birds with a similar form of song, such as British species of this family, may reinforce the impression that they exercise some freedom in this respect. If one concentrates on the structure of a Blackbird's song for some weeks the bird appears to be discriminat-ing and preferring certain phrases and sequences but this may mean little more than that the mechanisms involved are complex.† To what extent any process of selection involved can be regarded as free choice is a matter of opinion. If it be objected that even the evolution of preferential sequences may be determined the reply may be given that a similar, or closely related, effect is apparent in human artistic creation, particularly in Shakespeare's poetry in which the association of two images in an early play often determines the linkage of related images in later plays (Armstrong 1946b).

Craig shows that the 'sentences' of the Wood Pewee's song are not deliberately composed but are due to underlying tendencies, each of which is of a mathematical character. This does not imply that the bird has no aesthetic perception. Craig believes that it has. He reminds us of the authorities who have commented on the similarities between growth and the creation of a work of art. For example, tendencies towards symmetry and equilibrium are characteristic of both. Craig and Saunders agree, on the basis of analytical observations of the songs of a single remarkable bird, that the Wood Pewee exercises aesthetic choice. In their view the bird could and did compose. Significantly, this maestro stammered occasionally as if involved in a conflict or indecision as to which phrase to sing next. Craig indicates the nature of this conflict. It was due to a tendency towards a regular recurrence of three phrases and another tendency to sing sixty-two per cent of one of these phrases.

This raises the question of memory. Can a bird remember what he has sung so that he can deliberately vary the sequence of phrases? Craig found evidence that the Wood Pewee could recollect three or four successive phrases but not more. A Song Thrush disturbed from its perch in the middle of a phrase may complete it when it perches again. Hartshorne (1956, 1958b) holds that 'birds can stand a prolonged succession of songs or phrases separated by brief intervals of silence (less than two or three seconds) only if there is considerable variety among the songs or phrases'. He calls this the 'anti-monotony principle' and deduces from it that if a bird sings another phrase within a memory span such that it can recall the preceding phrase it tends to vary the next phrase, thus showing musical discrimination and exemplifying a tendency towards variety in unity.

While it is fairly generally true that, as he holds, many birds which sing a set phrase over and over again make pauses such that only about thirty per cent of the performance is song there are considerations which weaken his plea that these phenomena are indications of musical ability. There are birds, such as the Wren, whose pauses almost equal the length of the phrases and others, including the Cuckoo and Corncrake which re-iterate a monotonous phrase continuously. To argue, as Hartshorne does, that the 'notoriously monotonous' song of the House Wren is not really so because differences between songs are revealed by spectrographic analysis is not entirely convincing. Moreover, the duration of a bird's pauses may well be determined in large measure by the advantages of listening for other sounds and looking around to forestall the attacks of predators (p. 222). There is, however, some force in the argument that it would be easier for a bird such as a Song Thrush to repeat the same phrase again and again continuously—as many birds do—than to vary the phrases as it does. We may suppose, with Craig and Hartshorne, that when a bird sings again within the time-span of vivid memory of what it has already sung it avoids monotony and shows an anticipation of human music in which unpredictability is important. This view will appeal to us as valid according to the degree to which we are convinced that these variations have not come about through the selective advantage they confer. Such variety may be useful in proclaiming individual identity, capturing and holding attention, or even easing fatigue of the nervous system or vocal organs—all the more likely as some of these birds are apt to sing a great deal.

Hartshorne, endorsing the view that bird song is an anticipation of our own music, stresses as a 'pervasive fact' the correlation between quantity and quality in singing. He claims that the singers of the most musical songs spend a larger proportion of the minute, day, and year singing than poor singers. The evidence is not as cogent as he suggests. On the basis of the seasonal chart of bird song given by Nicholson and Koch (1936) he points out that of the resident British species in song for five and a third months or more five are reckoned good singers—Robin, Song Thrush, Blackbird, Woodlark, and Skylark—and eleven or twelve middling or poor. He claims that the odds against this distribution are 100 to 1. But if we take a more natural division of the year—six months—and enquire which birds are in song for this period of time or longer each year the list is, in order, Robin, Starling, Dipper, Song Thrush, Green Woodpecker, Hedgesparrow, Wren, Woodpigeon, and Corn Bunting. Three excellent singers, the Blackbird, Woodlark, and Skylark, are thus excluded and we have a preponderance of poor singers. Thus the correlation is with duration of breeding and territorialism rather than the musical quality of the song. My recollection of bird song during two years in tropical Asia, some months in north and tropical America and the West Indies, and several weeks in the Arctic, is that the quantity-quality correlation is no more valid in these areas than in the north temperate region. For example, the Cape Wagtail in Africa and the Orange-billed Sparrow in Central America sing practically throughout the year. They are not good singers (Skead 1954; Skutch 1954). However, the 'rule' may apply in some areas with mild winters, such as parts of the Southern United States and Australia, where many species maintain territory and sometimes also the pair-bond, outside the breeding season. This indicates that the explanation is, at least in large part, ecological.

Hartshorne (1960) adopts six standards for assessing songs—loudness, scope (variety and complexity), continuity, purity of tone, unity of pattern, and use of imitation. Each variable is allotted a score from 1 to

9 and the total gives the rating of the species. For example, the Mocking-bird scores about 42. Applied to British birds there is no constant correlation between high scoring and great output of song—as the data quoted above have already indicated. Discontinuity of song and lack of versatility seem to be associated in many species but some species which Hartshorne (1956) regards as very non-versatile singers have a repertoire of several song-versions (Marler and Isaac 1960). In this context it is not easy to define versatility.

The attractiveness of being able to obtain some sort of quantitative evidence for bird musicianship is so great that this theory demands a little further examination. The exclusion of migratory species from consideration involves the omission of some of our finest singers. Hartshorne endeavours to overcome the difficulty they present by commenting that when they sing in Africa they do not utter full song there for anything like the two or three months necessary to bring them into his category of birds which sing for five and a third months. In Africa the singers may be mainly young birds (Stresemann 1948). The Chiffchaff—a poor singer—is in song longer than the Nightingale. Cetti's Warbler is in full song in Italy for more than six and a half months and in fairly frequent song throughout the rest of the year but nobody would rate its explosive burst of sharp notes as high-quality song. If it be urged that the Nightingale sings by night as well as by day so does the Grasshopper Warbler—an indifferent performer. If mimicry is to be taken into consideration the Marsh Warbler is one of our finest singers, but its song period is very short. Despite these criticisms Hartshorne's attempt to correlate biological and aesthetic principles opens out possibilities of studying an elusive topic which are worth exploring further.

Attempts have been made to prove that birds have musical appreciation similar to our own by finding approximations in their songs to the pentatonic scale. Wing (1951), for example, considered that a Hermit Thrush sang thus, but in listening to bird songs and noting them down it is practically impossible for those with musical training in Western traditions to avoid finding closer resemblances to intervals familiar to them than in fact occur. However, this is a mathematical matter and it can hardly be fortuitous that some birds do sing and transpose in accordance with our musical scale (p. 29). Study of primitive music gives little justification for the assumption that human beings necessarily tend to make music according to the pentatonic scale.

We return to the problem that underlying every effort to show that birds have aesthetic taste is the difficulty of proving that any characteristic of bird song is non-utilitarian. Hartshorne maintains that 'to say aesthetic is to say non-utilitarian' and though he qualifies, if not contradicts, this by saying 'musicality is in some degree utilitarian' the solution of this problem remains elusive.† The aesthetic and utilitarian should not be set against each other thus, although it is attractive to suppose that the non-utilitarian, and hence the aesthetic, can be clearly separated from the utilitarian. Only on a pragmatic and materialistic definition of utilitarian would the activity of either the metaphysician or musician be considered non-utilitarian. Rather we must think of the aesthetic as biologically adaptive and involving a delicately refined sensitivity and responsiveness to the environment. If we regard freedom as identified with the measure in which an organism can be potentially responsive selectively in widest degree to the environment we need not consider utilitarian behaviour and aesthetic sensitivity or expression as antagonistic, nor may we think of them as clearly separable. Every advance in freedom of expression and finer sensitivity is a step towards deeper aesthetic experience. If we think thus of aesthetic experience, not as an achievement fully realized by humanity but as a road along which we have made some progress we can acknowledge that birds, though limited by their relatively stereo-typed responses, have advanced some way along the same road.

If harmony and rhythm are of the nature of reality aesthetic judg-ments reached through the application of capacities evolved from those basic to animal life are not merely subjective. Beauty, and the power to appreciate it—'their great Original proclaim'. But this is a realm for the poet, metaphysician, and theologian rather than the biologist.

> From harmony, from heavenly harmony,
>   This universal frame began:
> When nature underneath a heap
>   Of jarring atoms lay
> And could not heave her head,
> The tuneful voice was heard from high:
>   Arise ye more than dead.
> Then cold and hot and moist and dry
> In order to their stations leap
>   And music's power obey.
> From harmony, from heavenly harmony,
>   This universal frame began;
> From harmony to harmony
> Through all the compass of the notes it ran,
> The diapason closing full in man.

APPENDIX

ACOUSTIC COMMUNICATION IN THE ANIMAL KINGDOM AND THE ORGANS INVOLVED

MANY creatures use sounds for communication but comparatively few have elaborated them beyond the bare rudiments of a language. Alexander (1960) believes that sound production among the arthropods is of immense antiquity and has arisen independently hundreds of times. It has been known since 1863 that some are equipped with hearing organs. The snapping shrimps *Crangon* and *Synalpheus*, make clicks with their modified claws but evidence was lacking until recently that these noises have any function (Everest *et al*. 1948; Johnson *et al*. 1947); it is now reported that *Crangon californiensis* stuns tiny fish and other shrimps with its snapping sounds (MacGinitie and MacGinitie 1949). Calman pointed out in 1908 that some West African river crabs possess what appear to be stridulating organs (Gordon 1954). If a ghost crab, *Ocypode macrocerca*, is placed in the burrow of another individual the owner of the burrow protests in increasingly loud and shrill tones. Spiny lobsters, *Palinurus interruptus*, stridulate before fighting and there is some evidence that this may have a deterrent effect (Collias 1960) but there is still much uncertainty as to the efficacy of acoustic communication in the Crustacea.

Some spiders, including British species, also possess stridulating structures. The extent to which they serve for auditory communication needs further investigation (Bristowe 1958). Usually only the male is thus equipped. We may assume with some probability that the sound attracts and stimulates the female, though the female Australian 'barking spider', *Selenocosmia crassipes*, has been noted making a 'whistling noise' which could be heard eight or ten feet away. James Wood-Mason described the sound made by the great stridulating spider of Assam as like 'drawing the back of a knife along the edge of a small comb' (McKeown 1936). Some wolf spiders, *Lycosa* spp., communicate with the female by drumming with their palps on a dead leaf—a method somewhat resembling the supposedly ominous tapping of the death-watch beetle. The stridulatory hiss of the scorpion, *Opisthopthalmus latimanus*, deters mammalian predators.

Among insects able to communicate by acoustic methods are members of the Orthoptera, Homoptera, Coleoptera, and Heteroptera. These produce sounds by mechanical means though the structures employed vary greatly. Usually a vibratory apparatus and resonator are involved. The cicada's song is produced by vibrating a pair of tymbals. Beneath each is a tracheal air cavity which serves as resonator. Many Orthoptera use variations of the rod-and-comb technique (Faber 1953). The water beetle, *Hygrobia hermanni*, rubs the tip of the abdomen on the elytra, making a sound audible even under the water. Some tropical butterflies click their wings in flight and the death's head hawk moth is capable of uttering a squeak, reputed to be caused by air forced through the pro-boscis. The queen honey bee's piping is apparently produced by air vibrations in the trachea. Thus among the insects there has been consider-able 'experimentation' with sound-producing apparatus.

The sounds made by insects tend to be higher in pitch than those uttered by vertebrates and are broken up into short pulses of twenty to 500 per second. Pulse patterns are distinctive for each species. Usually the specific identity of the insect and its mood—the kind of activity it is ready to embark upon—are conveyed by the pattern of the pulses rather than by variations in pitch. This is correlated with relatively greater simplicity in the auditory apparatus than is characteristic of vertebrates. Thus insects are able to locate sounds directly as their auditory receptors, unlike those of mammals and birds, do not respond to changes in pressure. The hearing range of one species, *Thamnotrizon apterus*, lies somewhere about 435 to over 25,000 cycles per second (Regen 1914; Wever and Bray 1933; Pumphrey 1940; Pringle 1956; Alexander 1960).

Insect song serves fewer functions than bird song. Apart from such sounds as the 'squawk' of the cicada or the squeak of the death's head hawk moth when seized, which may tend to deter predators, most of the signal sounds made by insects have a significance in sexual relationships.†
Very few female insects are capable of making a sound more elaborate than a high-pitched click. The song informs the female of the proximity of a male belonging to her species in mating condition perched in a locatable place. Faber's study (1929, 1932) of grasshoppers (*Chorthip-pus*) indicates what must be about the maximum information communi-cable by insect songs. He distinguished twelve different songs or phrases, each expressing a different mood. The most significant are: the song of an isolated male, the serenade when the female is present, the cry of triumph, the rivals' duet, and the copulation song. Male katydids, *Ambly-corypha oblongifolia*, answer each other with chirps differing in character (Pierce 1948). The female, *Melampsalta cingulata*, a large New Zealand cicada, replies with wing-clicks to the singing male and may thus induce him to approach. Another species, *Scuderia curvicauda*, has two songs, one sung by day, the other by night (Myers 1929). Some cicadas sing strictly in unison. The significance of these performances is unknown

(Alexander 1957a, b). The calling of male crickets near the burrow appears to have some of the functions of territorial song. This also applies to the high-pitched buzzing of honey bees defending the hive.

Acoustic communication in vertebrates

Some aspects of the behaviour of certain groups of fish, notably forms of display, nest-building, and defence of territory, are remarkably convergent with the behaviour of birds. Auditory clues play a more important rôle in the life of fish than naturalists would have conceded some years ago but little is known concerning the communicatory function of these sounds. Fish and marine mammals utter a wide range of call-notes. As the toad fish, *Opsanus tau*, produces noises mainly during the breeding season they may attract the female. These sounds are created when the membraneous walls and gaseous contents of the air bladder are set in motion (Fish 1954; Tavolga 1958; Fish and Mowbray 1959). Probably the 'boat whistle' sound made by the toad fish has a rôle in territorial behaviour and species discrimination (Tavolga 1960). According to Jan ter Pelkwyk (1946), who was killed by the Japanese before he could publish details of his observations, an Indonesian fish utters a 'territorial song'.†

Apparently the Amphibia were the first animals to acquire structures specially adapted for producing communicatory sounds when out-breathed air is passed over them. Present-day Amphibia, including some salamanders, utter noises varying greatly from species to species, and there are frogs, as well as birds, equipped with sacs which become inflated during sound-production and greatly amplify the sound. One species of salamander can pitch sounds with intervals of a fourth or fifth (Bogert 1960). Some frogs sing under the water, thereby securing protection from non-aquatic predators. As in insects, sound production in Amphibia is very largely associated with the attraction and stimulation of the female, though, like cicadas, frogs and toads utter a squawk or scream when seized. Experiments with the chorus frog have shown that the calls of the male provide the stimulation which brings the sexes together (Martof and Thompson 1959). Three species of toad (*Bufo*) studied by Aronson (1944) were found to utter three distinct calls—a sex trill, a chirp, and warning notes. There is evidence that female frogs are most attracted by males which call vigorously and persistently (Bogert 1960). Territorialism occurs among frogs and in some species territorial calls drive off intruders. They are characteristic of species in which foraging is restricted to streams, pools, cliffs, or trees rather than to the ground (Bogert 1960). The smoky jungle frog, *Leptodactylus caliginosis*, guards its foam nest (Beebe 1950).

Although some reptiles, such as lizards, defend territory and others, including crocodiles, guard their nests, the sounds uttered are mainly relevant to threat or sex. Possibly the clicks made by geckos may have some territorial significance. Both sexes of *Teratoscinus* and *Ptenopus* have special scale rings on their tails with which they make sounds. The sound-producing structures on the hind legs of the Pennsylvanian Mud Terrapin, *Cinosternum*, consisting of a double row of horny warts, are found only in the male. Presumably they are used in courtship. Darwin described the bellowing of the Galapagos tortoises. Alligators are said to demarcate territory by scent as well as vocally (Hediger 1950). The female responds to the grunts of her newly-hatched young by removing earth from the nest and she calls them to her at the edge of the water by grunting (McIlhenny 1935). The sacred crocodiles at Heliopolis would come at the call of the priests (Loisel 1912). The bellowing of these creatures attracts females and probably defies other males. The noises made by snakes—hissing, the clatter of the rattlesnake, and the rustling which the blue racer makes in the undergrowth—are warning or threat sounds, but it is doubtful whether rattlesnakes are able to hear their own rattles.

Some terrestrial mammals have a considerable vocabulary. The black-tailed prairie dog utters about ten different calls (King 1955) and the howler monkey between fifteen and twenty. Gibbons also have a repertoire of calls (Carpenter 1934, 1940, 1944). These primates not only make mating calls but use their vocalizations to demarcate territory.

Some mammals make warning or threat noises non-vocally—beavers by slapping their tails on the water, porcupines by rattling their quills, and rats by gnashing their teeth. Chimpanzees drum on logs or tree trunks and stamp on the ground during screaming sessions. These performances are communicatory but their exact significance is obscure (Stott and Selsor 1959). Gorillas under stress thump their chests (Schäfer 1960) or trees. Porpoises and bats have evolved acoustic signalling in a specialized way for echo-location. Oil birds (Guacharos) and one species of sea-swift (Medway 1959) in common with bats use calls as a means of echo-location but, so far as is known, only bats and cetaceans utter ultrasonic echo-locatory sounds (Griffin 1953, 1958). House Finches, Chaffinches (Thompson 1960), and probably birds of other species make a whirring sound with their wings when flying in dim light or darkness. Such sounds, and particularly the wing-noises of the Chimney Swift (p. 144), may enable birds to avoid each other in poor light and, perhaps, in some species may function in echo-location but there is no definite evidence of this.

Thus in many groups we find incipient systems of sound-signalling which birds and men have succeeded in developing further. Non-acoustic methods have been evolved by comparatively lowly organisms. Bees in their dances are able to convey a great deal of information to their fellows (von Frisch 1923, 1954).† Structure sets limits to what can be achieved. Acoustic signalling obviously depends on the development of sensitive hearing organs and the capacity to interpret the signals received. Many primates are less able to communicate multiple information by sound than song-birds. Their powers of sight, smell, and touch serve them so well that they have not developed a comparably complex vocal language.

The evolution and structure of hearing organs

In vertebrate evolution hearing organs evolved prior to sense organs responsive to gravity. Strange as it may seem, the response to gravity may be considered a by-product of hearing and the faculty of frequency analysis is, in turn, a by-product of distinguishing between responses to sound and to gravity. Hearing is defined by Pumphrey (1950) thus : 'An animal hears when it behaves as if it had located a moving object (a sound source) not in contact with it.' Thus defined hearing is practically universal among animals. Hearing, quite apart from its being essential to acoustic signalling, can be of obvious advantage to an organism in escaping predators or locating prey. The use of sounds by a species to communicate with other individuals followed the evolution of hearing. For the investigator of bird vocalizations the clues which a bird receives by means of its ears are, of course, highly important, for we can ascertain the significance of sounds uttered only by noting the changes in behaviour which they evoke in other organisms, particularly individuals of the same species.

A bird's ear is similar to the human ear in consisting of outer, middle, and inner parts. At the termination of the outer ear is the tympanic membrane. The middle ear communicates with the pharynx through the Eustachian tube and with the inner ear by two membrane-covered 'windows', one oval, the other round. The oval window connects with the columella and extra-columella by which movements of the tympanic membrane are communicated to the liquid perilymph of the inner ear. The hearing part of the inner ear, or cochlea, is proportionately shorter than our own, and is not coiled. The ductus cochlearis projects into it, separating two channels, the scala vestibuli and the scala tympani. The roof of the ductus cochlearis, which separates it from the scala vestibuli, is the tegmentum vasculosum, and the floor, separating it from the scala tympani, is the basilar membrane. Acoustical vibrations of large amplitude from the ear drum are transformed into vigorous vibrations of small amplitude at the oval window. The amplitude change is effected through the area of the ear drum being relatively much larger than the oval window and the columella footplate which connects with it. The hair cells, which are believed to be the actual sound receptors, are situated on the basilar membrane and are stretched when the basilar membrane is displaced. These cells are innervated by nerve fibres from the cochlear ganglion. The basilar membrane has transverse fibres and apparently they are each tuned to a distinct frequency. Thus the avian basilar membrane is a frequency analyser but there are about eight times as many such fibres in the human cochlea as in the pigeon's. At the apex of the cochlea there are further hair cells set in a cap loaded with calcareous particles. This organ, the lagena, is found in fish and many higher reptiles but not in man. It is possible that the lagena registers low frequencies and the cochlea proper high, and that the ranges of the two organs may not overlap (Pumphrey 1949, 1950).

The arrangement of the cochlea varies little throughout the whole class of birds. It increases relatively but not absolutely with decreasing body size so that the cochlea of small birds which hear and sing well is smaller than those of larger members of the group. The basilar membrane of an Amazon Parrot is 2·6 mm. in length as compared with 31 mm. for man with about the same pitch discrimination (Schwartzkopff 1955a, b).

The hearing range of birds

The hearing range varies considerably in different species. Knecht (1940), experimenting with Budgerigars and Crossbills, found that they had a span of eight or nine octaves—less than that of a man with good hearing. Human hearing lies between 16 and 20,000 c.p.s. The Budgerigar's hearing ranges from 40 to 14,000 cycles and the Crossbill can hear up to 20,000. The span of human hearing varies not only with age but also in individuals. Exceptional hearing ability appears to accompany musical talent. Sir J. J. Thomson (1936) observed that Galton's whistle could not produce a note beyond the hearing range of a boy he had invited to his laboratory. There were young students present with excellent hearing but none of them had heard anything for a long time before the whistle reached its highest note. The boy became a famous musician. The lower limit for the Starling, Magpie, Long-eared Owl, and Tawny Owl is about 100 cycles and for the Bullfinch and Chaffinch around 100–200. The Great Horned Owl hears sounds as low as 60 cycles and the limit for the Mallard, American Sparrow-hawk, and various crows is about 300. The Starling's higher limit is 15,000 but the House Sparrow, Robin, Greenfinch, Bullfinch, Magpie, and Tawny Owl hear up to 18,000 or 20,000. Probably there is considerable individual variation. Some Bullfinches can reach 20,000 and the Chaffinch 29,000 cycles. As there is some correlation between the highest frequencies a bird can hear and the highest frequencies in its song it may be that some species have a higher range of hearing than those mentioned and even higher than our own, as Brand (1935) suggested, but he was mistaken in believing that the House Wren could sing beyond our hearing. Later Brand and Kellogg (1939) showed that Starlings could hear only frequencies equivalent to the four highest octaves on the piano and about two octaves above its range. Man can hear at least an octave higher than the pigeon. The limit for birds with low-pitched voices tends to lie lower than for birds which sing high notes. For the Mallard, Great Horned Owl, American Sparrowhawk, and crows it is around 8000 cycles and for the pigeon 12,000. Highest sensitivity lies in the middle range. For man 1000–2400, Starling 2000, finches 3200, Magpie 800–1600, crows 2000, Mallard 2000–3000, Pigeon 1000–2400. Some owls are exceptional in this respect. The Tawny Owl's greatest sensitivity lies around 3000–6000 and the Long-eared Owl's about 6000 cycles. This confirms what observation indicates, that these birds are able to detect the squeaks and rustlings of their prey in the undergrowth. The most sensitive band for the Great Horned Owl is about 1000 cycles. The animals on which it preys are larger than those taken by the other two species. This bird's hearing is more sensitive than our own (Knecht 1940; Edwards 1943; Trainer 1946; Schwartz-kopff 1952a, b, 1955a).†

Pitch discrimination

Pitch discrimination varies among birds as it does among human beings but is generally good, especially in the range of greatest sensitivity, where birds are able to detect differences as small or smaller than a quarter tone. The pitch discrimination of the Budgerigar and at least some song-birds surpasses ours. Good songsters distinguish pitch better than species less gifted, such as doves. Birds have absolute pitch and some can transpose correctly (p. 29). Thus the hearing of birds compares favourably with our own. However, they seem to be unable to discriminate dissonances and consonances, and although some birds can sing more than one note simultaneously (p. 256), harmony in the true sense is absent from their singing.

The location of sounds

The ability to locate sounds readily and exactly is obviously advantageous. An animal is thus enabled to receive warning of the approach of a predator or intimation of the proximity of prey. It is also valuable socially. A hen can locate her chicks within 2° in the horizontal plane.

The chicks are equally accurate in locating their mother (Katz 1937). We must take into consideration that, as Marler (1955) has shown, the sounds emitted are adapted for easy localization. There is a concentration of energy at the beginnning; phase-difference perception is facilitated by the low frequencies and time-difference is rendered appreciable by the segmented character of the sounds (Collias and Joos 1953) (Fig. 4). In locating ability Domestic Fowl are better than dogs but not quite so good as cats. They are superior to an inexperienced man but human beings improve with practice (Katz 1937). Pumphrey points out that man's capacity in this respect depends primarily on an unconscious comparison of signals arriving at each ear in respect both of time- or phase-difference and intensity. For high frequencies intensity is most important, for low frequencies time-difference. With hearing restricted to one ear a man can still locate a sustained noise if it is sufficiently sustained, complex, and familiar. His head casts a shadow which is more complete for high frequencies than for low. Sound shadows become of appreciable magnitude only when the wave-length approximates to the diameter of the obstructing object. If he moves his head, unconsciously making comparison with the memory of the sound as heard when coming from in front, he is able to locate it (Pumphrey 1949).

Normally birds and mammals, including man, locate sounds by binaural comparisons of differences in phase, intensity, and arrival-time. Phase-difference—the alterations in pressure due to the sound occurring at different moments in the two ears—gives clear information when the wave-length is less than twice the difference between the ears—that is at low frequencies; but intensity differences are most useful for sound location at high frequencies as then the sound shadows are most marked. Time difference is useful at both high and low frequencies. Sounds which provide clues of all three kinds will be most easily located. Marler, who stresses these points, shows that the song of the Chaffinch, which has a wide frequency spectrum allowing opportunity for binaural time-comparison and intensity differences, is adapted to proclaim the whereabouts of the singer. This bird's head is so small and the ears are set so close together that time- and phase-differences must be more difficult to perceive than with larger species. All this makes it apparent that there is a close correlation between the nature of a bird's hearing and its vocalizations. Relationships may also be traced between hearing and vocalization in other respects. Some alarm calls of passerines and mammals are such as to baffle the locating ability of predators but the ears of some owls are so constructed as to facilitate precise location of prey (Fig. 43).†

Birds such as Domestic Fowl and Waterhens are practically incapable of locating sounds in the vertical plane (Katz 1937). This is also true of

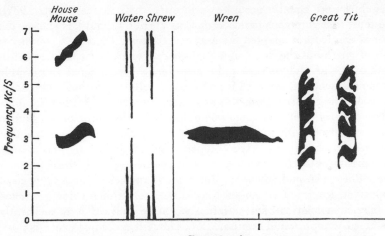

Fig. 43. A comparison of a house-mouse squeak and the chirp of a water shrew, the first difficult to locate accurately, the second quite easy. On the right is a similar comparison of the calls of a newly fledged Wren and a Great Tit. Again, the latter is easy to locate and the former is difficult, perhaps connected with the Wren's greater vulnerability when it leaves the nest. The ease of location of the water shrew's chirp may also be related to its aquatic habitat reducing its jeopardy from predators capable of responding to its auditory cues. (After Marler 1959b)

the dog. Probably it applies to all animals with ears set in the median plane. Moreover, experiments with human subjects show that they estimate tones of high pitch relative to other sounds as originating higher in space than comparable tones of lower pitch (Pedley and Hasker 1959). If this were true of four-footed predators it would probably add to their difficulty in locating exactly where birds were singing or calling, supposing, of course, that their hearing range extended to these high tones. For example, the cat has almost the same threshold of hearing as a man at frequencies from 100 to 3000 c.p.s., but the cat's threshold remains very low up to 13,000 c.p.s. (Wever 1930; Wever and Lawrence 1954). It seems that few, if any, predators rely on hearing birds sing in order to locate them.

In owls, particularly those which are most nocturnal, the outer ear is asymmetrical. They can locate brief sounds below them because their ears are apparently capable of resolving sound into at least three bands of frequency so that in each band independent comparison of the signals arriving at the two ears is possible, and also because the direction of maximum sensitivity of the ears differs for each band, and is different for the left and right ear for at least two of the bands (Pumphrey 1949).

Appendix

Miller (1952b) found that owls located owl calls quickly and accurately. This has been my experience also, with several species. For owls, resonance in the skull cavities may also magnify sound reception.

Sound production by birds

Sound production by birds may be vocal or non-vocal. The types of non-vocal noises made by birds have been discussed separately (Chapter VIII). To produce vocal sounds birds use as sound-box the syrinx, not the larynx. The essential features are membranes stretched across a bony or cartilaginous framework and muscles which control the tension of these membranes. The vocal muscles, on the lower end of the trachea (windpipe) or bronchi, are very differently modified in different groups of birds. In the ostriches, cassowaries, kiwis, and a number of other birds the trachea and syrinx have no intrinsic muscle attachments. The Turkey Vulture, *Cathartes aura*, has no syrinx (Miskimen 1957). The geese are among the birds with one pair of muscles on the distal end of the trachea, and there are many species with a pair of tracheo-bronchial muscles attached in other ways. Falcons and hummingbirds are among those with two pairs of such muscles, the parrots have three, and only a few species have four. Most of the singing birds proper (Oscines) have five or seven pairs of syringeal muscles. According to the position of the sound-producing membranes three types of syrinx are distinguishable—tracheal, bronchial, and tracheo-bronchial. Birds with the first type of structure are loud-voiced neo-tropical species, those of the second type include various cuckoos and nightjars, while most song-birds and a number of others belong to the third category (Gadow 1896).

Although there are general correlations between the character of the sound-producing organs and the sounds produced there are so many anomalies that inferences in regard to vocalization based on these structures are precarious. Cassowaries, with the simplest type of syrinx, can utter roaring noises whereas some birds with an elaborate syrinx, such as the Raven, produce relatively crude sounds. On the whole, the first-rate songsters have the most elaborate equipment. The birds with most syringeal muscles and greatest ability to move the membranes tend to produce the greatest variety of sounds. Enthusiastic as Craig is concerning the Wood Pewee's musical abilities he does not consider it to be in the first rank. It has only three pairs of syringeal muscles while the Blackbird has seven.

In birds with the less complex forms of vocal musculature the principal sound-producing structure resembles a wind instrument in which the resonator is modulated by a vibrator. The song-bird syrinx approximates in its operation rather to human vocal organs. Those species without intrinsic muscle attachments to the trachea and syrinx, or only a single pair, as in the Domestic Fowl, must produce sound by changes in the resonating tube rather than by the tympanic membranes. In this respect the amount of elongation and coiling of the trachea are important. For a long time it was supposed that song was produced while the bird drew in its breath. This belief was disproved in the early fifties. Miskimen (1951) showed that sound is produced as the bird exhales and that it originates in the vibrations of the syringeal membranes. The muscles attached to the syringeal cartilages are adapted to regulate with precision the tension on the vibrating membranes.

There is now evidence that, as has long been suspected, some birds, including the Brown Thrasher, Wood Thrush, Blue Jay, Gouldian Finch, and Reed Warbler can sing more than one note at the same time, and perhaps some birds such as the Wood Thrush as many as four (Saunders 1923, 1929, 1959; Potter *et al.* 1947; Borror and Reese 1956; Thorpe 1959, 1961) (Figs. 5, 6, 7 and 8) (pp. 32–35). The Blue Jay can sing the equivalent of a major chord, sustaining high and low notes simultaneously. The notes sung simultaneously may be of different intensities. Thus several vibrators must be involved—the two sets of tympaniform membranes, probably the semi-lunar membrane and perhaps structures in the superior larynx. On the basis of studies of the Indian Hill Mynah, which is among the very few imitative birds able to enunciate vowels, Thorpe concludes that it has three separately modifiable resonating chambers corresponding functionally to the human pharyngeal, oral, and nasal cavities. In the light of what is now known further study of the morphology of the structures involved is needed.

ADDENDA I

Owing to delays in publication the notes which follow have been added to take account of work which has been published during the last two and a half years.

Page 6.

† C. W. Morris (*Signs, Language and Behaviour*, 1946, New York) distinguishes signals by their function as identifiors, designators, appraisors and prescriptors. Marler (*J. Theoret. Biol. 1*: 295–317) shows the applicability of these to animal signals but points out that these often embody two of these functions.

Page 10.

† For a discussion of the function of vocalizations in facilitating individual recognition see P. Marler, *Amer. Inst. Biol. Sc. 7*: 348–367.

Page 12.

† Experiments with recordings of the voices of Adélie Penguins have shown that the chick is able to recognize the voice of the parent.

Page 13.

† Gompertz (1961) refers to quiet 'warbling' by male and female juvenile Great Tits and to two forms of 'quiet' song—'whispered' and 'intense'. The 'whispered' song is uttered only when the bird is in a relaxed state, according to her observations. The pre-copulation song noted by Gompertz is audible up to about twenty yards. She lists eighteen main categories of sounds made by Great Tits and mentions a bird with forty 'distinct utterances'.

Page 19.

† A Turnstone's call will attract the whole flock to feed. These birds sometimes devour carrion and other sporadically available forms of provender (S. O. Macdonald and D. F. Parmelee, *Brit. Birds 55*: 241–244).

Page 26.

† Observers in Africa have noted that mixed groups of mammals respond to each other's alarm responses more effectively than mixed parties of birds (J. M. Winterbottom, *Ibis 85*: 437–442. When shooting Woodpigeons French wildfowlers imitate their cooing to reassure perched birds (R. G. Busnel and J. Giban: *Colloque* 1958). See P. Pfeffer (*Oiseau 29*: 210–213) for the alerting of wild pigs by birds.

Page 29.

† Miss G. Page-Wood (MS deposited in Newton Library, Cambridge) shows in musical notation how a Blackbird gradually lowered pitch from A to E while singing. She maintains (*in litt.*) that Cuckoos and Blackbirds, if they do not (or cannot) answer a rival with the same phrase at the same pitch, will answer with that phrase truly transposed to another key in accordance with our western system of key-relationships. Mrs. J. Hall-Craggs (*in litt.*) comments that she has no example of a copied phrase differing widely in pitch

from the pattern phrase but would not say that such copying and transposing cannot occur. In the beautiful song of the Rufous and White Wren there are clear notes, *accelerando* and, apparently, changes of key. When several Long-eared Owls are within earshot of each other they raise or lower slightly the pitch of their calls so that they can be detected apart. (S. Palmér, Radions Fagel Skivor.)

Page 32.

† Thorpe and Griffin (*Ibis 104*: 220–27) show that although there are ultrasonic frequencies in many small birds' songs it is unlikely that they have a communicatory function. They may provide a significant component in the tonal quality of the notes as perceived by other birds.

Page 41.

† Andrew (1961b) defines song 'for present purposes' as 'vocalizations given persistently by a bird in breeding condition (and at no other time) before it acquires a mate (or when it loses contact with its mate)'. This is too limited and arbitrary to be accepted as a general definition and introduces confusion into his own discussion. Song need not be vocal nor limited to the breeding season. Thorpe (1961) defines it as 'a series of notes, generally of more than one type, uttered in succession and so related as to form a recognizable sequence or pattern in time'. But some birds utter distinctive sequences of notes as alarm or contact calls. Borror (1961) defines song as vocalization with one or more of three functions, to advertise the presence of the male, to attract a female, and to repel other males. This is too limited as is also M. Moynihan's definition (*Auk 79*: 319). W. C. Dilger (*Living Bird 1*: 86) would cavalierly discard 'song' from scientific terminology.

Andrew maintains that the causation of song may differ from its motivation and that a song is not necessarily aggressive because it repels males. However, it is evident that motivation and causation have evolved *pari passu*, with mutual interaction. He believes that song evolved from contact calls and retains much of this motivation. All social utterances are *ipso facto* contact calls but some, especially song, have become much more. They are basically elicitatory or inhibiting; that is, such as to evoke another response, initiate a chain of responses, maintain responsive behaviour or suppress certain behaviour.

Page 48.

† Page-Wood (MS) noted that Blackbird song develops from a single phrase by the addition of others. Blackbirds invent phrases which may be abandoned or accepted into the repertoire. New phrases are added in subsequent seasons. Thielcke-Poltz and Thielcke (1960) state that development is more rapid during the second year. Page-Wood states that imitation is marked during the dawn chorus and only then do some birds use their full repertoire. A phrase sung by one bird was sung by six others the next season. Two years later it could still be heard but it had disappeared after two more years. Hall-Craggs (*Ibis 104*: 277–300; in press) has independently confirmed some of these observations and added to them.

Page 49.

† J. A. Mulligan (*Abstr. XIII Int. Orn. Congr.*) shows that the repertoire of 12–23 song-versions is peculiar to the individual Song Sparrow.

Addenda I

Page 54.

† The critical period for song-learning in meadowlarks is between the learning of song at about four weeks of age and the first winter (Lanyon 1957). Bluebirds reared from the egg and isolated for six months showed no response to American Robin, Baltimore Oriole, and Wood Thrush songs but perked up a little when a Bluebird recording was played in reverse. When it was played correctly they perched motionless for thirty to forty seconds and then sang crude versions. Within five minutes they sang the song in recognizable form (A. A. Allen, *Nat. Geogr. Mag. 121*: 530–49). Marler, Kreith and Tamura (*Auk 79*: 12–30) studying hand-reared Oregon Juncos found 'no critical period in the life history for the development of song'. Gompertz (1961) suggests that the Great Tit's song repertoire includes (*a*) patterns under genetic control or acquired early in life, perhaps from the male parent, and (*b*) patterns conforming to those of Great Tits with which it comes into competition during the first or subsequent seasons.

Page 55.

† Marler *et al.* found that Oregon Juncos in acoustic isolation tended to sing more variable and longer songs with fewer, longer syllables than wild birds. Birds reared in a rich auditory environment had more song-versions with a more elaborate syllable structure. In such an environment imitation occurs and vocal improvisation is stimulated. These capacities are not restricted to any particular phase of the life history. A wild bird with several song-versions may repeat one version for very much longer than a Chaffinch or Great Tit. The latter has been known to continue for eight minutes (Gompertz 1961).

Poulsen (*Proc. XII Int. Orn Congr.*) points out that the Canary's imitations, which may be complete copies of alien songs, are always separate from the bird's own song. Apparently the learning of alien calls is not restricted to the sub-song period. In a list of species which learn mimicries all through life he mentions the Bluethroat. In a recording by S. Palmér a Bluethroat is heard mimicking reindeer bells as well as various birds.

Page 58.

† The bird referred to is evidently the Japanese Bush Warbler *Cettia diphone*.

Page 64.

† The term 'muted song' might be used in reference to quiet utterances of the normal, or nearly normal, territorial or advertising, song pattern, as occasionally noted of the Chaffinch, Wren, American Redstart, and some other birds. For the development of flycatcher sub-song see E. Curio, *J. Orn. 101*: 291–307.

Page 75.

† The Chinese take cage birds, such as Mongolian Larks, into the open to learn the songs and calls of other species, tapping the cage when the bird attempts to sing its own song. A 'good' mimic is able to reproduce the song or calls of at least 13 other species (Hoffmann, A., 1960. *Nachrichten der Gesellschaft für Natur- und Volkskunde. Hamburg. 88*: 45–79). In his studies of the Lyrebird's song, published in the *Victorian Naturalist 75*: 175–176; *78*:

79–81; *79*: 137–139, K. C. Halafoff claims that it is highly developed technically and aesthetically. On playing recordings at a slow tempo he found that in the mimicked twittering of two Scrub Wrens the sounds uttered by the individuals were intercalated and even the utterance of a third bird of another species which, at normal tempo, also seemed superimposed did not overlap. He believes that the musical intervals in the songs of some Australian birds are very close to our scale and suggests, as others have done, that the evolution of man's musical appreciation was influenced by hearing birds' songs. (Mrs. Hall-Craggs has independently suggested that such influence may have been subconscious). Halafoff states that certain percussive notes are synchronised with the Lyrebird's dance movements. He identifies distinctive dialects, a distinctive courtship song and a muted song uttered when preening.

H. and A. Ansley (Folkways Record FX 6115), using slowed recordings, claim to find similarities in bird songs to human musical scales and notations. They believe mimetic ability to be very widespread and consider the Mockingbird's capacity to mimic to be almost unlimited. A basic two-note phrase is so widespread that it is supposed to be an inheritance from reptilian ancestors. Song-learning in many species is believed to occur during a very brief early period.

Page 79.
    † A. R. Maclatchey (*L'oiseau* 7: 60–80) states that the male African Crowned Eagle whistles softly to attract monkeys, which it then seizes. This observation has not been confirmed.

Page 83.
    † Mr. Maxwell Knight informs me that his female African Grey Parrot performs a song-and-dance act learned from human beings, swaying rhythmically and whistling. (See Thorpe 1963.)

Page 87.
    † A Blackbird may complete another's phrase if it stops short (J. Hall-Craggs, *op. cit.*). Thus antiphonal song is not restricted to mated birds. Lyrebirds of like sex are also said to sing antiphonally (Chisholm 1934). Hall-Craggs also noted a Blackbird imitating a Blue Tit's alarm call immediately after it had been uttered (see p. 85). Thielcke (*Vogelwarte 21*: 199–202) believes that the Great Spotted Woodpecker's call, terminating the Chaffinch's song in some areas, is learned by one individual from another. Similarly the call of the Short-toed Treecreeper is added to the Treecreeper's song.

Page 89.
    † L. F. Brosnahan, in *The Sounds of Language* (Cambridge, 1961), discusses the evidence that genetic factors underlie certain differences between European languages.

Page 92.
    † The song of a Crested Lark, *Galerida theklae*, is said to be of longer duration as one passes from north to south in Africa (Huxley 1942). Probably the first literary reference to bird dialects is Aristotle's comment that Partridge calls differ according to locality, some being of a cackling type, others whistling (*H.A.*, 536b. 10–15).

Addenda I

Page 94.

† R. C. Stein (*Living Bird 1*: 61–71), studying five American warblers found that the song patterns showed a relationship parallel to that indicated by plumage. Where there are fewer species, greater separation of habitat and less risk of confusion, songs are more variable.

Marler and Tamura (*Condor 64*: 368–377), found distinctive and consistent differences in the song patterns of three populations of White-crowned Sparrows. Where separation was greatest divergence was also greatest.

Page 99

† Since this was written I have heard the Winter Wren singing at 6000 feet in the Great Smoky Mountains, Tennessee. The song pattern seemed to differ from that of the European Wren about as much, or rather less than, the North British island wrens' songs and the length of the phrase approximated to that of the European Wren. Its duration may have been a second or two longer. The terminal note seemed absent and the incorporation of three longish repetitive sections less apparent. Unfortunately no recording is available. Having listened at Cornell to recordings of the Winter Wren from other regions of the United States I believe that the recording figured in Armstrong, 1955, is of abnormal length.

Page 102

† Other examples of the spread of novel forms of acquired behaviour are cited by D. Stenhouse (*Ibis 104*: 250–52).

Page 107.

† Lanyon (*Condor 63*: 421–29), investigating reports of mass hybridization between the Ash-throated Flycatcher *Myiarchus cinerascens*, and Nutting's Flycatcher, *M. nuttingi*, shows that one of the basic vocal patterns is distinctive and diagnostic. He found no evidence of mixed pairing. A hand-reared *M. cinerascens* uttered its species-characteristic calls at sixteen days of age. C. J. O. Harrison (*Condor 63*: 450–55) observed differences in call-note between the Inca Dove, *Scardafella inca*, and the Scaly Dove, *S. squammata*, but considers that specific separation is incomplete and that the distinction is maintained by allopatric separation.

Page 108.

† Such intermediate songs may be the direct expression of structural modifications whereas inborn bird songs must be due, at least in many instances, to central nervous structure. For hybrid chickadee songs see R. Brewer, *Auk 80*: 9–47.

Page 111.

† Thielcke (1961) agrees that the Brown Creeper is more closely related to the European Treecreeper than to the Short-toed Treecreeper, but considers the evidence inconclusive as to whether the Brown Creeper should be regarded as a race of the European Treecreeper or a distinct species. In a later paper (*J. Orn.103*: 266–71) he considers it to be distinct. Löhrl (*J. Orn. 101*: 245–64 and *102*: 111–132) finds acoustic evidence that the Corsican and Canadian Nuthatches, *Sitta whiteheadi* and *S. canadensis*, are not conspecific.

Page 112.

† For a discussion of the authenticity of Leguat's narrative, see A. E. H. Swaen: *Ardea 12*: 25, and *29*: 19–44.

Page 116.

† Pied Flycatchers may be polyterritorial (Curio 1959a). The Seaside Sparrow *Ammospiza maritima* defends an area around the nest and a feeding strip along the sea shore (Welty, J. 1962, *The Life of Birds*, New York). The Greenshank may also hold a feeding territory as well as a nesting territory (Nethersole-Thompson 1951). H. E. Howard, in *An Introduction to the Study of Bird Behaviour* (Cambridge, 1929), records observing a Skylark with two territories.

Page 118.

† Hall-Craggs (*op. cit.*) found that a Blackbird which sang very vigorously held a particularly large territory.

Page 124.

† Dr. J. H. Crook tells me that his study of weavers confirms my views in regard to the relationship between availability of food and the nature of the pair-bond. (See *Ibis 104*: 444). Dr. J. Verner (*in litt.*), studying the Long-billed Marsh Wren, finds that the amount of attention by the male to the young depends largely on foraging conditions. D. W. Snow (*Zoologica 47*: 65–104), discussing the display of the Black and White Manakin, traces the evolution of such communal performances to easy foraging emancipating the male from tending the young and necessitating rapid synchronisation of male and female rhythms through exactly coordinated activities. Curio (*Vogelwelt 82*: 33–48), notes that in Germany and Finland the Pied Flycatcher is polygamous but the Spanish race is monogamous—a situation comparable with that among Wren subspecies. There are other differences between the two populations.

Page 126.

† Evidence accumulates that territorialism, including the calls, songs and displays associated with it, is important in controlling populations within the limits of the food supply. (For the Bellmagpie see R. Carrick, *Abstr. XIII Int. orn. Congr.* and for the Song Sparrow, F. S. Tompa (*Auk* 79: 687–97). See also Wynne-Edwards (1962). His argument that animals contend for conventional substitutes rather than directly for food, and that such behaviour determines dispersal, is in line with the accepted view that territorialism side-tracks or buffers dysgenic conflict. My view (1955, 1956) is that the whole integrated complex of behaviour-patterns, in correlation with the environment, and particularly in relationship to foraging and food supply, determines dispersal.

Page 128.

† Miss Page-Wood (MS.) noted that territorial competition increased the amount of song by a Blackbird. She considered that the effect was to 'improve' the song. Rufous Whistlers, when challenging and standing almost beak to beak sing more slowly and sweetly as feeling mounts (Erickson 1951). Thus belligerence does not necessarily reduce the aesthetic qualites of song. In some

species of grasshopper a male singing the courtship song will break off to sing the 'rivalry song' at an intruding male and either drive him away or keep him engaged in song until the female moves away (Haskell 1961).

Page 130.

† The Honeyeaters (*Meliphagidae*) have poorly developed threat displays, engage in combat, and utter fighting songs (K. Immelmann, *J. Orn. 102*: 164–207).

Page 132.

† The interpretation as displacement activity of certain forms of song by von Haartman, Löhrl, and Curio is open to question. C. H. F. Rowell (*Anim. Behav. 9*: 38–63), explains displacement grooming in terms of equilibrium of motivation rather than the degree of disinhibition.

Page 134.

† A distinction should be made between transference activities and 'non-correlation activities' (Armstrong 1961). The latter differ from transference activities in being initiated in the absence of the normal initiating object—as when a bird removes a pebble or a leaf in the absence of a faecal sac. On hearing a recording of its song a male bird may attack the nest (Allen 1961). As it is the song rather than the sight of a rival which initiates aggression this is a transference activity because it is normally activated.

Page 137.

† In areas where related species of wader are sympatric, their song-flights are usually readily distinguishable (R. G. B. Brown, *Ibis 104*: 1–12). O. von Frisch (1960) holds that the Redshank's display-flight is concerned with the delimitation of territory rather than courtship. D. Blume (*J. Orn. 103*: 140–149) distinguishes 'Erregungsflug' or 'excitement-flight' from display-flight, pointing out that the former is little ritualized. Cf. the distinction made on p. 136 between 'flight-song' and 'song-flight'. The song-flight utterances of the American Redstart resemble the territorial song (M. Ficken *Auk 79*: 687–97), but in other parulids and passerines of various species these utterances may differ in lesser or greater degree.

Page 144.

† Gould's Manakin makes six different kinds of non-vocal sound (H. Sick, *Proc. XII Int. orn. Congr.*). Two male Blue-backed Manakins perform a precisely coordinated dance and duet in front of the female (E. T. Gilliard, *Amer. Mus. Novit. 1942*; Snow 1956b: *Zoologica 47*: 65–104; *Condor 65*: 44–88.

Page 145.

† A White Bellbird called from his 'stud-post' for 78 per cent of the time during a 5½-hours watch (B. K. Snow, *Auk 78*: 150–61).

Page 147.

† The peacock butterfly makes a hissing sound with its wings when disturbed on settling down to hibernate. The 'eye-spots' are displayed simul-

taneously. Probably the sound, as well as the display, is deterrent. The hearing of rats and mice is particularly sensitive to high-frequency sounds (Haskell 1961).

Page 160.
† Modified song accompanies copulation in some American warblers (M. S. and R. W. Ficken, *Living Bird 1*: 102–22).

Page 162.
† The White-tailed Trogon lures the female to the site with a melodious twitter (A. F. Skutch, *Ibis 104*: 399–406), and the female Casqued Hornbill is led by the wailing male to the proposed nest-site (L. Kilham, *Smithsonian Misc. Coll. 131*).

Page 169.
† The female Nightingale-Thrush utters 'little ghosts of song' while approaching or leaving the nest, contemplating the nestlings or in the midst of scolding intruders with a churring note (Skutch 1958a).
The male Wren-Tit incubates but sings when he goes off the nest. The male Red-breasted Flycatcher and Great Reed Warbler cease to sing when the female begins incubation.

Page 173.
† Wynne-Edwards (1962) describes song and display-flights by a vast congregation of White-winged Crossbills before departing for the south.

Page 174.
† W. J. Hamilton (*Condor 64*: 390–401), finds that calls of birds on migration stimulate others to fly up and may provide orienting cues for flock maintenance.

Page 182.
† W. H. Thorpe informs me that the true reaction time of the female *L. erythrogaster* to the male's note is $0·125 - 0·053$ secs. $= 0·072$ secs. Over a series of duets the response time may be kept accurate to within $0·03$ secs. Two other East African species which duet are *Cisticola chubbi* and *C. hunteri*, birds of the long grass and misty habitats. A female Rufous Whistler may complete a phrase by the male when separated some yards from him (Erickson 1951). Among other species which duet are the Cardinal, Buff-throated Saltator (Skutch 1954) and the Queo. Male and female of this species may sing together when disturbed at the nest (Skutch *Auk 79*: 633–39). Among the Honeyeaters vocalizations grade from mutual responsive contact notes to highly-developed duetting and group singing (K. Immelmann, *J. Orn. 102*: 164–207).

Page 185.
† Saunders (1929) and G. F. Fisler (*Condor 64*: 184–97), note that the singing of one individual may stimulate an individual of the same or another species to sing. R. Brewer (*Auk 80*: 9–47) discusses song-rivalry between chickadee species.

Page 200.

† Leopold and Eynon (1961) note three, possibly four, types of daybreak song: (1) Departing from and returning to the Civil Twilight curve at about the same angle on both sides of the solstice (Field Sparrow); (2) Departing from the Civil Twilight curve at a medium angle until about the solstice and then returning to the Civil Twilight curve at a sharper angle (Cardinal); (3) Following the Civil Twilight curve closely (House Wren). The song of the Catbird becomes earlier and then becomes later more gradually. These writers quote Armstrong (1955) to the effect that the Wren arises about the same time in relation to Civil Twilight throughout the year but this generalization needs to be qualified in view of the data shown on the graph (Fig. 31) indicating that during the moult in August arising tends to be relatively late. Probably the correlation between the moult and late rising is fairly general among birds. G. F. Fisler (*op. cit.*), notes, as others have done, that the 'bird-clock' effect is only valid within certain limits and must be related to the breeding cycle. Some species maintain their relative positions better than others. Thus the Cardinal always precedes the Crow. J. Aschoff and R. Wever (*J. Orn. 103*: 2–27), summarize much data on the relationship between light and bird activities.

Page 203.

† See also L. Vlijm (*Ardea 49*: 158–64) and R. G. B. Brown (*Ibis 105*: 63–75), on the characteristics of the daily rhythm in high latitudes.

Page 204.

† Reports by 107 Scandinavian observers of the eclipse of 30 June 1954 were summarized by C. Ehrström (*Vår Fågelvärld 15*: 1–28. Totality was early in the afternoon and birds ceased singing for about fifteen minutes. After the eclipse they began song at higher light values than those at which they stopped singing before it. This reversal of the usual relationship of song to decreasing and increasing light might be used to support the theory that fatigue is important in causing birds to cease song in the evening at higher light values than they begin in the morning (Cf. Leopold and Eynon 1961). Ehrström noticed that the Willow Warbler sang throughout the eclipse. A Pied Flycatcher feeding young sang a phrase 27 minutes before and 22 minutes after the eclipse reached 99 per cent. Feeding the young proceeded normally during the eclipse (K. Elgmork, *Brit. Birds 55*: 385–87).

‡ These observations are in line with observations on other dark-adapted birds that activity begins in the evening at higher light values than it ceases in the morning. In diurnal birds song begins at lower and more precise light values than those at which evening song ends. The American Woodcock ceases song at more precise light values than it begins. The morning mean intensity was 0·028–0·002 foot-candle. Leopold and Eynon quote the following light intensities in foot-candles for first vocalization in European birds: Wren 0·003, Blackbird and Redstart 0·007, Red Grouse 0·036 (0·39 lux) for ten mornings but on four mornings 0·009 foot-candle (0·1 lux).

Page 205.

† It should be noted that moonlight affected the earliness of the American Robin's song in March, April, and May, but in June, when the birds were

active earlier in relation to Civil Twilight the influence of moonlight was not apparent. Leopold and Eynon also show that in the country birds tend to sing earlier than in the town. Dr. Eynon (*in litt.*) suggests that this may be due to the difficulty experienced by town birds, exposed to artificial illumination, in assessing light intensity. R. Graczyk (*Ekologia Polska 9*: 453–485) notes that urban Blackbirds are more sedentary, have simpler songs and more broods than forest birds. Evidence for a 'physiological clock' adjusted by the influence of light is available for insects and mammals as well as for birds.

Page 209.

† According to Hinde (1952) the Great Tit's output of song is greatly influenced by the weather. Morning fog or frost reduces song and sharp showers cause its immediate cessation. Low temperatures in England up to the third week of March 1962 had a strongly depressing effect on the song of several species, including the Great Tit, Wren, and Chaffinch. Rain after drought stimulates Blackbird song (Snow 1958).

Page 220.

† See B. K. Snow (*op. cit.*) for bellbird displays. The American Redstart displays orange side-spots and the Red-winged Blackbird red shoulder-patches when singing. The Meadowlark's chest adornments are conspicuous in song-flight or when singing on a post (Fig. 40). The scarlet crest of the Red-crowned Ant-Tanager is consistently raised only during the dawn song in dim light when it is more likely to be seen by the bird's mate than by a rival (E. Willis, *Condor 62*: 73–87).

‡ Among American warblers there is 'almost perfect correlation between average height at which the species forages and the average pitch of the song' (M. S. and R. W. Ficken, *Living Bird 1*: 102–21). E. Willis (*Condor 62*: 73–87), found that of two ant-tanagers (*Habia*) the species which feeds nearest the ground is the most secretive and has the greatest diurnal output of song.

Page 221.

† It should be remembered that a 'pure tone' is, to the physicist, a sine wave, but to the musicologist and ordinary listener a clear, smooth sound, free from harshness. Spectrograms reveal details, some of which are not apparent to our hearing but are probably important to birds. See G. Thielcke, *J. Orn. 102*: 285–300.

Page 231.

† For onomatopoeic and poetic renderings of bird songs cf. Armstrong (1923) and W. Garstang, *Songs of the Birds* (1935). The most ambitious attempt to present bird songs in musical notation is in Miss Page-Wood's MS. mentioned above.

Page 235.

† The problem of the subjectivity of our assessment of bird music is discussed by P. Szöke in *Studia Musicologica* (1962) 2: 33–85. His argument is to some extent on the lines of that in Chapter XIII—that man and bird possess common physical and physiological foundations for the 'appreciation' of sounds. By slowing down recordings it can be shown that the notes of birds

may be referred to the harmonic series. A parallelism is apparent between musical complexity and evolutionary status. The utterance of the crane *Grus leucogeranus* consists of fourths, up and down. The Chaffinch's song is a stereotyped structure of melodic lines more complex musically than the most primitive stage of human vocal music. The song of the Woodlark is rich in invention and approximates most closely to human vocal music. Remarkable transposing occurs, including to the fifth—a feature of folk music. Szöke maintains that bird song as perceived by ear is something 'higher' than the physical reality and so graphs of frequency changes represent it inadequately. Fully developed bird song is music in that it is a tonal system, based on the transposition of intervals and musical phrases. (These notes are partly based on a summary by Dr. L. Picken.) He suggests that as birds evolved elaborate musical utterances before the evolution of *Homo sapiens* we may suppose that primitive music was influenced by hearing and imitating bird vocalizations. In primitive culture, however, interest in bird sounds is utilitarian. Robert Bridges in *The Testament of Beauty* comments that birds 'gracefully schooling music to enliven leisure were the earlier artists' and may have been man's teachers.

Page 238.

† Lorenz (1935) stresses that in social play all the social inhibitions are maintained. Such play could be useful early experience in the exercise of restraint. M. Markgren (*Vår Fågelvärld 20*: 214–24), holds that 'play' and 'dance' should be eliminated from ethological discussion. Similarly, W. J. Dilger (*op. cit.*) would banish 'song'. The belief that a mechanistic terminology necessarily clarifies problems is naïve.

Page 240.

† While this seems to be true in general qualifications are needed; thus Hall-Craggs (*op. cit.*) points out that the complexity of full territorial song may overtax our appreciative capacity.

Page 241.

† I do not now consider this explanation adequate.
Although 'vocal inventiveness is a significant factor in the development of song in Oregon Juncos' (Marler, Kreith and Tamura, *Auk 79*: 12–30) each song-version is uttered for long periods without a break. This appears to be contrary to the 'anti-monotony principle'.

Page 245.

† Professor Hartshorne points out that he qualified this (*Ibis 100*: 439). We agree that the complexity of some bird songs goes beyond discernible biological advantage and that in so far as a bird 'appreciates' what it is doing in manipulating sounds an aesthetic mood may exist. I agree with him (*in litt.*) that 'the more a bird needs to sing musically the more it needs to feel musically'. As evidence increases it becomes more difficult to deny that birds possess some aesthetic sensitivity. For apes, see D. Morris, *The Biology of Art* (1962).

Page 247.

† In some groups sound signals have become specialized to serve a variety of functions. Some crickets appear to defend territory by stridulation, and certain notes serve as warnings among members of ant and termite colonies. Ants of the species *Megaponera foetans* stridulate when buried in sand and thus attract companions to rescue them. Apparently some Hymenoptera use sound signals to attract members of their colony to sources of food (Haskell 1961; Cf. also A. S. Weth, *Z. Tierpsychol 8*: 1–41).

Page 248.

† For a discussion of aggressive and territorial sounds uttered by fish see H. Schneider, *Naturwiss 48*: 513–18. Cf. also H. E. Winn and J. A. Marshall in *Physiol. Zool. 36*: 1–44 and W. N. Tavolga in *Bio-Acoustics Bull. 2*: 10–11. This journal summarises recent contributions on hearing and sound production in vertebrates and invertebrates including snakes. It gives references to the application of the analysis of the utterances of amphibia to problems of systematics. J. D. Roeder and A. E. Treat (*Amer. Sci. 49*: 135–148), show that noctuid moths can detect the echo-location utterances of bats at 100 feet. R. D. Alexander (*Behav. 17*: 130–223), demonstrates that the call-songs of field crickets show more differences than courtship songs among sympatric, synchronic species. This is in accord with the general principle that long-distance signals tend to be more distinctive than close-up utterances. The late-season songs of American warblers are less distinctive than the earlier definitely territorial songs.

Page 250.

† See also Lindauer, M. 1961. *Communication among Social Bees*. Harvard Univ. Press.

Page 252.

† Some of these results need verification as the testing of cochlear potential gives hardly any information concerning amplitude. Schwartzkopff (*Abstr. XIII Int. Orn. Congr.*), shows that the threshold of cochlear potential in passerines is 20 to 40 db., lower than in Striges, and states that 'in birds there is physiological evidence of a striking sensitivity to transitory stimuli'. This may be of importance in apprehending the details of rapidly uttered songs.

Page 253.

† R. S. Payne (*Living Bird 1*: 151–59), describes the procedure by which the Barn Owl locates prey by hearing.

ADDENDA II

Pre-natal communication and individual recognition

(pp. 9–12, 120, 148, 257). Unhatched chicks make various sounds, vocal and nonvocal. The most noticeable, apart from the bill-tapping with which the chick breaks the shell, are the regular clicks caused by respiration. This clicking probably occurs in many species, having been observed in the Coal Tit, Song Thrush, Herring Gull, Japanese Quail (*Coturnix coturnix japonica*), and domestic fowl. Unhatched ducklings perform 'bill-clapping' during the latter half of incubation (R. W. Oppenheim, 1970. *Anim. Behav. 18:* 335–352). Curlew and Greylag Goose chicks call within the egg when temperature falls.

The brooding bird reacts to information from the unhatched egg. In some species sounds from the eggs influence the pre-natal behaviour of other unhatched chicks and result in closer synchronization of hatching, an adaptation which has survival value, particularly among ground-nesting birds, enabling the whole brood to leave the nest with the parent (M. A. Vince, 1969. *In* R. A. Hinde, *Bird Vocalizations*, Cambridge, pp. 233–260; cited later as *B. V.*).

Chicks within the egg may react to other environmental sounds, including the species call. Pre-natal experience of the call of the Laughing Gull (*Larus atricilla*) influences the chick's post-natal responsiveness to it (M. Impekoven, 1971. *Anim. Behav. 19:* 475–480). During the 3–4 days before hatching Guillemot chicks begin to learn the calls of their parents and the parents those of their young (B. Tschanz, 1968. *Z. Tierpsychol. 4*). In ground-nesting species with young which gather together in groups, such as the King Penguin (*Aptenodytes patagonica*) and Sandwich Tern, parent and chick recognize each other individually by each other's calls. Common Terns 2–4 days old use auditory cues to distinguish their parents. As young as 24 hours after hatching Laughing Gulls recognize their parents' calls. Male and female Gannet recognize individually the mate's landing call. Probably such mutual recognition of the birds' vocalizations not only prevents 'misunderstandings' when one bird joins the other on the nesting ledge but enables them to breed together again in successive seasons (W. H. Thorpe, 1972. *In* R. A. Hinde, *Non-verbal Communication*, Cambridge, pp. 153–175).

Further evidence continues to accumulate indicating that birds, including mature songbirds, are able to recognize the individual utterances of their neighbours (C. G. Beer, 1970. *Adv. Study Behav. 3:* 27–74). J. B. Falls (*B. V.*, pp. 206–232) has shown that a bird's capacity to recognize other individuals by their songs restricts belligerency to situations in which a threat to its territory exists.

Social functions

(pp. 1–27, etc.). The social and communicative functions of bird utterances have been enumerated, discussed and the relevant literature reviewed by G. Thielcke (1970. *Vogelwarte 25:* 204–229).

A Study of Bird Song

Learning and imitation

(pp. 44–57, 70–87, 259–260, 264). Vocal learning by imitation is much more widespread and developed in the Passeriformes than in other groups. It is reported of one hummingbird as well as of parrots but, to give a few examples, doves and pigeons, the Domestic Fowl and Cuckoo can produce their repertoires of calls without hearing another bird of their own species. The extensive differentiation among song-birds may have been furthered through the direct and indirect consequences of such learning but the imitative ability of species, even of those closely related, may differ greatly. Thus, if the White-crowned Sparrow is to produce normal song it must be within hearing of it during its first 100 days whereas the Song Sparrow, although capable of imitation, may sing normally without ever hearing another of its kind sing. Even when reared with a singing Canary this bird's song is not copied. However, learning from other Song Sparrows determines whether an individual's song will be rich or poor. The White-crowned Sparrow sings virtually the same song all its life but the Song Sparrow averages sixteen song types in the San Francisco area and ten in Ohio. Two species of Junco are intermediate between these extremes (J. A. Mulligan, 1966. *Univ. Calif. Publ. Zool. 81:* 1–76. P. Marler, 1967. *Proc. 13th Int. Orn. Congr.*, pp. 231–244).

In birds such as the Chaffinch which learn their songs during a 'critical' period or periods it is assumed that there exists a template on which the full song is built up. At the beginning of the period the template is only a crude specification but is sufficient to exclude the songs of other species (P. Marler, 1970. *Journ. Comp. Physiol. Psychol. Monog. 71:* 1–25). Social singing, even with other immature birds, may facilitate the development of coded elements which would otherwise not appear (W. H. Thorpe, 1967. *Proc. 14th Int. Orn. Congr.*, pp. 245–263). Auditory social facilitation is important in many species. A male Chaffinch, castrated during its first winter, was implanted with testosterone and allowed to hear two song themes at the age of two years. It learned these, thus showing that the ability to develop song for the first time is not age-dependent (F. Nottebohm, 1967. *Proc. 14th Int. Orn. Congr.*, pp. 265–280).

Although call notes tend to be more innate than song, yet in some species they can be acquired while young. Willow Tits reared by other *Parus* species use calls characteristic of the foster-parents. But in this and other species the location call is species-specific, not learned, and therefore it can provide useful taxonomic data (H. Löhrl, 1963. *Proc. 13th Int. Orn. Congr.*, pp. 544–552). The application of evidence provided by avian vocalizations to systematics has been discussed by W. E. Lanyon (*B. V.*, pp. 291–310).

An extreme illustration of imitation is provided by the utterances of Widow-birds (Viduinae) which lay their eggs in the nests of various weaver-finch (Estrildine) species. The calls of the young and songs of the adults resemble closely those of the species victimised, thus facilitating the deception of the Estrildines. The songs consist of two groups of elements; in each case one is typically Widow-bird and the other includes the entire repertoire of the particular weaver-finch concerned. Thus it is possible to identify the species of weaver-finch parasitised by a particular Widow-bird by noticing what species its utterances resemble (J. Nicolai, 1964. *Z. Tierpsychol. 21:* 129–204. 1967. *J. Ornith. 108:* 309–319).

When a Robin is challenged by another's song he responds promptly with a motif used by his rival, declaring in effect: 'I am directing this challenge at you' (J. C. Brémond, pers. comm.). This is probably the significance of comparable imitation by other species, such as the Blackbird, Nightingale, and Chaffinch. The procedure amounts to 'naming' the other bird. Naming of a bird's mate also occurs. Captive Jackdaws learn to mimic sounds such as fragments of human speech, the 'klappering' of Storks and gobbling of Turkeys. Each individual bird in the course of time acquires his or her own repertoire which differs from that of all other Jackdaws, including its mate. When a pair become separated each begins using items from the other bird's repertoire, thus calling it back. If a male Shama absents himself from his mate—who is normally rather silent—she imitates his song. He returns in an aggressive mood, as if challenged by a rival, but on seeing his partner changes to his courtship song (E. Gwinner and J. Kneutgen, 1962. *Z. Tierpsychol. 19:* 692–696). Ravens also 'name' the absent partner by uttering its calls.

The antiphonal song of the Whipbird *(Psophodes olivaceus)* is effective in maintaining the pair-bond, as territorial advertisement and display. When a female reacts to a playback of the male's song it is with territorial defence. (M. Watson, 1969. *Behav. 35:* 157–177). Bou-bou Shrikes (*Laniarius aethiopicus*) are notable duettists. On the death of one of a pair the other sang the complete pattern, which it had never done before (T. and B. I. Hooker, *B.V.*, pp. 185–205). Much earlier it had been reported (p. 87) that when a Bellmagpie which had sung only its own part of an antiphonal duet lost its mate it began to sing the whole melody (Waite 1903). A monograph on antiphonal song discusses the various aspects of duetting and related types of song (W. H. Thorpe, 1972. *Behav. Monogr. Suppl. 18:* 1–200).

Despite the Mynah's ability to imitate speech and other sounds with great verisimilitude when in captivity it does not mimic other species or extraneous sounds in the wild, but males in a particular area imitate other males and females only imitate other females. The pair-bond is maintained from season to season and the birds recognize one another by their calls. A Mynah recognizes its mate by the fine structure of its calls even when these types are shared by neighbours. It tends to reply at once to its mate's calls with a reply type standard for the call type heard. Vocal learning has been selectively advantageous because of the stimulation of the females effected and the benefits accruing from the formation of local dialects (C. Bertram, 1970. *Anim. Behav. Monog. 3*, Pt. 2). Apparently the proclivity of birds such as Mynahs and parrots to imitate non-specific sounds when removed from their normal environment and early intercourse with their kind is due to thwarting and the re-direction of the tendency. They make exceptional efforts to establish *rapport* with a non-existent partner. The imitative expertise of the Lyrebird and some bower-birds may be attributed to the selective value to male birds calling and displaying in small, precise areas of declaring their precise location and identity in order to attract females.

The extent to which social stimulation is important in encouraging song learning varies in different species. In some it is dependent on non-auditory feedback as well as influences from the environment and normal feedback (P. Marler and M. Tamura, 1964. *Science 146*: 1483–1486). Budgerigars are stimulated to warble by hearing others, and hearing or uttering warbling promotes full gonadal activity in both sexes. Thus vocal-endocrinological feedback interactions play an essential role in breeding (B. F. Brockway, *B.V.*, pp. 131–158).

Song dialects

(pp. 88–111, 260–261). Song dialects are maintained and propagated by learning. Even where a dialect has persisted for more than twenty years other song-types may be superimposed. A new dialect becomes established gradually but may then be very persistent (K. Conrads, 1966. *Vogelwelt 87*: 176–182). This is true of a number of species. The geographical range of a dialect is dependent on historical, geographical, and ecological circumstances which have facilitated or prevented the occupation of territories in certain areas. Dialects must be influential in early stages of genetic divergence and may be useful in making the song more effective by reducing local variability (W. H. Thorpe, 1972. *In* R. A. Hinde, *Non-verbal Communication*, Cambridge, p. 160. G. Thielcke, *B.V.*, pp. 311–339).

Spectrographic analysis has resulted in a clearer understanding of the relationship between utterances and speciation. It has been noted that the area in Europe in which Long-tailed Tits show head coloration intermediate between the eastern and western forms roughly coincides with the area of overlap of the Treecreeper and the Short-toed Treecreeper, closely related species but differing in some behavioural characteristics, such as song. Together with other evidence this indicates that during the advance of the ice some 10,000 years ago populations were separated and evolved independently. Greater differentiation occurred with the treecreepers so that they are now separate species—probably due in part to adaptation to different types of tree (G. Thielcke, 1970. *Vogelstimmen*, Berlin, pp. 84–120). Once established, differences in vocalization tend to prevent interbreeding. Races of the Great Tit occur throughout much of Europe and Asia but when hybrids between English and Indian forms which resembled the Indian form were released in England no response among neighbouring birds was evoked by the song (T. Gompertz, 1967. *Vogelwelt 1*: 63–92). Studies of tits, nuthatches and flycatchers show that the location call is not learned and is the most useful characteristic in determining taxonomic relationship (H. Löhrl, 1963. *Proc. 13th Int. Orn. Congr.*, pp. 544–552).

Species recognition

(pp. 94–111, 118, 261). J. B. Falls (1963. *Proc. 13th Int. Orn. Congr.*, pp. 259–271. *B.V.*, pp. 207–232) has pointed out that in the Ovenbird and White-throated Sparrow several of the most obvious properties of the songs contribute to species recognition. Pitch, form and arrangement of sounds, their durations and intervals between are important, but timing is most significant in the former's song, form and pitch in the latter's. The inference is that features invariably present in these songs but unnecessary to convey any territorial message may have other functions than the deterrence of males, such as, for example, recognition by females. In regard to the Ovenbird, its crescendo may be useful in establishing individual identity. Experiments with Chiffchaffs have shown that frequency modulation conveys the important species-specific information (G. Schubert, 1971. *Behav. 38:* 289–314). According to S. T. Emlen (1972. *Behav. 41:* 130–171) the characteristics of song involved in species recognition are the most constant features in the repertoire. Characteristics constant in the repertoire of an individual but variable in the population are unimportant in species identification but often facilitate the identification of individuals. Variable aspects of territorial song often carry information concerning the motivational state of the singer.

Song structure

(pp. 88–111, 261). J. A. Mulligan's studies of the Song Sparrow (1963. *Proc. 13th Int. Orn. Congr.*, pp. 272–284) were directed to obtain information on the extent to which variations in song structure can be correlated with the divisions of the San Francisco Bay birds into four sub-species. The differences between the populations were found to be hardly greater than those within any one of these. There is greater variation between the songs of an individual and the individuals of a population than the variation between populations. The races have diverged in song less than they have done morphologically.

The essential characteristic of the Robin's song is its variability, attained by changes in the sequence of the elements. It is effective when played backwards as is not the case with some other species. All the consecutive motifs in a sequence are different but all proclaim the same territorial message. A normal aggressive reaction may be evoked by playing back a very simple schema of the song consisting of the alternating high and low notes at the correct time intervals, omitting all else. But doubtless elements omitted in such an experimental situation have significance in other situations. The Robin's Song achieves the effectiveness necessary for a highly territorial bird through its motifs being interchangeable without the semantic significance being altered (J.-C. Brémond, 1967. *Proc. 14th Int. Orn. Congr.*, pp. 217–229).

Ecological and meteorological

(pp. 188–230, 265–266). The behaviour of the Long-billed Marsh Wren illustrates some of the various factors which can be involved in a bird's seasonal output of song. Singing increases after pairing, remains at a constant level throughout laying and incubation, and as in many other species decreases greatly during the nestling and fledgling periods, but the maintenance of the song level during the latter periods by some males is due to their polygamy. The amount of song is thus related not only to the effects of weather and light duration but also to the nature of the pair-bond (J. Verner, 1963. *Proc. 13th Int. Orn. Congr.*, pp. 299–307). But in some wren species and sub-species the nature of the habitat may determine whether the pair-bond is monogamous or polygamous (Armstrong, 1955, pp. 102–109,

217–221). Thus the amount and incidence of song by a species or individual is the end-product of a network of endogenous and environmental factors.

J. H. Crook (*B.V.*, pp. 265–289), studying the 14 types of weaver-bird utterance in relation to their habitat preferences and feeding behaviour, has found that adaptation to grassland nidification has resulted in comparable adaptations in display and song in three genera, *Ploceus*, *Quelea*, and *Euplectes*. Nests in relatively concealed situations are not advertised by vocalizations owing to the danger of attracting predators, whereas colonial species nesting in protected sites advertise conspicuously and loudly. It seems that the diversity of songs evolved prior to and independently of visual advertisement displays. Comparison with the behaviour of wren species (Armstrong, 1955, *passim*) reveals convergences in behaviour even when some climatic and other conditions differ from those in tropical Africa.

The Skylark, living in open habitats, is particularly sensitive to meteorological conditions. Strong wind, rain, a fall in temperature or an overcast sky tend to suppress song while a burst of sunshine after rain stimulates it (J. D. Delius, 1963. *Z. Tierpsychol. 20:* 297–348). In contrast, the Nightingale, sheltering in low vegetation, is little affected by wind. Further evidence that high wind associated with cold reduces song has appeared (R. L. Smith, 1959. *Wils. Bull. 71:* 145–152).

The Zebra Finch ceases to be sensitive to song learning shortly after its 80th day—sooner than in a number of other Passerines but comparable with the song-learning of the White-crowned Sparrow. This seems to be an adaptation to its arid environment and its breeding in close proximity to other species of grass finch. Pairing is early and may occur in mixed flocks. Thus it is advantageous for the species-specific song to be acquired soon. Possibly the differences in song between individuals depend on the amount they hear of their father's singing, i.e. on whether their parents reared a second brood (K. Immelmann, *B.V.*, pp. 61–74).

The times when birds are first and last heard during the day (or night) are related to an endogenous, built-in, "circadian" rhythm, subject to adjustments synchronizing them to 24 hours by periodic factors in the environment, amongst which daily changes in light and temperature are most important (J. Aschoff, 1967. *Proc. 14th Int. Orn. Congr.*, pp. 81–105).

Neurological

(p. 133). Progress has been made in the location of the areas of the brain responsible for vocal control. It has become apparent that older theories based on drives and centres were too vague. Experiments on the Red-winged Blackbird show that both normal and abnormal calls may be evoked by stimulation of certain areas of the brain but song and flight calls were not elicited. Calls elicited from the mid-brain were of the 'annoyance' type, those from the anterior brain included various alarm calls (J. L. Brown, *B.V.*, pp. 79–96. 1971. *Behav. 28:* 91–127. J. D. Delius, 1971. *Exptl. Brain Res. 12:* 64–80. R. E. Phillips and O. M. Youngren, 1972. *Anim. Behav. 19:* 757–779). Birds, like human beings, may show partial restriction of vocal control to one hemisphere of the brain (F. Nottebohm, 1970. *Science 167:* 950–956).

Addenda II

Physiological

(pp. 45, 49, 87). R. J. Andrew (*B.V.*, pp. 97–130) has reviewed the data on the effects of testosterone on vocalization and concludes that the 'assumption that the main causal systems underlying instinctive behaviour have all been identified and clearly defined should be avoided'.

Vocal organs

(pp. 255–256). There is no parallel in the animal kingdom to the physiology and acoustics of bird utterances. Recent research has advanced our knowledge considerably and provided an explanation of some of the strange sounds emitted but there is much scope for further investigation of the working of organs involved. Control of sound production is due to precise simultaneous neural control of the whole complex of syringeal muscles. Sound is produced at the syrinx modulated by a membrane vibrating in a passage bounded by the walls of the bronchus. It contains two sources, independently controllable, one in each bronchus. Thus a bird may produce two notes or phrases simultaneously. These sounds can be modulated in frequency or amplitude, or both, with extreme rapidity (C. H. Greenewalt, 1968. *Bird Song: Acoustics and Physiology*, Washington. R. C. Stein, 1968. *Auk 85*: 229–243. P. L. Ames, 1971. *Peabody Mus. Nat. Hist. Bull. 37*: 1–194. R. W. Warner, 1971. *Journ. Zool. 164*: 197–207).

Bird song as music and in literature

(pp. 231–245, 266–267). The aesthetic content of bird song has been considered by J. Hall-Craggs (*B.V.*, pp. 367–381 and in Thorpe 1972). E. Tretzel (1965. *Z. Tierpsychol. 22*: 784–809) expresses enthusiastic admiration for the musical qualities of a Crested Lark's song. The topic will be discussed in a forthcoming book by Charles Hartshorne. A review of the treatment of bird song in literature by the present author has appeared (*B.V.*, pp. 343–365) and further comments on the subject occur in his work in course of publication—*St. Francis: Nature Mystic* (1973. Calif. Univ. Press).

REFERENCES

ADAMS, D. K., 1931. 'Restatement of the problem of learning'. *Brit. J. Psychol.* 22: 150–178.

ALEXANDER, C. J., 1917. 'Birds singing in their winter quarters'. *Brit. Birds* 11: 98–102.

—, H. G., 1927. 'The birds of Latium, Italy'. *Ibis 3* (12): 245–271.

—, —, 1931. 'The effect of severe weather on bird song'. *Brit. Birds 25:* 97–101.

—, —, 1942. 'Report on the bird song enquiry'. *Brit. Birds 36:* 65–72, 86–92, 102–109.

—, R. D., 1957a. 'Sound production and associated behaviour in insects'. *Ohio J. Sci. 57:* 101–113.

—, —, 1957b. 'The song relationships of four species of ground crickets'. *Ohio J. Sci. 57:* 153–163.

—, —, 1960. 'Sound communication in Orthoptera and Cicadidae'. *In* Lanyon and Tavolga, 1960.

ALLARD, H. A., 1930. 'The first morning song of some birds in Washington, D.C., its relation to light'. *Amer. Nat. 64:* 436–469.

—, —, 1937. 'Activity of the Screech Owl'. *Auk 54:* 299–302.

—, —, 1939. 'Vocal mimicry of Starling and Mockingbird'. *Science 90:* 370–371.

ALLEN, A. A., 1961. *The Book of Bird Life.* New York.

—, F. H., 1916. 'A nesting of the Rose-breasted Grosbeak'. *Auk 33:* 53–56.

—, R. P., 1960. 'Do we want to save the Whooping Crane?' *Audubon Mag. 62:* 122–124, 134–135.

ALLEY, R. and Boyd, H., 1950. 'Parent-young recognition in the Coot *Fulica atra*'. *Ibis 92:* 46–51.

ALTUM, B., 1868. *Der Vogel und sein Leben.* Munster.

AMADON, D., 1944. 'Results of the Archbold expedition. No. 50. A preliminary life history study of the Florida Jay, *Cyanocitta c. coerulescens*'. *Amer. Mus. Nov. 1252:* 1–22.

—, —, 1950. 'The Hawaiian honeycreepers'. *Bull. Amer. Mus. Nat. Hist. 95:* 151–262.

ANDERSON, A. H. and ANDERSON, A., 1957, 1959. 'Life history of the Cactus Wren'. *Condor 59:* 274–296, *61:* 186–205.

ANDRÉ, E., 1904. *A Naturalist in the Guianas.* London.

ANDREW, R. J., 1956a. 'Some remarks on behaviour in conflict situations with special reference to *Emberiza* spp.'. *Brit. J. Anim. Behav. 4:* 41–44.

—, —, 1956b. 'Territorial behaviour of the Yellow-hammer (*Emberiza citrinella*) and Corn Bunting (*E. calandra*)'. *Ibis 98:* 502–505.

—, —, 1956–57. 'The aggressive and courtship behaviour of certain Emberizines'. *Behaviour 10:* 255–308.

—, —, 1957. 'A comparative study of the calls of *Emberiza* spp. (Buntings)'. *Ibis 99:* 27–42.

—, —, 1961a. 'The motivational organization controlling the mobbing calls of the Blackbird'. *Behaviour 18:* 25–43.

ANDREW, R. J., 1961b. 'The displays given by passerines in courtship and reproductive fighting.' *Ibis 103a:* 315–348, 549–579.

APLIN, O. V., 1896. 'An ornithological tour in Norway'. *Zool. 20* (3): 416–432, 441–464.

ARMSTRONG, E. A., 1923. 'What the birds sing'. *Pageant of Nature 2:* 614–620. Ed. P. C. Mitchell. Cassell, London.

—, —, 1929. 'The Cuckoo'. *Sci. Progr. 24:* 81–96.

—, —, 1940. *Birds of the Grey Wind.* Oxford. 3rd. edn. 1946. London.

—, —, 1942. *Bird Display.* Cambridge.

—, —, 1944a. 'The song of the Wren'. *Brit. Birds 38:* 70–72.

—, —, 1944b. 'White plumage of sea-birds'. *Nature 153:* 527.

—, —, 1946a. 'The coloration of sea-birds'. *Birds of Britain No. 2:* 15–19.

—, —, 1946b. *Shakespeare's Imagination.* London. Neb. Univ. Press, 1963.

—, —, 1947. *Bird Display and Behaviour.* London. Dover edn., 1965.

—, —, 1949. 'Diversionary display. Pt. I. Connotation and terminology. Pt. II. The nature and origin of distraction display'. *Ibis 91:* 89–97, 179–188.

—, —, 1950a. 'The behaviour and breeding biology of the Iceland Wren'. *Ibis 92:* 384–401.

—, —, 1950b. 'The nature and function of displacement activities'. *Symp. Soc. Exper. Biol. 4:* 361–387.

—, —, 1950c. 'The significance of the dark ventral plumage of wading birds in high latitudes'. *Ibis 92:* 480–481.

—, —, 1950d. 'Bird Song'. *Chambers's Encyclopaedia.* London. New edn. 1962.

—, —, 1951a. 'The nature and function of animal mimesis'. *Bull. Anim. Behav. 9:* 46–59.

—, —, 1951b. 'The significance of a dark ventral surface in certain birds'. *Ibis 93:* 314–315.

—, —, 1952a. 'The behaviour and breeding biology of the Shetland Wren'. *Ibis 94:* 220–242.

—, —, 1952b. 'The distraction displays of the Little Ringed Plover and territorial competition with the Ringed Plover'. *Brit. Birds 45:* 55–59.

—, —, 1953a. 'The behaviour and breeding biology of the Hebridean Wren'. *Brit. Birds 46:* 37–50.

—, —, 1953b. 'The history, behaviour and breeding biology of the St. Kilda Wren'. *Auk 70:* 127–150.

—, —, 1953c. 'Island wrens'. *Brit. Birds 46:* 418–420.

—, —, 1953d. 'Territory and birds'. *Discovery 14:* 223–224.

—, —, 1954a. 'The behaviour of birds in continuous daylight'. *Ibis 96:* 1–30.

—, —, 1954b. 'The ecology of distraction display'. *Brit. J. Anim Behav. 2:* 121–135.

—, —, 1955. *The Wren.* London.

—, —, 1956. 'Territory in the Wren *Troglodytes troglodytes*'. *Ibis 98:* 430–437.

—, —, 1958a. 'Blackbird antics'. *Countryman 55:* 88–93.

—, —, 1958b. *The Folklore of Birds.* London. Dover edn., 1969.

—, —, 1959a. 'Bird of darkness—the South American Guacharo, or Oilbird'. *Audubon Mag. 61:* 256–257, 288.

—, —, 1959b. 'The behaviour and breeding environment of the St. Kilda Wren'. *Brit. Birds 52:* 136–138.

—, —, 1961. 'Birds on the horns of a dilemma'. *Animal Kingdom 74:* 138–142.

—, —, 1964. In *The New Dictionary of Birds*. Ed. Sir A. L. Thomson.

— and PHILLIPS, G. W., 1925. 'The breeding of the Short-eared Owl in Yorkshire'. *Brit. Birds 18:* 226–230.

— and THORPE, W. H., 1952, ' "Casting" by Shetland Wren nestlings'. *Brit. Birds 45:* 98–101.

— and WESTALL, P. R., 1953. 'The song-flights of some northern birds'. *Ibis 95:* 143–145.

ARONSON, L. R., 1944. 'The sexual behaviour of *Anura*'. *Amer. Mus. Nov. 1250:* 1–15.

ASHMORE, S. E., 1935. 'Time of singing of the Goatsucker'. *Brit. Birds 28:* 259–260.

BAERENDS, G. P., 1958. 'The contribution of ethology to the causation of behaviour'. *Acta Physiol. Pharmacol. Néerlandica 7:* 466–499.

—, —, 1959. 'The ethological analysis of incubation behaviour'. *Ibis 101:* 357–368.

BAGSHAWE, T. W., 1939. *Two Men in the Antarctic*. Cambridge.

BAILLY, J. B., 1853–55. *Ornithologie de la Savoie*. Paris.

BAKER, B. W., 1944. 'Nesting of the American Redstart'. *Wilson Bull. 56:* 83–90.

BAKUS, G. J., 1959a. 'Observations of the life history of the Dipper in Montana'. *Auk 76:* 190–207.

—, —, 1959b. 'Territoriality, movements and population density of the Dipper in Montana'. *Condor 61:* 410–425.

BALDWIN, J. M., 1914. 'Deferred imitation in West African Grey Parrots'. *Proc. 9th Int. Congr. Zool.,* 536–537.

—, P. H., 1947. 'The life history of the Laysan Rail'. *Condor 49:* 14–21.

—, S. P. and KENDEIGH, S. C., 1927. 'Attentiveness and inattentiveness in the nesting behaviour of the House Wren'. *Auk 44:* 206–216.

BALL, S. C., 1945. 'Dawn songs and calls of birds'. *Conn. Acad. Arts. Sci. 36:* 851–877.

BALLY, G., 1945. *Vom Ursprung und von der Grenzen der Freiheit*. Basel.

BANKS, R. C. and JOHNSON, N. K., 1961. 'A review of North American hybrid hummingbirds'. *Condor 63:* 3–28.

BANNERMAN, D. A., 1930–51. *The Birds of West Africa*. London.

BARBER, D. R., 1959. 'Singing pattern of the Common Chaffinch'. *Nature 183:* 129.

BARRETT, J. H., 1947. 'Some notes on the breeding habits of the Chaffinch'. *Ibis 89:* 439–450.

—, —, CONDER, P. J., and THOMPSON, A. J. B., 1948. 'Some notes on the Crested Lark'. *Brit. Birds 41:* 162–166.

BARRINGTON, D., 1773. 'Experiments and observations on the singing of birds'. *Philos. Trans. 63:* 249–291.

BASTOCK, M., MORRIS, D., and MOYNIHAN, M., 1953. 'Some comments on conflict and thwarting in animals'. *Behaviour 6:* 66–84.

BATESON, G., 1936. *Naven*. Cambridge.

BEACH, F. A., 1945. 'Current concepts of play in animals'. *Amer. Nat. 79:* 523–541.

—, —, 1948. *Hormones and Behaviour*. New York.

BECHSTEIN, J. M., 1795. *Naturgeschichte der Stubenvögel*. Gotha. English edn., Bohn's Library, 1864. London.

BEDFORD, DUKE OF, 1954. *Parrots and Parrot-like Birds*. Wisconsin.

BEEBE, W., 1917. *Tropical Wild Life*. New York.

—, —, 1918–22. *A Monograph of the Pheasants*. London.

—, —, 1925. 'The Variegated Tinamou, *Crypturus v. variegatus* (Gmelin)'. *Zoologica, N.Y. 6:* 195–227.

—, —, 1950. *High Jungle*. London.

BEER, J. R., FRENZEL, L. D., and HANSEN, N., 1956. 'Minimum space requirements of some nesting passerine birds'. *Wilson Bull. 68:* 200–209.

BELCHER, C. F., 1914. *The Birds of the District of Geelong, Australia*. Geelong.

BENÉ, F., 1945. 'The rôle of learning in the feeding behaviour of Black-chinned Hummingbirds'. *Condor 47:* 3–22.

BENSON, C. W., 1946. 'The genera *Turdus*, etc. in Nyasaland'. *Ostrich 17:* 156–164.

—, —, 1948. 'Geographical voice-variation in African birds'. *Ibis 90:* 48–71.

—, —, 1960. 'The birds of the Comoro Islands'. *Ibis 103b:* 5–106.

BENT, A. C., 1939. 'Life Histories of the North American woodpeckers'. *Bull. U.S. nat. Mus., 174:* 1–334.

—, —, 1948. 'Life Histories of North American nuthatches, wrens, thrashers and their allies'. *Bull. U.S. nat. Mus. 195:* 1–475.

—, —, 1953. 'Life Histories of North American warblers'. *Bull. U.S. nat. Mus., 203:* 1–134.

BERGER, A. J., 1953. 'Female American Goldfinch warbles while incubating'. *Wilson Bull. 65:* 217–218.

BERGMAN, G., 1946. 'Der Steinwälzer, *Arenaria i. interpres* (L) in seiner Beziehung zur Umwelt'. *Acta zool. fenn. 47:* 1–152.

—, —, 1950. 'Experimentella undersökningar ovaer sömndjupet hos olika smafagelarter'. *Ornis fenn. 27:* 109–124.

—, —, 1953. 'Über das Revierbesetzen und die Balz des Buchfinken, *Fringilla c. coelebs*'. *Acta Soc. Fauna Flora fenn. 69:* 1–15.

—, —, 1955. 'Milt väder efter höld utlöser sang hos talgoxen (*Parus major*) midvinterted'. *Ornis fenn. 32:* 8–16.

—, —, 1958. 'Auslösung von Übersprungseinschlafen sowie Ermüdung der akustisch ausgelösten Revierteidigung durch Magnetophonwiedergabe der Agressionlaute beim Steinwälzer (*Arenaria i. interpres*)'. *Ornis fenn. 35:* 151–154.

BEVEN, G., 1946. 'Some notes on song'. *Ostrich 17:* 51–74.

BICKNELL, E. P., 1884. 'A study of the singing of our birds'. *Auk 1:* 209–218.

BIERENS DE HAAN, J. A., 1929. 'Animal language in its relation to man'. *Biol. Rev. 4:* 249–268.

BLACKFORD, J. L., 1958. 'Territoriality and breeding behaviour of a population of Blue Grouse in Montana'. *Condor 60:* 145–158.

References

BLACKWALL, J., 1824. 'Observations on the notes of birds, etc.' *Mem. Manchr. lit. phil. Soc. 4:* (2) 289–323.

BLAIR W. F., 1955a. 'Differentiation of mating calls in spadefoots, Genus *Scaphropus*'. *Texas J. Sci. 7:* 183–188.

—, —, 1955b. 'Mating call and stage of speciation in the *Microhyla olivacea* —*M. carolinensis* complex'. *Evolution 9:* 469–480.

—, —, 1956. 'Call differences as an isolating mechanism in southwestern toads (Genus *Bufo)'. Texas J. Sci. 8:* 87–106.

—, —, 1958. 'Mating call in the speciation of American amphibians'. *Amer. Nat. 92:* 27–52.

—, — and LITTLEJOHN, M. J., 1960. 'Stage of speciation of two allopatric populations of chorus frogs *(Pseudacris)'. Evolution 14:* 82–87.

BLANCHARD, B. D., 1941. 'The White-crowned Sparrows *(Zonotrichia leucophrys)* of the Pacific seaboard; environment and annual cycle'. *Univ. Calif. Publ. Zool. 46:* 1–178.

BLASE, B., 1960. 'Die Lautäusserungen des Neuntöters *(Lanius c. collurio L.)*, Freilandbeobachtungen und Kaspar Hauser Versuche', *Z. Tierpsychol. 17:* 200–344.

BLUME, D., 1955. 'Über einige Verhaltensweisen des Grünspechtes in der Fortpflanzungszeit'. *Vogelwelt 76:* 193–210.

—, —, 1957. 'Verhaltensstudien an Grünspechten *(Picus viridis)'. Vogelwelt 78:* 41–48.

—, —, 1958. 'Über die instrumentalen Lautäusserungen bei Schwarzspecht, Grünspecht, Grauspecht und Buntspecht'. *Vogelring 27:* 1–13, 65–74.

BOEHM, E. F., 1950. 'Diurnal birds singing at night'. *Emu 50:* 62–63.

BOGERT, C. M., 1960. 'The influence of sound on the behaviour of amphibians and reptiles'. *In* Lanyon and Tavolga, 1960.

BOND, P., 1951. 'Timing the Nightingale'. *Field 198:* 695–696.

BORROR, D. J., 1956. 'Variations in Carolina Wren songs'. *Auk 73:* 211–229.

—, —, 1959a. 'Songs of the Chipping Sparrow'. *Ohio J. Sci. 59:* 347–356.

—, —, 1959b. 'Variation in the songs of the Rufous-sided Towhee'. *Wilson Bull. 71:* 54–72.

—, — and REESE, C. R., 1953. 'The analysis of bird song by means of a vibralyser'. *Wilson Bull. 65:* 271–276.

—, —, —, —, 1956. 'Vocal gymnastics in Wood Thrush songs'. *Ohio J. Sci. 56:* 177–182.

—, —, 1960. 'The analysis of animal sounds'. *In* Lanyon and Tavolga, 1960.

—, —, 1961. 'Intraspecific variation in passerine bird songs'. *Wilson Bull. 73:* 57–58.

BOURKE, P. A., 1947. 'Notes on the Horsfield Bush-lark'. *Emu 47:* 1–7.

—, —, 1949a. 'The breeding population of a thirty-five acre timber paddock'. *Emu 49:* 73–83.

—, —, 1949b. *In* Robinson, 1949.

BOYD, A. E., 1949. 'Display of Tree Sparrow'. *Brit. Birds 42:* 213–214.

BRACKBILL, H., 1948. 'A singing Wood Thrush'. *Wilson Bull. 60:* 98–102.

—, —, 1959. 'An avian predator alarm of the American Robin'. *Bird-Banding 30:* 46–47.

BRAND, A. R., 1935. 'A method for the intensive study of bird songs'. *Auk 52:* 40–52.

BRAND, A. R., 1938. 'Vibration frequencies of passerine bird song'. *Auk 55:* 263–268.

—, —, and KELLOGG, P. P., 1939. 'Auditory responses of Starlings, English Sparows and Domestic Pigeons'. *Wilson Bull. 51:* 38–41.

BRAUNER, J., 1952. 'Reactions of Poorwills to light and temperature'. *Condor 54:* 152–159.

—, —, 1953. 'Observations on the behaviour of a captive Poorwill'. *Condor 55:* 68–73.

BRAY, C. W. and THURLOW, W. R., 1942. 'Temporary deafness in birds'. *Auk 59:* 379–387.

BRISTOWE, W. S., 1958. *The World of Spiders.* London.

BROCK, S. E., 1910. 'The Willow-wrens of a Lothian wood'. *Zoologist 14:* 401–417.

BROOKS-KING, M., 1942. 'Song form in the thrush family'. *Brit. Birds 36:* 82–85.

BROWN, L. H., 1948. 'Notes on the birds of the Kabba, Ilorin and N. Benin provinces of Nigeria'. *Ibis 90:* 525–538.

—, —, 1953. 'On the biology of the large birds of prey of the Emou district, Kenya Colony'. *Ibis 95:* 74–114.

—, —, P. E. and DAVIES, M. G., 1949. *Reed Warblers.* East Molesey.

—, R. H., 1938. 'Breeding habits of the Dunlin'. *Brit. Birds 31:* 362–366.

BRYANT, A. A. and AMOS, B., 1945. 'Notes on the crakes of the genus *Porzana* around Melbourne, Victoria'. *Emu 48:* 249–275.

BULLOUGH, E., 1919. ' "Psychical distance" as a factor in art and an aesthetic principle'. *British J. Psychol. 5:* 87–118.

—, W. S., 1942. 'The reproductive cycles of the British and continental races of the Starling'. *Philos. Trans. Series B. 231:* 165–246.

—, —, 1945. 'Endocrinological aspects of bird behaviour'. *Biol. Rev. 20:* 89–99.

BURCKHARDT, D., 1948. 'Zur Brutbiologie der Beutelmeise *Remiz pendulinus* (L)'. *Orn. Beob. 45:* 207–227.

BURGER, J. W., 1953. 'The effect of photic and psychic stimuli on the reproductive cycle of the male starling (*Sturnus vulgaris*).' *J. Exp. Zool. 124:* 227–239.

BURKITT, J. P., 1935. 'An attempt to chart fluctuations in the song of Song Thrush, Blackbird and Chaffinch'. *Brit. Birds 28:* 364–367.

BUSSMAN, J., 1935. 'Der Terragraph am Schleiereulenhorst'. *Orn. Beob. 32:* 177–179.

BUXTON, A., 1946. *Fisherman Naturalist.* London.

BUXTON, J., 1950. *The Redstart.* London.

—, —, 1953. *Rödstjärten.* Stockholm.

CAIN, A. J. and GALBRAITH, C. J., 1956. 'Field notes on birds of the eastern Solomon Islands'. *Ibis 98:* 262–295.

CALMAN, W. T., 1954. *In* Gordon, 1954.

Cambridge Bird Club Report, 1945. p. 46.

CAMPBELL, A. J., 1901. *Nests and Eggs of Australian Birds.* Sheffield.

CARPENTER, C. R., 1934. 'A field study of the behaviour and social relations of howler monkeys'. *Comp. Psychol. Monogr. 10:* No. 2. 1–168.

—, —, 1940. 'A field study in Siam of the behaviour and social relations of the Gibbon (*Hylobates lar*)'. *Comp. Psychol. Monogr. 16: No. 5.* 1–112.

—, —, 1944, 'Societies of monkeys and apes'. *Bull Anim. Behav. 1:* 1–15.

CARTER, J., 1883. 'Fighting of Dipper'. *Field 61:* 65.

CASTORO, P. L. and GUHL, A. M., 1959. 'Pairing behaviour of Pigeons related to aggressiveness and territory'. *Wilson Bull. 70:* 57–69.

CAWKELL, E. M. and HAMILTON, J. E., 1961. 'The Birds of the Falkland Islands'. *Ibis 103a:* 1–27.

CHAFFER, N., 1945. 'The Spotted and Satin Bower-birds: a comparison'. *Emu 44:* 161–181.

—, —, 1958. 'Mimicry of the Stagemaker'. *Emu 58:* 53–55.

—, —, 1959. 'Bower-building and display of the Satin Bowerbird'. *Austral. Zool. 12:* 295–305.

CHAPMAN, H. H., 1942. 'Trumpeter Swans in British Columbia'. *Auk 59:* 100–103.

—, F. M., 1904. *Birds of Eastern North America.* New York.

—, —, 1928. 'The nesting habits of Wagler's Oropendola (*Zarhynchus wagleri*) on Barro Colorado Island'. *Bull. Amer. Mus. nat. Hist. 58:* 123–166.

—, —, 1930. *My Tropical Air Castle.* London and New York.

—, —, 1935. 'The courtship of Gould's Manakin (*Manacus m. vitellinus*) on Barro Colorado Island, Canal Zone'. *Bull. Amer. Mus. nat. Hist. 68:* 471–525.

—, —, 1940. 'The post-glacial history of *Zonotrichia capensis*'. *Bull. Amer. Mus. nat. Hist. 77:* 381–438.

—, F. S., 1958. *In* Gatty, 1958.

CHISHOLM, A. G., 1932. 'Vocal mimicry among Australian birds'. *Ibis 2* (13): 605–624.

—, —, 1936. 'Annotations'. *Emu 35:* 212–215.

—, —, 1937. 'The problem of vocal mimicry'. *Ibis 1* (14): 703–719.

—, —, 1946a. *Nature's Linguists: A study of the Problem of Vocal Mimicry.* Melbourne.

—, —, 1946b. 'Observations and reflections on birds of the Victorian mallee'. *Emu 46:* 168–186.

—, —, 1948. *Bird Wonders of Australia.* Melbourne.

—, —, 1949a. 'Strange vocal mimicry'. *Emu 49:* 60–61.

—, —, 1949b. 'Further notes on vocal mimicry'. *Emu 49:* 232–234.

—, —, 1951. 'More about vocal mimicry'. *Emu 51:* 75–76.

CHRISTOLEIT, E., 1927. 'Muss der Vogel seinen Gesang lernen?' *Beitr. FortPflBiol. Vögel 3:* 147–152.

CINAT-TOMSON, H., 1962. 'Die geschlechtliche Zuchtwahl beim Wellensittich (*Melopsittacus undulatus* Shaw)'. *Biol. Zbl. 46:* 543–552.

CLARK, A., 1938. 'Morning song commencement'. *Brit. Birds 31:* 265–266.

—, R. B., 1947. 'Seasonal fluctuations in the song of the Sky-lark'. *Brit. Birds 40:* 34–43.

—, —, 1949. 'Statistical information about Wren song'. *Brit. Birds 42:* 337–346.

—, X., 1879. 'Animal music, its nature and origin'. *Amer. Nat. 13:* 209–223.

COBB, N. A., 1897. 'The sheep fluke'. *N.S.W. Agric. Gazette 8:* 453–480.

COLLETT, R., 1876. *In* Sharpe, R. B. and Dresser, H. E., 1876. *A History of the Birds of Europe* 7: 631–639.

COLLIAS, N. E., 1950a. 'Social life and the individual among vertebrate animals'. *Ann. N.Y. Acad. Sci. 51:* 1074–1092.

—, —, 1950b. 'Hormones and behaviour with special reference to birds and the mechanisms of hormone action'. *In* Gordon, 1950.

—, —, 1952. 'The development of social behaviour in birds'. *Auk 69:* 127–159.

—, —, 1960. 'An ecological and functional classification of animal sounds. *In* Lanyon and Tavolga, 1960.

—, —, and JOOS, M., 1953. 'The spectrographic analysis of sound signals of the Domestic Fowl'. *Behaviour 5:* 175–187.

COLQUHOUN, M. K., 1939. 'The vocal activity of Blackbirds at a winter roost'. *Brit. Birds 33:* 44–47.

—, —, 1940. 'A note on song and the breeding cycle'. *Brit. Birds 35:* 98–104.

CONDER, P. J., 1948. 'The breeding biology and behaviour of the Continental Goldfinch *Carduelis c. carduelis*'. *Ibis 90:* 493–525.

—, —, 1953. Lecture to Cambridge Bird Club, cited as pers. comm.

—, —, 1956, 'The territory of the Wheatear *Oenanthe oenanthe*'. *Ibis 98:* 453–459.

CONRADI, E., 1905. 'Song and call-notes of English Sparrows when reared with Canaries'. *Amer. J. Psychol. 16:* 190–199.

COOKE, D., 1959. *The Language of Music.* Oxford.

COTT, H. B., 1940. *Adaptive Coloration in Animals.* London.

—, —, 1947. 'The edibility of birds, etc.'. *Proc. zool. Soc. Lond. 116:* 371–524.

COX, P. R., 1944. 'A statistical investigation into bird-song'. *Brit. Birds 38:* 3–9.

CRAIG, W., 1908. 'The voices of Pigeons regarded as a means of social control'. *Amer. J. Sociol. 14:* 66–100.

—, —, 1909. 'The expression of emotion in the Pigeons. I. The Blond Ring-Dove (*Turtur risorius*)'. *J. comp. Neurol. 19:* 29–80.

—, —, 1913. 'The stimulation and the inhibition of ovulation in birds and mammals'. *J. Anim. Behav. 3:* 215–221.

—, —, 1918. 'Appetites and aversions as constituents of instincts'. *Biol. Bull. 34:* 91–107.

—, —, 1921–22. 'A note on Darwin's work on the expression of the emotions in man and animals'. *J. abnorm. soc. Psychol.* 356–366.

—, —, 1943. 'The song of the Wood Pewee *Myiochanes virens* Linnaeus: A study of bird music'. *N.Y. State Mus. Bull. 334:* 1–186.

CREUTZ, G., 1943. 'Die Brutbiologie des Trauerfliegenschnäppers (*Muscicapa h. hypoleuca* Pallas)'. *Ber. Ver. schles. Orn. 28:* 1–10.

—, —, 1955. 'Der Trauerschnäpper (*Muscicapa hypoleuca* Pallas). Eine Populationsstudie'. *J. Orn. 96:* 241–326.

—, —, 1961. 'Kreutzungen zwischen Hohltaube und Ringeltaube'. *J. Orn. 102:* 80–87.

CROOK, J. H., 1958. 'Études sur le comportement social de *Bubalornis a. albirostris* (Vieillot)'. *Alauda 26:* 161–195.

CROSS, F. C., 1951. 'Apparant song imitation by Field Sparrow *Spizella pusilla*'. *Auk 68:* 122.

References

CROWCROFT, P., 1957. *The Life of the Shrew*. London.

CULLEN, E., 1957. 'Adaptation in the Kittiwake to cliff-nesting'. *Ibis 99:* 275–302.

CURIO, E., 1959a. *Verhaltensstudien am Trauerschnäpper*. Berlin and Hamburg.

—, —, 1959b. 'Beobachtungen am Halbringschnäpper, *Ficedula semitorquata*, in mazedonischen Gebiet'. *J. Orn 100:* 176–209.

DAANJE, A., 1941. 'Ueber das Verhalten des Haussperlings (*Passer d. domesticus L.)'. Ardea 30:* 1–42.

—, —, 1950. 'On the locomotory movements of birds and the intention movements derived from them'. *Behaviour 3:* 48–98.

DARLING, F. F., 1952. 'Social behaviour and survival'. *Auk 69:* 183–191.

DARWIN, C., 1872. *The Expression of the Emotions in Man and Animals*. London.

DAVIS, D. E., 1940. 'Social nesting habits of the Smooth-billed Ani'. *Auk 57:* 179–218.

—, —, 1941a. 'Social nesting habits of *Crotophaga major'. Auk 58:* 179–183.

—, —, 1941b. 'The relation of abundance to territorialism in tropical birds'. *Bird-Banding 12:* 93–97.

—, —, 1941c. 'Notes on Cuban birds'. *Wilson Bull. 53:* 37–40.

—, —, 1942. 'The phylogeny of social nesting habits in the Crotophaginae'. *Qrt. Rev. Biol. 17:* 115–134.

—, —, 1954. 'The breeding biology of Hammond's Flycatcher'. *Auk 71:* 164–171.

—, —, 1959. 'Territorial rank in Starlings'. *Anim. Behav. 7:* 214–221.

, J., 1958. 'Singing behaviour and the gonad cycle of the Rufous-sided Towhee'. *Condor 60:* 308–336.

—, —, 1960. 'Nesting behaviour of the Rufous-sided Towhee in coastal California'. *Condor 62:* 434–456.

—, L. I., 1958. 'Acoustic evidence of relationship in North American crows'. *Wilson Bull. 70:* 151–167.

—, T. R. A. W., 1949. 'Communal display of the Black-chinned Antcreeper *Hypocnemoides melanopogon* Sclater'. *Ibis 91:* 351.

DE KIRILINE, L., 1954. 'The voluble singer of the tree-tops'. *Audubon Mag. 56:* 109–111.

DELACOUR, J., 1943. 'A revision of the subfamily Estrildinae of the family Ploceidae'. *Zoologica N.Y. 28:* 69–86.

DE LAGUNA, G. A., 1928. *Speech: Its Function and Development*. Newhaven. Yale Univ. Press.

DELAMAIN, J., 1938. *Portraits d'Oiseaux*. Paris.

DILGER, W. C., 1949. 'Duetting in the Coppersmith'. *Abstr. A.O.U. meeting,* 1949.

—, —, 1956a. 'Hostile behaviour and reproductive isolating mechanisms in the avian genera *Catharus* and *Hylocichla'. Auk 73:* 313–353.

—, —, 1956b. 'Relationships of the thrush genera *Catharus* and *Hylocichla'. Syst. Zool. 5:* 174–182.

Dixon, K. L., 1949. 'Behaviour of the Plain Titmouse'. *Condor 51*: 110–136.

—, —, 1955. 'An ecological analysis of the interbreeding of Crested Titmice in Texas'. *Univ. Calif. Publ. Zool. 54*: 125–306.

Domm, L. V., 1939. 'Modifications in sex and secondary characters in birds'. *In* E. Allen, 1939. *Sex and Internal Secretions*. London.

—, —, and van Dyke, H. B., 1932. 'Precocious development of sexual characters in the fowl by daily injections of hebin. I. The male'. *Proc. Soc. exp. Biol. N.Y. 30*: 349–351.

Dubois, A. D., 1924. 'A nuptial song-flight of the Short-eared Owl'. *Auk 41*: 260–263.

Dunnett, G. E. and Hinde, R. A., 1953. 'The winter roosting and awakening behaviour of captive Great Tits'. *Brit. J. Anim. Behav. 1*: 91–95.

Durango, S., 1948. 'Om beteenden och spelyttringar hos törnskathanen (*Lanius c. collurio* L.) under tiden för revirbesattandet, innan honan anlänt'. *Vår Fågelvärld 7*: 145–156.

—, —, 1956. 'Territory in the Red-backed Shrike'. *Ibis 98*: 476–484.

Dyer, E., 1943. 'Songs of California Thrasher'. *In* Nice, 1943, 145.

Edgerton, H. E., Niedrach, R. J., and Van Riper, W., 1951. 'Freezing the flight of hummingbirds'. *Nat. Geogr. Mag. 100*: 245–261.

Edwards, E. P., 1943. 'Hearing ranges of four species of birds'. *Auk 60*: 239–241.

Eggebrecht, E., 1937. 'Brutbiologie der Wasseramsel *Cinclus cinclus aquaticus* (Bechst.)'. *J. Orn. 85*: 636–676.

Eibl-Eibesfeldt, I., 1950. 'Über die Jugendentwicklung des Verhaltens eines männlichen Dachses (*Meles meles* L.)'. *Z. Tierpsychol. 7*: 327–355.

Eisner, E., 1960. 'The relationship of hormones to the reproductive behaviour of birds, referring especially to parental behaviour: A review'. *Anim. Behav. 8*: 155–179.

Elliott, H. F. I. and Fuggles-Couchman, N. R., 1948. 'An ecological survey of the birds of the Crater Highlands and Rift Lakes, Northern Tanganyika Territory'. *Ibis 90*: 394–425.

Emlen, J. T., 1937. 'Morning awakening time of a Mockingbird'. *Bird-Banding 8*: 81.

—, —, 1954. 'Territory, nest-building and pair-formation in the Cliff Swallow'. *Auk 71*: 16–35.

—, —, 1957. 'Display and site-selection in the whydahs and bishopbirds'. *Ostrich 28*: 202–213.

England, M. D., 1945. 'Singing of breeding female Chaffinch'. *Brit. Birds 38*: 274.

—, —, 1960. *In* Ferguson-Lees, 1960.

Erickson, M. M., 1938. 'Territory, annual cycle and numbers in a population of Wren-tits (*Chamaea fasciata*)'. *Univ. Calif. Publ. Zool. 42*: 247–334.

—, R., 1950. 'Inheritance of territory in Rufous Whistlers and notes on begging in courtship by both sexes'. *Western Austral. Nat. 2*: 145–160.

—, —, 1951. 'Notes on the Rufous Whistler'. *Emu 51*: 1–10, 153–165.

—, —, 1953. 'Musical values of bird songs at Bolgart, W.A.' *Emu 53*: 319–323.

Evans, F. C. and Vevers, H. G., 1938. 'Notes on the territory of the Faeroe mouse (*Mus musculus faeroensis*)'. *J. Anim. Ecol. 7*: 290.

References

EVEREST, F. A., YOUNG, R. V., and JOHNSON, M. W., 1948. 'Acoustical characteristics of noise produced by the snapping shrimp'. *J. Acoust. Soc. Amer. 20:* 137–142.

EYGENRAAM, J. A., 1947. 'Het gedrag van de zwarte specht, *Dryocopus m. martius* (L)'. *Ardea 35:* 1–44.

FABER, A., 1929. 'Die Lautäusserungen der Orthopteren. I.' *Z. morph. Ökol. Tiere 13:* 745–803.

—, —, 1932. 'Die Lautäusserungen der Orthopteren. II.' *Z. morph. Ökol. Tiere 26:* 1–93.

—, —, 1953. *Laut und Gebärdensprache bei Insekten*. Stuttgart.

FALCONER, D. S., 1941. 'Observations on the singing of the Chaffinch'. *Brit. Birds 35:* 98–104.

FALKNER, G., 1943. 'Mimicking the Woodpecker'. *Field 182:* 460.

FARKAS, T., 1955. 'Zur Brutbiologie und Ethologie des Steinrötels (*Monticola saxatilis*)' *Vogelwelt 76:* 164–180.

FARNER, D. S., 1959. 'Photoperiodic control of annual gonadal cycles in birds'. In *Photoperiodism and Related Phenomena in Plants and Animals*. Amer. Soc. Adv. Sci. Washington, D.C.

FARREN, W., 1912. In Kirkman *3:* 529–540.

FERGUSON-LEES, I. J., 1943. 'Song of female Greenfinch'. *Brit. Birds 39:* 244.

—, —, 1959. 'Terek Sandpiper'. *Brit. Birds 52:* 85–90.

—, —, 1960a. 'Studies of less familiar birds: Black-necked Grebe'. *Brit. Birds 53:* 77–80.

—, —, 1960b. 'Studies of less familiar birds: the Black Wheatear'. *Brit. Birds 53:* 553–558.

FEUERBORN, H. J., 1939. 'Die Instinktbegriff und die Archetypen C. G. Jung's'. *Biol. Generalis 14:* 456–506.

FICKEN, M. S. and DILGER, W. C., 1960. 'Comments on redirection with examples of avian copulation with substitute objects'. *Anim. Behav. 8:* 219–222.

—, R. W., VAN TIENHOVEN, A., FICKEN, M. S., and SIBLEY, F. C., 1960. 'Effect of visual and vocal stimuli on breeding in the Budgerigar (*Melopsittacus undulatus*)'. *Anim. Behav. 8:* 104–106.

FINN, F., n.d. *Bird Behaviour*. London.

—, —, 1902. 'Notes on the Painted Snipe (*Rostratula capensis*) and Pheasant-tailed Jacana (*Hydrophasianus chirurgus*)'. *Proc. zool. Soc. Lond.* 261–264.

FISCHER, R. B., 1958. 'The breeding biology of the Chimney Swift *Chaetura pelagica* (Linnaeus)'. *N.Y. State Mus. Sci. Service Bull. 368:* 1–141.

FISH, M. P., 1954. 'The character and significance of sound production among fishes of the North Atlantic'. *Bull. Bingham Ocean. Coll. 14:* 1–109.

—, —, and MOWBRAY, W. H., 1959. 'The production of underwater sounds by *Opsanus* sp., a new toadfish from Bimini, Bahamas'. *Zoologica 44:* 71–76.

FITCH, F. W., 1950. 'Life History and ecology of the Scissor-tailed Flycatcher *Muscivora forficata*'. *Auk 67:* 145–168.

FONTAINE, V., 1955. 'Bastarder mellan björktrast (snöskata) och koltrast (*Turdus pilaris* L. × *Turdus merula* L.)'. *Fauna och Flora 6:* 225–233.

A Study of Bird Song

FORBUSH, E. H., 1929. *Rep. Mass. Bd. Agric. 3*: 350–352.

FRANCK, D., 1959. 'Zum Drohverhalten der Lachmöwe (*Larus ridibundus*) ausserhalb der Brutzeit'. *Vogelwarte 20*: 137–144.

FRANZ, F., 1949. 'Jahres- und Tagesrhythmus einiger Vögel in Nordfinnland'. *Z. Tierpsychol. 6*: 309–329.

—, —, 1950. 'Wann erwachen die Vögel?' *Columba 2*: 23.

FRENCH, N. R., 1959. 'Life history of the Black Rosy Finch'. *Auk 76*: 159–180.

FREUCHEN, P. and SALOMONSEN, F., 1959. *The Arctic Year*. London.

FRIEDMANN, H., 1955. 'The honeyguides'. *Bull. U.S. nat. Mus. 208*: 1–292.

—, —, 1958. 'Advances in our knowledge of the honey guides'. *Proc. U.S. nat. Mus. 108*: 309–320.

FRINGS, H., COX, B., and PEISSNER, L., 1955. 'Auditory and visual mechanisms in food-finding behaviour of the Herring Gull'. *Wilson Bull. 67*: 155–170.

—, and FRINGS, M., 1956. *Sci. Amer.* Aug.

—, —, 1957. 'Recorded calls of crows as attractants and repellants'. *J. Wildlife Mgmt. 21*: 91.

—, —, JUMBER, J., BUSNEL, R. H., GIBAN, J., and GRAMET, P., 1958. 'Reactions of American and French species of *Corvus* and *Larus* to recorded communication signals tested reciprocally'. *Ecology 39*: 126–131.

FRISCH, K. VON, 1923. 'Über die "Sprache" der Bienen'. *Zool. Jb. 40*: 1–186.

—, —, 1954. *The Dancing Bees*. London.

—, O. VON, 1956. 'Zur Brutbiologie und Jugendentwicklung des Brach (*Numenius arquata* L.)'. *Z. Tierpsychol. 13*: 50–81.

—, —, 1959. 'Zur Jugendentwicklung, Brutbiologie und vergleichenden Ethologie der Limicolen'. *Z. Tierpsychol. 16*: 545–583.

—, —, 1960. 'Zum Thema Balzflug'. *J. Orn. 101*: 496–497.

FROHAWK, F. W., 1892. 'Description of a new species of rail from Laysan'. *Ann. Mag. Nat. Hist. 9*: 247–249.

FUERTES, L. A., 1916. 'Impression of the voices of tropical birds'. *Ann. Rep. Smithsonian Inst.*, 299–323.

FULTON, B. B., 1931. 'Inheritance of song in hybrids of two subspecies of *Nemobius fuscatus* (Orthoptera)'. *Ann. ent. Soc. Amer. 26*: 368–376.

—, —, 1937. 'Experimental crossing of subspecies of *Nemobius* (Orthoptera; Gryllidae)'. *Ann. ent. Soc. Amer. 30*: 201–207.

GADOW, H., 1896. Art. 'Syrinx' in Newton, 1896.

GÄTKE, H., 1896. *Heligoland as an Ornithological Observatory*. Edinburgh.

GATTY, H., 1958. *Nature is your Guide*. London.

GAUKRODGER, D. W., 1922. 'Spotted Bowerbirds at home'. *Queensland Nat.* April, 81.

GERBER, R., 1956. 'Singende Vogelweibchen'. *Beitr. Vogelkunde 5*: 36–45.

GÉROUDET, P., 1946. 'Le tambourinage des pics'. *Les Oiseaux 184*: 145–150.

GEWALT, W., 1959. *Die Grosstrappe*. Wittenberg.

GIBB, J., 1951. 'The birds of the Maltese Islands'. *Ibis 93*: 109–127.

—, —, 1954. 'Feeding ecology of tits, with notes on Treecreeper and Goldcrest'. *Ibis 96*: 513–543.

—, —, 1956a. 'Territory in the genus *Parus*'. *Ibis 98*: 420–429.

—. —, 1956b. 'Food, feeding habits and territory of the Rock Pipit *Anthus spinoletta*'. *Ibis 98:* 506–530.

GILBERT, P. A., 1928. 'Female birds in plumage, display and song-mimicry'. *Austral. Zool. 5:* 141–147.

—, —, 1937. 'Field notes from New South Wales'. *Emu 37:* 28–31.

GILLIARD, E. T., 1959. 'Notes on the courtship behaviour of the Blue-backed Manakin (*Chiroxiphia pareola*)'. *Amer. Mus. Novit. 1942:* 1–19.

GIVENS, T. V. and HITCHCOCK, W. B., 1953. '*Cisticola juncides* in the Northern Territory'. *Emu 53:* 193–200.

GODDARD, M. T., 1947. 'Bower painting by the Regent Bowerbird'. *Emu 47:* 73–74.

GODMAN, S., 1954. Ed. *The Bird Fancyer's Delight*. (Richard Meares, London, 1717).

—, —, 1955. 'The Bird Fancyer's Delight'. *Ibis 97:* 240–246.

GOETHE, F., 1937. 'Beobachtungen und Untersuchungen zur Biologie der Silbermöwe (*Larus a. argentatus* Pontopp.) auf. der Vogelinsel Memmertsand'. *J. Orn. 85:* 1–119.

—, —, 1954. 'Experimentelle Brutbeendigung und andere brutbiologische Beobachtungen bei Silbermöwen (*Larus a. argentatus* Pontopp.)'. *J. Orn. 94:* 160–174.

—, —, 1956. *Die Silbermöwe*. Wittenberg.

GOMPERTZ, T., 1961. 'The vocabulary of the Great Tit'. *Brit. Birds 14:* 369–394, 409–418.

GOOCH, G. B., 1938. 'Domestic habits of the Spotted Flycatcher'. *Brit. Birds 32:* 269.

—, —, 1940. 'The bill-snapping of the Little Owl'. *Brit. Birds 33:* 316.

—, —, 1952. 'Variations in Cirl Bunting song while bathing'. *Brit Birds 45:* 407–408.

GOODACRE, M. J. and LACK, D., 1959. 'Early Breeding in 1957'. *Brit. Birds 52:* 74–83.

GOODWIN, D., 1946. 'Speculations on the mimicry of the Jay'. *Avic. Mag. 52:* 204–206.

—, —, 1949. 'Notes on the voice and display of the Jay'. *Brit. Birds 42:* 278–287.

—, —, 1951. 'Some aspects of the behaviour of the Jay *Garrulus glandarius*'. *Ibis 93:* 414–442, 602–625.

—, —, 1952. 'A comparative study of the voice and some aspects of behaviour in two old-world jays'. *Behaviour 4:* 294–316.

—, —, 1956. 'Further observations on the behaviour of the Jay *Garrulus glandarius*'. *Ibis 98:* 186–219.

GORDON, E. S., 1950. Ed. *A symposium on Steroid Hormones*. Madison. Univ. of Wisconsin Press.

—, I., 1954. 'Obituary of W. T. Calman'. *Proc. Linn. Soc. Lond. 165:* 83–87.

GRAY, L., 1912. Art. 'Duelling' in *Enc. Rel. Eth. 5:* 116–117.

GREELEY, F. and MEYER, R. K., 1953. 'Seasonal variation in testis-stimulating activity of female Pheasant pituitary glands'. *Auk 70:* 350–358.

GREENBAUM, M. and GUNBERG, D. L., 1960. 'A note on the effect of early blindness on sexual arousal in the male rat'. *Anim. Behav. 8:* 107–108.

GRIFFIN, D. R., 1953. 'Acoustic orientation in the Oil Bird *Steatornis*'. *Proc. Amer. nat. Acad. Sci. 39*: 884–893.

GRIFFIN, D. R., 1958. *Listening in the Dark; the acoustic orientation of bats and men.* Newhaven. Univ. of Yale Press.

GRIMEYER, D., 1943. 'Geslachtelijk geluidsverschil en enkele voorlopige mededelingen aangaande het gedrag den Meerkoet'. *Ardea 43*: 273–278.

GRINNELL, J., 1920. 'Sequestration notes'. *Auk 37*: 84–88.

GROOS, K., 1898. *The Play of Animals.* New York.

GROSS, A. O., 1930. 'The Wisconsin Prairie Chicken investigation'. *American Game. Conn.* 1–112.

—, —, 1952. 'Nesting of Hicks' Seedeater at Barro Colorado Island. Canal Zone'. *Auk 69*: 433–446.

GROEBBELS, F., 1956. 'Untersuchung über den Morgenlichen Beginn und die abendliche Beendigung der Stimäusserungen von Vogelarten'. *Orn. Mitt. 8*: 61–66.

GROSSKOPF, G., 1959. 'Zur Biologie des Rotschenkels'. *J. Orn. 100*: 210–236.

GROVE, SIR G., 1954. *Dictionary of Music and Musicians.* 5th edn. London.

GULLION, G. W., 1950. 'Voice differences between sexes in the American Coot'. *Condor 52*: 272–273.

—, —, 1952. 'The displays and calls of the American Coot'. *Wilson Bull. 64*: 83–97.

GWINNER, E., 1961. 'Beobachtungen über die Aufzucht und Jugendentwicklung des Weidenlaubsängers'. *J. Orn. 102*: 1–23.

HAARTMAN, L. VON, 1949. 'Der Trauerfliegenschnäpper. I. Ortstreue und Rassenbildung'. *Acta zool. fenn. 56*: 1–104.

—, —, 1951. 'Successive polygamy'. *Behaviour 3*: 256–274.

—, —, 1952. 'Über den Einfluss der Temperatur auf den morgendlichen Gesangsbeginn des Buchfinken, *Fringilla c. coelebs* L.' *Orn. fenn. 29*: 73–76.

—, —, 1956. 'Territory in the Pied Flycatcher'. *Ibis 98*: 460–475.

—, —, and LÖHRL, H., 1950. 'Die Lautäusserungen des Trauer- und Halsbandfliegenschnäppers *Muscicapa h. hypoleuca* (Pall.) und *M. a. albicollis* Temminck'. *Orn. fenn. 27*: 85–97.

HAECKER, V., 1900. *Der Gesang der Vogel.* Jena.

—, —, 1916. 'Reizphysiologisches über Vogelzug und Fruhgesang'. *Biol. Zbl. 36*: 403–431.

—, —, 1924. 'Reizphysiologisches über den Abendgesang der Vögel'. *Pflug. Arch. ges. Physiol. 204*: 718–725.

HAILMAN, J. P., 1959. 'Convergence in passerine alarm calls'. *Bird-Banding 30*: 232.

HALE, W. G., 1956. 'The lack of territory in the Redshank'. *Ibis 98*: 398–400.

HAMERSLEY, J., 1714. Cf. Godman, 1955.

HAMILTON, W. J., 1959. 'Aggressive behaviour in migrant Pectoral Sandpipers'. *Condor 61*: 161–177.

HANN, H. W., 1937. 'Life history of the Oven-bird in southern Michigan'. *Wilson Bull. 49*: 145–237.

HANSEN, L., 1952. 'The diurnal and annual rhythm of the Tawny Owl (*Strix a. aluco* L.)'. *Dansk. orn. Foren. Tidsskr. 46*: 158–172.

References

HARDY, SIR A., 1959. *The Open Sea*. II. London.

HARTLEY, P. H. T., 1937. 'The sexual display of the Little Grebe'. *Brit. Birds* 30: 266–275.

—, —, 1946. 'The song of the White Wagtail in winter quarters'. *Brit. Birds* 39: 44–47.

—, —, 1949. 'The biology of the Mourning Chat in winter quarters'. *Ibis 91*: 393–413.

—, —, 1950a. 'Interspecific competition in chats'. *Ibis 92*: 482.

—, —, 1950b. 'An experimental analysis of interspecific recognition'. *Symp. Soc. exp. Biol. 4*: 312–336.

HARTSHORNE, C., 1953. 'Musical values in Australian bird songs'. *Emu 53*: 109–127.

—, —, 1956. 'The monotony threshold in singing birds'. *Auk. 73*: 176–192.

—, —, 1958a. 'The relation of bird song to music'. *Ibis 100*: 421–445.

—, —, 1958b. 'Some biological principles applicable to song behaviour'. *Wilson Bull. 70*: 41–56.

—, —, 1960. 'Freedom, individuality and beauty in nature. *Snowy Egret* 24. No. 2 Rome, Ga.

HARVIE-BROWN, J. A., 1861. 'Dipper display'. *Zoologist*, 7005.

HASKELL, P. T., 1961. *Insect sounds*. London.

HAVERSCHMIDT, Fr., 1946. 'Observations on the breeding habits of the Little Owl'. *Ardea 34*: 214–246.

—, —, 1947. 'Duetting in birds'. *Ibis 89*: 357–358.

HAVILAND, M. D., 1916a. 'Notes on the breeding-habits of Temminck's Stint'. *Brit. Birds 10*: 157–165.

—, —, 1916b. 'Notes on the Lapland Bunting on the Yenesei River'. *Brit. Birds 9*: 230–238.

—, —, 1926. *Forest, Steppe, and Tundra*. Cambridge.

HAWKINS, C. J., 1920. 'Song as a sexual stimulant'. *Smithsonian Report*, 1918, 461–473.

HEDIGER, H., 1950. *Wild Animals in Captivity*. London.

HEILFURTH, F., 1938. 'Beitrag zur Faunistik, Ökologie und Besiedelungs-geschichte der Vogelwelt der Tres-Marias Inseln (Mexico)'. *Proc. VIII. Int. orn. Congr. Oxford, 1954*. 456–475. Oxford.

HEINRICH, G., 1958. 'Zur Verbreitung und Lebensweise der Vögel von Angola'. *J. Orn. 99*: 121–141.

HEINROTH, O., 1909. 'Beobachtungen bei der Zucht des Ziegenmelkers (*Caprimulgus europaeus* L.)'. *J. Orn. 57*: 56–83.

—, —, 1910. 'Zimmerbeobachtungen an selten gehaltenen Europäischen Vögeln'. *Proc. VI Int. orn. Congr. 1910*. Berlin.

—, —, 1924. 'Lautäusserungen der Vögel'. *J. Orn. 72*: 223–244.

—, —, and HEINROTH, K., 1959. *The Birds*. London.

—, —, —, —, M., 1924–33. *Die Vögel Mitteleuropas*. Berlin.

—, —, —, —, 1948. 'Verhaltensweisen der Felsentaube *Columba livia livia* L'. *Z. Tierpsychol. 6*: 153–201.

HENSCHEL, SIR G., 1903. 'Bullfinch and Canary'. *Nature 67*: 609–610.

HEYDER, R., 1931. 'Amselbeobachtungen'. *Mitt. Ver. sächs. Orn. 3*: 105–129.

HEYDER, R., 1933. 'Das Zuruhegehen der Amsel *Turdus merula* L., in seinem Verhaltnis zur Tageshelle'. *Mitt Ver. sächs. Orn. 4:* 57–81.

HICKLING, R. A. O., 1950. 'Joint "injury-feigning" by Shoveler and Mallard'. *Brit. Birds 43:* 304.

HILL, C. H., 1955. 'Notes on the habits and breeding of the Tasmanian Masked Owl'. *Emu 55:* 203–210.

HINDE, R. A., 1952. 'The behaviour of the Great Tit'. *Behaviour Suppl. 2:* 1–201.

—, —, 1954. 'Changes in response to a constant stimulus'. *Brit. J. Anim. Behav. 2:* 41–55.

—, —, 1955–56. 'A comparative study of the courtship of certain finches (Fringillidae)'. *Ibis 97:* 706–745.

—, —, 1956a. 'Breeding success in Cardueline interspecies pairs, and an examination of the hybrid's plumage'. *J. Genetics 54:* 304–310.

—, —, 1956b. 'The behaviour of certain Cardueline F1. interspecies hybrids' *Behaviour 9:* 202–213.

—, —, 1956c. 'The biological significance of the territories of birds'. *Ibis 98:* 340–370.

—, —, 1958. 'Alternative motor patterns in Chaffinch song'. *Anim. Behav. 6:* 211–217.

—, —, 1959. 'Behaviour and speciation in birds and lower vertebrates'. *Biol. Rev. 34:* 85–128.

HINDWOOD, R. A., 1955. 'Long use of nest by Lyrebird'. *Emu 55:* 257–258.

HINGSTON, R. W. G., 1933. *The Meaning of Animal Colour and Adornment.* London.

HOGARTH, W. M., 1753. *The Analysis of Beauty.* London.

HÖHN, E. O., 1953. 'Display and mating behaviour of the Black Grouse *Lyrurus tetrix* (L.)'. *Brit. J. Anim. Behav. 1:* 48–58.

HØJGAARD, M., 1958. 'Observations and experiments conducted on a tame Blue Tit (*Parus caeruleus* L.)'. *Dansk. orn. Foren. Tidsskr. 52:* 12–40.

HOLLOM, P. A. D., 1955. 'A fortnight in South Turkey'. *Ibis 97:* 1–17.

HOLMAN, F. C., 1947. 'Birds of the Gold Coast'. *Ibis 89:* 623–650.

HOLST, E. VON, and SAINT PAUL, U., 1960. 'Vom Wirkungsgefüge der Triebe'. *Naturwissenschaften 47:* 409–422.

HOMANN, P., 1960. 'Beitrag zur Verhaltensbiologie des Weidenlaubsängers (*Phylloscopus collybita*)'. *J. Orn. 101:* 195–224.

HOMEYER, A. VON, 1897. 'Über Locktone, Gesang und Balz des *Calcarius lapponicus* (L.)'. *Orn. Mber. 5:* 2–3.

HOSKING, E. and NEWBERRY, C., 1940. *Intimate Sketches from Bird Life.* London.

—, —, and SMITH, S., 1943. 'A pair of Reed Warblers'. *Brit. Birds 37:* 131–133.

HOWARD, H. E., 1900. 'Variation in the notes and songs of birds in different districts'. *Zoologist 58:* 382–383.

—, —, 1902a. 'On Mr. Selous' theory of the origin of nests'. *Zoologist 60:* 145–148.

—, —, 1902b. 'The birds of Sark, and variation in song'. *Zoologist 60:* 416–422.

—, —, 1907–14. *The British Warblers.* London.

References

—, —, 1920. *Territory in Bird Life*. London.

—, —, 1929. *An Introduction to the Study of Bird Behaviour*. Cambridge.

—, —, 1935. *The Nature of a Bird's World*. Cambridge.

—, L., 1952. *Birds as Individuals*. London.

HÜCHTKER, R. and SCHWARTZKOPFF, J., 1958. 'Soziale Verhaltensweisen bei hörenden und gehörlosen Dompfaffen (*Pyrrhula pyrrhula* L.)'. *Experientia 14:* 106–107.

HUDSON, W. H., 1892. *The Naturalist in La Plata*. London.

—, —, 1920. *The Birds of La Plata*. London.

HULME, D. C., 1959. 'Breeding season calls of the Chaffinch and Greenfinch'. *Brit. Birds 52:* 83–85.

HUMBOLDT, A. VON, 1852. *Personal Narrative of a Journey to the Equinoctial Regions of the New Continent*. Bohn's edn. London.

HUTSON, H. P. W., 1956. *In* Thorpe, 1956.

HUXLEY, J. S., 1919. 'Some points in the sexual habits of the Little Grebe, with a note on the occurrence of vocal duets in birds'. *Brit. Birds 13:* 155–158.

—, —, 1938. 'The present status of the theory of sexual selection'. In *Evolution*, ed. G. R. de Beer, Oxford.

—, —, 1942. *Evolution: the modern synthesis*. London.

—, —, and MONTAGUE, F. A., 1926. 'Studies on the courtship and sexual life of birds. VI. The Black-tailed Godwit *Limosa limosa* (L.)'. *Ibis 2* (12): 1–25.

ILJIN, N. A., 1941. 'Wolf-dog genetics'. *J. Genet. 42:* 359.

IMMELMANN, K., 1960. 'The sleep of the Emu'. *Emu 60:* 193–195.

INGRAM, C., 1956. 'Mechanical sounds in bird life'. *Illust. Lond. News. 20 Oct. 1956:* 673.

—, W. J., 1907. 'On the display of the King Bird of Paradise (*Cicinnurus regius*)'. *Ibis 1* (9): 226–229.

IVOR, H. R., 1944. 'Bird study and some semi-captive birds: the Rose-breasted Grosbeak'. *Wilson Bull. 56:* 91–104.

JACK, N., 1949a. 'Territory and nesting in the Rufous Whistler'. *Emu 49:* 26–34.

—, —, 1949b. 'Wren with flower and mimicry by Whistler'. *Emu 49:* 142–144.

JACKSON, M., 1932. 'A warning call of the American Robin, *Turdus migratorius*'. *Auk 69:* 466.

—, S. W., 1912. 'Haunts of the Spotted Bowerbird (*Chlamydera maculata* Gld.)'. *Emu 12:* 65–104.

JAHN, T. L. and WULFF, V. J., 1950. 'Phonoreception'. *In* Prosser, C.L. (ed.). *Comparative Animal Physiology*. Philadelphia.

JENKINS, D., 1961. 'Social behaviour in the Partridge *Perdix perdix*'. *Ibis 103a:* 155–188.

JEWETT, S. G., 1944. 'Hybridization of Hermit and Townsend Warblers'. *Condor 46:* 23–24.

JOHNSON, M. W., EVEREST, F. A., and YOUNG, R. W., 1947. 'The rôle of snapping shrimps (*Crangon* and *Synalpheus*) in the production of underwater noise in the sea'. *Biol. Bull. 93:* 122–138.

JOHNSTON, R. F., 1960. 'Behaviour of the Inca Dove'. *Condor 62:* 7–24.

KATZ, D., 1937. *Animals and Men.* London.

—, —, and REVESZ, G., 1921. 'Experimentelle Studien zur vergleichenden Psychologie (Versuche mit Hühnern)'. *Z. f. angew. Psychol. 18:* 307–320.

KELLOGG, P. P. and STEIN, R. C., 1953. 'Audio-spectrographic variations of the song of the Alder Flycatcher'. *Wilson Bull., 65:* 75–80.

KENDEIGH, S. C., 1941a. 'Territory and mating behaviour of the House Wren'. *Biol. Monogr. Illinois 18:* 1–120.

—, —, 1941b. 'Birds of a prairie community'. *Condor 43:* 165–174.

—, —, 1945a. 'Nesting behaviour of wood warblers'. *Wilson Bull. 57:* 145–164.

—, —, 1945b. 'Effect of temperature and season on energy resources of the English Sparrow'. *Auk 66:* 113–127.

KENNEDY, I., 1797. 'Anmerkungen über das Singen der Vögel'. *Neue philos. Abh. Baier. Akad. Wiss. 7:* 169–206.

KESSEL, B., 1957. 'A study of the breeding biology of the European Starling in North America'. *Amer. Midl. Nat. 58:* 257–331.

KETTLEWELL, H. B. D., 1956. 'Further selection experiments on industrial melanism in the Lepidoptera'. *Heredity 10:* 278–301.

KIDD, B., 1921. *A Philosopher with Nature.* London.

KILHAM, L., 1956. 'Notes on courtship behaviour of wild and tame Blue Jays'. *Auk 73:* 128–129.

—, —, 1958. 'Pair-formation, mutual tapping and nest hole selection of Red-bellied Woodpeckers'. *Auk 75:* 318–329.

—, —, 1959a. 'Mutual tapping of the Red-headed Woodpecker'. *Auk 76:* 235–236.

—, —, 1959b. 'Behaviour and methods of communication of Pileated Woodpeckers'. *Condor 61:* 377–387.

—, —, 1960. 'Early reproductive behaviour of Flickers'. *Wilson Bull. 71:* 323–336.

KING, J. A., 1955. 'Social behaviour, social organization and population dynamics in a black-tailed prairiedog town in the Black Hills of South Dakota'. *Contr. Lab. Vert. Zool. 67.* Ann Arbor.

KIPPS, C., 1953. *Sold for a Farthing.* London.

KIRCHER, P. A., 1650. *Musurgia universalis, sive ars magna consoni et dissoni.* Rome.

KIRILINE, L. DE, 1954. 'The voluble singer of the tree-tops'. *Audubon Mag. 56:* 109–111.

KIRKMAN, F. B., 1911–13. *The British Bird Book.* London.

—, —, 1937. *Bird Behaviour: A Contribution chiefly based on a Study of the Black-headed Gull.* London.

KLOPFER, P. H., 1957. 'Empathic learning in ducks'. *Amer. Nat. 91:* 61–63.

—, —, 1959. 'Social interaction in discrimination learning with special reference to feeding behaviour in birds'. *Behaviour 14:* 282–299.

KLUIJVER, H. N., 1933. 'Bijdrage tot de biologie en de ecologie van den spreeuw (*Sturnus v. vulgaris* L.) gedurende zijn voortplantingstijd'. *Versl. en Meded. Plantenziektenk Dienst. Wageningen 69:* 1–146.

—, —, 1950. 'Daily routines of the Great Tit *Parus m. major* L.' *Ardea 38:* 99–135.

References

—, —, 1951. 'The population ecology of the Great Tit, *Parus m. major* L.' *Ardea 24:* 133–166.

—, —, LIGTVOET, T., VAN DEN OUWELANT, C., and ZEGWAARD, F., 1940. 'De levenswijse van der Winterkoning'. *Limosa 13:* 1–51.

KNECHT, S., 1940. 'Uber den Gehörsinn und die Musikalität der Vogel'. *Z. vergl. Physiol. 27:* 169–232.

—, —, 1955. 'Gesangsformen der Mönchgrasmücke'. *Orn. Mitt. 7:* 1–51.

KOEHLER, O., 1937. 'Können Tauben zahlen?' *Z. Tierpsychol. 1:* 39–48.

—, —, 1943. ' "Zahl"-versuch an einem Kohlkraben und Vergleichsversuche an Menschen'. *Z. Tierpsychol. 5:* 575–712.

—, —, 1950. 'The ability of birds to "count" '. *Bull. Anim. Behav.* No. 9: 41–45.

—, —, 1951. 'Der Vogelgesang als Vorstufe von Musik und Sprache'. *J. Orn. 93:* 3–20.

—, —, 1954. 'Vorbedingungen und Vorstufen unserer Sprache bei Tieren'. *Verh. dtsch. Zool. Ges. Tübingen.* 1954.

—, —, 1956. 'Thinking without words'. *Proc. 14th Int. Congr. Zool. Copenhagen, 1953.* 75–88.

—, W., 1921. 'Zur Psychologie der Schimpansen'. *Psychol. Forsch. 1:* 2–46.

—, —, 1927. *The Mentality of Apes.* London.

KOENIG, O., 1951. 'Der Aktionssystem der Bartmeise'. *Öst. Zool. Z. 3:* 1–81.

KÖNIG, D., 1938. 'Paarung der Amsel'. *Beitr. FortPflBiol. Vögel 14:* 69–70.

KORTLANDT, A., 1940a. 'Eine Übersicht der angeborenen Verhaltungsweisen des Mittel-Europäischen Kormorans *Phalacrocorax carbo sinensis* (Shaw and Nodd) ihre Funktion, ontogenetische Entwicklung und phylogenetische Herkunft'. *Arch. néerl. Zool. 4:* 401–442.

—, —, 1940b. 'Wechselwirkung zwischen Instinkten'. *Arch. néerl. Zool. 4:* 442–520.

—, —, 1959a. 'An attempt at clarifying some controversial notions in animal psychology and ethology'. *Arch. néerl. Zool. 13:* 196–220.

—, —, 1959b. 'Analysis of pair-forming behaviour in the Cormorant, *Phalacrocorax carbo sinensis* (Shaw and Nodd.)'. *Proc. 15th Int. Congr. Zool. London. 1958.*

KOZLOWA, E. V., 1947. 'On the spring life and breeding habits of the pheasant (*Phasianus colchicus*) in Tadjikistan'. *Ibis 89:* 423–429.

KUHK, R., 1943. Paper to D.O.G. *J. Orn. 91:* 361–364.

—, —, 1949. 'Aus der Fortpflanzungsbiologie des Rauhfusskauzes, *Aegolius funereus* L.' *In* Mayr and Schüz, 1949.

KULLENBERG, B., 1955. 'Biological observations during the solar eclipse in southern Sweden (Province of Öland) on 30 June 1954'. *Oikos 6:* 51–60.

KUUSISTO, O., 1941. 'Studien über die Ökologie und Tagesrhythmick von *Phylloscopus trochilus acredula* (L.) mit besonderer Berücksichtigung der Brutbiologie'. *Acta zool. fenn. 31:* 1–120.

LACK, D., 1939a. 'The behaviour of the Robin'. *Proc. zool. Soc. London. A 109:* 169–178.

—, —, 1939b. 'The behaviour of the Blackcock'. *Brit. Birds 32:* 290–303.

—, —, 1941a. 'Some aspects of instinctive behaviour and display in birds'. *Ibis 83:* 407–441.

LACK, D., 1941b. 'Notes on territory, fighting and display in the Chaffinch'. *Brit. Birds 34:* 216–219.

—, —, 1943. *The Life of the Robin.* London.

—, —, 1944. 'Early references to territory in bird life'. *Condor 46:* 108–111.

—, —, 1947. *Darwin's Finches.* Cambridge.

—, —, 1954. *The Natural Regulation of Animal Numbers.* Oxford.

—, —, 1956. *Swifts in a Tower.* Oxford.

—, —, and SOUTHERN, H. N., 1949. 'Birds on Tenerife'. *Ibis 91:* 607–626.

LANG, E. M., 1946. 'Ueber die Brutgewohnheiten des Schneefinken *Montifringilla n. nivalis* (L.)'. *Orn. Beob. 43:* 33–43.

LANYON, W. E., 1957. 'The comparative biology of the meadowlarks (*Sturnella*) in Wisconsin'. *Publ. Nuttall Orn. Cl. 1:* 1–67.

—, —, 1960a. 'The Middle American populations of the Crested Flycatcher *Myiarchus tyrannulus*'. *Condor 62:* 341–351.

—, —, 1960b. 'The ontogeny of vocalizations in birds'. *In* Lanyon and Tavolga, 1960.

—, —, 1960c. 'Relationship of the House Wren (*Troglodytes aedon*) of North America and the Brown-throated Wren (*Troglodytes brunneicollis*) of Mexico'. *Proc. XII Int. orn. Congr.* 450–459. Helsinki.

—, —, and Tavolga, W. N., 1960. *Animal Sounds and Communication.* Washington, D.C.

LASHLEY, K. A., 1913. 'Reproduction of inarticulate sounds by the parrot'. *J. Anim. Behav. 3:* 361–366.

—, —, 1915. 'Notes on the nesting activities of the Noddy and Sooty Tern, Washington, D.C.' *Carnegie Inst. Washington 7:* 301–366.

—, —, 1938. 'Experimental analysis of instinctive behaviour'. *Psychol. Rev. 45:* 445–471.

LASKEY, A. R., 1935. 'Whisper songs and night singing'. *Migrant 6:* 1–2.

—, —, 1936. 'Fall and winter behaviour of Mockingbirds'. *Wilson Bull. 48:* 241–255.

—, —, 1944a. 'A study of the Cardinal in Tennessee'. *Wilson Bull. 56:* 27–44.

—, —, 1944b. 'A Mockingbird acquires his song repertory'. *Auk 61:* 213–219.

—, —, 1948.'Some nesting data on the Carolina Wren at Nashville,Tennessee'. *Bird-Banding 19:* 101–121.

—, —, 1950. 'Cowbird behaviour'. *Wilson Bull. 62:* 157–174.

LAVEN, H., 1940. 'Beiträge zur Biologie des Sandregenpfeifers (*Charadrius hiaticula* L.).' *J. Orn. 88:* 183–288.

—, —, 1941. 'Beobachtungen über Balz und Brut beim Kiebitz (*Vanellus vanellus* L.)' *J. Orn. Ergänzungsband. 3:* 1–64.

LAWRENCE, L. DE K., 1953. 'Notes on the nesting behaviour of the Blackburnian Warbler'. *Wilson Bull. 65:* 135–144.

—, —, 1957. 'Displacement singing in a Canada Jay (*Perisoreus canadensis*)'. *Auk 74:* 260–261.

LEHRMAN, D. S., 1959. 'Hormonal responses to external stimuli in birds'. *Ibis 101:* 478–496.

LEHTONEN, L., 1947. 'Zur Winterbiologie der Kohlmeise *Parus m. major*'. *Orn. fenn. 24:* 32–47.

—, —, 1959. 'On the effect of the sun on the daily rhythm and behaviour of birds'. *Orn. fenn. 36:* 41–42.

References

LEOPOLD, A. and EYNON, A. E., 1961. 'Avian daybreak and evening song in relation to time and light intensity'. *Condor 63:* 269–293.

LINSDALE, J. M., 1928. 'Variation in the Fox Sparrow (*Passerella iliaca*) with reference to its natural history and osteology'. *Univ. Calif. Publ. Zool. 30:* 251–283.

—, —, 1938a. 'Bird life in Nevada with reference to modifications in structure and behaviour'. *Condor 40:* 173–180.

—, —, 1938b. 'Environmental responses of vertebrates in the Great Basin'. *Amer. Midl. Nat. 19:* 1–206.

—, —, 1950. 'Observations on the Lawrence Goldfinch'. *Condor 52:* 255–259.

LISTER, M. D., 1953a. 'Secondary song; a tentative classification'. *Brit. Birds 46:* 139–143.

—, —, 1953b. 'Secondary song of some Indian birds'. *J. Bombay Nat. Hist. Soc. 51:* 699–706.

LOCKIE, J. D., 1952. 'The food of Great Skuas on Hermaness, Unst, Shetland'. *Scot. Nat. 64:* 158–162.

LÖHRL, H., 1951. 'Balz und paarbildung beim Halsbandfliegenschnäpper'. *J. Orn. 93:* 41–60.

—, —, 1958. 'Das Verhalten des Kleibers'. *Z. Tierpsychol. 15:* 191–252.

—, —, 1960. 'Ökologie und Verhalten des Felsenkleibers'. *J. Orn. 101:* 232.

LOISEL, G., 1912. *Histoire des ménageries de l'antiquité à nos jours.* Paris.

LORENZ, K., 1931. 'Beiträge zur Ethologie sozialer Corviden'. *J. Orn. 79:* 67–127.

—, —, 1935. 'Der Kumpan in der Umwelt des Vögels'. *J. Orn. 83:* 137–213, 289–413.

—, —, 1938. 'A contribution to the comparative sociology of colonial-nesting birds'. *Proc. 8th Int. orn. Congr. Oxford,* 1934. 204–218. Oxford.

—, —, 1941. 'Vergleichende Bewegungsstudien an Anatinen'. *J. Orn. 89:* (*Ergänzungsband iii*) 194–294.

—, —, 1943a. *In* Nice, 1943.

—, —, 1943b. *In* Craig, 1943.

—, —, 1952. *King Solomon's Ring.* London.

LUCANUS, F. VON, 1923. 'Das Sprechen der Papageien und ihre geistigen Fähigkeiten'. *Orn. Mber. 31:* 97–102, 121–127.

—, —, 1925. *Das Leben der Vögel.* Berlin.

LUDLOW, F., 1928. 'Birds of the Gyantse neighbourhood, Southern Tibet'. *Ibis 4* (12): 51–73, 211–232.

LUNDEVALL, C. F., 1952. 'The bird fauna in the Abisko National Park and its surroundings'. *Kungl. Svensk. Vetensk. Akad. 7:* 1–72.

LUTZ, F. E., 1931. 'Light as a factor controlling the start of daily activity of a wren and stingless bees'. *Amer. Mus. Novit. 468:* 1–7.

LYNES, H., 1913. 'Early "drumming" of the Snipe and its significance'. *Brit. Birds 6:* 354–359.

—, —, 1930. 'Review of the genus *Cisticola*'. *Ibis Suppl. 6 (12):* 1–673.

—, —, 1938. 'A contribution to the ornithology of the southern Congo basin'. *Rev. Zool. Bot. afr. 31:* 1–122.

McCABE, R. A., 1951. 'The song and flight-song of the Alder Flycatcher'. *Wilson Bull. 63:* 89–98.

McEvey, A., 1949. 'Notes on the Australian Pipit and its territory'. *Emu 49:* 35–43.

Macginitie, G. E. and Macginitie, N., 1949. *The Natural History of Marine Animals.* New York.

McIlhenny, E. A., 1935. *The Alligator's Life-history.* Boston.

McKeown, R. C., 1952. *Australian Spiders.* 2nd edn. Sydney and London.

McLennan, C., 1946. *In* Chisholm. 1946.

Macqueen, P. M., 1950. 'Territory and song in the Least Flycatcher'. *Wilson Bull. 62:* 144–205.

Makkink, G. F., 1931. 'Die Kopulation der Brandente (*Tadorna tadorna* L.)'. *Ardea 20:* 18–21.

—, —, 1936. 'An attempt at an ethogram of the European Avocet (*Recurvirostra avosetta* L.)', with ethological and psychological remarks'. *Ardea 25:* 1–63.

Maljchevskij, A. S., 1959. 'Grezdovaya zhiznj perchikh ptic'. *Izdat. Leningrad Univ.* Leningrad.

Mannichie, A. L. V., 1910. 'Terrestrial mammals and birds of north-east Greenland. Biological observations'. *Medd. Grönland 45:* 1–199.

Marler, P., 1952. 'Variation in the song of the Chaffinch *Fringilla coelebs*'. *Ibis 94:* 458–472.

—, —, 1955. 'Characteristics of some animal calls'. *Nature 176:* 6–8.

—, —, 1956a. 'The behaviour of the Chaffinch *Fringilla coelebs*'. *Behaviour (Suppl.) 5:* 1–184.

—, —, 1956b. 'The voice of the Chaffinch and its function as language'. *Ibis 98:* 231–261.

—, —, 1956c. 'The voice of the Chaffinch'. *New Biology 20:* 70–87.

, —, 1957. 'Specific distinctiveness in the communication signals of birds'. *Behaviour 11:* 13–39.

—, —, 1959a. 'Song development in hand-raised Oregon Junuos'. *Abstr. Camb. Eth. Conf.*

—, —, 1959b. 'Developments in the study of animal communication'. In *Darwin's Biological work; some aspects reconsidered.* Ed. P. R. Bell. 150–206. Cambridge.

—, —, 1960a. 'Bird songs and mate selection'. In Lanyon and Tavolga, 1960.

—, —, 1960b. 'Song variation in a population of Brown Towhees'. *Condor 62:* 272–283.

—, —, and Boatman, D., 1951. 'Observations on the Birds of Pico, Azores'. *Ibis 93:* 90–99.

—, —, and Isaac, D., 1960. 'Physical analysis of a simple bird song as exemplified by the Chipping Sparrow'. *Condor 62:* 124–135.

Marples, G., 1939. 'Some notes on the diurnal song of birds'. *Brit. Birds 33:* 4–11.

Marshall, A. J., 1949. 'Weather factors and spermatogenesis in birds'. *Proc. zool. Soc. Lond. 119:* 711–716.

—, —, 1950a. 'The function of the bower of the Satin Bowerbird in the light of experimental modifications of the breeding cycle'. *Nature 165:* 388–389.

—, —, 1950b. 'The function of vocal mimicry in birds'. *Emu 50:* 5–16.

—, —, 1951. 'Leaf-display and the sexual cycle in the Tooth-billed Bowerbird

References

(*Scenopoeetes dentirostris* Ramsay)'. *Proc. zool. Soc. Lond. 120:* 749–759.

—, —, 1952a. 'Display and the sexual cycle in the Spotted Bowerbird (*Chlamydera maculata* Gould)'. *Proc. zool. Soc. Lond. 122:* 239–252.

—, —, 1952b. 'The interstitial cycle in relation to autumn and winter sexual behaviour in birds'. *Proc. zool. Soc. Lond. 121:* 727–740.

—, —, 1954. *Bower-birds; their displays and breeding cycles.* Oxford.

—, —, 1959. 'Internal and environmental control of breeding'. *Ibis 101:* 456–478.

—, J. T. 1960. 'Interrelations of Abert and Brown Towhee'. *Condor 62:* 49–64.

MARTOF, B. S. and THOMPSON, E. F., 1959. 'Reproductive behaviour of the chorus frog'. *Behaviour 13:* 241–258.

MAY, D. J., 1949. 'Studies on a community of Willow Warblers'. *Ibis 91:* 24–54.

MAYR, E., 1935. 'Bernard Altum and the territory theory'. *Proc. Linn. Soc. N.Y.* Nos. 45–46.

—, —, 1942. *Systematics and the origin of Species.* New York.

—, —, 1946. 'History of the North American bird fauna'. *Wilson Bull. 58:* 3–41.

—, —, 1956. 'Gesang und Systematik'. *Beitr. Vogelkunde 5:* 112–117.

—, —, ANDREW, R. J. and HINDE, R. A., 1956. 'Die systematische Stellung der Gattung *Fringilla*'. *J. Orn. 97:* 112–117.

—, —, and SCHUZ, E. 1949. *Ornithologie als Biologisches Wissenschaft,* Heidelberg.

MEDWAY, LORD, 1959. 'Echo-location among *Collocalia*'. *Nature,* Lond. *184:* 1352–1353.

MEGAW, J. V. S., 1960. 'Penny whistles and prehistory'. *Antiquity 34:* 6–13.

MEHNER, J. F., 1952. 'Notes on song cessation'. *Auk. 69:* 466–469.

MEIKLEJOHN, M. F. M., 1948. 'Summer notes on birds of Teheran and the Alburz mountains'. *Ibis 90:* 376–386.

MEINERTZHAGEN, R., 1930. *Nicoll's Birds of Egypt.* London.

—, —, 1943. 'Physiological races'. *Bull. Brit. orn. Cl. 63:* 78–80.

MEISE, W., 1936b. 'Über Artenstehung durch Kreuzung in der Vogelwelt'. *Biol. Zbl. 56:* 590–604.

MESSMER, E. and MESSMER, I., 1956. 'Die Entwicklung der Lautäusserungen und einiger Verhaltensweisen der Amsel (*Turdus merula merula* L.), unter naturlichen Bedingungen und nach Einzelaufzucht in schalldichten Raumen'. *Z. Tierpsychol. 13:* 341–441.

METFESSEL, M., 1935. 'Roller Canary song produced without learning from external sources'. *Science 81:* 470.

MEYER, P. O., 1929. 'Beiträge zur Biologie der Vögel von Vuaton (Bismarck-Archipel)'. *Orn. Mber. 37:* 105–107.

MICHENER, H. and MICHENER, J. R., 1935. 'Mockingbirds, their histories and individualities'. *Condor 37:* 97–140.

MICKEY, F. W., 1942. 'Breeding habits of the McCown's Longspur'. *Auk 60:* 181–209.

MILKEIV, A. V., 1939. 'Contributions to the biology of the Lapland Bunting'. *Zool. Zh. 18:* 924–938. (Russian, with English summary.)

MILLER, L., 1938. 'The singing of the Mockingbird'. *Condor 40:* 216–219.

A Study of Bird Song

MILLER, L., 1952a. 'Songs of the Western Meadowlark'. *Wilson Bull. 64:* 106–107.

—, —, 1952b. 'Auditory recognition of predators'. *Condor 54:* 89–92.

—, R. C., 1958. 'Morning and evening song of Robin in different latitudes'. *Condor 60:* 105–107.

MISKIMEN, M., 1951. 'Sound production in passerine birds'. *Auk 68:* 493–504.

—, —, 1957. 'Absence of syrinx in the Turkey Vulture (*Cathartes aura*)'. *Auk 74:* 104–105.

MIYADI, D., 1959. 'On some new habits and their propagation in Japanese monkey groups'. *Proc. 15th Int. Congr. Zool. Lond.* 1958. 857–860.

MOFFAT, C. B., 1903. 'The spring rivalry of birds'. *Irish Nat. 33:* 25–29.

MONTAGU, G., 1802. *Ornithological Dictionary.* London.

MORASSI, A., 1958. 'Oublié et retrouvé'. *L'oeil. No. 41:* 40–47.

MOREAU, R. E., 1930. 'On the age of some races of birds'. *Ibis 6 (12):* 229–239.

—, —, 1949. 'The breeding of a Paradise Flycatcher'. *Ibis 91:* 256–279.

—, —, 1960. 'Conspectus and classification of the Ploceine weaver-birds Pt. ii'. *Ibis 102:* 443–471.

—, —, and MOREAU, W. M., 1928. 'Some notes on the habits of Palaearctic migrants'. *Ibis 4 (12):* 233–252.

MÖRIKE, K. D., 1935. 'Der Leier-Überschlag der Mönchgrasmücke'. *Orn. Mitt. 5:* 90–95.

MORLEY, A., 1941. 'Behaviour of resident British Starlings from October to March'. *Naturalist 788:* 55–61.

—, —, 1943. 'Sexual behaviour in British birds from October to January'. *Ibis 85:* 132–158.

MORRIS, D., 1954. 'The reproductive behaviour of the Zebra Finch *Poephila guttata*, etc'. *Behaviour 6:* 271–322.

—, —, 1956. 'The feather postures of birds and the problem of the origin of social signals'. *Behaviour 9:* 75–113.

—, —, 1957. 'The reproductive behaviour of the Bronze Mannikin'. *Behaviour 11:* 156–201.

—, —, 1958. 'The comparative ethology of grassfinches (*Erythrurae*) and mannikins (*Amadinae*)'. *Proc. zool. Soc. London. 131. Pt. 3:* 389–431.

MORRISON, R. I., 1949. 'Common Sandpiper singing sub-song on nest'. *Brit. Birds 42:* 92–93.

MOWRER, O. H., 1950. 'On the psychology of "talking birds" '—a contributon to language and personality theory. In *Learning Theory and Personality Dynamics.* New York.

—, —, 1952. 'Speech development in the young child'. *J. Speech and Hearing Disord. 17:* 263–268.

MOUNTFORT, G. M., 1954. 'The larks of Andalucia'. *Ibis 96:* 111–115.

—, —, 1957. *The Hawfinch.* London.

MOYNIHAN, M., 1955b. 'Remarks on the original sources of displays'. *Auk 72:* 240–246.

—, —, 1959a. 'Some aspects of reproductive behaviour in the Black-headed Gull (*Larus r. ridibundus*) and related species'. *Behaviour (Suppl.)* 4.

—, —, 1959b. 'Notes on the behaviour of some North American Gulls. IV. The ontogeny of hostile behaviour and display patterns'. *Behaviour 14:* 214–239.

References

—, —, and HALL, M. F. 1954. 'Hostile, sexual and social behaviour patterns of the Spice Finch (*Lonchura punctulata*) in captivity'. *Behaviour 7*: 33–76.

MURASAKI, LADY, 1935. *The Tale of Genji*. Tr. A. Waley, London.

MYERS, J. G., 1929. *Insect Singers*. London.

NETHERSOLE-THOMPSON, C. and NETHERSOLE-THOMPSON, D., 1943. 'Nest-site selection by birds'. *Brit. Birds 37*: 70–74, 88–94, 108–113.

—, —, —, 1944. *In* Witherby *et al.* 1944.

—, —, —, 1951. *The Greenshank*. London.

NEWTON, A., 1896. *A Dictionary of Birds*. London.

NICE, M. M., 1937. 'Studies in the life history of the Song Sparrow. I. A population study on the Song Sparrow'. *Trans. Linn. Soc. N.Y. 4*: 1–247.

—, —, 1939.'Territorial song and non-territorial behaviour of Goldfinches in Ohio'. *Wilson Bull. 51*: 123.

—, —, 1943. 'Studies in the life history of the Song Sparrow. II. The behaviour of the Song Sparrow and other passerines'. *Trans. Linn. Soc. N.Y. 6*: 1–328.

—, —, 1945. 'Seven baby birds in Altenberg'. *Chicago Nat. 8*: 66–74.

—, —, 1946. 'Jan Joost ter Pelkwyk, Naturalist'. *Chicago Nat. 9*: 26–35.

—, —, and TER PELKWYK, J. J., 1941. 'Enemy recogntion by the Song Sparrow'. *Auk. 58*: 195–214.

NICHOLSON, E. M., 1927. *How Birds Live*. London.

—, —, and KOCH, L., 1936. *Songs of Wild Birds*. London.

—, —, —, —, 1937. *More Songs of Wild Birds*. London.

NICOLAI, J., 1956. 'Zur Biologie und Ethologie des Gimpfels (*Pyrrhula pyrrhula* L.)'. *Z. Tierpsychol. 13*: 93–132.

—, —, 1959. 'Familientradition in der Gesangentwicklung des Gimpel (*Pyrrhula pyrrhula* L.)'. *J. Orn. 100*: 39–46.

NICOLL, M. J., 1930. Cf. Meinertzhagen, 1930.

NIETHAMMER, G., 1955. 'Jagd auf Vogelstimmen'. *J. Orn. 96*: 115–118.

NOBLE, G. K., 1936. 'Courtship and sexual selection of the Flicker (*Colaptes auratus luteus*)'. *Auk 53*: 269–282.

—, —, 1939. 'The rôle of dominance in the social life of birds'. *Auk 56*: 263–273.

—, —, and WURM, M., 1940. 'The effect of testosterone propionate on the Black-crowned Night Heron'. *Endocrinology 26*: 837–850.

—, —, and ZITRIN, A., 1942. *Endocrinology 30*: 327–334.

NÖHRING, R., 1958. 'Einige Bemerkungen über das Verhalten von *Regulus regulus* während der Wintermonate'. *Abstr. 12th Int. orn. Congr. Helsinki*.

NOLAN, V., 1958a. 'Singing by female Indigo Bunting and Rufous-sided Towhee'. *Wilson Bull. 70*: 287–288.

—, —, 1958b. 'Anticipatory food-bringing in the Prairie Warbler'. *Auk 75*: 263–278.

NORTON, D. D., 1929. *In* Forbush, 1929.

NÖTEL, E., 1921. 'Kuckuck'. *Orn. Monatschr. 46*: 63–64.

ODUM, E. O., 1941–42. 'Annual cycle of the Black-capped Chickadee'. *Auk 58*: 314–333, 518–535, *59*: 499–531.

ODUM, E. O., 1947. 'More about Chimney Swifts'. *Bird-Banding 18:* 84.

O'GARA, W., 1946. 'The vanishing Sharp-tail'. *Nat. Hist. N.Y. 55:* 167–171.

OLDFIELD, R. C. and BEST, A. T., 1938. 'Verbal learning in parrots'. *Research Rep. Inst. Study Anim. Behav.,* 1936–37.

OLDYS, H., 1907. 'Bird duets'. *Independent 63:* 604–608.

—, —, 1913. 'A remarkable Hermit Thrush song'. *Auk 30:* 538–541.

—, —, 1917. 'The meaning of bird music'. *Amer. Mus. J. 17:* 123–127.

OLINA, G. P., 1622. *Uccelliera.* Rome.

ORR, R. T., 1945. 'A study of captive Galapagos finches of the genus Geospiza'. *Condor 47:* 177–201.

OSMASTON, B. B., 1941. ' "Duetting" in birds'. *Ibis 5* (14): 310–311.

PAATELA, J. E., 1934. 'Havaintoja lintujen laulun tai ääntelyn alkamisajoista'. *Orn. fenn. 11:* 87–89.

—, —, 1938. 'Beobachtungen über das Verhalten der Vögel in der Sommernacht'. *Orn. fenn. 15:* 65–69.

PAKENHAM, R. H. W., 1943. 'Field notes on the birds of Zanzibar and Pemba'. *Ibis 85:* 165–189.

PALLIS, M., 1939. *Peaks and Lamas.* London.

PALMER, R. S., 1941. 'A behaviour study of the Common Tern'. *Proc. Boston Soc. Nat. Hist. 42:* 1–119.

—, —, 1949. 'Maine Birds'. *Bull. Mus. Comp. Zool. Harv. 102:* 1–656.

PALMGREN, P., 1935. 'Ueber den Tagesrhythmus der Vögel im arktischen Sommer'. *Ornis fenn. 12:* 107–121.

—, —, 1944. Studien über Tagesrhythmik gekäfigter Zugvögel'. *Z. Tierpsychol. 6:* 44–86.

—, —, 1949. 'On the diurnal rhythm of activity and rest in birds'. *Ibis 91:* 565–575.

PARKS, M., 1947. *Bird-Banding. 20:* 61.

PATKAI, I., 1939. 'A Magyarországi seregély (rendszertani tanulmáni)'. *A. M. Kir. Madártani Intézet Kiadványa.* Budapest.

PATTERSON, A. H., 1904. *Notes of an East Coast Naturalist.* London.

PAYN, W. H., 1943. 'Notes on a pair of Common Teal × Shoveler hybrids'. *Ibis 85:* 219–220.

PEDLEY, P. E. and HASKER, R. S., 1959. 'Pitch and the vertical localization of sound'. *Amer. J. Psychol. 72:* 447–449.

PEITZMEIER, J., 1949. 'Uber nicht erbliche Verhaltensweisen bei Vögeln'. *In* Mayr and Schüz, 1949.

—, —, 1955. 'Zur Deutung des "Regenrufs" des Buchfinken (*Fringilla coelebs* L.)'. *J. Orn. 96:* 147–152.

PELKWYK, J. TER, 1946. *In* Nice, 1946.

PERDECK , A. C., 1958. 'The isolating value of specific song patterns in two sibling species of grasshoppers (*Chorthippus brunneus* Thunb. and *C. biguttulus* L.)'. *Behaviour 12:* 1–75.

PERNAU, BARON VON, 1707. *In* Stresemann, 1947.

PERRY, R., 1940. *Lundy, Isle of Puffins.* London.

—, —, 1946. *A Naturalist on Lindisfarne.* London.

—, —, 1948. *In the High Grampians.* London.

PETERS, J. L., 1931. *Check-list of Birds of the World.* Harvard Univ. Press.

References

PETRIDES, G. A., 1938. 'A life history of the Yellow-breasted Chat'. *Wilson Bull. 50:* 184.

PICKWELL, G. B., 1931. 'The Prairie Horned Lark'. *Trans. Acad. Sci. St. Louis 27:* 1–153.

PIERCE, G. W., 1948. *The Songs of Insects.* Cambridge, Mass.

PIIPARINEN, T. and TOIVARI, L., 1958. 'Über die Tagesrhythmik im Gesang des Sprosser *Luscinia luscinia'. Orn. fenn. 35:* 65–70.

PITELKA, F. A., 1943. 'Territoriality, display and certain ecological relationships of the American Woodcock'. *Wilson Bull. 55:* 88–114.

POLLARD, J., 1930. 'Whisper songs'. *Emu 30:* 62–63.

POPHAM, H. L., 1891. 'Notes on birds observed on the Yenesei river, Siberia, in 1895'. *Ibis 7* (3): 89–108.

POTTER, R. K., KOPP, G. A., and GREEN, H. C., 1947. *Visible Speech.* New York.

POULSEN, H., 1951. 'Inheritance and learning in the song of the Chaffinch *Fringilla coelebs* L'. *Behaviour 3:* 216–228.

—, —, 1954. 'On the song of the Linnet (*Carduelis cannabina* L.)'. *Dansk. orn. Foren. Tidsskr. 48:* 32–37.

—, —, 1958. 'The calls of the Chaffinch (*Fringilla coelebs* L.) in Denmark'. *Dansk. orn. Foren. Tidsskr. 52:* 89–105.

—, —, 1959. 'Song learning in the domestic Canary'. *Z. Tierpsychol. 16:* 173–178.

PRATT, A., 1937. *The Lore of the Lyrebird.* Melbourne.

PRINGLE, J. W. S., 1956. 'Insect song'. *Endeavour 15:* 68–72.

PROMPTOFF, A. N., 1930. 'Die geographische Variabilität des Buchfinkenschlags (*Fringilla coelebs* L.') *Biol. Zbl. 50:* 478–503.

—, —, and LUKINA, E. V., 1945. 'Conditioned reflex differentiation of calls in passerines and its biological value'. *C.R. (Dokl.) Acad. Sci. U.S.S.R. 46:* 382–384.

PUGSLEY, —, 1946. *News from Bird Banders. 21:* 32–36.

PUMPHREY, R. J., 1940. 'Hearing in insects'. *Biol. Rev. 15:* 107–132.

—, —, 1948. 'The sense organs of birds'. *Ibis 90:* 171–199.

—, —, 1949. 'The sense organs of birds'. *Smithsonian Rep. 1948. No. 3967:* 305–330.

—, —, 1950. 'Hearing'. *Symposia Soc. Exp. Biol. 4:* 3–18.

PURCHON, R. D., 1948. 'The nesting activities of the Swallow'. *Proc. zool. Soc. Lond. 118:* 146–170.

PYCRAFT, W. P., 1912. *In* Kirkman, 1912, 3: 304.

PYNNONEN, A., 1939. *Beiträge zur Kenntnis der Biologie Finnischer Spechte.* Helsinki.

QUAINTANCE, C. W., 1938. 'Context, meaning, and possible origin of male song in the Brown Towhee'. *Wilson Bull. 40:* 97.

RAINES, R. J., 1945. 'Notes on the territory and breeding behaviour of the Blackcap and Garden Warbler'. *Brit. Birds 38:* 202–204.

RAMSAY, A. O., 1951. 'Familial recognition in domestic birds'. *Auk 68:* 1–16.

—, E. P., 1946. *In* Chisholm, 1946a.

RAND, A. L., 1941a. ' "Duetting" in birds'. *Auk 58:* 57–59.

RAND, A. L., 1941b. 'Development and enemy recognition of the Curve-billed Thrasher *Toxostoma curvirostra*'. *Bull. Amer. Mus. nat. Hist. 78:* 213–242.

—, —, and RAND, R. M., 1943. 'Breeding notes on the Phainopepla'. *Auk 60:* 334–341.

RANGER, G. A., 1955. 'On three species of honey-guide; the Greater (*Indicator minor*) and the Scaly-throated (*Indicator variegatus*)'. *Ostrich 26:* 70–87.

RANKIN, M. N. and RANKIN, D. H., 1940. 'The breeding behaviour of the Irish Dipper'. *Irish Nat. J. 7:* 273–282.

REGEN, J., 1914. 'Untersuchungen über die Stridulation von *Thamnotrizon apterus* Fab.' *S. B. Akad. Wiss. Wien, 132:* 81–88.

RENNIE, J., 1883. *Domestic Habits of Birds.* London (published anonymously).

RICHARDSON, R. A., 1947. 'Courtship feeding of Chaffinch and song of female'. *Brit. Birds 40:* 307.

RICHDALE, L. E., 1941. 'A brief summary of the history of the Yellow-eyed Penguin'. *Emu 40:* 265–287.

—, —, 1945. 'Courtship and allied behaviour of Penguins'. *Emu 44:* 305–319, *45:* 37–54.

RINEY, T., 1951. 'Relationships between birds and deer'. *Condor 53:* 178–185.

RINGLEBEN, H., 1944. *In* Witherby *et al.*, 1944.

RITTINGHAUS, H., 1953. 'Adoptionsversuche mit Sand- und Seeregenpfeifern'. *J. Orn. 94:* 144–159.

ROBERTS, A., 1948. *The Birds of South Africa.* London and Johannesburg.

—, N. L., 1953. 'Choosing the nest site'. *Emu 53:* 128–130.

ROBINSON, A., 1945. 'The application of territory and the breeding cycle to some Australian birds'. *Emu 45:* 100–109.

—, —, 1946. 'Territory and bird song. *Emu 45:* 335–336.

—, —, 1946–47. 'Magpie-larks: a study in behaviour'. *Emu 46:* 265–281, 382–391, *47:* 11–28, 147–153.

—, —, 1949. 'The biological significance of bird song in Australia'. *Emu 48:* 291–315.

—, —, 1956. 'The annual reproductory cycle of the Magpie *Gymnorhina dorsalis* Campbell, in south-western Australia'. *Emu 56:* 233–236.

ROBSON, F. D., 1948. 'Kiwis in captivity'. *Bull. Hawkes Bay Art Gallery and Mus.* 1–8.

RODGER, G., 1943. *Red Moon Rising.* London.

ROLLIN, N., 1931. 'The varying length of lark song'. *Scot. Nat.* 47–54.

—, —, 1943. 'Skylark song'. *Brit. Birds 36:* 146–150.

—, —, 1953. 'Dawn chorus. April 13th.' *Dawn Song and all Day I:* 73–82.

—, —, 1958a. 'Late season singing of the Yellowhammer'. *Brit. Birds 51:* 290–303.

—, —, 1958b. 'The daily behaviour of birds on the Farne Islands'. *Trans. Nat. Hist. Soc. N'land 12:* 161–184. .

—, —, 1959. *The Times*, 3 October.

ROOKE, K. B., 1947. 'Notes on Robins wintering in North Africa'. *Ibis 89:* 204–210.

ROWAN, M. K., 1955. 'The breeding biology and behaviour of the Red-winged Starling *Onychognathus morio*'. *Ibis 97:* 663–705.

References

ROWELL, C. H. F., 1957. 'The breeding of the Lapland Bunting in Swedish Lapland'. *Bird Study 4*: 33–40.

RUPPELL, W., 1933. 'Physiologie und Akustik der Vogelstimme'. *J. Orn. 81*: 433–542.

RUSSOW, W. V., 1940. 'Lokale, resp-geographische Gesangsunterscheide bei den Weindrossel *Turdus musicus*'. *Orn. Mber. 48*: 57–58.

ST. JOHN, H. C., 1880. *The Wild Coasts of Nipon*. London.

SANBORN, H. C., 1932. 'The inheritance of song in birds'. *J. comp. Psychol. 13*: 345–364.

SAUER, F., 1954. 'Die Entwicklung der Lautäusserungen von Ei ab Schalldicht gehalten Grasmücken (*Sylvia communis* Latham)'. *Z. Tierpsychol. 11*: 10–93.

—, —, 1955. 'Uber variationen der Artgesänge bei Grasmücken'. *J. Orn. 96*: 129–146.

—, —, 1956. 'Uber das Verhalten junger Gartengrasmücken (*Sylvia borin*)'. *J. Orn. 97*: 156–189.

SAUNDERS, A. A., 1923. 'A double song of the Cardinal'. *Auk 40*: 539–541.

—, —, 1924. 'Recognizing individual birds by song'. *Auk 41*: 242–259.

—, —, 1929. 'Bird Song'. *New York State Mus. Handb. 7*: 1–121.

—, —, 1935. *A Guide to Bird Songs*. New York and London. New edn. 1951.

—, —, 1942. 'The Brown Thrasher and the territory theory'. *Bird-Banding 13*: 75–76.

—, —, 1947. 'The beginning of song in spring'. *Auk 64*: 97–107.

—, —, 1948a. 'Note on Starling mimicry'. *Condor 50*: 276.

—, —, 1948b. 'The seasons of bird song—the cessation of song after the nesting season'. *Auk 65*: 19–30.

—, —, 1951. 'The song of the Song Sparrow'. *Wilson Bull. 63*: 99–109.

—, —, 1958. 'Differences in vocalization in subspecies'. *Auk 75*: 379.

—, —, 1959. 'Octaves and kilocycles in bird songs'. *Wilson Bull. 71*: 280–282.

—, D. C., 1951. 'Territorial songs of the White-winged Dove'. *Wilson Bull. 63*: 330–332.

—, F. A., 1924. *In* Townsend, 1924.

SCHAEFER, E., 1953. 'Contribution to the life history of the Swallow Tanager'. *Auk 70*: 403–460.

SCHAFER, E., 1960. 'Uber den Berggorilla (*Gorilla gorilla beringei*)' *Z. Tierpsychol. 17*: 376–381.

SCHALDACH, W. J., 1960. 'Occurrence of Slaty and Dwarf Vireos in Jalisco, Mexico'. *Condor 62*: 139.

SCHEER, G., 1941. 'Ueber den Frühgesang der Vögel'. *Verh. Orn. Ges. Bayern. 22*: 137–160.

—, —, 1950. 'Vom Vogelgesang am frühen Morgen'. *Orn. Mitt. 2*: 3–6.

—, —, 1951. 'Ueber die zeitlange Differenz zwischen Erwachen und gesangsbeginn'. *Vogelwarte 16*: 13–15.

—, —, 1952a. 'Beobachtungen und Untersuchungen über die Abhängigkeit des Frühgesanges der Vögel von inneren und ausseren Faktoren'. *Biol. Abhl. 3-4*: 1–68. Darmstadt.

SCHEER, G., 1952b. 'Ueber den Einsfluss der Temperatur auf den morgend-lichen Gesangsbeginn der Buchfinken in verschiedenen Jahren'. *Ornis fenn. 29:* 77–82.

—, —, 1952c. 'Über Schlafgewohnheiten einiger Vögel'. *Schrift. Naturschutz-stelle Darmstadt-Stadt. 3:* 13–25.

—, —, 1952d. 'Gibt es eine für ganz Deutschland gultige Vogeluhr?' *Deutsch Jäger Zeitung.* Das Waidwerk. No. *1–3.*

SCHENKEL, R., 1956, 1958. 'Zur Deutung der Balzleistungen einiger Phasianiden und Tetraoniden. I'. *Orn. Beob. 53:* 182–201; II *55:* 65–95.

SCHILLER, C. H., 1957. (Ed.) *Instinctive Behaviour.* London.

SCHJELDERUP-EBBE, T., 1922. 'Die Stimme der Hühner'. *Z. Psychol. 92:* 60–87.

SCHOLES, P., 1938. *The Oxford Companion to Music.* Oxford.

SCHUZ, E., 1942. 'Biologische Beobachtungen am Staren in Rossitten'. *Vogelzug. 13:* 99–132.

SCHWARTZKOPFF, J., 1952a. 'Untersuchungen über die Arbeitsweise des Mittelohres und der Richtungshoren der Sangvogel unter Verwendung von Cochlea-Potentialen'. *Z. vergl. Physiol. 34:* 46–68.

—, —, 1952b. 'Uber den Gehörsinn der Vögel'. *J. Orn. 93:* 91–103.

—, —, 1955a. 'On the hearing of birds'. *Auk 72:* 340–347.

—, —, 1955b. 'Schallsinnesorgane, ihre Funktion u. biologische Bedeutung bei Vögeln'. *Proc. 11th Int. orn. Congr. Basel,* 1954. 189–208.

SCLATER, W. L. and MOREAU, R. E., 1933. 'Taxonomic and field notes on some birds of north-eastern Tanganyika territory. Pt. IV'. *Ibis 3* (13): 187–219.

SCOTT, J. W., 1942. 'Mating behaviour of the Sage Grouse'. *Auk 59:* 477–498.

—, W. E. D., 1901. 'Data on song in birds. Observations on the song of the Baltimore Oriole in captivity'. *Science, N.S. 14:* 522–526.

—, —, 1904. 'The inheritance of song in passerine birds'. *Science, N.S. 19:* 154, 95–956; *20:* 282–283.

SEAVER, G., 1937. *Edward Wilson, Naturalist.* London.

SEDGWICK, E. H., 1951. 'Nocturnal bird song'. *Emu 50:* 268.

SELANDER, R. K., 1959. 'Polymorphism in Mexican Brown Jays'. *Auk 76:* 385–417.

—, —, and GILLER, D. R., 1959. 'Interspecific relations of woodpeckers in Texas'. *Wilson Bull. 71:* 107–124.

SELOUS, E., 1905. *Bird-life Glimpses.* London.

—, —, 1914. 'The earlier breeding habits of the Red-throated Diver'. *Wild Life 3:* 138–144, 206–213.

SELVAGE, J. J., 1954. *In* Marshall, 1954, and *N. Q. Bird Notes,* 1948.

SEPPÄ, J., 1938. 'Observations on the influence of light and weather on the beginning of daily activity of birds'. *Ann. Soc. zool.-bot. fenn. Vanamo 6:* 52–64.

SERLE, W., 1957. 'Birds of eastern Nigeria'. *Ibis 99:* 371–418, 628–685.

—, —, and BRYSON, D., 1935. 'Distribution and numbers of the Dipper on the N. and S. Esks (Midlothian)'. *Brit. Birds 28:* 327–331.

SHAVER, J. M. and ROBERTS, M. B., 1933. 'A brief study of the courtship of the Eastern Cardinal (*Richmondena c. cardinalis* Linnaeus)'. *J. Tenn. Acad. Sci. 5:* 116–123.

—, —, and WALKER, G., 1930. 'A preliminary study of the effects of tempera-

References

ture on the time of ending of the evening song of the Mockingbird'. *Auk 47:* 385–396.

SIBLEY, C. G., 1955. 'Behavioural mimicry in the titmice and certain other birds'. *Wilson Bull. 67:* 128–132.

—, —, 1957. 'The evolution and taxonomic significance of sexual dimorphism and hybridization in birds'. *Condor 59:* 166–191.

—, —, 1959. 'Hybridization in birds: Taxonomic and evolutionary implications'. *Bull. Brit. orn. Cl. 79:* 154–158.

—, —, and PETTINGILL, O. S., 1955. 'A hybrid Longspur from Saskatchewan'. *Auk 72:* 423–425.

—, —, and WEST, D. A., 1959. 'Hybridization in the Rufous-sided Towhees of the Great Plains'. *Auk 76:* 326–338.

SICK, H., 1935. 'Spiegeln die Gesänge der Spötter die sie umgebende Avifauna wieder?' *Ber. Ver. schles. Orn. 20:* 12–17.

—, —, 1939. 'Ueber die Dialektbildung beim "Regenruf" des Buchfinken'. *J. Orn. 87:* 568–592.

—, —, 1950. 'Der Regenruf des Buchfinken (*Fringilla coelebs*)'. *Vogelwarte 15:* 236–237.

—, —, 1954. 'Zur Biologie des amazonischen Schirmvogels *Cephalopterus ornatus*'. *J. Orn. 95:* 233–244.

—, —, 1959. 'Die Balz der Schmuckvögel (Pipridae)'. *J. Orn. 100:* 269–302.

SICKER, H. L., 1946. 'Mating display of the Magpie'. *Emu 46:* 75–76.

SIELMANN, H., 1959. *My Year with the Woodpeckers.* London.

SIIVONEN, L., 1939. 'Zur Oekologie und Verbreitung der Singdrossel (*Turdus ericetorum philomelos* Brehm)'. *Ann. Soc. zool.-bot. fenn. Vanamo 7:* 1–289.

SIMMONS, K. E. L., 1951. 'Interspecific territorialism'. *Ibis 93:* 407–413.

—, —, 1954. 'The behaviour and general biology of the Graceful Warbler *Prinia gracilis*'. *Ibis 96:* 262–292.

—, —, 1956. 'Territory in the Little Ringed Plover *Charadrius dubius*'. *Ibis 98:* 390–397.

SIMMS, E., 1958. 'The conversational calls of birds as revealed by new methods of recording'. *Acta XI Int. orn. Congr. 1954.* 623–626.

SKEAD, C. J., 1954. 'A study of the Cape Wagtail *Motacilla capensis*'. *Ibis 96:* 91–103.

SKUTCH, A. F., 1942. 'Life history of the Mexican Trogon'. *Auk 59:* 341–363.

—, —, 1944. 'Life history of the Quetzal'. *Condor 46:* 213–235.

—, —, 1945a. 'Life history of the Allied Woodhewer'. *Condor 47:* 85–94.

—, —, 1945b. 'Life history of the Blue-throated Green Motmot'. *Auk 62:* 489–517.

—, —, 1946a. 'Life history of the Costa Rican Tityra'. *Auk 63:* 327–362.

—, —, 1946b. 'The hummingbirds' brook'. *Sci. Month. 63:* 447–457.

—, —, 1946c. 'Life histories of the Panamanian antbirds'. *Condor 48:* 16–28.

—, —, 1948a. 'Life history of the Golden-naped Woodpecker'. *Auk 65:* 225–260.

—, —, 1948b. 'Life history of the Citreoline Trogon'. *Condor 50:* 137–147.

—, —, 1948c. 'Life history notes on puff-birds'. *Wilson Bull. 60:* 81–97.

—, —, 1950. 'Life history of the White-breasted Blue Mockingbird'. *Condor 52:* 220–227.

A Study of Bird Song

SKUTCH, A. F., 1951a. 'Life history of the Boat-billed Flycatcher'. *Auk* PB: 30–49.

—, —, 1951b. 'Congeneric species of birds nesting together in Central America'. *Condor 53:* 3–15.

—, —, 1953. 'How the male bird discovers the nestlings'. *Ibis 95:* 1–37, 505–542.

—, —, 1954. 'Life histories of Central American birds'. *Pacific Coast Avifauna. Cooper Orn. Soc. 31:* 1–448.

—, —, 1958. 'Life history of the Violet-headed Hummingbird'. *Wilson Bull. 70:* 5–19.

—, —, 1959. 'The singing of the Wood Rail'. *Audubon Mag. 61:* 20–21

—, —, 1960. 'Life histories of Central American birds'. *Pacific Coast Avifauna. Cooper Orn. Soc. 34:* 1–593.

SLADEN, W. J. L., 1958. 'The Pygoscelid penguins. I. Methods of study. II. The Adélie Penguin'. *F.I.D.S. Scientific Report. No. 17:* 1–97.

SLUD, P., 1958. 'Observations on the Nightingale Wren in Costa Rica'. *Condor 60:* 243–251.

SMART, A. D. G., 1943. 'Variation in Chaffinch song'. *Brit. Birds 37:* 50–53.

SMITH, R. L., 1959. 'Songs of the Grasshopper Sparrow'. *Wilson Bull. 71:* 141–152.

—, S., and HOSKING, E., 1955. *Birds Fighting.* London.

SMYTHIES, B. E., 1960. 'Subspecific variation in birds' songs and call-notes'. *Ibis 102:* 134–135.

SNOW, D. W., 1952. 'A contribution to the ornithology of north-west Africa'. *Ibis 94:* 473–498.

—, —, 1956a. 'Territory in the Blackbird *Turdus merula*'. *Ibis 98:* 438–452.

—, —, 1956b. 'The dance of the manakins'. *Animal Kingdom 59:* 86–91.

—, —, 1958. *A Study of Blackbirds.* Oxford.

SNYDER, B. E., 1954. 'A nesting study of Crossbills'. *Wilson Bull. 66:* 32–37.

SOTAVALTA, O., 1956. 'Analysis of the song pattern of two Sprosser Nightingales *Luscinia luscinia* (L.)'. *Ann. Soc. zool.-bot. fenn. Vanamo 17:* 1–30.

STADLER, H., 1929. 'Die Vogelstimmung als Wissenschaft'. *Verh. 6th Int. orn. Congr. Copenhagen, 1926,* 338–357.

—, —, 1930. 'Vogeldialekt'. *Alauda 2 (Suppl.):* 1–66.

—, —, 1932. 'La voix des chouettes de l'Europe Moyenne'. *Alauda 4:* 174–191, 271–283, 407–415.

—, —, 1934. 'Der Vogel kann Transponieren'. *Orn. Mber. 59:* 1–9.

—, —, 1935. 'Das Spotten der Vogel'. *Orn. Mber. 60:* 168–187.

STANFORD, J. K., 1945. 'Variation in birds' songs and call-notes in different localities'. *Ibis 87:* 102–103.

—, —, 1954. 'A survey of the ornithology of northern Libya'. *Ibis 96:* 449–473, 606–624.

STEIN, R. C., 1956. 'A comparative study of advertising song in the Hylocichla thrushes'. *Auk 73:* 503–512.

—, —, 1958. 'The behavioural, ecological, and morphological characteristics of the two populations of the Alder Flycatcher *Empidonax traillii* Audubon'. *Bull. N.Y. State Mus. 371:* 1–63.

STEINFATT, O., 1937. 'Aus dem Leben des Grossbuntspechtes'. *Beitr. FortPfl. Biol. Vögel 13:* 45–54, 144–147.

References

—, —, 1939. 'Beobachtungen beim Kleinspecht'. *Beitr. Fortpfl. Biol. Vögel* 15: 9–14.

—, —, 1940. 'Beobachtungen über das Leben der Goldammer (*Emberiza citrinella*)'. *Ber. Ver. Schles. Orn. 25:* 11–27.

STENGER, J. and FALLS, J. B., 1959. 'The utilized territory of the Ovenbird'. *Wilson Bull. 71:* 125–139.

STEWART, R. E., 1953. 'A life history study of the Yellowthroat'. *Wilson Bull.* 65: 99–115.

STIEVE, H., 1950. 'Der Gesang der Vogel und seine Abhängigkeit von dem Keimdrusen'. *Syllegomena Biologica (Akad. Verl. Ges. Geest und Portig. Leipzig):* 413–428.

STILLWELL, J. E. and STILLWELL, N. J., 1952. 'Notes on some songs of the Pine-woods Sparrow'. *Wilson Bull. 65:* 118.

—, —, —, 1955. 'Notes on the Songs of Lark Buntings'. *Wilson Bull. 67:* 138–139.

STODDARD, H. L., 1931. *The Bob-white Quail, its habits, preservation and increase.* New York.

STOKES, A. W., 1950. 'Breeding behaviour of the Goldfinch'. *Wilson Bull. 62:* 102–127.

—, —, 1961. 'Voice and social behaviour of the Chukar Partridge'. *Condor 63:* 111–127.

STOTT, K., and SELSOR, C. J., 1959. 'Chimpanzees in Western Uganda'. *Oryx 5:* 108–115.

STRESEMANN, E., 1947. 'Baron von Pernau, pioneer student of bird behaviour'. *Auk 64:* 35–52.

—, —, 1948. 'Nachtigall und Sprosser, ihre Verbreitung und Biologie'. *Orn. Ber.* 193–200.

SUMMERS-SMITH, D., 1955. 'Display of the House Sparrow *Passer domesticus*'. *Ibis 99:* 296–305.

SUTTON, G. M., 1945. 'At a bend in a Mexican river'. *Audubon Mag. 47:* 239–242.

—, —, and PARMELEE, D. F., 1955. 'Summer activities of the Lapland Bunting in Baffin Island'. *Wilson Bull. 67:* 110–127.

SVÄRDSON, G., 1949. 'Competition and habitat selection in birds'. *Oikos 1:* 11.

SWANBERG, P. O., 1951. 'Food storage, territory and song in the Thick-billed Nutcracker'. *Proc. X Int. orn. Congr. Uppsala.* 110–127.

—, —, 1956. 'Territory in the Thick-billed Nutcracker'. *Ibis 98:* 219–412.

SWIFT, J. J., 1959. 'Le guêpier d'Europe *Merops apiaster* L. en Camargue'. *Alauda 27:* 97–143.

SWINBURNE, SIR J., 1920. 'Mental processes in music'. *Proc. Music. Assn. 72:* 29–52.

TARR, H. E., 1948a. 'Notes on the King Quail'. *Emu 48:* 103–106.

—, —, 1948b. 'Courtship display of the Little Wattle Bird'. *Emu 47:* 318.

TASKER, R. R., 1955. 'Chipping Sparrow with song of a Clay-coloured Sparrow'. *Auk 72:* 303.

TAVOLGA, W. N., 1958 'Underwater sounds produced by two species of toadfish, *Opsanus tau* and *Opsanus beta*'. *Bull. Marine Sci. of Gulf and Caribbean 8:* 278–284.

A Study of Bird Song

TER PELKWYK, J., 1946. *In* Nicc, 1946.

THIELCKE, G., 1959a. 'Über Schlafgewohnheiten des Gartenbaumläufers (*Certhia brachlactyla*) und des Waldbaumläufers (*Certhia familiaris*)'. *J. Orn. 100:* 25–38.

—, —, 1959b. Review. *Vogelwarte 20:* 191.

—, —, 1960. 'Mischgesang der Baumläufer, *Certhia brachydactyla* und *C. familiaris*'. *J. Orn. 101:* 281–287.

—, —, 1961. 'Stammesgeschichte und geographische Variation des Gesanges unserer Baumläufer (*Certhia familiaris* L. und *Certhia brachydactyla* Brehm.)'. *Z. Tierpsychol. 18:* 188–204.

THIELCKE-POLTZ, H. and THIELCKE, G., 1960. 'Akustisches Lernen verschieden alter schallisolierter Amseln *Turdus merula* L. und die Entwicklung erlernter Motive ohn und mit küntstlichem Einfluss von Testosteron'. *Z. Tierpsychol. 17:* 211–244.

THOMAS, R. H., 1946a. 'A study of Eastern Bluebirds in Arkansas'. *Wilson Bull. 58:* 143–183.

—, —, 1946b. 'An Orchard Oriole colony in Arkansas'. *Bird-Banding 17:* 61–67.

—, —, 1952. *Crisp, come Home.* New York.

THOMPSON, W. L., 1960. 'Agonistic behaviour in the House Finch. I. Annual cycle and display patterns'. *Condor 62:* 245–271.

THOMSON, G. M., 1922. *The Naturalisation of Plants and Animals in New Zealand.* Cambridge.

—, SIR J. J., 1936. *Recollections and Reflections.* London.

THORPE, W. H., 1951. 'The learning abilities of birds'. *Ibis 93:* 1–52, 252–296.

—, —, 1955. 'Comments on *The Bird Fancyer's Delight*, together with notes on imitation in the sub-song of the Chaffinch'. *Ibis 97:* 247–251.

—, —, 1956. *Learning and Instinct in Animals.* London. New edn. 1963.

—, —, 1958. 'The learning of song patterns by birds, with especial reference to the song of the Chaffinch *Fringilla coelebs*'. *Ibis 100:* 535–570.

—, —, 1959. 'Talking birds and the mode of action of the vocal apparatus of birds'. *Proc. zool. Soc. London. 132:* 441–455.

—, —, 1961. *Bird Song: The Biology of Vocal Communication and Expression in Birds.* Cambridge.

—, —, and PILCHER, P. M., 1958. 'The nature and characteristics of sub-song'. *Brit. Birds 51:* 509–514.

—, —, and LADE, B. I., 1961. 'The songs of some families of the Passeriformes. II. The songs of the buntings *Emberizidae*'. *Ibis 103a:* 246–259.

THREADGOLD, L. T., 1960. 'A study of the annual cycle of the House Sparrow at various latitudes'. *Condor 62:* 190–201.

TICEHURST, C. B., 1938. *A Systematic Review of the the Genus Phylloscopus.* London.

TINBERGEN, L., 1946. *Die Sperwer als Roofvijand van Zangvogels.* Leiden.

—, N., 1935. 'Field observations of Greenland birds. I. The behaviour of the Red-necked Phalarope (*Phalaropus lobatus* L.) in spring'. *Ardea 24:* 1–42.

—, —, 1939. 'The behaviour of the Snow Bunting in spring'. *Trans. Linn. Soc. N.Y. 5:* 1–95.

—, —, 1940. 'Die Uebersprungbewegung'. *Z. Tierpsychol. 4:* 1–40.

References

—, —, 1952. ' "Derived" activities: their causation, biological significance, origin and emancipation during evolution'. *Quart. Rev. Biol. 27:* 1–32.

—, —, 1953. *The Herring Gull's World.* London.

—, —, 1957. *In* Schiller, 1957.

—, —, and VAN IERSEL, J. J. A., 1947. ' "Displacement reactions" in the three-spined stickleback'. *Behaviour I:* 56–63.

TOOK, G. E., 1947. 'Singing of juvenile Tree Pipit'. *Brit. Birds 40:* 83–84.

TOWNSEND, C. W., 1905. 'The birds of Essex County, Massachusetts'. *Mem. Nuttall. Orn. Cl. Mass. No. 3.*

—, —, 1924. 'Mimicry of voice in birds'. *Auk 41:* 541–552.

TRAINER, J. E., 1946. 'The auditory acuity of certain birds'. Cornell thesis. *Abstr. of Theses,* 246–251.

TREBESIUS, J., 1930–32. 'Beeinflussen meteorologische Faktoren den Beginn des Vogelsanges?' *Mitt. Vogelwelt.* Stuttgart. *29:* 139–140, *30:* 14–37, 106–108, *31:* 40–45.

TREUENFELS, H. VON, 1937. 'Beitrag zur Brutbiologie des Waldlaubsängers (*Phylloscopus sibilatrix*)'. *J. Orn. 85:* 605–623.

—, —, 1940. 'Zur Biologie und Psychologie des Weidenlaubsängers (*Phylloscopus collybita*)'. *J. Orn. 88:* 509–536.

TRISTRAM, H. B., 1889. 'Ornithological notes on Gran Canaria'. *Ibis 1* (6): 13–22.

TUCKER, A. C. G., 1809. *Ornithologia Danmoniensis, or, an History of the Habits and Economy of Devonshire Birds. I.* London.

—, B. W., 1944. 'Song of female Chaffinch associated with normal sex behaviour'. *Brit. Birds 38:* 94–95.

TURNER, E. L., 1924. *Broadland Birds.* London.

—, —, 1929. *Stray Leaves from Nature's Notebook.* London.

TUSSER, T., 1580. *Five Hundred Pointes of good Husbandric.* London.

TYLER, J. G., 1916. 'Migration and field notes from Fresno county, California'. *Condor 18:* 167–169.

TWINING, H., 1938. 'The significance of combat in Rosy Finches'. *Condor 40:* 246–247.

—, —, 1940. 'Foraging behaviour and survival in the Sierra Nevada Rosy Finch'. *Condor 42:* 64–72.

UEXÜLL, J. VON, 1926. *Theoretical Biology.* London.

USSHER, R. J. and WARREN, R., 1900. *The Birds of Ireland.* London.

UTTENDÖRFER, O., 1939. *Die Ernährung des deutschen Raubvögel und Eulen.* Neudamm.

—, —, 1952. *Neue Ergebnisse über die Ernährung der Greifvögel und Eulen.* Stuttgart.

VAN IERSEL, J. J. A. and BOL, A. C. A., 1958. 'Preening of two species. A study on displacement activities'. *Behaviour 15:* 1–88.

VAN SOMEREN, V. D., 1946. 'The dancing display and courtship of Jackson's Whydah (*Coliuspasser jacksoni* Sharpe)'. *Jour. E. Afr. Nat. Hist. Soc. 18:* 131–141.

—, —, 1947. 'Field notes on some Madagascar birds'. *Ibis 89:* 235–267.

VAN TYNE, J. and BERGER, A. J., 1959. *Fundamentals of Ornithology*. New York and London.

VERHEYEN, R., 1953. 'Les migrateurs chantent-ils dans leurs quartiers d'hiver?' *Gerfaut 43:* 1–11.

VINCENT, A. W., 1936. 'The Birds of north-eastern Africa, etc.' *Ibis 6:* 48–123.

—, —, 1947–49. 'On the breeding habits of some African birds'. *Ibis 89:* 163–210; *91:* 313–345.

VOGT, W., 1944. 'Ueber die Territorien der Wasseramsel *Cinclus cinclus* (L.) in Winter 1943/44 an der Aare bei Bern'. *Orn. Beob. 41:* 36–43.

VOIGT, A., 1901. 'Über das Nachahmungstalent der Vögel'. *Orn. Mschr. 26:* 328–330.

—, —, 1913. *Exkursionsbuch zum Studium der Vogelstimmen*. Leipzig.

VOIPIO, P., 1952. 'Disguised calls of birds as defence mechanisms'. *Orn. fenn. 29:* 63–67.

WAGNER, H. O., 1941. 'Lange "Verlobungzeit" Mexikanischen Tyrannidae'. *Orn. Beob. 41:* 36–43.

—, —, 1944. 'Notes on the life history of the Emerald Toucanet'. *Wilson Bull. 56:* 65–76.

—, —, 1945a. 'Observaciones sobre el comportamiento de *Chiroxiphia linearis* durant su propagacion'. *An. Inst. Biol. Univ. Mex. 16:* 539–546.

—, —, 1945b. 'Notes on the life history of the Mexican Violet-ear'. *Wilson Bull. 57:* 165–187.

—, —, 1946. 'Observaciones sobra la vida de *Calothorax lucifer*'. *An. Inst. biol. Univ. Mex. 17:* 283–299.

WAITE, E. R., 1903. 'Sympathetic song in birds'. *Nature 68:* 322.

WALKINSHAW, L. H., 1944. 'The Eastern Chipping Sparrow in Michigan'. *Wilson Bull. 56:* 193–215.

WALLACE, A. R., 1896. *A Narrative of Travels on the Amazon and Rio Negro*. London.

—, H. J., 1939. 'Bicknell's Thrush, its taxonomy, distribution and life history'. *Proc. Boston Soc. Nat. Hist. 41:* 211–402.

WALLRAFF, H. G., 1953. 'Beobachtungen zur Brutbiologie des Stares (*Sturnus v. vulgaris* L.) in Nürnberg'. *J. Orn. 94:* 36–67.

WALPOLE-BOND, J., 1933. 'The Marsh Warbler as a Sussex species'. *Brit. Birds 27:* 58–65.

WARBURG, G. O., 1941. 'Song of the female Chaffinch'. *Brit. Birds 34:* 261.

WARD, T., 1714. *In* Godman, 1954.

WARHAM, J., 1954. 'The behaviour of the Splendid Blue Wren'. *Emu 54:* 135–140.

WARWICK, T. and VAN SOMEREN, V. D., 1936. 'The roding of the Woodcock (*Scolopax rusticola* Linné)'. *Scot. Nat.* 165–172.

WATERTON, C., 1903. *Wanderings in South America in the years 1812, 1816, 1820 and 1824*. London.

WATSON, J. B. and LASHLEY, K. A., 1915. 'An historical and experimental study of homing'. *Carnegie Inst. Wash. 7:* 9–60.

WEEDEN, J. S. and FALLS, J. B., 1959. 'Differential responses of male Ovenbirds to recorded songs of neighbouring and more distant individuals'. *Auk 76:* 343–351.

WEISMANN, A., 1889. 'Gedanken ueber Musik bei Tieren und bei Menschen'. *Deutsche Rundschau 61:* 50–79.

WELDON, W. F. R., 1903. 'Bullfinch and Canary'. *Nature 67:* 609–610.

WELTER, W. A., 1935. 'The natural history of the Long-billed Marsh Wren'. *Wilson Bull. 47:* 3–34.

WESTON, H. G., 1947. 'Breeding behaviour of the Black-headed Grosbeak'. *Condor 49:* 54–73.

WEVER, E. G., 1930. 'The upper limit of hearing in the cat'. *J. comp. Psychol. 10:* 221–233.

—, —, and BRAY, C. W., 1933. 'A new method for the study of hearing in insects'. *J. cell. comp. Physiol. 4:* 79–93.

—, —, and LAWRENCE, M., 1954. *Physiological Acoustics.* Princeton.

WEYDEMEYER, W., 1930. 'An unusual case of mimicry by a Catbird'. *Condor 32:* 124–125.

WHARTON-TIGAR, N., 1946. 'Wild bird notes from the Isle of Thanet', *Avic. Mag. 52:* 225–227.

WHEELWRIGHT, H. W., 1871. *A Spring and Summer in Lapland.* London.

WHITE, G., 1789. *The Natural History and Antiquities of Selborne, in the County of Southampton.* London.

WHITEHOUSE, H. L. K. and ARMSTRONG, E. A., 1953. 'Rhythms in the breeding behaviour of the European Wren'. *Behaviour 5:* 261–288.

WHITMAN, C. O., 1919. *The Behaviour of Pigeons.* Ed. H. A. Carr. Washington.

WHITTLE, H. G., 1928. 'The biography of a Cedar Waxwing'. *Bull. Northeastern Bird-banding Assn. 1:* 26–30.

WILLIAMS, G. R., 1960. 'The Takahe (*Notornis mantelli* Owen, 1848): A general survey'. *Trans. Roy. Soc. N.Z. 88:* 235–258.

—, L., 1952. 'Breeding behaviour of the Brewer Blackbird'. *Condor 54:* 3–47.

WILLIAMSON, K., 1958. 'Population and breeding environment of the St. Kilda and Fair Isle Wrens'. *Brit. Birds 52:* 369–393.

—, —, 1959a. 'The behaviour and breeding environment of the St. Kilda Wren'. *Brit. Birds 52:* 138–140.

WILSON, E., 1937. *In* Seaver, 1937.

WING, L., 1946. 'Drumming flight in the Blue Grouse, and courtship characters of the Tetraonidae'. *Condor 48:* 154–157.

—, —, 1951. 'Notes on the song-series of a Hermit Thrush in the Yukon'. *Auk 68:* 189–193.

—, L. W., 1956. *Natural History of Birds.* New York.

WITCHELL, C. A., 1896. *The Evolution of Bird Song.* London.

WITHERBY, H. F., JOURDAIN, F. C. R., TICEHURST, N. F., and TUCKER, B. W., 1938–41. *The Handbook of British Birds.* London.

WOLFE, L. R., 1954. 'The Australian Snipe in Japan'. *Emu 54:* 198–203.

WOLSTENHOLME, H., 1926. 'Birds singing in their nests'. *Emu 25:* 295–296.

WYNNE-EDWARDS, V. C., 1962. *Animal Dispersion in relation to Social Behaviour.* Edinburgh and London.

A Study of Bird Song

YARRELL, W., 1856. *A History of British Birds*. London.

YERKES, R. M. and YERKES, A. W., 1929. *The Great Apes; a study of anthropoid life*. New Haven, Yale U.P.; London, Oxford.

YOUNG, H., 1951. 'Territorial behaviour in the Eastern Robin'. *Proc. Linn. Soc. N.Y. 58–62:* 1–37.

ZIMMER, C., 1919. 'Der Beginn des Vogelsanges in der Frühdämmerung'. *Verhandl. Orn. Ges. Bayern München 14:* 152–180.

ZIMMERMAN, E. C., 1960. 'Possible instances of rapid evolution'. *Evolution 14:* 137–139.

INDEXES

I. BIRDS

315

Index I

321

II. ORGANISMS OTHER THAN BIRDS

III. AUTHORITIES

Index

IV. GENERAL INDEX

Abstract relationships, 83
  thought, 239
Abbreviation, of song, 240
Accelerando, 42, 268
Acoustic characters, 8
  principles, 31
Activity, displacement, 3, 126, 130, 131,
    132, 133, 134, 148, 150, 161, 262,
    263
  redirection, 134
  non-correlation, 263
  overflow, 159
  transference, 134, 263
Adaptations, 126
  ecological, 109
  feeding, 99
  loud song, 116
Adornments, bright, 130, 224, 226–30
  display of, in flight, 157
  in duet displays, 164
Advertising behaviour, 8, 114, 121, 226,
    227
  self, 228
Advertising song, 41, 69, 121; *see* song
Aerobatics, 138, 209
After-discharge, 159
Aggression, 12, 13, 15, 16, 63, 146; *see*
    threat
  absence of, 166
  and song, 154
  and utterances, 240
Alarm calls, 4, 5, 6, 15, 69, 132, 260, *see*
    call-notes, escape, warning
Allopatric species, 90
Androgen output, 168
Altitude, effects of on song, 194
Anticipation, 19, 82
Anti-monotony principle, 242
Antiphonal song, 180, 183; *see* song
Appeasement, 148
Associations, anticipatory, 2
  relationship to learning, 21, 81, 83
Autumnal mimicry, 84
Awakening, 191–200, 215

Bathing, song during, 29
  sun-, 65
Batrachians, songs of, 221
Beak, closure of, 49
  form of, 98
  use of, in display, 148, 158–219, 223

Beauty, criteria of, 231
  objectivity of, 231
Bivalent repertoire, 102; *see* repertoire
Brain stem, 134
Broods, second, 154

Callnotes,
  aggressive, 5, 15, 16, 148; alarm, 3–6,
    12, 15–18, 20–27, 47, 61, 63, 77,
    80, 115; dialects of, 101, 132,
    157, 224; begging, 5, 13, 14, 170;
    clicking, 148; composite, 3; con-
    stancy of, 91; contact, 14–18, 258;
    —— as source of song, 154; ——
    reciprocal, 80; contentment, 15, 168;
    copulation, 13, 14, 159; corporate,
    185–7; courtship, 5; defensive, 16;
    deterrent, 99; development of, 18;
    dialects of, 101; dispersal, 14, 17;
    display, 135; distance adjustment,
    18; distinctive, 76; distress, 15;
    escape, 4, 13; female attraction,
    145; flight, 7, 15; flying raptor, 17;
    functions of, 2; food, 19, 69, 257;
    greeting, 14, 18; ground-predator
    warning, 23; gull-warning, 132;
    in relation to habitat, 217–30;
    imitative, 26; inborn, 21, 45, 48,
    106; incorporated into flight-song,
    19; individual, 10; insect-like,
    121; interspecific alarm, 25–27;
    investigatory, 16; juvenile, 13, 25;
    learning, significance of, 21, 22;
    location, 6, 14, 18–27, 226; mating,
    112; mimicry of, 72, 76–85; modi-
    fication of, 3; mutual, 148, 168;
    need, 15; nest-invitation, 154, 162;
    nest-relief, 162; nest-site, 20, 161,
    162, 165; perch, 117, 127; preco-
    cious, 44; predator-warning, 20, 21,
    25, 27, 230; rallying, 18, 69; rally-
    ing to food, 69, 257; recognition,
    9, 10; repertoires of, 2, 45;
    seasonal differences in, 90–92, 97;
    sequestration, 18; signal, 169; simi-
    larity in, 14, 98; social, 4, 5, 15,
    194; solicitation, 161; specific, 26,
    27; stimulating, 14; study of, 149;
    subdued, 149; territorial, 115;
    threat, 15; types of, 4, 24; ultra-
    sonic, 24, 249; ventriloquial, 167;

A CATALOGUE OF SELECTED DOVER BOOKS
IN ALL FIELDS OF INTEREST

AMERICAN FOOD AND GAME FISHES, David S. Jordan and Barton W. Evermann. Definitive source of information, detailed and accurate enough to enable the sportsman and nature lover to identify conclusively some 1,000 species and sub-species of North American fish, sought for food or sport. Coverage of range, physiology, habits, life history, food value. Best methods of capture, interest to the angler, advice on bait, fly-fishing, etc. 338 drawings and photographs. 1 + 574pp. 6⅝ x 9⅜.
22383-1 Paperbound $4.50

THE FROG BOOK, Mary C. Dickerson. Complete with extensive finding keys, over 300 photographs, and an introduction to the general biology of frogs and toads, this is the classic non-technical study of Northeastern and Central species. 58 species; 290 photographs and 16 color plates. xvii + 253pp.
21973-9 Paperbound $4.00

THE MOTH BOOK: A GUIDE TO THE MOTHS OF NORTH AMERICA, William J. Holland. Classical study, eagerly sought after and used for the past 60 years. Clear identification manual to more than 2,000 different moths, largest manual in existence. General information about moths, capturing, mounting, classifying, etc., followed by species by species descriptions. 263 illustrations plus 48 color plates show almost every species, full size. 1968 edition, preface, nomenclature changes by A. E. Brower. xxiv + 479pp. of text. 6½ x 9¼.
21948-8 Paperbound $5.00

THE SEA-BEACH AT EBB-TIDE, Augusta Foote Arnold. Interested amateur can identify hundreds of marine plants and animals on coasts of North America; marine algae; seaweeds; squids; hermit crabs; horse shoe crabs; shrimps; corals; sea anemones; etc. Species descriptions cover: structure; food; reproductive cycle; size; shape; color; habitat; etc. Over 600 drawings. 85 plates. xii + 490pp.
21949-6 Paperbound $3.50

COMMON BIRD SONGS, Donald J. Borror. 33⅓ 12-inch record presents songs of 60 important birds of the eastern United States. A thorough, serious record which provides several examples for each bird, showing different types of song, individual variations, etc. Inestimable identification aid for birdwatcher. 32-page booklet gives text about birds and songs, with illustration for each bird.
21829-5 Record, book, album. Monaural. $2.75

FADS AND FALLACIES IN THE NAME OF SCIENCE, Martin Gardner. Fair, witty appraisal of cranks and quacks of science: Atlantis, Lemuria, hollow earth, flat earth, Velikovsky, orgone energy, Dianetics, flying saucers, Bridey Murphy, food fads, medical fads, perpetual motion, etc. Formerly "In the Name of Science." x + 363pp.
20394-8 Paperbound $2.00

HOAXES, Curtis D. MacDougall. Exhaustive, unbelievably rich account of great hoaxes: Locke's moon hoax, Shakespearean forgeries, sea serpents, Loch Ness monster, Cardiff giant, John Wilkes Booth's mummy, Disumbrationist school of art, dozens more; also journalism, psychology of hoaxing. 54 illustrations. xi + 338pp.
20465-0 Paperbound $2.75

MATHEMATICAL PUZZLES FOR BEGINNERS AND ENTHUSIASTS, Geoffrey Mott-Smith. 189 puzzles from easy to difficult—involving arithmetic, logic, algebra, properties of digits, probability, etc.—for enjoyment and mental stimulus. Explanation of mathematical principles behind the puzzles. 135 illustrations. viii + 248pp.
20198-8 Paperbound $1.75

PAPER FOLDING FOR BEGINNERS, William D. Murray and Francis J. Rigney. Easiest book on the market, clearest instructions on making interesting, beautiful origami. Sail boats, cups, roosters, frogs that move legs, bonbon boxes, standing birds, etc. 40 projects; more than 275 diagrams and photographs. 94pp.
20713-7 Paperbound $1.00

TRICKS AND GAMES ON THE POOL TABLE, Fred Herrmann. 79 tricks and games— some solitaires, some for two or more players, some competitive games—to entertain you between formal games. Mystifying shots and throws, unusual caroms, tricks involving such props as cork, coins, a hat, etc. Formerly *Fun on the Pool Table.* 77 figures. 95pp.
21814-7 Paperbound $1.00

HAND SHADOWS TO BE THROWN UPON THE WALL: A SERIES OF NOVEL AND AMUSING FIGURES FORMED BY THE HAND, Henry Bursill. Delightful picturebook from great-grandfather's day shows how to make 18 different hand shadows: a bird that flies, duck that quacks, dog that wags his tail, camel, goose, deer, boy, turtle, etc. Only book of its sort. vi + 33pp. 6½ x 9¼. 21779-5 Paperbound $1.00

WHITTLING AND WOODCARVING, E. J. Tangerman. 18th printing of best book on market. "If you can cut a potato you can carve" toys and puzzles, chains, chessmen, caricatures, masks, frames, woodcut blocks, surface patterns, much more. Information on tools, woods, techniques. Also goes into serious wood sculpture from Middle Ages to present, East and West. 464 photos, figures. x + 293pp.
20965-2 Paperbound $2.00

HISTORY OF PHILOSOPHY, Julián Marias. Possibly the clearest, most easily followed, best planned, most useful one-volume history of philosophy on the market; neither skimpy nor overfull. Full details on system of every major philosopher and dozens of less important thinkers from pre-Socratics up to Existentialism and later. Strong on many European figures usually omitted. Has gone through dozens of editions in Europe. 1966 edition, translated by Stanley Appelbaum and Clarence Strowbridge. xviii + 505pp. 21739-6 Paperbound $3.00

YOGA: A SCIENTIFIC EVALUATION, Kovoor T. Behanan. Scientific but non-technical study of physiological results of yoga exercises; done under auspices of Yale U. Relations to Indian thought, to psychoanalysis, etc. 16 photos. xxiii + 270pp.
20505-3 Paperbound $2.50

Prices subject to change without notice.
Available at your book dealer or write for free catalogue to Dept. GI, Dover Publications, Inc., 180 Varick St., N. Y., N. Y. 10014. Dover publishes more than 150 books each year on science, elementary and advanced mathematics, biology, music, art, literary history, social sciences and other areas.